# 100 MILES AROUND
# YELLOWSTONE

Jim and Madonna Zumbo

Trailer Life Books

All photographs are by the authors unless otherwise credited.

Editorial Director: Bob Livingston
Production Director: Nan Caddel
Production Manager: Ann Forman
Interior design: Dianne Nelson, Shadow Canyon Graphics
Map illustrations: Robert Schram, Bookends


This book was set in Bookman and Bauhaus and
Printed and bound by R. R. Donnelley and Sons.


ISBN: 0-934798-52-4

9  8  7  6  5  4  3  2  1

**CAUTION**

As with any outdoor recreation or activity that occurs in a moving vehicle, there is a potential danger. Those who engage in such activities must assume responsibility for their own actions and safety, and the consequences of said behavior. This guidebook contains information that by its very nature is subject to change through natural circumstances and acts of God, and man-made developments. In addition, the scope of this guidebook does not allow for complete disclosure of all the potential risks involved in such activities. The information in this guidebook cannot replace good judgment and prudent decisions that help reduce risk exposure to hazards.

The overall experience you have will be made more safe and enjoyable through learning as much as possible about the outdoor recreation activities in which you participate. Consult several possible sources of information, especially the current firsthand knowledge of U.S. Forest Service officers and other authorities working in the activity areas. Beyond that, you should always prepare for the unexpected.

# CONTENTS

# ACKNOWLEDGMENTS

A bunch of folks were instrumental in helping us put this book together. First, we'd like to thank General Chuck Yeager for taking time out of his busy schedule to write the foreword. And busy it was—when we asked Chuck to write it, he was preparing to celebrate the 50th anniversary of his legendary feat of being the first person to break the speed of sound in 1947. A special thanks also goes to Thayne Smith and Jayco Inc. for supporting us in our field work research. Bob Livingston gets special thanks, too. Bob is our editor and was responsible in getting this book from the idea stage to a real project. Lots of hugs go to Mary Williams, our neighbor who, in her lovely almost-snowbound home, volunteered to proof and help organize sections of this book into a logical journal that made sense. We'd also like to thank all the chambers of commerce and visitors bureau folks who offered tons of literature and friendly advice. Finally, a big bow to our friend Patty Mayfield. She made zillions of phone calls to confirm the facts we wrote and ensured that every business was RV-friendly. Heartfelt thanks also go from Madonna to her parents, and Patty, for all their support and encouragement.

# INTRODUCTION

With some 4 million visitors each year, Yellowstone National Park is a major attraction to travelers around the world. But, unknown to many tourists, the scope of sights and activities doesn't begin and end at Yellowstone's borders. To be sure, the 2-million-acre park is surrounded by a wealth of spectacular places offering a fascinating array of things to see and do. These include not only wondrous natural features, but man-made events and creations as well.

Living just 25 miles from the park as we do, and traveling extensively in the greater Yellowstone area, we've seen firsthand the frustrations of travelers who are unaware of the region's sights and attractions. We've also talked to many out-of-towners who couldn't find a camping site for their RV during the peak season, even though we knew of nifty little campgrounds just a mile or two off the beaten track that had plenty of vacant spots.

Aware of these problems, we decided to write this book especially for RV travelers. We soon learned that the old saying "Ignorance is bliss" is an accurate phrase when one innocently undertakes a project that is a far more monumental task than anticipated. Little did we know what we were getting into, though we'll admit the field work was a pleasure (well, most of the time). Towing our camp trailer, accompanied by our two labrador retrievers, we poked around in practically every nook and cranny within the 100-mile area included in the book, traveling thousands of miles. Though it was great fun exploring back roads that we'd never driven before, it was nonetheless exasperating to see the road suddenly deteriorate to a muddy, rutted tank trap that not only defied travel, but also had no decent place to turn around. Our hands-on experiences taught us places to avoid in RVs, as well as gems of places tucked away in the mountains that were well worth the drive. In every case, we tried our best to evaluate roads as to their RV-friendliness. Because of unpredictable weather, as well as the varying sizes and capabilities of RVs, we obviously can't guarantee travel on unpaved roads. Then, too, we traveled many roads when weather conditions were good and had to rely on the advice of others to have them appraised during bad weather. For the most part, our sources were U.S. Forest Service workers, information officers, ranchers and other folks intimately familiar with the roads we traveled. We strongly advise that you inquire locally before you drive on dirt or gravel, especially with government agencies who administer the management of most of the public lands around Yellowstone.

It immediately became obvious that the 100-mile designation provided plenty of challenges. We drew a line, as the crow flies, 100 miles from the perimeter of Yellowstone's borders, taking in huge chunks of Idaho, Montana and Wyoming. We cheated a bit if a location was just a mile or two outside the area, incorporating it in the book. But we agonized over other places that were just a bit far out, and then grudgingly omitted them, realizing that we had to draw a line and adhere to it.

Road systems being what they are, we decided to start at each of Yellowstone's five gates and work away from the park. We used the logic that most folks make Yellowstone a priority, and once having seen it, they look for other attractions outside the park.

The practical information in the introductory section sets the stage for traveling the greater Yellowstone area. We begin by telling you how to see Yellowstone National Park in one day if you have a time crunch. We've listed the major attractions, knowing that it's tough to bypass some during your brief visit, requiring you to make some sacrifices. We list the campgrounds in the park and information on road construction which will go on for several more years. We also provide a brief history of Yellowstone.

We've included a special chapter on backcountry driving tips that describes some of the perils you might find, along with unwritten rules of the road. Because you'll undoubtedly see wildlife, we've listed all the large animals you'll see in and around Yellowstone. We give descriptions of their typical environments and list specific places in the greater Yellowstone area where you can generally see animals. Another kind of wild life is the sort you'll see in a rodeo arena. In that regard, there's a chapter that tells you how to see and understand a rodeo, since these events are enormously popular. It's practically impossible to find an incorporated town that doesn't have rodeo grounds.

We thought it would be interesting to include a chapter that briefly describes the general histories of each of the states bordering Yellowstone. First we discuss Native Americans, mountain men, explorers, trappers and fur traders, then settlers and pioneers who flocked to the west in search of fertile farming lands, or gold, silver and copper, followed by those whose interests were more tuned to fossil fuels such as coal and oil.

Then it's time to hit the road! There are many roads that we've come to know and love over the years; many of them lead to lovely campgrounds. These are listed as Favorite Drives in the book, and we're betting you find them to be special places just as we did. The state-designated scenic byways are also incredible, and we've selected a few favorites among them as well. We've also listed RV Cautions that describe a hazard or a place requiring extra wariness, such as roads that become impassable when wet, extraordinarily steep grades over mountain passes, or roads that are closed to RV use.

Throughout the book we've sprinkled fishing information at appropriate locations and also included a special chapter in the introductory section that describes famous waters in the area, as well as those where you can find some elbow room. Because many of the top rivers are dedicated to fly-fishing enthusiasts, we've listed several where you can walk from your RV with a lawn chair and a can of worms and enjoy the western landscape, catching a few fish while you're at it.

We chronicle the origins of most of the towns along the routes, as well as local activities, events and interesting places. We describe historic spots, famous hotels, saloons, suggested dining establishments, golf courses, museums, state parks, spas—you name it; if we felt it was worth seeing, it's in here. Outfitters such as those providing adventures on horseback, rafts and boats are also mentioned. In case you're visiting off-season, we've listed winter activities such as skiing and snowmobiling. Not all local events are listed because some aren't annual affairs and dates can change from year to year. We encourage you to visit chamber of commerce offices for details. In some towns where streets are narrow and RV parking is limited, we direct you to specific nearby locations where parking is available. Telephone numbers for emergency medical and pharmaceutical services, towing and RV repair, and veterinarians are listed.

No doubt, your greatest concern while free-wheeling around the sights is where to camp for the night (unless you're among those who, unlike us, are able to plan ahead, make reservations and then stick with the plan). To help you out, we included the RV parks and campgrounds that are most likely to have an opening even on the busiest weekends. We've designated these places as a Best Shot for a Camp Spot, and you'll find them throughout our 100-mile territory.

We've also canvassed hundreds of bed and breakfasts and guest ranches in the region, listing those that are exclusively RV-friendly. Even though many folks traveling with RVs have self-contained units and do their own cooking, we thought that a night or two at a B&B or ranch would enable you to become acquainted with local folks and experience their customs and values in a firsthand way. Many ranches offer horseback riding and chuckwagon feasts, and some allow you to participate in a real live cattle roundup. Remember, too, that most communities offer all sorts of outdoor recreation. Just because we haven't mentioned it doesn't mean it's not available, especially in regard to fishing and hiking.

Finally, the routes that connect towns are described as to the general countryside they travel through, as well as adjacent features that you see as you drive. Our hopes are that this book will allow you to discover those wonderful "everythings" to see while you visit our first, and finest (in our opinion), national park.

*The Grand Teton mountain range, just outside Yellowstone National Park, is one of the best known and most widely photographed ranges in the Rockies.*

## SECTION 1

# All About Traveling the Greater Yellowstone Area

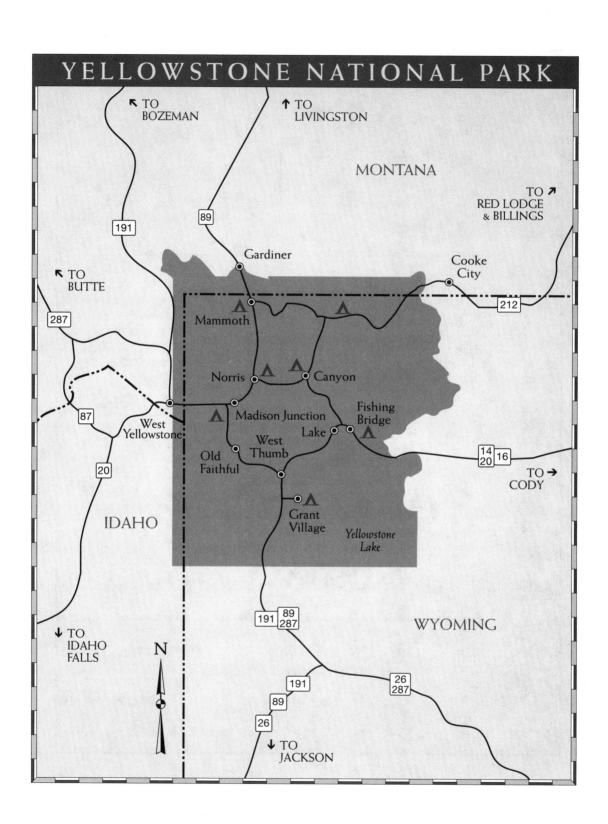

# YELLOWSTONE NATIONAL PARK

↖ TO BOZEMAN

↑ TO LIVINGSTON

MONTANA

TO ↗ RED LODGE & BILLINGS

191

89

Gardiner

Cooke City

↖ TO BUTTE

212

287

Mammoth

Norris

Canyon

87

West Yellowstone

Madison Junction

Fishing Bridge

Lake

14 20 16

TO → CODY

20

Old Faithful

West Thumb

Grant Village

Yellowstone Lake

IDAHO

↓ TO IDAHO FALLS

N

191 89 287

WYOMING

191

26 287

89

26

↓ TO JACKSON

# PRACTICAL INFORMATION ABOUT YELLOWSTONE NATIONAL PARK

## SEEING YELLOWSTONE NATIONAL PARK IN ONE DAY

At 2.2 million acres, and with countless sights worth seeing, it takes several days to really view everything Yellowstone National Park offers. However, some travelers find themselves with just a few hours to see the park, perhaps because of a tight schedule, unexpected problems or delays, or a myriad of other reasons. While we'd be the last to suggest that you can see what the park offers in a day, there are a number of attractions that shouldn't be missed. Here's a thumbnail sketch of the major sights if your schedule is tight.

Before entering the park, be aware that the road system is definitely not engineered for speed. Construction is underway in many areas, causing delays. Some roads may be closed for certain periods each day. Many of the roads are narrow, steep and winding, making for slow travel. And, of course, there will be plenty of traffic in the summer, and you can count on frustrating jams when animals are spotted near the road—especially a bear sighting, which is guaranteed to result in a huge bottleneck. The fastest legal speed you can travel in Yellowstone is 45 mph, and many sections require slower speeds. Keep a light-hearted attitude when you see people do dumb things, and remember that 3 million folks want to see the park just as you do, many of them enthusiastic foreigners who may not understand English.

During your abbreviated visit, realize that most of the park is composed of timbered mountains, with creeks, streams and willow bottoms—similar to what you'll see in other western forests. If there's anything unique about Yellowstone's forest environment, it's the incredible devastation caused by the 1988 fires. Park personnel have done a nice job in explaining the role of fire, and you won't have to drive to any specific point to view the burn. You'll see it practically everywhere on your travels throughout the park.

That leaves one major feature—Yellowstone's amazing thermal activity. Thousands of geysers, boiling cauldrons, steam vents, spluttering mud pots, steaming turquoise pools and other bizarre features will keep you spellbound. Many visitors are so enthralled when they get their first glimpse of thermal activity that they spend a great deal of time at lesser sites. We're not saying that there are places not worth stopping at, but simply that if you have a short time window, you must select priorities and see the primary attractions.

Other than thermal features, an absolute must is the Grand Canyon of the Yellowstone. You'll never forget it. (More on that below.)

Of course, if you don't see Old Faithful, you haven't seen the granddaddy of all natural attractions, not only in Yellowstone, but also on the continent. This geyser gets its name for its consistent eruptions, which occur on the average of once every 80 minutes or so. There's plenty of room for RV parking, and it's a short and level walk from the parking lot to the geyser viewing area. Try to get to Old Faithful early in the day. If you've just missed an eruption, you'll have to wait more than an hour for the next one, taking up plenty of your constrained time budget. If you arrive late in the afternoon, a long wait may interfere with your plans on exiting the park. If you must wait for an eruption, you'll have plenty to see at Old Faithful Inn. This enormous log-and-stone structure was built in 1904. The giant stone fireplace in the lobby sets the stage for this lovely building, and you'll undoubtedly marvel at the fine craftsmanship that went into the inn.

There are a number of geyser areas in the park, and it is difficult to choose only one. Norris Geyser Basin is one of the most extensive, with an interesting assortment of thermal features. The world's largest geyser, called Steamboat, is located here, as is Echinus, which erupts once every hour. A nearby museum houses many fascinating exhibits that explain geyser activity.

Near Canyon Village, you should head for the Grand Canyon of the Yellowstone and take a breathtaking look at the Upper and Lower Falls, which are 109 and 308 feet, respectively. Take the time to go to Artist's Point and Inspiration Point, which will give you incredible views. Fair warning: Bring plenty of film, because you'll never see the fabulous panorama of colors, as painted on the river walls, duplicated anywhere else.

The three attractions just mentioned are all on the Grand Loop Road and are easily driven to in sequence. If you have the time to head toward the North Gate near Mammoth, be sure to pay a visit to Mammoth Hot Springs. The name *hot springs* implies a spa, which is a common sight throughout the country, but don't let the name fool you. These springs are actually a spectacular series of travertine terraces laced with all sorts of little bubbly fissures, vents and exceedingly colorful deposits. A boardwalk allows access throughout this amazing feature.

These four sights are our favorites and should take up most of your day. If you still have time and are headed out the West Gate, you'll be enormously impressed with the Imax theater at West Yellowstone. Here, a huge six-story-high screen presents the Yellowstone story in vivid color with stereo surround-sound. The theater has a seating capacity of 348 with special wheelchair spaces.

If you intend on camping inside Yellowstone, be aware that of the twelve campgrounds, five take advanced reservations, and seven are on a first-come, first-served basis. To find a site in the latter, get there as early in the day as possible, since most are full by midday. For more information on camping in the park, see the Overnighting information for Yellowstone National Park on page 6.

## RV COURTESY

Many roads in the greater western Yellowstone area are steep and winding, and RVs commonly move slower than automobile traffic. As a matter of courtesy, RV drivers should pull over where safe pullouts exist to allow following vehicles to pass. This is especially true in Yellowstone National Park, which has an exceptional amount of RV traffic, wildlife along the roads and narrow highways with long stretches that have no passing lanes. The Wyoming legislature is considering a law requiring RVs to pull over if five vehicles are following. Whether this becomes law or not, it's a matter of good road etiquette to do so.

## ROAD CONSTRUCTION IN YELLOWSTONE NATIONAL PARK AS OF 1998

Yellowstone's roadways were established more than 100 years ago when stagecoaches slowly made their way about, and the winding routes were not designed for speedy, direct travel. Those same passageways are used today. Since traffic is extremely heavy in the summer and the roads are subjected to the extremes of sub-zero temperatures and thermal heating, the pavement has been badly damaged over the years. A program to widen and improve the highways was started several years ago and will continue for several more. Here are construction areas to be aware of:
- From Madison Junction to Old Faithful, expect periodic closures with 30-minute delays.
- From the Northeast Gate to Tower Junction—the newest construction area in the park—expect delays of 30 minutes or more.
- From Fishing Bridge to the East Gate, expect 30-minute delays along with some nightly closures.

Here's a tip: Check with the gate attendants before you enter, or call chamber of commerce offices in towns close to the gates you wish to use. These offices keep updated information on construction.

## YELLOWSTONE NATIONAL PARK CAMPING INFORMATION

There are two types of campgrounds in Yellowstone: those managed by the National Park Service and those managed by the official concessionaire AMFAC. You may make reservations at the concessionaire-operated campgrounds; these are Canyon Village, Grant Village, Bridge Bay and Madison. Camping at the park's other seven campgrounds is offered on a first-come, first-served basis. Park personnel at the entrance gates have current information as to which campgrounds are fully occupied. Remember to check the campground status as you enter the park. The campground's opening and closing dates are weather-based and subject to change.

## OVERNIGHTING

### Campgrounds & RV Parks

AMFAC campgrounds are those operated by the official concessionaire for Yellowstone National Park, AMFAC, Inc. For reservations at AMFAC campgrounds, call (307) 344-7311.

### Canyon
Canyon Village—AMFAC Campground, .25 mile east of Canyon Junction. 272 RV sites, sewer hook-up, but no electrical or water hook-ups, no dump station; hot showers, laundry and drinking water; open June 4 through September 6; for reservations, call AMFAC.

Norris—National Park Service Campground, 1 mile north of Norris Junction. 116 RV sites (max. length 35 feet), no hook-ups or services; open May 19 through September 18.

### Grant Village
Grant Village—AMFAC Campground, 2 miles south of West Thumb Junction on the West Thumb of Lake Yellowstone. 425 RV sites, dump station, hot showers, laundry and drinking water; open June 25 through September 5; for reservations, call AMFAC.

Lewis Lake—National Park Service Campground, 10 miles south of West Thumb Junction. 85 RV sites (max. length 45 feet), no services; open June 9 through October 31.

### Lake Village
*(Best spot to stay—the only complete RV park in Yellowstone)*
Fishing Bridge RV Park—AMFAC Campground, 26 miles west of the East Gate, then 1 mile east of Lake Junction. 345 RV sites, hook-ups, dump station, hot showers, laundry and drinking water; open May 24 through September 8; for reservations, call AMFAC.

Bridge Bay—AMFAC Campground, 3 miles southwest of Lake Village. 420 RV sites, no hook-ups; dump station and drinking water; open May 25 through September 15; for reservations, call AMFAC.

### Mammoth

Indian Creek—National Park Service Campground, 7 miles south of Mammoth Junction. 75 RV sites (max. length 45 feet), no services; open June 4 through September 13.

Mammoth—National Park Service Campground, .5 mile north of Mammoth Junction. 85 RV sites (max. length 45 feet), no services; open year-round.

Pebble Creek—National Park Service Campground, 7 miles south of northeast entrance. 36 RV sites (max. length 25 feet), no services; open June 9 through September 5.

Slough Creek—National Park Service Campground, 10 miles northeast of Tower Junction. 29 RV sites (max. length 25 feet), no services; open May 26 through October 31.

Tower Falls—National Park Service Campground, 3 miles southeast of Tower Junction. 32 RV sites (max. length 25 feet), no services; open May 26 through September 11.

### Old Faithful

Madison—AMFAC Campground, .25 mile west of Madison Junction. 280 RV sites, no hook-ups; dump station and drinking water; open May 5 through October 25; for reservations, call AMFAC.

## YELLOWSTONE NATIONAL PARK VISITOR INFORMATION

Yellowstone National Park Service, Visitor Services, PO Box 168, Yellowstone Park, WY 82190; (307) 344-7381.

Current information on Yellowstone National Park roads is available at the entrance gates or through the Communication Center's automated service: (307) 344-2132.

Reservations for all accommodations, including campgrounds and hotels, within Yellowstone National Park are handled by AMFAC, Inc., PO Box 165, Yellowstone Park, WY 82190; (307) 344-7311; fax: (307) 344-7456.

*Fishing is superb in the rivers around Yellowstone National Park.*

## THE HISTORY OF YELLOWSTONE NATIONAL PARK

When John Colter first explored the Yellowstone area in 1807, he was undoubtedly awestruck at the bizarre geyser eruptions and goings-on that he observed. The boiling springs, bubbling mud-pots, steam clouds and churning and frothing waters must have left him spellbound. As the first non-Native in the park, Colter is commonly credited with Yellowstone's discovery.

Colter was a member of the famous Lewis and Clark Expedition. He wasn't ready to settle down in St. Louis with the others when their long journey was over. He struck out alone, investigating an immense part of the Rockies that no white man had ever seen. When Colter returned to St. Louis after three years of trapping and exploring, his tales of Yellowstone were considered ludicrous. He was called a madman (in so many words) and had no credibility.

As the years passed, other mountain men journeyed into the park, trapping for beaver and other fur-bearing animals. They found a wealth of animals and enjoyed a lucrative but temporary business. Beaver suddenly was no longer fashionable nor as plentiful, and this prompted most trappers to depart. The park was once again left to the Sheepherder Natives who were a part of the Shoshone tribe. They moved about and migrated with the seasons and the supply of animals.

*These bear warning signs near Yellowstone should be taken seriously.*

*Pronghorn antelope are common residents of the prairies and lowlands surrounding Yellowstone National Park.*

A major factor in Yellowstone's development was the visit by Dr. Ferdinand V. Hayden, director of the U.S. Geological Survey, in 1871. Hayden left Ogden, Utah, with seven wagons, 34 men and an appropriation of $40,000. Two of the men in the party were to become important in establishing Yellowstone as a real place and agree with the descriptions by John Colter.  Thomas Moran, a landscape painter, and William Henry Jackson, a photographer, made it clear through their paintings and photographs that Yellowstone was truly real. Besides their artwork, a 500-page report on Yellowstone impressed Congress. So much so, in fact, that Hayden was able to persuade the legislators to make Yellowstone America's first national park. This historic day was March 1, 1872. (More details on Moran and Jackson are in the South Gate section, page 183.)

Prior to the Hayden visit, two other expeditions were responsible for setting the wheels in motion for recognizing Yellowstone. In 1869, three prospectors from around Helena journeyed to the area to see for themselves what the rumors were all about. Known as the Falsom-Cook-Petersen Expedition, they spent 36 days mapping and traveling the Yellowstone area. When they first gazed upon the Grand Canyon of the Yellowstone, Cook was reported to have said, "It seemed to me that it was five minutes before anyone spoke." They wrote a magazine article about their adventure when they got home and suggested that the area be set aside for the public.

Spurred on by the article and other stories, another expedition left Helena in 1870 to explore the area even more. This one, known as the Washburn-Langford-Doane Expedition, was made up of 19 men and 40 horses. The group was comprised of many respected Montana territorial leaders. They spent about 30 days exploring and naming many of Yellowstone's features.

*Coyotes are numerous around Yellowstone. They provide entertainment to campers with their nightly music.*

One of the group's leaders, Nathaniel P. Langford, traveled to the East Coast to promote Yellowstone's amazing treasures. Among his listeners was Ferdinand V. Hayden, who then set out with Moran and Jackson to bring back irrefutable proof of the area's existence. When the park was created in 1872, the honor of the first superintendent position was bestowed on Nathaniel P. Langford.

After Yellowstone achieved park status, curious travelers made the rugged trip west. At best, about 1,000 people were able to see the park each year, traveling on narrow paths and game trails. It wasn't until 1883 that overnight accommodations were established in Yellowstone. This was due to increased numbers of visitors traveling on the new roads built by the U.S. Army Corps of Engineers. Because of the expense, only wealthy people could afford to travel there.

Railroads were built to bring people to Yellowstone, and as a result, tourism rapidly increased. The Union Pacific and Northern Pacific Railroads reached the perimeter of the park in 1907 at West Yellowstone. From there, stagecoaches carried people to the interior, but they were replaced with automobiles in 1917. Rail service to West Yellowstone was terminated in the 1950s.

In 1997, Yellowstone National Park celebrated its 125th anniversary amidst a great deal of dust, dirt and blackened trees. Despite a catastrophic fire in 1988, and an intensive project to modify the entire road system, Yellowstone is still America's oldest—and premiere—park.

## BACKCOUNTRY DRIVING TIPS

Any time you turn your RV off a paved highway, you're headed for either a pleasant adventure or a disaster, depending on the condition of the road and/or your vehicle. Check your RV thoroughly, ensuring that all batteries are charged and that you have extra coolant, oil and necessary fluids, as well as a well-stocked toolbox and full containers of propane. It's expensive, time-consuming and frustrating to be towed out of a rural area. Be aware that your cellular phone might be useless in the backcountry if no communication towers are within signal range. The newer satellite phones are dependable but are relatively expensive and haven't yet had widespread acceptance. Tire chains are good to have along in the event you're caught in a long-term storm and can't drive out—maybe. Read on.

Unpaved roads in the greater Yellowstone area may be treacherous during rainstorms. Well-graveled roads with a solid base are usually okay for foul weather travel, but they might have unstable areas where they pass through low marshy areas. Dirt roads, especially those with a high percentage of clay, may become absolutely impassable, defying tire chains and every manner of extricating equipment short of a D-8 bulldozer. Despite your best intentions, you might find yourself in an awful predicament. For example, say you're merrily cruising along in your RV, enjoying the sunshine and splendid scenery. The road is dry, the birds are singing and life is peachy fine. Around noon you notice a fluffy cloud peeking over the western horizon, but you don't give it much thought. You're so enchanted with the backcountry landscape that you've forgotten you're 30 miles from the pavement on a road that can turn into a nightmare in a matter of minutes.

The cloud looms larger, and in a half-hour, the sky is changing from blue to gray to black. Presently a raindrop hits the windshield, and you're suddenly involved in a storm that instantly douses your world. Before you know it, your RV is sliding a bit, and you have difficulty steering it. As the road gets wetter, you've lost total control and are unable to move. You're stuck, big time. Even chains won't get you moving, because the clay builds up under and on top of the links, making your wheels as slick as fresh bagels.

All you can do is wait for the sun to shine. Most western storms last no longer than an hour or two, and the hot sun dries the road quickly. You can usually be on your way in a couple hours. If, however, you're caught in the middle of a storm that lasts a day or more, you'll have no choice but to camp where you are. That's a good reason to have plenty of food, propane and fully-charged batteries.

To eliminate this sort of dilemma, get a dependable, updated weather forecast before you strike off into the hinterlands. Use good sense. There are times in the summer when storms strike practically every afternoon, just like clockwork. This storm schedule can continue for a week or two. Avoid unstable backcountry roads when these conditions persist. To get expert advice on a particular road, visit the government office that administers management of the area in which you're traveling. The U.S. Forest Service has ranger district offices in many small communities. The U.S. Bureau of Land Management (BLM) likewise has district offices, but they're not as prevalent as Forest Service offices. Ask to speak to one of the field personnel, since the nice helpful clerk at the front desk may have no clue as to the potential problems of the roads you're soliciting information about.

Backcountry travel is a lot more fun if you know where you're headed and what to expect along the way. For around $4 each, you can buy Forest Service or BLM maps that indicate all sorts of nifty features on your route. Many folks find it great fun to navigate with a map as they're exploring a brand-new area. Then, too, if you're driving a long travel trailer or large motorhome, you might not want to commit yourself on a strange road if you don't know where it leads. Always have a contingency route in mind where you can be assured of turning around or taking an alternate road if necessary. You don't want any unpleasant surprises on a backcountry road.

Be extra cautious if the road you're traveling on is being used by logging or mining trucks. If workers are logging or mining ahead of you, you can normally count on them driving toward you at the end of the shift.

If you meet up with another vehicle on a narrow road and one must back up to a wide spot, it's typically good etiquette and more convenient for the smaller vehicle to do the backing. On the other hand, if you encounter a vehicle on a steep road, the unwritten rule of the road suggests that the uphill driver back uphill because he or she has far better control in reverse than a driver who must back downhill.

# WILDLIFE IN THE AREA

## TIPS ON VIEWING AND PHOTOGRAPHING WILDLIFE

As a general rule, you'll see most animals around sunup and sunset when they're actively foraging. Most animals feed all night, beginning in late afternoon and ending in early morning. To spot game, focus your attention on areas with the sun at your back, since the rays of the early or late sun will often "light up" the animals, making them easier to see. Look for animals along the edges of fields and meadows rather than in the middle, and don't always expect to see the entire animal but just a part of it. Sometimes the animal will be partially shielded by brush or be in a shaded area where it's difficult to see. Pull your RV entirely off the road to observe wildlife so traffic isn't obstructed. If necessary, drive to a pullout where you can park and walk back. Remember, wild animals, even small ones, can be dangerous, so keep your distance.

Binoculars are a must if you're serious about viewing wildlife. A small, compact six- or seven-power binocular will stow conveniently, but for better viewing under low-light conditions, consider an eight- or ten-power binocular.

Most serious photographers use a 35mm single-reflex camera and shoot slide film; any film will work as long as the film speed is fast enough when you're shooting under low-light conditions. To get quality photos, consider a camera that accepts a telephoto lens of at least 70mm. A tripod is a good idea to steady the camera if you're using slow shutter speeds.

Keep your film cool. Your RV refrigerator will do nicely. Be sure to keep cameras and film off the hot dash or any place exposed directly to the sun.

## ELK

These are high-elevation animals that are seldom seen during hot summer days. Elk are most active early in the morning and late in the afternoon. Because grass is high on their menu, they commonly feed in large meadows, often called *parks* in the west. You'll also see them in areas burned by forest fires and in places recently logged, since those areas often support lush vegetation. Elk are famous for their mating calls, referred to as *bugling*, but don't expect to hear them vocalizing unless you're visiting the region in September or early October. That's their breeding season, and vocalizations seldom occur before and after. Male elk, called bulls, grow very large antlers and are among the most handsome animals in the west. Each mature bull gathers as many females (cows) as possible prior to the breeding season, and guards his harem from other bulls. Competition for females is fierce, and bulls have been known to kill each other. Elk are large in size; the bulls weigh from 600 to 800 pounds or more. Typically you'll see elk in herds year-round, since they're very social animals.

There are a number of places where you may see elk outside Yellowstone. As a rule, look for them in areas that contain evergreen forests. Elk are timber-oriented animals, preferring to be in the cool shade. You won't see them readily in the forests, but you can often catch a glimpse of them as they're traveling out into the meadows just before dark. If you rise early enough in the morning, you might see

*This bull elk is taking life easy. Tens of thousands of elk live in and around Yellowstone National Park.*

them slowly drifting out of the openings and into the forests.

Specifically, you can look for elk in these areas. In Yellowstone National Park itself, you can see elk 12 months out of the year in and around the park headquarters at Mammoth just south of the North Gate at Gardiner. Animals loaf around houses, government buildings, in campgrounds and just about anywhere. Crowds of people have little effect on them. Other good spots to see elk in the park are in meadows from Mammoth to Norris Junction, and then to Madison Junction. You may also see some around Canyon Village and Old Faithful. Outside Yellowstone, look for them between the town of West Yellowstone and Big Sky. In Idaho, good spots are in Island Park and in the Targhee National Forest. You're also apt to see elk outside Cooke City toward and along the Beartooth Highway and in the vicinity of the Chief Joseph Highway in Wyoming.

## MULE DEER

It's said that Lewis and Clark gave the mule deer its name because it reminded them of a deer with large mule-like ears. This is strictly a western animal that lives in every western state and in western Canada. Commonly called the "muley," this deer inhabits more open country than elk, preferring to be in brush and drier country. Nonetheless, muleys are amazingly adaptable and live in habitats from lowland deserts to alpine tundra above timberline.

*Mule deer are considered the deer of the West. They live in the mountains and prairies around Yellowstone National Park.*

Mule deer populations are often ravaged by severe winters when deep snows blanket their forage and extreme cold saps their energy. These massive declines are cyclic, and herds bounce back during years of mild winters. Muleys are migratory, often traveling long distances from high summer ranges to lowland winter areas where snow is not as deep and food is more available.

You can expect to see mule deer anywhere around Yellowstone, but especially in sagebrush areas. In the summer you'll see them high in the mountains, often in fields of wildflowers or along rocky, brushy slopes. Along rural roads you'll often spot them feeding in fields, especially in alfalfa, one of their favorite summer foods. In the late spring and summer, look for animals with rust-colored fur. In the early morning and late afternoon, they appear to be almost orange. In the fall, this summer coat is shed and deer then take on a gray winter pelt. In sunshine, their distinctive white rumps are often the first thing you'll see.

Unlike male whitetails, the antlers of mature mule deer bucks typically have double forks that are often high and wide. Young bucks may have single, spike-like antlers or small single-forked antlers.

Muleys have a peculiar gait when they run, called stotting; they jump as if they're on pogo sticks. These animals commonly live in herds. If you spot one, keep looking, since there might be more.

Here's where you can see mule deer. In Yellowstone, most deer are seen in the drier habitat from Gardiner and Mammoth out toward the Lamar Valley. The best time to view deer here is in late fall when they migrate to lower elevations to seek does and find more food. Muleys live in scattered locations in the park, and you're apt to see them anywhere in the summer. Outside the park, look for them in the Driggs-Victor area in Idaho, as well as in the sagebrush country west of Freedom, Wyoming. A prime spot to see them is along the Chief Joseph Highway, especially in the area along the Clark Fork River.  Another superb region is around Roscoe, Montana, and along the rural roads and farm fields there.

## WHITETAIL DEER

Many people believe whitetails are an "eastern" species, but they thrive in the west. These are the most common deer in America, so named because of their huge tails that are brown on top and white below. When a whitetail is running from danger, it "flags" its tail, waving it about and signaling other animals.

A buck's antlers typically have a pair of curved main beams with several tines growing off each. In the fall, bucks fight viciously in a battle of dominance to win does. Like mule deer, whitetails breed from mid-November to mid-December.

Unlike mule deer, whitetails are much more at home around people. Some live all their lives on a relatively small chunk of landscape no bigger than 30 or 40 acres. Whitetails are fond of farmlands and are mostly seen in agricultural areas.

There are occasional reports of whitetails in Yellowstone, but they're very rare. You can see plenty along the Yellowstone River along I-90. Look for them in agricultural areas around Powell and Lovell east of Cody, Wyoming. There are also good numbers of them around Clark, Wyoming.

*Whitetail deer are inhabitants of farm and ranch country and the brushy lowlands.*

## ANTELOPE

Often called pronghorns, these animals are prairie dwellers, living in large herds. These are the fastest mammals in North America, capable of running at speeds in excess of 55 mph. They also have tremendous vision, equal to that of a powerful telescope. Unlike other animals that seek heavy vegetation for escape cover, pronghorns are more secure in the open where their superior eyesight allows them to spot danger at long distances. These animals are tough, able to withstand ferocious prairie blizzards without seeking shelter. They're tolerant to severe cold because their hair is hollow, offering more insulation in strong winds. Antelope are unique in that they rarely jump fences, unlike all other large hoofed mammals. Instead, they go under the bottom wire, or find a spot where the fence has been damaged, allowing them to get through.

Antelope are found in sizable herds throughout the west with the exception of Washington. They're fond of sagebrush prairies, but are also quite happy in lush alfalfa fields. The only place you'll regularly see them in Yellowstone is in the area between Gardiner and Mammoth. Outside Yellowstone, look for them along I-15 north and south of Dillon, Montana; in the desert and farmland country around Clark, Wyoming; and along the highway between Cody and Thermopolis, Wyoming.

## MOOSE

The largest member of the deer family inhabits wet places like willow bottoms and alder swamps, but it is also quite at home in evergreen and aspen forests. This is the Shiras or Wyoming moose, one of three subspecies found in North America. Only the Shiras dwells in the Rockies; it is well distributed through the entire Yellowstone area. The other two, the Canadian and Alaska-Yukon moose, live farther north. Although a big bull moose can weigh a half-ton or more, they aren't easily spotted when they're in a dense willow thicket. Moose are best known for their giant antlers, which can exceed a tip-to-tip spread of 50 inches. In Alaska, a bull's antlers may be wider than 75 inches. Look for moose early and late in the day, since they often

*Bull moose are very common in the marshes and mountains around Yellowstone.*

*Cow moose near Greys River
in western Wyoming*

bed in evergreen forests or willow thickets where they're very tough to see. You may observe a clump of willows and swear no moose are anywhere around, but when they stand up, they look as big as a barn.

To see moose in Yellowstone National Park, look for them in the willow areas between Mammoth and Norris and in the wetlands around Fishing Bridge. Outside the park, you can see them in marshy spots around Jackson Lake; north and west of West Yellowstone, Montana; along the North Fork of the Shoshone River near the East Gate (Cody entrance); and in and around Red Rock Lakes Refuge west of Henry's Lake.

## MOUNTAIN GOATS

These amazing animals inhabit the most precarious terrain in North America. Mountain goats are strictly high-altitude residents, preferring to live in and around sheer rock walls and cliffs where they seemingly defy gravity. Pure white in color, the goats are easy to spot in the summer. Conversely, they're almost impossible to see in the winter when they blend in with snow. Females are called nannies; males are billies. Both sexes have black horns that are seven to nine inches in length. Typically, a billy's horns are a bit thicker than those of the female.

Goats are very rare in Yellowstone, but you can see them quite frequently along the Beartooth Highway in Wyoming and Montana.

## BIGHORN SHEEP

These are among the most noble of our large mammals. Males, called rams, have huge horns that curl out from the skull. Both sexes live in the high country, commonly migrating to low elevations in late fall where they seek food. On a disconcerting note, bighorn sheep are extremely susceptible to a variety of diseases. Entire herds have been known to die. In the 1970s, an enormous number of sheep died in the Mammoth-Gardiner area in Yellowstone.

During the late November breeding season, rams butt heads fiercely in a dominance battle. The winner is rewarded with the object of his attention, a ewe in heat. It's not uncommon for rams to battle for days. Though the impact of their heads striking together is tremendous, they have special muscles in their necks that act like shock absorbers.

*Bighorn sheep live high in the mountains and are sometimes seen around Yellowstone, especially in the fall.*

Sheep are scattered in Yellowstone but are most commonly seen in the steep hills below Mammoth along the highway to Gardiner. The best time to see rams is in late fall. Outside the park, sheep are often viewed along the Yellowstone River north of Gardiner; along the North Fork of the Shoshone River between the East Gate and Wapiti, Wyoming; and in the vicinity of Dubois, which has one of the largest sheep herds in the country.

## BISON

It's practically impossible to visit Yellowstone and not see bison. These huge animals, weighing up to a ton, are visible in grassy areas as well as in open forests. Most of us are aware of the tragic slaughter of these great beasts when the country was settled. Luckily, remnant herds survived, including those in Yellowstone, though some bison were introduced to bolster the herd at the beginning of this century.

Currently about 2,000 bison remain in Yellowstone. During the 1996–97 winter, 1,100 were either shot by government agents or sent to slaughter houses, because these animals wandered out of the park's boundaries. Many also died from the severe winter. Since bison carry brucellosis, which is allegedly transmitted to cattle, the livestock industry is not anxious to allow bison to mix with cattle. Several options other than killing migrating bison have been proposed and may be implemented.

Seeing bison outside the park boundaries is rare, unless they're fenced in on a ranch. In the park, you can usually see large herds in Hayden Valley, around Fishing Bridge, most geyser areas and in the Lamar Valley.

Bulls are much larger than cows and are usually the most dangerous. Bison may attack humans with little or no provocation and have seriously injured many unsuspecting tourists. Be cautious around these peaceful-looking animals. If irritated, they can reach a full charge in just a few seconds, easily catching a fleeing human. Keep a safe distance, and if you want to photograph them, stay in or very close to your vehicle.

## GRIZZLY BEARS

This is the most formidable predator in the lower 48 states, weighing in at 500 pounds or more. Only Alaska's brown bear and polar bear are larger. Because of widespread persecution by settlers, grizzlies have vanished from most of their original habitat. The last of the great bears were killed in the 1920s and 1930s, except for those in Yellowstone and parts of Montana where they were protected. Now, about 300 grizzlies live in and around Yellowstone.

*Grizzly bears are numerous in and around Yellowstone National Park, requiring campers to take special precautions.*

Contrary to popular belief, grizzlies don't hibernate, but go into a semi-dormant state in the winter. They often wander about outside their dens during periods of mild weather. Their dietary preferences include practically anything digestible, but in the summer, they feed extensively on seeds of whitebark pines as well as moths. Grizzlies are efficient hunters, capable of running down and catching large animals. In the spring and early summer, calf elk are especially prized. With enormous, needle-sharp claws, bears easily dig out marmots and squirrels. These claws, combined with a powerful tooth-studded mouth, make the grizzly indeed a beast to be avoided. Unfortunately, grizzlies are often involved in human conflicts and end up the losers.

The best place to see grizzlies in Yellowstone is in the Mount Washburn area, in Hayden Valley and in the general vicinity of Fishing Bridge. Outside the park, you can often see grizzlies outside the East Gate, from the gate to Pahaska Tepee and along the Shoshone River toward Cody.

## BLACK BEARS

Some of the most memorable wildlife photographs in Yellowstone show black bears begging food from tourists. Those days are gone, since the practice was highly discouraged in the early 1970s, and bears were managed to be "wild." Nowadays, black bears are where they belong—as residents of the park's natural environment. Like grizzlies, black bears do not hibernate. They awake from a deep sleep in the spring and feed extensively to gain back much of the weight they lost during the winter. Though black bears are smaller than grizzlies, large individuals can easily weigh several hundred pounds. Some bears in the east have been weighed at more than 700 pounds. Black bears are largely nocturnal, moving about and feeding in the dark. Like grizzlies, they're not above raiding campgrounds, scaring the wits out of human visitors.

*Black bears are common in and around Yellowstone but are rarely seen.*

Seeing a black bear in or outside Yellowstone is iffy at best, since they're so widely scattered. You might see a bear in such widely diverse habitats as in sagebrush, along a stream or at timberline. The best time to spot them is just before dark. You might spot a black bear in the area around Sunlight Basin and Crandall along the Chief Joseph Highway in Wyoming.

## MOUNTAIN LIONS

These large cats roam throughout the west, and lately have been causing problems in urban areas. Increased attacks on humans and pets most likely are because of civilization's encroachment into habitat normally occupied by lions. In the Yellowstone area, mountain lions, also known as cougars, are residents of the backcountry and are rarely seen. These predators may weigh up to 170 pounds and reach lengths of eight feet from nose to tail. Males are larger than females. Lions are meat-eaters and prefer their menu fresh. Deer are among their favorite prey species, but they'll also catch other animals such as beavers, rabbits, porcupines and various rodents. Contrary to popular belief, lions do not ambush their prey from a tree limb as the hapless quarry walks underneath. Instead, the cat makes an incredibly stealthy stalk, using vegetation as screening cover. When it's just a short distance away, the lion makes a quick charge and either catches the prey in the first few bounds or misses it. During long chases, deer can usually outrun a lion, but the initial surprise attack is a most successful strategy.

Seeing a lion anywhere in the west is cause for great celebration. Don't expect to see one, but if you do, consider yourself very fortunate. Typically, lions dwell in places where there are plenty of deer.

## WOLVES

Thanks to a controversial but very successful reintroduction program, wolves are now back in Yellowstone after an absence of almost 70 years. Several dozen wolves were captured in Canada and turned loose in Yellowstone in March 1995. Those animals have done remarkably well, reproducing at a rapid rate. Packs are now located in various parts of the park. Wolves prey on a variety of species, notably elk in the Yellowstone area, but will also pursue moose, deer, sheep and other animals.

*Wolves are now common residents in and around Yellowstone due to their reintroduction in the mid-1990s.*
DONNIE SEXTON/COURTESY TRAVEL MONTANA

Although wolf packs have wandered outside Yellowstone, the best place to see them is in the Lamar Valley between Mammoth and Cooke City. Get there very early in the morning when it's still dark, park your RV in a pullout and listen very quietly. Chances are good you'll hear them howl, and you may see them in this vast open sagebrush area as they hunt for breakfast. At this time, it will be tough to see them outside the park, although there are often consistent sightings around Nye and Fishtail, Montana. Inquire locally for updated information.

## COYOTES

This member of the dog family is quite possibly the most successful predator on the continent. Despite widespread efforts to eliminate coyotes, they've not only failed to go away, but they've enormously expanded their range. Just a few decades ago, coyotes were animals of the West. Now they're in such far-removed places as Maine and Florida. A big coyote will weigh 30 to 40 pounds, and the animals are fond of anything they can catch and subdue. Rodents are their mainstay, but they're known to take birds, reptiles and even large mammals such as deer and antelope. You may hear coyotes early in the morning and throughout the night as they roam about searching for food. In Yellowstone, their yips and barks are much shriller than the deep, throaty howl of a wolf.

Trying to describe where you can see coyotes is fruitless, since you're apt to see them everywhere, both in the park and outside its borders. Though most of their hunting is in early morning and late afternoon, you can often see them during the day.

## FISHING OUTSIDE
## YELLOWSTONE NATIONAL PARK

Regardless of the season you visit the greater Yellowstone area, you can count on good fishing somewhere. Thousands of miles of creeks and rivers, and hundreds of lakes, will provide all the angling opportunities you can handle.

With a few minor exceptions, trout are about all you'll find in this region, and lots of them at that. That's the good news. The bad news is that many of the best spots are not secret, so you can expect plenty of company. On the other hand, there are plenty of places that are truly outstanding but haven't yet been trampled by crowds of anglers. We're going to give you a mix of places to wet your line. We'll describe some of the mothers of all fishing waters in each of the three states within the 100-mile limit of this book, but we'll also tell you where to find some quiet spots. Some of the places we'll recommend will be famous fly-fishing areas, but recognizing the fact that many RVers simply like to use spinning lures or bait, we'll suggest those too. And we'll include lakes where you can park your RV in a campground, walk to the shore with a can of worms and a lawn chair, and relax in the sun.

If your visit is in June or July, be aware that many of the top rivers may look like chocolate milk. The disconcerting color is due to geologic erosion, which in turn is caused by snow melting in the high country. During years of exceptional winter snows, the high runoff can continue into late July. Do not despair if you find this to be the case. Instead, check out some rivers below dams, since the impounded reservoirs collect the high water and filter the mud out before it emerges at the dams. You should also know that rivers can instantly turn muddy if there's a severe summer storm in the headwaters. These are temporary conditions, but nonetheless can ruin your day. It's also quite possible, and frustrating, to see a river turn to mud before your very eyes, even though there hasn't been a cloud in the sky for a week. Some of those erosion-causing high-elevation storms may be dozens of miles away, and you won't know it.

As a rule of thumb, expect the heaviest fishing pressure around campgrounds, since people are concentrated and typically take a walk from their unit to the nearby water. The same is true along highways. Since an RV requires a larger roadside pullout than a smaller vehicle, it's tough to park where few other people do. Here's a tip: When you turn into a roadside pullout, walk a few hundred yards along the

*Rainbow trout, an important fish species in the greater Yellowstone area*

highway, and fish as far from the parking spot as you can. It's surprising how easy it is to find water that isn't heavily fished, but you must expend a little energy.

Be sure you thoroughly check the angling regulations for the water you're fishing. Some streams have entirely different sets of rules depending on the section being fished. We know at least one lake that has different seasons, depending on which side of an imaginary line drawn between two points that you're fishing. Some waters have minimum lengths, requiring your fish to be a certain size before you keep it. Some have maximum lengths, requiring you to release it if it's bigger than a set size. More common these days is a "slot" limit, requiring you to release fish between certain sizes, or allowing you to keep fish between certain sizes. If you intend to keep fish for dinner, be sure to bring a ruler along to stay within the law. Be aware that many streams, or parts of them, are either catch-and-release or artificial lures only. When buying a license, be aware that you can purchase a single-day license or one good for a certain number of days. Each state has different license structures.

An important matter is to be able to identify fish species if you intend on keeping some. Some waters require you to release cutthroat trout; in many waters there's a bonus limit of brook trout under a certain size, etc. If you're unsure of trout identification, take along a book or pamphlet showing trout and their characteristics.

# FAMOUS WATERS

**IDAHO:
Henry's Fork of
the Snake River**

If a poll were taken among the nation's top trout anglers, the Henry's Fork would no doubt garner the most votes as the Holy Grail of fishing. Every truly serious trout angler has either fished the Henry's Fork or *wishes* he or she had fished it. John Randolph, longtime editor of the prestigious *Flyfishing* magazine, says the Henry's Fork is the greatest trout river in the *world*. This western river offers the quintessence of everything that trout fishing is all about—wonderful insect hatches, superb water conditions and quality trout that fight like crazy. That, in a nutshell, is the heart and soul of trout fishing, not to mention magnificent mountain scenery and hearty camaraderie among other anglers who are just as happy to be on the Henry's as you are.

The river, named after fur trader Andrew Henry, runs 120 miles from where it exits Henry's Lake to the Snake River near Rexburg. It is Idaho's claim to fame among anglers, with no close second. Of its entire length, a single 10-mile stretch is considered to be the only place to fish, and that's the stretch between Island Park Dam and the Osborne Bridge. Only fly fishing is allowed here, and all fish must be released. For that reason, there are plenty of trout in the river, and most of them are sophisticated enough to spurn all but the finest fly offerings, which must be precisely presented at the right time at the right place. Rainbows are the prize in the river, including some monsters that are easily two feet long.

Other famed stretches of the Henry's are the Last Chance Run, which is one of the most popular of all, and the Railroad Ranch. If you aren't familiar with the river, visit one of the numerous fly shops in the Island Park area. Plenty of campgrounds are available in the region, but they're extremely busy when the hatches are on and the trout are biting. Show up early in the day to get a campsite.

The river is accessed via U.S. 20, which runs from West Yellowstone to Ashton.

**IDAHO:
Henry's Lake**

Like the famous river that runs out of it, Henry's Lake is a favorite trout mecca whose followers fish out of boats, float tubes or wade the shoreline. The lake, in the Centennial Mountains less than 20 miles from Yellowstone, regularly produces lunker trout. Known by locals as "Hank's Pond," the lake gives up brook trout, cutthroats and hybrid cuttbows. The hybrids are the biggest, some running up to 10 pounds. The lake covers about 15 square miles and is relatively shallow with an average depth of 18 feet.

Unlike the Henry's Fork, spinning lures are allowed and are responsible for a good share of the fish caught. Popular lures are

*This campground at Henry's Lake in Idaho is popular with trout anglers.*

Mepps spinners, Panther Martins, Roostertails and pop gear trailed by a small worm. Since trolling is one of the most effective techniques, anglers have been experimenting on flies rather than lures because flies have been proven to cause less injury to released fish.

Fishing from shore is best when flies are cast by float tube anglers or those who wade along the shallows. A heavy layer of vegetation covers much of the lake in summer; fly fishing is much more effective than lures.

Fishing season usually opens the Saturday before Memorial Day and runs to late October. Veteran anglers catch fish throughout the season, but favorite periods for the biggest trout are in September and October.

Two public campgrounds are available: Henry's Lake State Park and Fremont County Camp. They are accessible via U.S. 20 and Montana 87.

**MONTANA: Gallatin River**

This 80-mile-long river, which begins deep in Yellowstone National Park and joins the Missouri at Three Forks, runs along U.S. 191 for much of its length. There are plenty of turnouts to accommodate RVs, making the river highly accessible, and much of the river courses through public land in either the Gallatin National Forest or Yellowstone National Park. Despite the proximity to the highway, it remains an outstanding river with plenty of trout. If you head north out of West Yellowstone, you'll enter Yellowstone for a short distance, and see the Gallatin River for the first time. If you fish this stretch in the park, (which, incidentally, is very good), you'll need a Yellowstone National Park fishing permit. You can pick one up at the West Gate at West Yellowstone at a cost of $10 for seven days or $20 for the season.

The Gallatin isn't known for producing big trout, primarily because of the cold water temperatures that inhibit food and, subsequently, fish growth. It takes about five years for a rainbow to grow to 14 inches in the river. Most of the fish in the Gallatin are rainbows running up to 14 inches, though it's not uncommon to tie into a two- or three-pounder. Besides rainbows, you may tangle with an occasional brown or cutthroat.

The river enters private land as you near Gallatin Gateway, and much of it is posted. Fish tend to run bigger in these lower waters. A Montana law allows anglers to fish anywhere in a river up to the high-water mark, provided access is made at a legal entry point. If you do this, be sure you don't exit the water and climb the bank onto private land above the high-water mark.

## MONTANA: Yellowstone River

This magnificent waterway has the distinction of being the longest undammed river in the United States. The 678-mile river is born high in Yellowstone National Park, traveling through Wyoming, then into Montana where it runs north to Livingston and then east to the border, and finally into North Dakota, joining the Missouri. Within the park, the river commonly has elbow-to-elbow anglers any place there's reasonable access. Outside the park, you'll find far fewer crowds. From Gardiner, the river follows U.S. 89 for some 50 miles to Livingston, then along I-90 and I-94 to the border. Access is outstanding along several hundred miles.

The river flows away from Gardiner quickly, and fishing is tough in this stretch. As it enters Yankee Jim Canyon, it continues to roar along, but it deepens considerably. Three rapids offer an exciting ride to those brave enough to float it. The depths of the Yankee Jim stretch reportedly hold some monster trout.

The Yellowstone slows down as it leaves the canyon, and spreads wider. As you near the towering Emigrant Peak, you'll begin to see islands in the river. From that point down, you'll see long pools mixed with riffles. Much of this is perfect for bank fishing; there are a number of access points along the highway.

Mallard's Rest Fishing Access above Livingston is a popular spot to put in and take out boats, or to simply wade. From that point to Livingston, trout tend to be bigger in size than upriver. Rainbows and browns are the dominant trout in the Yellowstone. Whitefish are also plentiful, and are encouraged to be kept since they compete with trout. Montana allows each angler to keep 100 fish. On a good day you can easily catch your limit. Whitefish are outstanding when smoked. See page 34 for a great recipe.

Below Livingston, the river makes a dramatic easterly swing, following I-90. Many access points are available along the interstate. In the Billings area, the river warms considerably. Here you begin seeing walleye, channel catfish, sauger and paddlefish. Trout continue to show up, but in lesser numbers as you go downstream.

**WYOMING: Snake River**

This big western river is Wyoming's largest blue-ribbon water, offering exceptional fishing throughout its entire length. Beginning in Yellowstone National Park, the river descends through remote forests and is unseen by travelers until it becomes visible a few miles below the park's South Gate.

The good news is that a fair share of the Snake flows across public land, requiring no permission to gain access, especially in the downstream sections. The bad news is that the banks are often steep, precluding an easy descent to much of it. There are, however, places where access is fairly good. RV parking is possible in dozens of spots. Here's a tip: Because annual spring flooding can alter the course of the river, creating new pools and holes where none existed before, it's a good idea to visit one of the fly shops in Jackson to see what's hot and what's not. It's also wise to buy a few flies and then ask your questions. Some busy clerks are more prone to talk to bona fide customers than tire-kickers. This river also offers an outstanding opportunity to fish from a raft with the assistance of an outfitter. There are plenty in the greater Jackson area.

If you visit the area early in the spring, the river is apt to be clear, but in May it suddenly becomes transformed into a muddy mess, thanks to snow melting in the high country. You can usually count on the river being clear in late July.

The lower part of the Snake between Hoback Junction and Alpine Junction has dozens of parking spots allowing access. Be cautious when wading, because the underlying rocks and boulders can be extremely slick.

By far the majority of fish in the river are the Snake River cutthroat trout. There are also some brookies and browns and lots of whitefish.

*Kayaking is a popular activity on the Snake River near Jackson, Wyoming.*

## PLACES TO BEAT THE CROWDS

**MONTANA:**
**Clark Canyon**
**Reservoir**

Though this reservoir is well known and is no secret, it offers fishing for really big rainbow and brown trout, many of them easily surpassing the five-pound mark and closer to ten. You'll find less angling pressure here in the early spring and late fall, which happen to be prime times to fish. In the summer, you can expect plenty of weekend anglers from Utah and Idaho.

Clark Canyon is easily accessible, since it lies just west of I-15, which connects Salt Lake City to Butte. Montana 324 follows along much of the northwest shore.

Many anglers use float tubes, and boating is extremely popular, though caution is advised because of frequent heavy winds. The most popular spot for fly fishing is at the southern end of the lake where the Red Rocks River flows in. At the dam on the opposite end, the famous Beaverhead River, legendary among anglers everywhere, runs out.

For anglers who simply want to toss out a bait and let the fish do the work, there are a number of places along the shoreline that are accessible. If you're unfamiliar with the lake, talk to some of the locals; most are willing to share information. Two campgrounds offer overnighting on the lake, one on the east side and one on the west. Both have boat ramps.

To fish lures from either boats or shore, try sinking Rapalas, large Mepps spinners and Daredevles. The lake holds an interesting fish called a burbot or ling. These cod-like fish look terrible but are unbelievably good on the table. Unfortunately, for those passing by in the summer, the best burbot fishing is through the ice; they're not consistently caught any other time of the year.

**MONTANA:**
**Stillwater River**

The name of this river is no indication of its characteristics. In reality, it's one of the swiftest-flowing rivers in the state. Perhaps an early explorer with a penchant for practical jokes came up with the name. If this river was located someplace where there was a dearth of trout fishing, it would be beat to death by hordes of anglers. Though it offers superb fishing, it's largely ignored except by locals, because so many other famous waters are close by. Most anglers come from Billings or are residents who work in nearby mines.

A favorite spot to begin fishing its upper waters is in the vicinity of Woodbine Campground. A hiking trail runs along the river, allowing access to deep pools that hold plenty of feisty brookies, as well as some rainbows and cutthroats. As you continue downstream, rainbows and browns show up in greater numbers, replacing the brookies.

The river is noted for huge boulders that create eddies on the downstream side. These pockets often hold trout, and astute anglers fish every boulder eddy they come to. The fast water requires the utmost caution for waders. The East and West Forks of the Rosebud River join the Stillwater just above Absarokee, adding a large volume of water. Here the large boulders give way to smaller stones, and the current slows down a bit. Fish tend to run bigger as the Stillwater approaches the Yellowstone, which it joins at Columbus.

Hundreds of Montana waters hold whitefish, but the Stillwater is one of the best. Many anglers deliberately fish for whitefish, normally catching all they want on flies or bait. Though anglers typically toss whitefish back in disgust, folks in the know put them in a smoker and enjoy a superb treat.

Flies, lures and bait all work well on the river. Worms seem to catch plenty of fish, and spin fishermen do well on small spoons, spinners and jigs.

Several public fishing areas provide access, but, like everywhere else, it's a good idea to walk as far as you can from parking areas. Where private land is present, be sure to ask permission from landowners.

To reach the river, take Montana 78 south from Columbus to Absarokee, then County Road 420 to Nye, and then to the Woodbine Campground.

## WYOMING: North Fork of the Shoshone River

As you leave the East Gate of Yellowstone Park, headed to Cody, you travel along the Shoshone River to its entry to the Buffalo Bill Reservoir about 35 miles downstream. Throughout this length, the river, simply known as the "North Fork" among locals, gives up rainbows, cutthroats, browns and a few brookies.

Different seasons govern various sections of the river, so be sure to check the angling regulations carefully. Part of the river is open to year-round fishing, part of it closes April 1, and other sections open in July.

The North Fork drainage receives a great deal of water from melting snow, rendering the river unfishable until July. When the water clears, fish are eager to bite, but anglers are few and far between. Most nonresidents are so busy driving as fast as they can to fish Yellowstone National Park that they ignore the North Fork. That's a big mistake, as most anglers learn when they try the river.

The water is a good mix of rapids, riffles, runs and pools, offering excellent opportunities to anglers using flies, lures or bait. There are no restrictions anywhere on the river. Most trout run 12 to 16 inches.

All of the river from Pahaska Tepee, just outside Yellowstone, flows through public land in the Shoshone National Forest to the point where the river leaves the canyon and enters ranchlands in

*Floating down the Shoshone River near Cody, Wyoming*

the valley. Access is difficult to obtain on private land, but there are several public entry points along the lower section. Numerous campgrounds are scattered down through the Shoshone National Forest, and there's a new campground at Buffalo Bill State Park, located where the river joins the reservoir. There are also plenty of turnouts along the highway, allowing good access.

As a fair warning, be aware that the river flows through prime grizzly bear country, which is no surprise for anglers who fish on streams outside Yellowstone. Anglers are cautioned to be careful and to carry a container of bear repellent spray.

The river is a natural spawning ground, and produces wild fish, many from adults that swim upriver from the reservoir. The widely varying seasons were established to protect spawning fish.

### WYOMING: Wind River

The Wind River south of Thermopolis is perhaps the most ignored trout water in the state. This waterway actually has its beginnings high in the Wind River Mountains, flowing almost 150 miles to a point below Thermopolis where it is joined by a warm-water canal and essentially ceases to be a trout fishery. The river exits 19,000-acre Boysen Reservoir and runs rapidly through the Wind River Canyon, paralleling U.S. 20 along the entire stretch. At the mouth of the canyon from which it emerges near Thermopolis, it undergoes a name change and becomes known as the Bighorn River.

In the canyon, the river is characterized by serious rapids, runs and tantalizing pools. Rainbows and browns live in the river, some reaching large sizes. The river doesn't turn to mud as do most others in the spring and early summer, because it emerges from Boysen Dam. The reservoir above the dam collects the sediment, allowing it to settle before the water leaves. For this reason, the Wind is a fine fishery when other rivers are in bad shape.

A drawback to the river is the steep, rocky slopes that must be negotiated to reach it from the highway. There are trails from most turnouts, and a bit of care is suggested. Rarely is a descent of more than 30 to 50 yards required; some are much shorter.

The river runs through the Wind River Indian Reservation, and an Indian permit must be purchased. They're available in surrounding communities.

*The Wind River Canyon south of Thermopolis, Wyoming*

Curiously, few people fish the river, even though it runs a few yards from a major highway throughout its length in the canyon, with numerous parking turnouts along the route. Even on holiday weekends, it's tough to count more than a dozen vehicles parked alongside, and most of them have out-of-state license plates.

It's said that the absence of anglers is because the locals fish the river on either end of the canyon and are hesitant to pay the extra fee within the reservation. Non-residents, on the other hand, are so anxious to sample the outstanding fishing in the canyon that the fee is immaterial.

**WYOMING: Buffalo Bill Reservoir**

This lake collects water from both the South and North Forks of the Shoshone River that flow from widely divergent watersheds. Biologists claim it's a "sleeper" in that it's one of the most productive waters in the state as well as being one of the most unknown. Rainbows dominate the lake, with cutthroats and hybrids also present, along with lake trout.

In early summer, both forks of the Shoshone deposit muddy water in the lake, and it takes some time for the particles to settle. During high-water years, the entire reservoir takes on a murky color, but it begins clearing in mid-summer. Because trout spawn chiefly in the North Fork, the lake is closed from April 1 to July 15 each year, west of an imaginary line drawn from Rattlesnake Creek to Spring Creek, which drain into the reservoir on opposing shorelines. This closure is meant to protect spawners concentrated in the west end of the lake.

The eastern portion of the lake that remains open all year offers very good fishing and remains clear longer than the rest of the reservoir. Boat ramps allow access, and bank fishing is excellent around the shoreline. U.S. 14/16/20 runs along the entire north side, offering good shore fishing. Numerous turnouts allow access, and the Buffalo Bill State Park campground provides excellent overnight accommodations along the lake shore. Many campers stroll to the bank and enjoy fishing with bait or lures. Another campground, also in Buffalo Bill State Park, is at the west edge of the lake where the river joins it. This campground is on the river, offering good access to the water. The portion of river adjacent to the campground opens July 1 each year.

Both campgrounds are seldom crowded, even on peak holiday weekends. They're a good alternative for RV travelers who are unable to find a space in nearby Cody. The downside is that they're a 15-minute drive to town.

There is a four-trout limit in the lake and a three-trout limit in the river above the Red Pole Bridge near the campground. Fish normally average 15 to 16 inches.

## TIPS ON CATCH-AND-RELEASE FISHING

1.  If you have a choice of artificial lures, flies and bait, avoid bait if you intend on releasing fish, since their mortality rate is much higher from fully ingesting hooks.

2.  Use barbless hooks. If they aren't barbless, you can pinch the barb down with needle-nose pliers.

3.  Play and land the fish as quickly as possible to reduce stress, especially if the water is warm. Use stronger line if necessary to land fish more quickly.

4.  Never take the fish out of the water. If you intend to photograph it, gently hold it on the surface of the water, and release it immediately after the photo is taken.

5.  Never touch the fish in the gills, and don't squeeze it or allow it to flounder about on the bank.

6.  Gently remove the hook. Special pliers called hemostats (available in fly-fishing shops) allow you to clamp onto the hook and quickly slip it free.

7.  Release fish in calm water, never in strong current. Hold it upright and gently move it back and forth slowly to push water through its gills. Allow it to swim away freely.

8.  **Here's reality**: If an injured fish is bleeding from the gills, it will undoubtedly die. If regulations allow you to do so, take it home and release it in hot butter.

## VISITOR INFORMATION

**State Guide and Outfitters Associations**

Wyoming Outfitters and Guides Association, PO Box 284, 329 Yellowstone Ave., Suite 3, Cody, WY 82414; (307) 527-7453.

Montana Outfitters and Guides Association, Box 1248, Helena, MT 59624; (406) 449-3578; fax: (406) 443-2439.

Idaho Guide and Outfitters Board, PO Box 95, Boise, ID 83701; (208) 342-1438; 1-800-VISITID; 1-800-847-4843.

**State Fish and Game Departments**

Wyoming Game and Fish, 5400 Bishop Blvd., Cheyenne, WY 82006; (307) 777-4600.

Montana Department of Fish, Wildlife and Parks, 1420 E. 6th Ave., Helena, MT 59620; (406) 444-2535.

Idaho Department of Fish and Game, 600 S. Walnut St., Boise, ID 83707; (208) 334-3700; 1-800-635-7820.

**To report game and fish violations:**
- Wyoming: 1-800-442-4331
- Montana: 1-800-847-6668
- Idaho: 1-800-632-5999

## FAVORITE FISH RECIPES

These are simple recipes that you can use in your RV. Most of the fish you'll catch in the greater Yellowstone area will be trout. Easiest of all to cook are brook trout, which are over-populated and stunted in many waters. Many states encourage you to keep brookies under a certain length (usually six inches) by allowing an additional bonus limit.

### Hot Buttered Brookies (or any trout)

cleaned trout
1 cup flour
¼ teaspoon salt or salt substitute
¼ teaspoon pepper
¼ teaspoon onion salt

¼ teaspoon garlic salt
pinch of dried parsley
crumbs of three crushed crackers
2 tablespoons butter or substitute

Mix all dry ingredients except trout thoroughly in a bag. Put trout in and toss until well coated. Cook in hot butter until golden brown.

## Fish in Foil

This is a nice recipe that works either in your RV oven or on the campfire grill.

four or five cleaned fish
¼ cup butter
3 tablespoons freshly squeezed lime juice
1 tablespoon dried parsley
¼ teaspoon salt
¼ teaspoon Tabasco sauce, or similar hot sauce
½ cup chopped onion
aluminum foil

Melt butter in small pan, and stir in lime juice, parsley, salt and hot sauce. Allow to heat through. Place fish on foil, and dab small amount of butter sauce in each cavity. Sprinkle onions on top, drizzle with remaining butter sauce (if fish are too large and you don't have enough butter sauce to pour over fish, make another adequate quantity) and fold up sides of foil, sealing tightly. Place on barbecue or campfire grill and allow to cook 10 or 15 minutes. Carefully turn over and cook the other side. To bake in oven, cook in preheated oven at 400 degrees for 20 minutes.

## Smoked Whitefish

Once you try this recipe, you'll never again cuss whitefish that steal your offering intended for trout. Smoked whitefish are extremely expensive, if you can find them at all in a store. Here's how to do it in your backyard. To smoke fish, you'll need a small electric smoker. Because the unit will give off a constant smoky smell after being used, you won't want to haul one around in your RV. It's best to do the smoking at home. When you catch whitefish, gut, scale, and behead them, and freeze them in your RV freezer, or put them in an iced cooler until you get home.

Brining is a mandatory part of the smoking process. This step introduces the correct amount of salt to the fish. Most recipes also call for sugar, either white or brown. Once the brine solution is made (see next page), immerse the fish and allow them to remain for at least 6 hours in a refrigerator. The brining container should be glass or plastic, never metal of any sort. After removing the fish from the brine, wipe them dry and allow them to stand at room temperature for one hour. This produces a sort of a glazed finish called a pellicle. Place the fish in the smoker and follow directions. The smoker will have a small hot plate in the bottom. You place a pan of wood chips on the hot plate and allow them to smolder until finished, then continue the process. Smokers are available in sporting goods stores and from mail order catalogs.

## Brine Solution

2 quarts water
1 cup non-iodized salt
½ cup brown sugar
2 tablespoons lemon concentrate
    or ¼ cup fresh lemon juice
¼ tablespoon garlic powder
¼ tablespoon onion powder

Mix all ingredients and stir until dissolved. Add fish, and follow instructions on page 34.

# HOW TO SEE A RODEO

Touring the greater Yellowstone area and not seeing a rodeo is like visiting New York City and not viewing the city from the top of the Empire State Building. There's really no good excuse for missing a rodeo, since practically every community has one in the summer. In Cody, Wyoming, dubbed the "Rodeo Capital of the World," you can see one every night from June through late August.

The hero of the rodeo is the cowboy, an amazing human who seemingly knows no pain, or if he *is* in pain, won't dare show it. Older cowboys have no use for whiners or pouters, and you'll never see more pride than in the rodeo arena. A cowboy who has never broken a bone is a rarity, and when he does, his pals sort of shrug it off and wonder when their turn will come. Nowhere else does a sport participant wade into a violent confrontation with absolutely no protection. Athletes on a playing field wear all sorts of safety devices, but a cowboy has nothing other than a pair of jeans, a thin shirt, boots, and a light hat that normally flies off his head as soon as he goes into action. Rest assured there is a ready and waiting ambulance parked at every rodeo, and when a cowboy is hauled away to the emergency room, it's normally not a big deal—it's just a fact of life with rodeo. But sometimes it *is* a big deal. More serious injuries than broken bones can occur, and losing one's life is also a reality in the rodeo arena. It happens all too often.

What possesses a person to get involved in this dangerous sport? Most are born into it, following in the footsteps of other male members of the family. Others like the fast action and love working with horses and livestock. A few come from big cities, never having ridden a horse until they were adults. There is, of course, a monetary reward, but it isn't all that much until a cowboy gets into the finals,

*The Cody Nite Rodeo is held every evening from mid-June to late August.*
COURTESY PARK COUNTY TRAVEL COUNCIL

and if he makes it, he'll have earned it the hard way, with plenty of bumps and bruises to show for it. Winners of an average event at a local rodeo may win a few hundred dollars and a belt buckle. At the annual National Finals Rodeo in Las Vegas, however, which is the Super Bowl of Rodeos, the all-time winner of an event will earn about $33,000, and about $12,000 each day that he wins that particular event. That's chicken feed when compared to professional golf and other sports, and remember that these fees are paid only to the winning cowboy. Second- and third-place winners earn much less.

Another rodeo hero is often overlooked by spectators. He's the clown, who jokes constantly with the commentator (using a microphone so the audience can listen in), and performs goofy antics to generate laughs from the crowd. But the clown has a deadly serious role during the bull-riding event, which is the most dangerous of all. When the cowboy is thrown from the bull's back, the huge animal typically wants revenge and is intent on making mush of the rudely vacated rider. To prevent this would-be catastrophe, the clowns tantalize the bull, beckoning it to chase them. The idea is to divert the bull's attention from the cowboy, who may have been injured during the ride and cannot move quickly. Clowns are so quick on their feet they can out-maneuver a bull, and some jump into a barrel, teasing the bull to knock it around. Don't let the clown costumes fool you. They conceal brave and extremely athletic men who ask nothing other than a few laughs and a bull ride without injury to the riders.

There are basically seven events in rodeo; all but one involves males. The exception is barrel racing, which is typically an all-female event.

*The Stampede Parade in downtown Cody occurs every July 4.*
COURTESY PARK COUNTY TRAVEL COUNCIL

## SADDLE BRONC RIDING

This is the oldest event, for obvious reasons. Young horses must be broken to accept a rider, and in the old days, there were challenges and wagers among cowboys when they mounted a "green" horse. In the rodeo arena, the cowboy mounts his horse while it is confined in one of several "chutes," a small pen that holds the unhappy bronc. When the rider signals to the attendants to open the gate, his feet must be positioned over the horse's back, or the cowboy will be penalized. Before the ride begins, his feet are firmly planted in stirrups, and he holds onto a thick rope. Once in the arena, he pumps his legs rapidly back and forth in sort of a rocking motion, as the horse leaps and bucks about, trying to throw the menace on its back. No score is possible unless the cowboy hangs on for eight seconds, indicated by a loud horn. At that point, two pick-up men ride up and pluck the cowboy from the horse, allowing him to swing down to the ground. The score is awarded according to the bucking ability of the horse, and the cowboy's actions in the saddle. Since the horse's performance is critical to the score, some horses are better judge-pleasers than others. To make it fair, cowboys draw their horses in a lottery.

## BAREBACK BRONC RIDING

Established in the 1920s, this event is similar to the saddle bronc ride, except the cowboy doesn't have the luxury of sitting in a saddle (the term "sitting" is taking the word loosely, because there's not a whole lot of sitting going on during the wild and crazy ride). The bareback rider holds onto a suitcase-like handle rigging made of leather and rawhide. When he exits the chute, he must be correctly positioned so he's lying back on the bronc with his heels above the horse's shoulders. Anything less and he's disqualified. From there on, he tries to hold on for eight seconds, and as in saddle bronc riding, he's judged by his performance as well as the horse's actions.

## BULL RIDING

This is the main event, always last, and always the most popular. If a cowboy can get hurt badly, here's where it's likely to happen. He must sit atop a wildly gyrating beast that can weigh a ton, holding onto a rope with one well-resined leather glove. If he can ride for eight seconds, he'll be happy and earn a score, providing he doesn't violate any rules. There's seldom a graceful way to dismount from the mighty upset bull. With luck the cowboy will make a flying leap and land on his feet, or he'll be dumped unceremoniously and hopefully keep all his bones intact. The clowns will then keep the bull busy and distracted until the cowboy dusts his jeans off and scampers out of the arena.

## BARREL RACING

This is a timed event where a cowgirl must race her horse in a cloverleaf pattern around three barrels positioned in triangle fashion within the arena. The object is simply to do it faster than anyone else without knocking over any barrels. This is a crowd-pleaser as ladies urge their horses around the course. Many rodeos have a juvenile event where it's not uncommon to see a five-year old-lass putting her horse through the paces.

## STEER WRESTLING

All sorts of talent come into play here: horsemanship, the willingness to leap off a moving object and grab a pair of sharp horns, also moving, and then physically to maneuver the steer off its feet and bring it to the ground. This event, also called bulldogging, is accomplished with a teammate called a "hazer," whose assignment is to ride along the steer and keep it running straight ahead. The cowboy with the wrestling chore begins behind a barrier, giving the steer a 30-foot head start. He rides up alongside the steer, and when he's correctly positioned, he lowers himself off his horse, and grabs the horns. By digging in with his bootheels, the cowboy slows the steer's forward progress and twists the neck to bring the animal down. The score will count only if the steer's feet all face the same direction when it's on the ground. The fastest time wins this event.

## CALF ROPING

Working cowboys on the range often catch calves by roping them, and this practice logically became a popular rodeo event. The calf is turned loose from a chute, and the waiting cowboy must give the calf a designated head start before making his move. Then he races out of the waiting area, throws a loop around the calf's head, dismounts, runs up to the calf, throws it to the ground, and ties three legs together with a rope called a "pigging string." When the knot is completed, the cowboy throws his hand in the air to signal the judge that he's done. The calf must then remain tied for six seconds, and the fastest time wins. The horse plays a major role here, keeping just the right distance from the calf as it's running, and maneuvering backward and keeping the rope taut as the cowboy ties the legs.

## TEAM ROPING

This event is the only one where two cowboys are teamed together for equal roles. The idea is for one cowboy to throw a loop around the head of a steer, and the second man to rope the two hind legs. Once the steer is properly trussed, the cowboys turn their horses to face each other. If the ropes are properly dallied and everything holds, the judge waves his flag and records a time. This event is more apt to fail than others because of the split-second coordination required as well as the ability to throw a rope around two wildly moving feet.

# A BRIEF LOOK AT THE STATE HISTORIES OF MONTANA, IDAHO, AND WYOMING

This is a general overview of the major developments that led to the settlement of the three states that surround Yellowstone. More detailed accounts of local history are given along with the descriptions of individual towns throughout the book.

## MONTANA

There's an interesting misconception about our fourth biggest state. Known as Big Sky Country, Montana is perceived to be a mountainous land with snow-capped peaks throughout. To be sure, plenty of that exists, but less than half the state is mountain country. The majority of it, east of the Rockies, is enormous rolling prairie and badlands, with huge ranches and rural areas where towns are light years apart (well, almost).

Montana is a land of countless rivers and streams, but the best-known are the Yellowstone and the Missouri, each crossing most of the state, primarily in the east. The Missouri's claim to fame is its role in the famous Lewis and Clark expedition. The Yellowstone is unique in that it is the longest undammed river in the United States.

Historians tell us the earliest inhabitants of Montana arrived during the Ice Age 10,000 years ago by crossing the frozen Bering Sea. Many Native American tribes settled in various parts of the state as the centuries progressed, with territories established and terminated due to constant battles. Some tribes came from the east and northwest, and some came from Canada. The Blackfeet were considered the most dangerous, along with the Shoshone, who were among the earliest tribes in the area. The Crow, Assiniboine, Sioux, Northern Cheyenne, Cree, Chippewa, Salish and Kootenai also took up residence, trading boundaries as skirmishes were bitterly fought.

In 1804, in response to President Thomas Jefferson's desire to find a route to the Pacific Ocean, Meriwether Lewis and William Clark left St. Louis, heading up the Missouri River with a crew of 27. President Jefferson had purchased the Louisiana Territory from France in 1803, and he was eager to learn what this enormous region comprised, as well as in finding a passageway to the West Coast.

*Wild horses still roam the deserts and prairie outside Yellowstone.*

Lewis and Clark made it as far as Mandan, North Dakota, that fall, when winter weather shut down their travel plans. In addition to charting new territory, the expedition gathered all sorts of natural items to send back to Washington, including bird and animal skins, fossils, plants, ore and a variety of other unique objects. At their North Dakota winter camp, the explorers met Sacajawea, a Shoshone woman who spoke French and English fluently. Lewis and Clark understood her value, not only because of her language skills, but also because her presence would reassure other Natives of the expedition's peaceful mission. Some historians say Sacajawea actually guided the party a considerable distance upriver, but that claim is disputed by others.

The next spring, the intrepid explorers crossed into Montana on April 26, 1805. Continuing upstream in enormous dugout canoes, the party eventually reached the headwaters of the Missouri near current-day Three Forks, Montana. The journey became far more difficult in the shallow river, and ultimately, the adventurers struck out overland to cross the Continental Divide and find a downstream route to the Columbia River. After several more months of very difficult travel, they left Montana on September 13 at Lolo Pass and entered Idaho. Lewis and Clark fulfilled their mission when they finally reached the Oregon Coast; they spent the winter there, eating unfamiliar food such as salmon and other treasures of the sea.

The next spring, they reversed their earlier route and headed back up the Columbia. They entered Montana on June 27, 1806, and a few days later, split their party in two. Lewis, with nine men, followed the Bitterroot River downstream and then traveled overland up the Blackfoot River drainage to Great Falls, intending to discover a better route over the Continental Divide. Clark, with 20 men and 50 horses, made his way back to Three Forks, where the party split again. One of the sergeants took nine men and floated down the Missouri, while Clark and the rest of the party worked their way into the Yellowstone Valley near Livingston. Following the river downstream, Clark rejoined Lewis on August 12 on the Missouri River, about 125 miles below its confluence with the Yellowstone. Unfortunately, the 50 horses Clark had herded downstream were stolen by Crow; he had intended to barter them with Natives at Mandan where the explorers had wintered during their upstream journey.

When the expedition arrived back in St. Louis on September 23, 1806, it had covered a distance of 8,000 miles, on foot, horseback and boats. It had been an incredibly successful mission, and Montana immediately felt the impact of the journey. Storytelling by members of the party of fur-rich regions motivated trappers to head west. Within a year of the expedition's arrival in St. Louis, the first trading post was built in Montana. A frenzy of trading and trapping continued, and more than 35 fur-trading forts were established.

The mountain-man era was essentially over by 1840. Many animals had been trapped to the point where few remained, especially beaver. When the supply of pelts dwindled, so did the fledgling industry.

Besides the trappers and mountain men, other white people penetrated Montana in the early part of the 1800s. These were Catholic missionaries; one of the most notable was Father Pierre Jean De Smet. St. Mary's Mission near Stevensville was established in 1841. Later, St. Ignatius Mission came into being at the town that bears its name today. Protestant missionaries entered the state at about the time gold and silver were discovered—no doubt in response to the large amount of sinning that was going on.

Now that the west had been opened, it was inevitable that Montana's enormous mineral wealth would be discovered. One of the first gold strikes occurred in 1860 when James and Granville Stuart made their find near Deer Lodge in a place aptly called Gold Creek. Two years later, another big strike was made on Grasshopper Creek near Bannack. Virginia City was the next gold town, and a year later the gold boom hit Helena. Within ten years of the first gold discovery, about $100 million had been extracted.

Gold wasn't the only valuable ore mined in those days. Silver was discovered by two gold miners in 1864 at the headwaters of the Clark Fork River, but there was a problem. Unlike gold, which could be panned easily and isolated in its pure form, silver had to be separated from its parent rock in a highly complicated smelter operation. Thus, the giant corporate smelting industry was born in Butte, but silver was only the beginning. On its heels was the discovery of copper, which also had to be smelted, but ended up being far more lucrative than silver. Because the area around Butte held an enormous amount of silver and copper, the community flourished and became Montana's wealthiest and largest city.

Riverboats were the only form of transportation into Montana with the exception of horse-drawn wagons and stagecoaches until 1881. That year, railroads punched into the state's borders, opening a new and vital link to the rest of the nation. The first line was a spur rail constructed from Utah to Butte, and within two years, a railroad line traversed the entire length of Montana, joining Chicago with Portland.

The mining frenzy subsequently engendered the livestock industry. Miners had to eat, and ranches were established to feed the hungry workers. This livestock industry was essentially born in the 1860s, but soon blossomed into investor-backed operations. Huge herds of cattle were trailed on the open range from Texas to lush (and free) Montana grasslands and were fattened and then sold in the east (shades of *Lonesome Dove*!). As railroads became established, cattle barons began shipping stock on trains to distant markets. And so sprang up the cattle towns of Billings, Miles City and Wibaux. In 1870, about 50,000 cattle roamed in Montana. Fifteen years later, there were almost three-quarters of a million.

Incredibly, a single severe winter killed off at least half of Montana's cattle; some historians place the loss at three-fourths of the total cattle population. It all happened during the devastating 1886–87 winter, when weeks of sub-zero cold sapped the life out of Texas longhorns that were incapable of dealing with the arctic conditions. Though cattle ranching continued, the big cattle-drive era with southern cows had come to a halt. Ranchers looked to hardier breeds, such as herefords and black angus, that were better able to cope with severe winter weather.

Homesteaders followed the railroad to find their dream, and some settled the fertile valleys away from major rail lines. The government offered each settler 320 acres; most of the settlers were farmers rather than livestock producers. Dreams sometimes turned to nightmares, though, as settlers learned they could not grow crops on the parched, windy prairies.

The 1900s brought drought and despair, with almost 60,000 people leaving the state by 1925. Not long afterward, the Depression forced many more to flee rural areas and find employment in cities if they could. But times change, and after the war years, Montana slowly began a building process. Ironically, that huge expanse of nothingness that spelled tragedy for many early homesteaders has now become the dream of urban Americans seeking escape from the rat race. Movie stars and corporate CEOs have discovered Big Sky, and Montana is now *the* place to live, embodying a rapidly disappearing American way of life.

# IDAHO

Idaho is a most diverse state, from the northern, slender Panhandle to the broad base in the south. In the north, dense timber is the norm, supported by a moist climate. Southern Idaho is more arid, with agriculture a major industry. Mountains are located throughout; it's difficult not to see a mountain range from most parts of the state.

The Snake River is Idaho's most famous and important waterway. Born in Wyoming, the majestic Snake crosses the entire width of Idaho, ultimately emptying into the Columbia.

As elsewhere, Idaho was first settled by Natives who traveled to North America from Asia during the Ice Age about 10,000 or more years ago. Most prevalent tribes were the Nez Perce in the north,

*A Native American powwow. These dances can be seen in various towns around Yellowstone National Park.*
DONNIE SEXTON/COURTESY TRAVEL MONTANA

and the Shoshone and Bannock in the south. The advent of the horse, brought in by Spanish conquistadors in the southwest, allowed Idaho's Natives to travel long distances. The people made many excursions into Montana and Wyoming, with small bands splintering off and establishing new colonies. When Lewis and Clark made their epic journey up the Missouri and eventually penetrated Idaho, about 10,000 Natives were in residence.

When Lewis and Clark returned to St. Louis and broadcast the news of the great wealth to be had in the fur-rich Rockies, many instant explorers hit the trail west. One of the first, John Colter (who was, in fact, a member of Lewis and Clark's Expedition) made several journeys into the unmapped mountains. He is credited with being the first white man to set foot in Yellowstone National Park.

Another trapper, David Thompson, established Idaho's first trading post in 1809 on the shore of Lake Pend Oreille. In 1810, a trader by the name of Andrew Henry constructed a winter outpost on a branch of the Snake River after being driven there by warring Blackfeet.

More mountain men traveled through the region, including several under the British flag. Two of the most intrepid adventurers were Peter Skene Ogden and Donald Mackenzie. Prior to 1846, Idaho was part of the Oregon Territory, jointly claimed by the United States and Britain. Subsequently, the powerful British Hudson's Bay Company established many trading posts and forts, while a new American venture, the Rocky Mountain Fur Company, was organized by William Ashley. Some of the mountain men dealing with Ashley were notables, such as Jedediah Smith and Jim Bridger.

In order to create a meeting place for mountain men and trappers to sell and buy goods, the rendezvous was born. These gatherings were often less than civil, with all sorts of shenanigans carried on. Among the rendezvous with the most notoriety were two at Pierre's Hole near Driggs, held in 1829 and 1832, respectively. The second one ended in a bloody battle between trappers and Natives from several tribes, leaving six trappers and 17 Natives dead. As a consequence, relations between mountain men and Natives, particularly members of the Blackfoot tribe, were not good for the next several years.

A number of missionaries, both Catholic and Protestant, moved into Idaho as early as 1834. They included Marcus and Narcissa Whitman, Jason Lee, Asa Smith, and Henry and Eliza Spaulding, all Protestants. For the most part, their efforts in converting the Nez Perce were unsuccessful; the Whitmans were killed by Cayuse. Jesuit missionaries, especially Father Pierre Jean De Smet, founded missions in Montana and then moved into Idaho, where De Smet built the Mission of the Sacred Heart on the St. Joe River in 1842. Another religious settlement occurred in the south as Mormons, following Brigham Young's orders, moved into Idaho from Utah to establish new colonies. Their first settlement, Franklin, was well underway by the mid-1850s.

In the meantime, tens of thousands of settlers moved across Idaho on the Oregon Trail. Following the Snake River, they ignored Idaho, seeking rich farmlands in Oregon and gold in California. During that period, Idaho was not a state but was part of Washington Territory. Idaho's unpopularity came to an end when Elias Pierce struck gold on Orofino Creek in 1860. Idaho suddenly became a hot destination, and within a year, cities sprang up in the new gold-bearing region, with Lewiston becoming the center of river transportation and supply headquarters for the boom. Two years later, a bigger strike was made on Grimes Creek, a tributary to the Boise River. Almost instantly, Idaho City sprang up from nowhere and became the largest city in the entire Pacific Northwest, with a population of almost 6,500.

In 1863, when Idaho was finally proclaimed a territory of its own, Idaho City was made the capital. That status was short-lived, and the capital was changed to Lewiston, and finally to Boise. As gold fever continued, so did battles with the Natives. The worst occurred in 1863 when the cavalry murdered more than 350 Shoshone, including women and children, in the infamous Bear River Massacre.

But perhaps the most notorious of the Native encounters was the Chief Joseph retreat. In 1877, Chief Joseph and Chief White Bird, both of the Nez Perce tribe, were ordered by the U.S. Army to move to a tiny reservation, thus abandoning their ancestral homelands. Both chiefs spurned the orders for years, but were about to give in when three young braves from White Bird's band killed four white settlers. The U.S. Army attacked, but it was badly beaten by White Bird. The battle left 34 cavalrymen dead and only two Natives wounded. Realizing they would now be a primary target of an overwhelming cavalry force, White Bird and Joseph retreated, intent on escaping into Canada. Their route took them across Wyoming and Montana. Joseph's party was captured just a few days' march from the border, but White Bird and his band made it through, avoiding the dreaded expulsion to a reservation. In one of the most repeated speeches in western history, Chief Joseph uttered these words when he surrendered:

> *I am tired of fighting. Our chiefs are killed. The old men are all dead. It is cold, and we have no blankets. The little children are freezing to death. My people, some of them, have run away to the hills. I want to have time to look for my children, and to see how many of them I can find; maybe I shall find them among the dead. Hear me, my chiefs: My heart is sick and sad. From where the sun now stands, I will fight no more forever.*

Joseph and his band initially were sent to Oklahoma in 1885, but most were reassigned to the Nez Perce reservation near Lewiston. Joseph and his followers were sent to the Colville Reservation in Washington, where he died in 1904.

Soon after, the Mormons established Idaho's first town in Franklin. Church members spread deeper into the territory, farming the desert and building new towns. In the meantime, a rail line was punched into Idaho, connecting Salt Lake City with Butte, Montana, the site of a silver and copper boom. In 1880, a silver strike near Sun Valley started a mad rush to mine the new riches, and five years later, an even bigger silver strike was made near Coeur d'Alene. The towns of Wallace, Kellogg and Osburn sprang up overnight, and Spokane, Washington, expanded to serve the needs of the booming communities. Both the gold and silver mines helped Idaho earn statehood in 1890.

Agriculture became an important industry when farmers learned how to irrigate the barren sagebrush prairie. The fertile Snake River Valley was one of the most important areas, along with the rolling hills near Lewiston. Various grains were successfully grown, and then it was discovered that potatoes grew well in Idaho's climate. Today, the Idaho potato is unquestionably the most popular in the country. One man, Jack R. Simplot, is credited with starting the potato's success. Timber became an important industry early on, not only to support the mines but also as a competitive product in demand around the country. Livestock production was also a vital factor in Idaho's growth, especially sheep raised for meat and wool.

With interstate highways spanning Idaho in the north and the south, and a wealth of things to see and do, the state enjoys a large tourist trade, both in summer and winter. River floaters enjoy trips down several large rivers, and skiers play on world-class slopes. Fishing and hunting are outstanding, and together with a myriad of other activities, make Idaho a superb place to visit.

## WYOMING

Look at the shape of Wyoming on a map, and you'll see a rather boring rectangle. Drive across the southern part of the state, and you'll gaze out at several hundred miles of sagebrush. But if you strike out from the prairie and head into the numerous mountain ranges, and some of the more rural areas, you'll discover an amazing world—one that is largely unknown to much of America. Of course, Yellowstone National Park is Wyoming's claim to fame, but many other natural features offer a reason to visit. In addition to tourism, livestock has always been important here, as well as oil, gas and coal. In fact, Wyoming is the top coal-producing state, offering the "cleanest" coal in the country.

Wyoming has the distinction of being the least populated of all 50 states. There's an old joke suggesting that Wyoming has more antelope than people; the last census showed less than 500,000 residents. To be sure, Wyoming will never be an important retirement state but people who do retire here, come for a western way of life rather than for palm trees and sunshine. A common bumper sticker proclaims: "Wyoming—Where the Old West Still Is."

The Plains tribes were thought to be the first humans in Wyoming. Many tribes wandered across the state, including the Arapaho, Crow, Cheyenne, Shoshone and Comanche. Since there were no geographic boundaries, bands moved in and out of the territories depending on weather and the food supply. From time to time, the dangerous Blackfoot passed through what is now Wyoming, along with the Ute and the Sioux. Native wars displaced many tribes; the Sioux pushed the Crow north into Montana, and the Arapaho and the Cheyenne forced the Comanche to move south.

Although John Colter gets the credit for being the first white man in the state, he may have been preceded by Louis-Joseph and Francois Verendrye some 70 years earlier. The two brothers, with their father Pierre, left Montreal in hopes of seeking their fortunes in fur and ocean riches. On their first trip west, they were able to reach North Dakota. They went back to Canada but intended to return and explore more of the west. Pierre was then too old to make the rugged journey, but his sons made the trip, and historians believe they penetrated as far as Sheridan, Wyoming. Unfortunately, historical accounts vary because many explorers left no written record; some mountain men and adventurers were illiterate.

John Colter, part of the famous Lewis and Clark Expedition, was not interested in staying in St. Louis when the explorers returned from their historic journey. He headed west once again, entering a strange land filled with sulfurous steam, geysers and bizarre thermal activity. Colter continued his solo journey, traveling in and out of many rugged mountain areas.

Other white explorers entered Wyoming as a result of their travels with John Jacob Astor, who tried to establish a major fur business. He built Fort Astoria at the mouth of the Columbia River in 1811, but the stockade was abandoned two years later because of the War of 1812. Astor's followers, called Astorians, did much to shape the west. One of them, Pierre Dorian, explored Wyoming's northern mountains on his way to the Columbia. Robert Stuart entered Wyoming in 1812, discovering South Pass. Little did he know then that this pass was to be used by hundreds of thousands of settlers making their way along the Oregon Trail years later. Stuart also built the first cabin in Wyoming, near Casper. Later, in 1824, Thomas Fitzpatrick claimed to have discovered South Pass, and from that point on, it was identified as the best route across the Rockies.

The western migration had its beginning when a small wagon train traveled the Oregon Trail in 1841, but it wasn't until 1843 that the great crush of humanity crossed Wyoming. Most of the 350,000 people who used the trail over the next three decades were headed for California, Oregon, Washington and Utah. They came for different reasons—some wanting to make their fortunes in the gold and silver boom areas, some wanting to grow crops on fertile northwest lands, and others to find a place to practice religion without being persecuted. Many died on the great trail, and many were born on it.

For the most part, the Natives were at first friendly to travelers, since the white people were only passing through. But when it became obvious that some whites intended to stay, Native raids on

*An angler fishes Granite Creek near Jackson, Wyoming.*

*Campers enjoy solitude along the Clark's Fork River in Wyoming.*

white settlements became more common. The cavalry interceded, leading to serious battles. The most well known was Custer's tremendous loss in Montana, but much blood was spilled on Wyoming soil. Two of the largest battles occurred near Fort Phil Kearney, which was one of the forts constructed to guard the Bozeman Trail, the fastest route between Fort Laramie and the Powder River, used extensively by people feverishly heading to Montana's rich goldfields. The Fetterman Battle resulted in the loss of 81 cavalrymen, including their leader, Lt. William J. Fetterman. Shortly afterward, during the Wagon Box Fight, about 60 Lakota were killed by soldiers. For several years the Bozeman Trail earned the name, Bloody Bozeman Trail.

Unlike other surrounding states such as Idaho, Montana, Utah and Colorado, Wyoming possesses no big deposits of rich ores such as gold, silver and copper, which undoubtedly accounted for its slow growth. An exception is Black Hills gold, but it never amounted to the frenzied boom that had occurred elsewhere. Wyoming made up for those deficits in the form of coal, which underlies the state in such widely scattered areas as Rock Springs and Gillette on opposite ends of the state. In 1870, Wyoming's first mining efforts got underway when coal was extracted near Hanna and Rock Springs. The advent of the Union Pacific rail line in 1867 contributed to the expansion of coal mines as new lodes were discovered and the coal could be easily whisked away. Oil and gas were discovered afterward, starting another industry in the state.

The first successful well was drilled on Salt Creek near Casper in 1890, and from then on, the industry went through cycles of boom and bust. Livestock in the form of cattle and sheep were important in Wyoming's early history, with extensive grazing occurring in the lush grasslands as Texas cattle were moved north to fatten. Those days came to a halt during the blizzard of 1886–87 that killed tens of thousands of cows in Wyoming and Montana.

Though Wyoming is popularly known as the Cowboy State, its official nickname is the Equality State. This is a bit of trivia largely unknown by outsiders. In 1869, Wyoming was the first state to give women the right to vote, serve on juries and hold office. The following year, Louisa "Grandma" Swain cast her vote in Laramie City, becoming the first American woman to do so. In 1924, Nellie Ross became the first woman governor in the United States. The first all-female town council took office in Jackson in 1920—the first in the country. Why did a rough-and-tumble state like Wyoming allow women these unprecedented firsts? Good question, and one that has no good answers.

*An angler tries his luck in a picturesque Wyoming river.*

# SECTION 2

# NORTH GATE

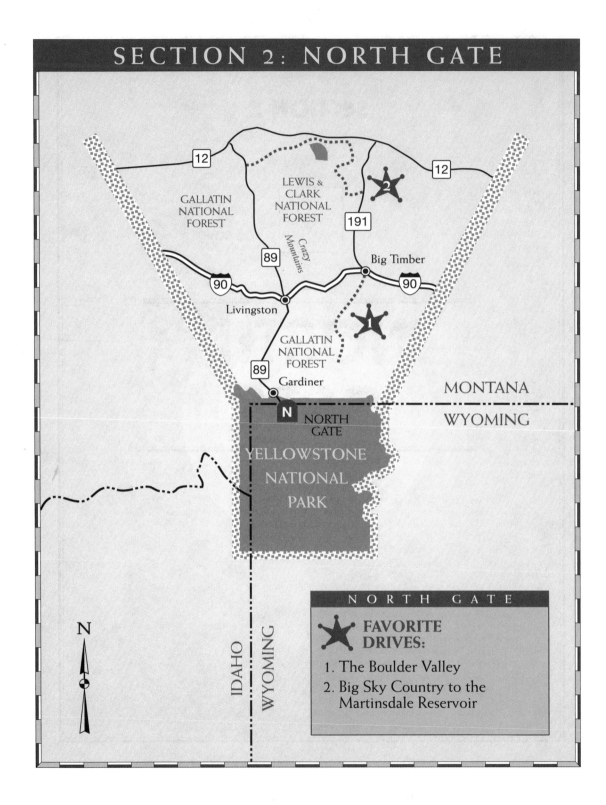

12

12

2

GALLATIN
NATIONAL
FOREST

LEWIS &
CLARK
NATIONAL
FOREST

*Crazy Mountains*

191

89

Big Timber

90

90

Livingston

1

GALLATIN
NATIONAL
FOREST

89

Gardiner

N

NORTH
GATE

MONTANA

WYOMING

YELLOWSTONE
NATIONAL
PARK

IDAHO

WYOMING

N

### NORTH GATE

**FAVORITE
DRIVES:**

1. The Boulder Valley
2. Big Sky Country to the
   Martinsdale Reservoir

# GENERAL OVERVIEW

Gardiner, Montana (pronounced Gardner) is the north gateway to Yellowstone, though Mammoth shares the position as well since it's just a few miles up the road. Once leaving Gardiner, you can only travel one route—U.S. 89 to Livingston, which is on I-90. This segment covers the area through Big Timber and east to Columbus via I-90, west on I-90 to Bozeman, and north on U.S. 89 to White Sulphur Springs and vicinity.

## MAMMOTH HOT SPRINGS

Fort Yellowstone, the home of Yellowstone National Park Headquarters, is at Mammoth Hot Springs. The Park Service succeeded the Army in directing the park and has used the facility since 1918.

Be sure to view the massive hot springs terrace, and create your own picture postcard. Current park information and quality historical exhibits are at the Horace Albright Visitor Center. However, the center's most noteworthy holdings are the photographs of Yellowstone taken in the 1850s by W. H. Jackson. The majestic photographs, taken on the Hayden Expedition, were the tangible evidence needed to persuade the government to preserve the wonders of Yellowstone as a public park. See more about Yellowstone National Park on page 3.

## GARDINER

Gardiner, the original entrance to Yellowstone, is the only year-round drive-in entrance to the park. Despite winter snows, plows keep the roads open, and the town is busy every season. Throughout, Gardiner has somehow retained its own character. The western-type show put on by Jackson, West Yellowstone, and even Livingston, has not been adopted in Gardiner. Tourism is mighty important, but this gateway town also caters to snowmobilers, cross-country skiers, and late-season elk hunters. Blaze orange is still an accepted winter color by most locals.

Controversy has become a common element in the lives of Gardiner's 600 residents. The Church Universal and Triumphant, known locally as CUT, purchased some 25,000 acres near Gardiner. The massive presence of the church made locals wary, and when the group began drilling geothermal wells, it was too much. Even environmentalists jumped in, demanding studies to determine the impact on area geysers. Subsequently, the well was capped. Studies by the USGS and the National Park Service were dissimilar, and the situation remains unresolved. Church members have since worked hard at good relations. The Ranch Kitchen at Corwin Springs is run by the church and serves up home-cooked meals and pleasant conversation. (406) 848-7891.

*Hay bales are common in Montana's big ranch country.*

Another hurdle for Gardiner residents is the ongoing controversy over Yellowstone National Park's migrating buffalo. Overpopulated herds seeking new winter feeding grounds migrate out of the park. The problem is brucellosis, a bacterial infection that can be carried by buffalo and potentially transmitted to cattle. Whether danger of the disease to cattle is only perceived or real, the problem it has created is absolute. Traditionally, the bison were harvested and the meat was donated to the Crow tribe. In 1997, several hundred buffalo were killed by Montana government hunters, drawing national attention to the situation. The future solution, best left to biologists skilled in game management, may end up in the wrong hands. Led by a public seeking the cessation of this killing, politicians seeking votes may determine the outcome.

Conflict has never been a stranger in these parts. Gardiner's first settlers battled the Crow, who fought to keep their ancient hunting grounds. The settlement was named for mountain man and fur trapper Johnston Gardiner. He hunted along the Yellowstone River and its tributaries in the 1830s.

The Northern Pacific Railroad made it to Cinnabar, a few miles to the north, in 1883, but disputes over the townsite's location caused a 20-year delay. James McCartney, who was in charge of the town, argued almost endlessly with Robert "Buckskin Jim" Cutler, who claimed ownership of the gold diggings. The NP branch line, bringing trainloads of park visitors, didn't reach Gardiner until 1903. That was a year of celebrations. In April, President Theodore Roosevelt arrived to dedicate the Roosevelt Arch before a bustling, cheering crowd of 5,000 spectators. The grand arch of basaltic rock still welcomes visitors today. The inscription, "For the Benefit and Enjoyment of the People" confirms the purpose of Yellowstone, the nation's first national park.

The Yellowstone River earned the designation of a blue-ribbon trout stream. Anglers can test their skills against the wily trout. Fishing guides, familiar with every bend of the river, will show you their hot spots. The Chamber of Commerce is a good source for information on guides. Another source is the Fishing Outfitters Association of Montana (FOAM); (406) 763-5436.

White-water rafting or kayaks await the adventuresome. The scenery is awesome for those who can keep their eyes open. Local outfits offer trips down the Yellowstone; motorized boats are not allowed. Contact Absaroka Rafting Adventures, Box 342, Gardiner, MT 59030; (406) 848-7414; 1-800-755-7414; or the Yellowstone Raft Company, Box 46, Gardiner, MT 59030; (406) 848-7777; 1-800-858-7781.

A variety of Yellowstone snowmobile trails begin at Gardiner. Rentals are available in Gardiner. The Gardiner Ranger District, Gallatin National Forest, has maps. Write Box 5, Gardiner, MT 59030; or call (406) 848-7375. The season runs mid-December through April.

Every fall, big-game hunters are welcomed to Gardiner. Skilled outfitters offer guided hunts through some of Montana's best big-game territory. Contact the Chamber of Commerce for outfitter information.

Weary of being behind the wheel? TW Services runs daily bus tours of the park from Gardiner. Tours depart each morning from the end of May through mid-September. Call (307) 344-7311 for reservations.

**ATTRACTIONS**

The Gardiner Rodeo takes place in mid-June. Specific dates for each year may be obtained through the Chamber of Commerce; (406) 848-7971.

Gardiner celebrates the end of each summer season with its Buffalo Days Parade and Celebration. The town party, complete with dancing in the streets and a western barbecue, is held on Labor Day weekend. Proceeds from the event help fund the volunteer Gardiner Ambulance Service.

Gardiner boasts about the quality of wildlife viewing around the town. Antelope often can be seen on the slopes and open meadow across from Park Street, and bears occasionally wander into town. Winter brings out the best viewing opportunities as animals move down from the higher elevations to winter feeding grounds. Look for them from Gardiner to Corwin Springs and throughout the valley. See antelope especially in October; and bighorn sheep, mule deer and elk, from November through January. Watch eagles soar above the Yellowstone River. Every weekend in winter, ranger-naturalists lead camera safaris on tours through the winter range of the park's northern big-game herds. More information is available from the Gardiner Chamber of Commerce.

## OVERNIGHTING

## CAMPGROUNDS & RV PARKS

▲ *Best Shot for a Camp Spot*
Rocky Mountain Campground, 1 block east of U.S. 89 at 4 Jardine Road, Gardiner, MT 59030. 50 RV sites, hook-ups, dump station, showers and laundry; open May 1 through November 1; (406) 848-7251.

Carbella—U.S. Bureau of Land Management Campground, 20 miles north of Gardiner on U.S. 89, then 1 mile west at Miner. Primitive campground, RVs allowed (max. length 35 feet), no services; boat-launch ramp for 4-wheel drive; open year-round.

Eagle Creek—U.S. Forest Service Campground, 2 miles northeast of Gardiner on Jardine Road. RVs allowed (max. length 30 feet), no services; open year-round.

Tom Miner—U.S. Forest Service Campground, 16 miles northwest of Gardiner on U.S. 89, then 12 miles southwest on County Road 63, 4 miles southwest on Forest Road 63. RVs allowed (max. length 22 feet), no services; open May 15 through November 30.

## BED & BREAKFAST ESTABLISHMENTS

Cabin by the River is a secluded cabin that has been operating since 1993. Open year-round; busiest in August, slowest in winter; no credit cards accepted; no pets allowed. Contact Chris and Warren Wagner, 1047 U.S. 89 South, Gardiner, MT 59030; (406) 848-2223; fax: (406) 848-7170.

Yellowstone Inn Bed & Breakfast has rooms with parlors and fireplaces. The inn has been operating since 1990. Some credit cards accepted; no pets allowed. Contact Barbara Brown, Box 515, U.S. 89 and Main, Gardiner, MT 59030; (406) 848-7000; fax: (406) 848-7000.

Yellowstone Suites, built in 1904, is off the highway on a gravel road. The establishment has been operating since 1996. Open year-round; busiest in summer, slowest in winter; credit cards accepted; no pets or smoking allowed. Contact David and Joy Perius, Box 277, 506 4th St., Gardiner, MT 59030; (406) 848-7937.

**SUGGESTED DINING**

Yellowstone Mine Steak & Shrimp, U.S. 89 North, Gardiner, MT; (406) 848-7336.

The Town Café, Corner of Park St. and U.S. 89, Gardiner, MT; (406) 848-7322.

**VISITOR INFORMATION & SERVICES**

Gardiner Chamber of Commerce is on 3rd Street, just off Park Street. Information is available at PO Box 81, Gardiner, MT 59030; (406) 848-7971; e-mail: gardinerchamber@gomontana.com website: http://www.gomontana.com/gardinerchamber.html

The Gallatin National Forest Ranger Station has maps, road and trail conditions, and other information. U.S. 89, Gardiner, MT; (406) 848-7375.

**MEDICAL SERVICES**

Mammoth Clinic, PO Box 447, Yellowstone National Park, WY, 82190. Open Monday through Friday, 8:30 A.M. to noon, 1 P.M. to 5 P.M. The clinic is open seven days a week from June through August. (307) 344-7965; fax: (307) 344-7336.

Gardiner Ambulance Service is in operation seven days per week on a 24-hour basis; dial 344-911.

Gardiner Drug Store, 24-hour services, Park St., Gardiner, MT 59030.

**REPAIR & TOWING**

Yellowstone Park Service Station, Mammoth, WY; (307) 347-7381.

Gray's Road Rescue, 1016 E. Park, Livingston, MT; (406) 540-4729.

**VETERINARY SERVICES**

Livingston Veterinary Hospital, Dr. John Murname, 1104 E. Park, Livingston, MT; (406) 222-3011.

Mill Creek Veterinary Hospital, Dr. John Sudduth, U.S. 89 South, Mill Creek, MT; (406) 333-4263.

## FAVORITE DRIVE

Explore Jardine, a ghost town northeast of Gardiner. The short trip up a steep gravel road leads to the old gold mine. The post office was opened in 1898 and named for the secretary of the Bear Gulch Mining Company, A. C. Jardine. The ore washers, bunkers and stamp mill testify to the bygone mining days that founded the town. Arsenic was also mined here for use by the government during World War II. The area is a good place to view elk and buffalo herds that leave Yellowstone in the winter.

# GARDINER TO LIVINGSTON: U.S. 89

U.S. 89 traverses Paradise Valley from Yellowstone to Livingston. The 53-mile scenic drive cuts along the valley bordered by some of Montana's highest peaks. The Absaroka Range (pronounced Ab-SOR-kee) is on the east; the Gallatin Range is on the west. The Yellowstone River, the longest undammed river in the United States, is visible for most of the drive. South of Livingston, the valley widens into rich ranchland. Fortuitous or not, many ranches are being subdivided into lots that move quickly on the real estate market. U.S. 89 is open year-round, but winter driving can be extremely hazardous with raging winds and icy conditions.

North of Gardiner, and about five miles north of Corwin Springs, U.S. 89 curves into Yankee Jim Canyon. James George, a rowdy gold prospector, earned the nickname Yankee Jim. A shrewd player, he built the first road through the narrow canyon and charged a toll. When the boom was in full swing, Yankee Jim wrangled with the Northern Pacific. He forced NP to build him a new road in trade for rights to lay its tracks along his original roadbed. NP was working to bring its branch line toward Yellowstone National Park. Yankee Jim was known for telling the tallest of all tall tales, as reported by his famous acquaintance, Rudyard Kipling.

## EMIGRANT

The majestic, steep and rugged Absaroka Mountains were ancient volcanoes. The catastrophic eruptions pushed up mighty peaks like Emigrant, which rises to an altitude of 10,960 feet. The small community of Emigrant takes its name from the grand mountain, as does Emigrant Gulch. In 1862, Thomas Curry discovered gold in Emigrant Gulch. The site of several mines, Emigrant Gulch is actually located closer to Chico Hot Springs and a few miles southeast of current-day Emigrant. Trappers and miners bathed in the hot springs, a welcome amenity in the harsh mountain men's life. Today, Chico Hot Springs is the site of the Chico Hot Springs Lodge and Resort (see Overnighting for more information on the resort).

## OVERNIGHTING

### CAMPGROUNDS & RV PARKS

Dailey Lake—Montana Department of Fish, Wildlife and Parks Campground, 1 mile east of Emigrant, then 4 miles south on Route 540, 6 miles southeast on County Road. RVs allowed, no services; boat-launch ramp for 2-wheel drive; open year-round.

## BED & BREAKFAST ESTABLISHMENTS

Paradise Gateway Bed & Breakfast is a log cabin on 26 acres located on U.S. 89 South near Yellowstone. Operating since 1991; open year-round; busiest May through October, slow rest of year; some credit cards accepted; no pets allowed. Contact Carol Reed, PO Box 84, Emigrant, MT 59027; (406) 333-4063; website: http://www.wtp.net/go/paradise

Querencia Bed & Breakfast, on the Yellowstone, has fishing on the property. The establishment has been operating since 1996. Open year-round; busiest July through August, slowest in January; credit cards accepted; pets allowed. Contact Joe Skaggs, Box 184, Milepost 3674, U.S. 89 South, Emigrant, MT 59027; (406) 333-4500; fax: (406) 333-4500.

Yellowstone Country Bed & Breakfast has new, private log cabins. Operating since 1992; some credit cards accepted; no pets allowed. Contact Tim and Judy Powell, PO Box 1002, 2850 U.S. 89 South, Emigrant, MT 59027; (406) 333-4917.

*The Paradise Valley near Livingston attracts many Hollywood stars.*
DONNIE SEXTON/COURTESY TRAVEL MONTANA

Yellowstone Riverview Lodge Bed & Breakfast, log home. The lodge has been operating since 1992. Open year-round; busiest in summer, slowest November through March; some credit cards accepted; no pets allowed. Contact Steve Koster and Bill Wagner, 186 E. River Rd., Emigrant, MT 59027; (406) 848-2156; e-mail: riverview@imt.net website: http://www.wtp.net/go/riverview

4M Ranch Bed & Breakfast, log-home country setting on 21 acres. The bed and breakfast has been operating since 1989. No credit cards accepted; pets allowed. Write Box 398, 194 Bridger Hollow Rd., Pray, MT 59065; (406) 333-4784; fax: (406) 333-4784.

High Country Outfitters is located 1.5 miles from Road 540. This fly-fishing lodge has been in operation since 1987 and features a fly-fishing school. Fishing season is May through October. RV hook-ups are available. No credit cards accepted; no pets allowed; reservations required for bed & breakfast. Contact Chip and Francine Rizzotto, 158 Bridger Hollow Rd., Pray, MT 59065; (406) 333-4763; e-mail: rizzotto@mcm.net

## GUEST RANCHES

Castle Lodge, 30 miles north of Yellowstone Park off U.S. 89. This secluded retreat has been in operation since 1977. No credit cards accepted; no pets allowed; open mid-July through September. Contact Castle and Linda Smith, Box 281, Emigrant, MT 59027; (406) 333-4726.

Keenan Ranch/Bugle Ridge Outfitters, on the Old Yellowstone Trail South. This working cattle ranch has been operating since 1991. No credit cards accepted; pets are conditional; open May 15 through October 15. Contact John Keenan, Box 1060, Emigrant, MT 59027; (406) 848-7525.

Chico Hot Springs Lodge, on Old Chico Road in the heart of Paradise Valley. Get to it by turning south at Emigrant. The grounds of the historic lodge extend over 154 acres. The resort has 90 guest rooms, chalets and log cabins, plus the famous natural hot pools. This is a family place that advertises itself as "dog friendly." There are two restaurants and a saloon that serve the inn. Guests can enjoy horseback riding, mountain biking, and winter dog-sledding and cross-country skiing. For more information, send inquiry to Drawer D, Old Chico Rd., Pray, MT 59065; or call (406) 333-4933; 1-800-HOT-WADA; fax: (406) 333-4694.

**LIVINGSTON**

Right from the start, railroads have been foremost in Livingston. The Northern Pacific planned the townsite of Livingston along its tracks in 1882. Destined to become a major railroad division point, Livingston incorporated in 1883. It was named after a Northern Pacific director, Crawford Livingston.

The NP officials established the town with high hopes of success. Coal mines, limestone ledges, tourist travel to Yellowstone National Park by rail, and local cattle ranches were to be the mainstays of a growing population. The predictions they made for a permanent population of 1,500 were conservative. The first issue of the *Livingston Enterprise*, published in 1883, claimed a population of 893 residents. When the spur rail line to Gardiner was completed, the population boomed. The 1890 census placed it sixth among Montana cities, with a population of 2,850. By 1910 the population had doubled, but the rank had slipped to tenth. In 1930, Livingston ranked ninth with a population of 6,391. Today, it's holding its own, and beginning to grow again. Livingston ranks eleventh in Montana among incorporated cities with a population of 7,414 (1994 U.S. Census).

Famous personalities have visited Livingston since William Clark camped by the Yellowstone River in 1806 on his homeward-bound journey. Today, the town is back in the spotlight because of its growing popularity for would-be ranchers from Hollywood.

Calamity Jane (Martha Jane Cannary) came to Livingston in the 1880s. The town was one of her haunts, or watering holes, as the stories go. The notorious woman was as tough as the times in which she lived. There are more stories than facts, but her exploits were popular with reporters. Calamity Jane worked as an Army scout, prospector and prostitute. She's said to have earned a coin or two from the tourists and indeed worked for a time in Buffalo Bill's Wild West Show. Her weakness for alcohol was her undoing, and she could never hold on to what she earned. She died at age 51 in South Dakota.

One of the most famous visitors arrived by rail. In April 1903, President Theodore Roosevelt traveled to Yellowstone via train, stopping briefly at the Livingston Depot. A large gathering of enthusiastic townsfolk and settlers came out to welcome him. The greeters followed the president's train to Gardiner on one of Northern Pacific's regular trains. Roosevelt spent two weeks in the park. He culminated the early spring excursion with a ceremony dedicating the gateway arch that marks Yellowstone's north entrance.

Riding the rails was the most popular and comfortable mode of travel for visitors from the east. Livingston was the gateway exchange point, and park visitors changed trains at the impressive Livingston Depot. The trains carried visitors to the park until 1948 when buses and automobiles became the new mode of transportation.

Livingston's downtown area is a slice of the past. Many buildings have been restored, and the western frontier atmosphere pervades the senses. You'd feel right at home in buckskins. The downtown area is a designated historic district listed on the National Register and encompasses scores of buildings. Geared toward tourism, the town features ten art galleries, several gift shops, boutiques, antique shops, and outfitters, guides and fly shops. Livingston is a western blend of shopping memorabilia and glamorized outdoor pastimes. Hang onto your hat, and enjoy a stroll down the wind-churned streets of this very charming town.

## OUTDOOR RECREATION

Safari Yellowstone and Grand Teton are widely noted for excellent, naturalist-guided, one-to-seven-day wildlife and photography tours. These safaris are filled with education on natural and cultural history, including bird-watching and ghost towns. Wilderness walks or hikes can be geared to all ages and abilities. Safari Yellowstone is offered by Sierra Safaris Wilderness Tours. For brochure, call 1-800-SAFARIS, or write PO Box 963, Livingston, MT 59047.

The Livingston Country Club has a beautiful golf course along the Yellowstone River with a stunning view of the Absaroka Mountains. The 9-hole course is open to the public. For tee times, call (406) 222-1031.

Even before the filming of *A River Runs Though It*, Livingston and the Paradise Valley were hotspots for anglers. Livingston's preferred outdoor activity can be pursued independently or with the aid of local guides. The Montana Travel Planner lists 37 outfitters and guides (available by calling 1-800-VISIT-MT). The two local fly shops can also hook you up with a guide. George Anderson's Yellowstone Angler shop is one-half mile south of Livingston on U.S. 89; PO Box 660, Livingston, MT 59047, or call (406) 222-7130. Guided float and wade trips and fly-fishing lessons are available. Dan Bailey's Fly Shop is in town at 209 W. Park St., Livingston, MT 59047, or call 1-800-356-4052; (406) 222-1673.

For a quick stretch and picnic lunch, Sacajawea Park on Yellowstone Avenue is a pleasant place. Sit by the Yellowstone River and view the Crazy Mountains in the distance. The energetic can play a game of tennis, or enjoy the swimming pool.

A popular hiking trail heads up at the Pine Creek Campground. The relatively easy trail leads to a lovely set of waterfalls, and the walk is good exercise. To get there from U.S. 89, turn east on Pine Creek Road, which is about 11 miles south of Livingston. From the Pine Creek village, turn south on East River Road and then go left on Forest Road 202, following the signs to the campground. Beyond Pine Creek, the area has several hiking trails that lead into the wilderness. The Gallatin National Forest Map is a good source for details on more extensive hikes.

**ATTRACTIONS**

The International Fly Fishing Center is at 215 East Lewis, in Livingston. Home of the Federation of Fly Fishers, the center is the only fly-fishing education center in the nation. There are displays of flies and tackle, live game fish and instructional habitat exhibit, and the angling sport's complete history. A "must visit" for all who wield a fly rod, or want to some day soon. (406) 222-9369; 1-800-618-0808.

The biggest ongoing community project is the restoration and preservation of the Livingston Depot Center. The historic Northern Pacific Depot has been transformed into a cultural center promoting visual and performing arts, the history of the Yellowstone region and many educational programs in the arts and humanities. Built in 1902, the grand, Italian-style passenger depot welcomed the eastern traveler to Yellowstone National Park, which lies 50 miles to the south. The architecture resembled that of the east, lessening the traveler's disorientation. With calmer spirits, the traveler continued on a rail line, which clung in places to cliffs above the Yellowstone River.

The City of Livingston received the building in rundown condition from Burlington Northern in 1985. Burlington, the successor to Northern Pacific, closed its southern Montana lines in 1985–86. Since that time, the Herculean efforts of Livingston's citizens to renovate the facility have received national acclaim. The restoration required over $800,000.

The exhibits and activities are of the highest quality. The Buffalo Bill Historical Center in Cody, Wyoming, provides an exhibition from mid-May to Mid-October every year. True to the BBHC reputation, the displays are outstanding. The Livingston Depot Foundation opened the "Rails Across the Rockies: A Century of People and Places" museum, which houses the history and culture of the region. The Festival of the Arts is held every Fourth of July weekend, and the Holiday Bazaar every November. In addition, ongoing concerts, art exhibits and conventions create a "can't miss" stop for the traveler's schedule. For a current schedule of activities, call (406) 222-2300, or write to the Livingston Depot Center, 200 W. Park St., Livingston, MT 59047. The center is open from June through mid-October and for winter conventions and special events. A fee is charged.

Known as the "House of Memories," the Park County Museum is open June 1 through Labor Day, daily from noon to 5 P.M., or by appointment; (406) 222-4184. Stop here to enjoy the interesting historic collection of items from Yellowstone National Park, schools, churches, ranches, and even an 1889 caboose. There's a pioneer home and displays of Native cultures and archaeology. The location, across the tracks from the Depot Center, is 118 W. Chinook in Livingston, MT 59047.

Year-round entertainment abounds at the Blue Slipper Theater and Fire House 5 Playhouse. The community theater offers live entertainment nightly. (406) 222-1420.

Like all western towns, Livingston hosts an annual rodeo. The Livingston Roundup is held over the July 4th weekend at the Park County Fairgrounds. The Livingston Chamber of Commerce has tickets and information.

## OVERNIGHTING

## CAMPGROUNDS & RV PARKS

▲ *Best Shot for a Camp Spot*
Osen's Campground, one-half mile south of Livingston on U.S. 89. 35 RV sites (14 pull-throughs), hook-ups, cable TV, dump station, showers and laundry; open April 1 to November 1; call (406) 222-1028.

▲ *Best Shot for a Camp Spot*
Paradise Valley/Livingston KOA, 9 miles south on U.S. 89, then 1 mile east, on the banks of the Yellowstone River. 52 RV sites (22 pull-throughs), hook-ups, dump station, showers, laundry, indoor pool, tent sites and cabins; open May 1 through October 31. Contact Paradise Valley/Livingston KOA, 163 Pine Creek Rd., Livingston, MT 59047; (406) 222-0992; 1-800-KOA-2805.

▲ *Best Shot for a Camp Spot*
Mallard's Rest—Montana Department of Fish, Wildlife and Parks Campground, 13 miles south of Livingston on U.S. 89 to Milepost 42. RVs allowed, no services; boat-launch ramp for 4-wheel drive; open year-round.

Paradise Livingston Campground, Exit 333 off I-90, then 1 block north on U.S. 89, then west off Rogers Lane. 25 RV sites, hook-ups, cable TV, dump station, showers, laundry and heated pool; open May 1 to October 31; call (406) 222-1122.

Rainbow Motel & Campgrounds, 5574 E. Park, Livingston, MT 59047. RV facilities at motel area just one and a half blocks from Yellowstone River; (406) 222-3780; 1-800-222-3780.

Paradise Greenhouse & Campground is behind the Livingston Inn, at 5 Rodgers Lane, Livingston, MT 59047. 45 RV sites (9 full hook-ups, 10 water and electric hook-ups); easy access to tour the sights of downtown; open May through September; (406) 222-2112.

Rock Canyon RV Park, 3 miles south on U.S. 89. 26 RV sites (5 pull-throughs), hook-ups, showers and laundry; open May 1 to October 31; (406) 222-1096.

Windmill Park, 1 mile south on U.S. 89, turn at RR crossing to Bill-man Lane. 15 RV sites (no pull-throughs), hook-ups, dump station, showers and laundry; open year-round, very busy in summer; (406) 222-2784.

Yellowstone's Edge RV Park, 3501 U.S. 89 South, 18 miles south of Livingston on U.S. 89. 81 RV sites, hook-ups, dump station, showers and laundry, open May 1 through November 1; (406) 333-4036.

Loch Leven—Montana Department of Fish, Wildlife and Parks Campground, 9 miles south of Livingston on U.S. 89 to Milepost 44, then 2 miles east, 4 miles south on Route 540. RVs allowed; no services; open year-round.

Pine Creek—U.S. Forest Service Campground, 4 miles south of Livingston on U.S. 89, then 6 miles east on Pine Creek Road. RVs allowed (max. length 22 feet), no services; open May 26 through September 15.

Snow Bank—U.S. Forest Service Campground, 15 miles south of Livingston on U.S. 89, then 12 miles southeast on Mill Creek Road 486. RVs allowed (max. length 22 feet), no services; open May 26 through September 15.

## BED & BREAKFAST ESTABLISHMENTS

The Blue Winged Olive Bed & Breakfast is perfect for anglers since it's just minutes from Paradise Valley. Operating since 1993; open April through October; some credit cards accepted; no pets allowed; horses boarded. Contact Joan Watts, 5157 U.S. 89 South, Livingston, MT 59047; (406) 222-8646; 1-800-471-1141; website: http://www.travel.mt.gov

Davis Creek Bed & Breakfast, in a rural setting. The establishment has been operating since 1985. Open year-round; busiest July through August, slowest March through April; some credit cards accepted; pets allowed. Contact Alan and Laurie Redfield, Norma Shapiro, 575 Mill Creek Rd., Livingston, MT 59047; (406) 333-4768; (406) 333-4353.

Greystone Inn Bed & Breakfast, historic home, operating since 1990. Open year-round; busiest May through September, slowest rest of year; no credit cards accepted; no pets allowed. Contact Lin Lee, 122 S. Yellowstone St., Livingston, MT 59047; (406) 222-8319.

Island Guest House and Bed & Breakfast, in a rural location with private fishing ponds. The establishment has been operating since 1993. Open May 1 through October 1 for bed & breakfast, winter for guest house; no credit cards accepted; no pets allowed. Contact Fran Eggar, 77 9th St. Island Dr., Livingston, MT 59047; (406) 222-3788; 1-800-438-3092.

Remember When Bed & Breakfast, in a Victorian home furnished with antique furniture. Open year-round; busiest in summer; no credit cards accepted; no pets allowed. Contact David Kinslow, 320 S. Yellowstone, Livingston, MT 59047; (406) 222-8367; e-mail: remember@mcn.net

The River Inn on the Yellowstone, 4950 U.S. 89 South, Livingston, MT 59047. Secluded on the riverbank, the inn is a restored historic farmhouse complete with cowgirl cabin and sheepherder's wagon. For details, call (406) 222-2429; website: http://www.wtp.net/go/riverinn

## GUEST RANCHES

Beartooth Wilderness Lodge & Llama Ranch, 50 miles north of Yellowstone National Park. This secluded getaway has been in operation since 1993. Pets conditional; no credit cards accepted; open year-round; busiest July through August, slowest February through March. Contact Suzanne Huelsmeyer, Box 1038, Livingston, MT 59047; (406) 220-2895; fax: (406) 220-2895; e-mail: THEBTWL@aol.com

Jumping Rainbow Ranch, 8 miles south of Livingston. This is a fly-fishing ranch along the Yellowstone River with private ponds. No credit cards accepted; outside pets allowed; open April through November. Contact Charles Lakovitch and Galen Ives, 110 Jumping Rainbow Rd., Livingston, MT 59047; (406) 222-5425; fax: (406) 222-5508; e-mail: jrr@mcn.net; website: http://www.mcn.net/jrr

63 Ranch, 50 miles north of Yellowstone National Park. This working dude ranch has been operating since the 1930s. Open June 15 through September 15; no credit cards accepted; no pets allowed. Contact Sandra Cahill, Box MA979, Livingston, MT 59047; (406) 222-0570; fax: (406) 222-9939; winter (406) 222-9446.

Lodge at Loch Leven, 17 miles south on U.S. 89 in Paradise Valley. Enjoy comfort and privacy on a bend of the Yellowstone River. Operating since 1995; no credit cards accepted; pets allowed; open year-round; busiest June through October, slowest January through February. Contact Fred and Anita Paoli, 46 Loch Leven, Livingston, MT 59047; (406) 222-4420; (406) 222-2710.

Pine Creek Store, Cafe & Lodges, 12 miles south on U.S. 89 in Paradise Valley. No credit cards accepted; pets allowed; open year-round; busiest June through October, slowest January through February. Contact Fred and Anita Paoli, 46 Loch Leven, Livingston, MT 59047; (406) 222-3628.

Yellowstone International Fly Fisherman's Lodge is a fishing ranch. Contact Don Charvat, RR 62, Box 3187, 5 Blue Rd., Livingston, MT 59047; (406) 222-7385; fax: (406) 222-6655.

Yellowstone Valley Ranch, 3840 U.S. 89 South on the Yellowstone River, which flows through the property. Credit cards accepted; pets allowed; open June through October. Contact the ranch at Route 38, Box 2202, 422 S. Main St., Livingston, MT 59047; (406) 333-4787; 1-800-626-3526; fax: (406) 333-4787.

**SUGGESTED DINING**

Winchester Cafe and Murray Lounge & Grill, Murray Hotel, 201 W. Park, Livingston, MT; (406) 222-2708.

Buffalo Jump Steak House, South of Livingston, Livingston, MT; (406) 222-7001.

Livingston Bar & Grille, 130 N. Main, Livingston, MT; (406) 222-7909.

The Sport, 114 S. Main, Livingston, MT; (406) 222-3533.

Uncle Louie's, 119 W. Park, Livingston, MT; (406) 222-7177.

**VISITOR INFORMATION & SERVICES**

The Livingston Chamber of Commerce is in the Livingston Depot Center on Main and Park Streets at 212 W. Park, Livingston, MT 59047; (406) 222-0850; fax: (406) 222-0852.

Unfortunately, it's difficult to park an RV in the downtown area here; there aren't any RV parking lots and the limited street parking quickly disappears.

**MEDICAL SERVICES**

Livingston Memorial Hospital, 504 S. 13th St., Livingston, MT; (406) 222-3541.

Pamida Pharmacy, open Monday through Friday, 9 A.M. to 7 P.M.; 100 W. Washington, Livingston, MT; (406) 222-7082; 1-800-246-7082.

Western Drug, open weekdays, 9 A.M. to 9 P.M.; weekends, 10 A.M. to 6 P.M.; 1313 W. Park, Livingston, MT; (406) 222-7332.

**REPAIR & TOWING**

J & J Towing, 24-hour services, 519 W. Park St., Livingston, MT; 1-800-939-8343.

Crash Repair Center, 24-hour services, 1324 W. Front, Livingston, MT; 1-800-383-2420.

**VETERINARY SERVICES**

Colmey Veterinary Services, Dr. Duane Colmey, U.S. 89 South, Livingston, MT; (406) 222-1700.

# LIVINGSTON TO BIG TIMBER, BOZEMAN AND VICINITY: I-90

### RV CAUTION

Be prepared to be buffeted by strong winds when you enter the Livingston area from any direction. This region typically has powerful gusts when the rest of the area is calm. If you take I-90 west to Bozeman and beyond, you'll go over Bozeman Pass, which winds through pretty mountain country laced with some lavish homes that you can't see well from the interstate. Although you wouldn't know it if you're a summer visitor, the pass can be a nightmare in the winter. Curiously, it doesn't seem to be much of a pass at all, just a rolling highway that ascends a slope and then gradually drops down into Bozeman. It can be a bearcat, so be extra careful if you're traveling in the spring and fall when unusual snowstorms can make this road a mess.

Driving east, you'll follow the Yellowstone River to Big Timber and beyond. The river parallels I-90 to Billings, and then follows I-94 all the way to North Dakota where it merges with the Missouri. The route from Livingston to Big Timber is fairly flat, passing through ranches and grand mountain ranges on each side.

## BIG TIMBER

The name conjures up immense forests, however, that's an image that remains only in one's imagination. The area is mostly wide-open grassland. But way back in the 1800s, some of the largest cottonwood trees in the state lined the banks of Big Timber Creek. Captain William Clark named the creek after the cottonwoods. Ranchers settled the grasslands about 60 years later. The first stage station, which was located at the mouth of Big Timber Creek, went by the name of Big Timber. Later, in 1880 when the first post office opened, it also took the creek's name. The town was officially established in 1883.

Big Timber is the county seat for Sweet Grass County. The community of about 1,600 depends mostly on sheep and cattle ranching and recreation tourism for support. There are many artists, poets, sculptors and history buffs in the town. Several antique stores, art galleries and craft shops offer pleasant ways to spend the afternoon. The nearby Crazy Mountains offer loads of outdoor fun, and the Boulder Valley to the south has interesting sights like Natural Bridge State Park. Big Timber itself is one of the friendliest towns in south central Montana.

The Boulder River flows into the Yellowstone River near Big Timber. Anglers can enjoy the blue ribbon trout streams of Boulder Valley or a variety of fishing in the warmer waters of the Yellowstone River. There are several competent fishing guides in the area, and if fishing doesn't interest you, simply enjoy an excursion down the river. The Chamber of Commerce has information on guide companies.

## OUTDOOR RECREATION

The Overland Golf Course is a 9-hole course at the Big Timber Exit off I-90. The course, one of the longest in the state, is open to the public. (406) 932-4297.

The Big Timber Waterslide will cool you off on a hot summer day. There are three waterslides, two tube pools and other amusements to keep the kids entertained. The pool is open Memorial Day to Labor Day; fee charged. To get there, take Exit 377 off I-90, and go 8 miles east of Big Timber. (406) 932-6570.

Half Moon Park campground is a great spot for fishing, hiking and a spectacular view of the Crazy Mountains. There's an easy walk to a waterfall and several clearly marked trails to nearby lakes. The area has camping for smaller RVs and is very popular in summer. (See directions under Campgrounds & RV Parks, page 73.)

## ATTRACTIONS

The newly designed Crazy Mountain Museum is just off I-90 at the West Big Timber Exit. Take the exit and go south. The museum is directly east of the cemetery.

The story of the Great American West is portrayed here, revealing the people who settled the land by the treasures they left behind. The archives of the museum are extensive, and many people who have ties to Sweet Grass County come to trace their family lines.

*Judi Zumbo proudly shows off her trout in the mountains east of Yellowstone.*

One of the most fascinating displays is a miniature of Big Timber in 1907. The display is historically accurate in every detail. New displays include a restored, one-room schoolhouse and a Norwegian *stabbur*. The schoolhouse is typical of those found in Montana in the pioneer days. The log cabin *stabbur*, used for storage, is of a unique Scandinavian design where the second story is larger than the ground level. No one could be trapped in by deep or drifting snow.

Another new feature is a magnificent rodeo exhibit. The Cremer Rodeo Company was one of the biggest rodeo companies west of the Mississippi. It is featured along with the saddle of 1997 All-Round Cowboy, Dan Mortenson; the story of cowboy Scott Breding, a native of Big Timber; and many others.

The free museum is open Memorial Day to Labor Day. Regular hours are 1 P.M. to 4:30 P.M., Tuesday through Sunday. If you're short on time, special tours are available. Call (406) 932-5126, and the friendly museum folks will be happy to help. Join the fun at the annual Grand Opening Celebration held each Memorial Day.

Visitors are welcome to browse the showroom of the Shiloh Rifle Manufacturing Company at 201 Centennial Drive in Big Timber; (406) 932-4454. The owners, Robert and Phyllis, and Kirk and Heather Bryan, combine Old World craftsmanship with modern technology to reproduce 1874 Sharps rifles. All rifles are custom-made to specification.

The Yellowstone Fish Hatchery offers free tours and is open daily 8 A.M. to 4:30 P.M. Yellowstone cutthroat trout are maintained here, and eggs are distributed to hatcheries across the state. More than 1 million eggs are harvested annually. In the fall, the 500,000 fry raised at the hatchery are transported to mountain lakes. Visitors can tour the indoor and outdoor raceways used to raise the trout. From Big Timber, take McLeod Street north for .5 mile to the hatchery. (406) 932-4434.

Every June, Big Timber hosts the annual Big Timber Rodeo at the Sweet Grass Fair Grounds. Dates vary each year and are available through the Chamber of Commerce.

The premier annual show, the Cutting Horse Event, is held at the Fair Grounds in late July. Competition is keen as talented riders and exquisite horses vie for cash prizes. Contestants come from across the western states to participate. The skill and communication between rider and horse, as they work to cut cattle from the herd, are a sight to behold and a true element of western culture. Specific dates are available from the Chamber of Commerce, or call (406) 932-5996.

# FAVORITE DRIVE: THE BOULDER VALLEY

If you have time, explore the Boulder Valley. The road south to McLeod is paved. To sample great fishing, you can get to the Boulder River at Big Rock, 3.5 miles south of Big Timber, and Boulder Forks, just past McLeod.

McLeod was originally a trading post until 1886 when the post office was opened. Named for W. F. McLeod, the quiet community hosts the ranchers, merchants and artisans of the valley.

Traveling south of McLeod, the scenery and fishing spots are top-notch, but the road is not. The area is one of our favorites but requires a great deal of discretion regarding how far to go. **RV Caution:** The Boulder River Road is paved up to Natural Bridge State Park. Don't go much more than a half dozen miles past the pavement; the road becomes very narrow and winding. The larger the RV, the more caution should be exercised.

The Natural Bridge State Park is RV accessible. Drive through the beautiful canyon along the main Boulder River and see the spectacular falls 27 miles south of Big Timber, where the Boulder River flows over an 80- to 100-foot precipice. There once was a natural bridge or arch across the Boulder River, carved out by water in the limestone. In recent years, the arch has fallen; the heavy rushing spring waters finally proved too much for the limestone rock. In the drier months, the river flows under the limestone and reappears as a waterfall pouring out from the cliff face. Interpretive signs explain the geologic formations and history of the gorge. (406) 252-4654.

As you continue south on Boulder River Road, travel becomes slower and the road more bumpy and narrow. Eventually the drive ends at Box Canyon, about 50 miles from Big Timber. For those towing vehicles, there are lots of side trips along the gravel roads to the East and West Forks of the Boulder River. There are many hiking trails along the way and several fishing access points on the Boulder River. The area here, at the heart of the Absaroka-Beartooth Wilderness, is steep; extensive hiking is for those who are fit and sure of foot.

## OVERNIGHTING

## CAMPGROUNDS & RV PARKS

### Big Timber
Big Timber KOA, 9 miles east of Big Timber, I-90 Exit 377. Send mail to Box 3634, Big Timber, MT 59011. 75 RV sites (49 pull-throughs), hook-ups, dump station, hot showers, laundry, pool, hot tubs; camping cabins; reservations advised; open May 15 through September 15; (406) 932-6569; 1-800-562-5869.

### ▲ *Best Shot for a Camp Spot*
Spring Creek Camp & Trout Ranch, 3 minutes off I-90, 2.5 miles south of Big Timber on Montana 298; PO Box 1063, Big Timber, MT 59011. Great fly fishing on Boulder River, horse rides, float/raft trips, golf, trout fishing pond. 50 RV sites, hook-ups, dump station, hot showers, laundry; open April 1 through November 30; (406) 932-4387.

# BOULDER VALLEY

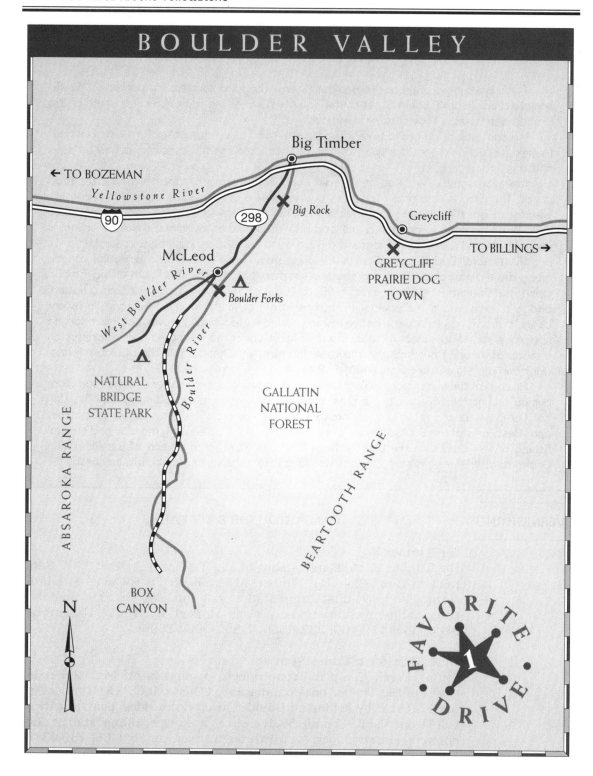

Big Timber

← TO BOZEMAN

*Yellowstone River*

90

298    Big Rock

Greycliff

TO BILLINGS →

McLeod

*West Boulder River*

Boulder Forks

GREYCLIFF
PRAIRIE DOG
TOWN

*Boulder River*

NATURAL
BRIDGE
STATE PARK

GALLATIN
NATIONAL
FOREST

ABSAROKA RANGE

BEARTOOTH RANGE

N

BOX
CANYON

FAVORITE · DRIVE
1

Big Beaver—U.S. Forest Service Campground, 36 miles south of Big Timber on Route 298. RVs allowed (max. length 32 feet), no services; open year-round.

Half Moon—U.S. Forest Service Campground, 12 miles north of Big Timber on Route 298. RVs allowed (max. length 22 feet), no services; open year-round.

### McLeod

McLeod Resort, 16 miles south of Big Timber on Route 298. 10 RV sites (6 pull-throughs), water and electric hook-ups only, dump station, hot showers, laundry; busiest mid-June through mid-August, especially on weekends July and August; will accept reservations; open May 1 through October 31; (406) 932-6167; fax: (406) 932-6167.

West Boulder—U.S. Forest Service Campground, 14 miles south of Big Timber on Route 298, then 16 miles west on County Road 35 (West Boulder Road). RVs allowed (max. length 20 feet), no services; open year-round.

East Boulder—U.S. Forest Service Campground, 19 miles south of Big Timber on Route 298, then 6 miles east on East Boulder Road (Forest Service Road 205). RVs allowed (max. length 16 feet), no services except drinking water; open year-round.

Falls Creek—U.S. Forest Service Picnic Ground, 34 miles southwest of Big Timber on Route 298. Day use only; 11 picnic units with trailer space available, drinking water, toilets and fishing access.

Aspen—U.S. Forest Service Campground, 37 miles southwest of Big Timber on Route 298. 11 camping sites, RVs allowed (max. length 32 feet), no services except drinking water; open year-round.

Chippy Park—U.S. Forest Service Campground, 38 miles southwest of Big Timber on Route 298. 4 camping sites, small RVs allowed, no services; open year-round.

Hells Canyon—U.S. Forest Service Campground, 45 miles southwest of Big Timber on Route 298. 11 camping sites, small RVs allowed (max. length 16 feet), no services; open year-round.

Hicks Park—U.S. Forest Service Campground, 48 miles southwest of Big Timber on Route 298. 23 camping sites, RVs allowed (max. length 32 feet), no services except drinking water; open year-round.

## BED & BREAKFAST ESTABLISHMENTS

### Big Timber

Big Timber Inn Bed & Breakfast, on Yellowstone River Lane, 1 mile gravel road. The inn has been operating since 1992. Open year-round; busiest in summer and early fall, slowest in winter; no credit cards accepted; outside pets only. Contact Bob Bovee, PO Box 328, Big Timber, MT 59011; (406) 932-4080.

The Grand Hotel, newly remodeled hotel. Built in 1890, it's listed in the National Register of Historic Places. Operating since 1985; open year-round; busiest May through September, slowest in winter; credit cards accepted; pets at additional charge. Contact Larry Edwards, Box 1242, 139 McLeod, Big Timber, MT 59011; (406) 932- 4459; fax (406) 932-4248.

Java Inn Bed & Breakfast, working family ranch that was once part of the old Crow Reservation. The ranch has been operating since 1990 as a bed & breakfast. Open year-round; busiest October through September, slowest in January; no credit cards accepted; pets are allowed. Contact Arlene Pile, HC 88, Box 3625, on Lower Deer Creek Rd., Big Timber, MT 59011; (406) 932-6595.

## GUEST RANCHES

### Big Timber

Burnt Out Lodge, off I-90, Exit 377 west. This working ranch has been operating since 1976. New log lodge located on Upper Deer Creek; no credit cards accepted; outside pets allowed; open May through November or on special request. Contact Ruth and Marlyn Drange, HC 88, Box 3620, Big Timber, MT 59011; (406) 932-6601.

Lazy K Bar Ranch, historic 22,000-acre working cattle ranch that was established in 1880. The ranch has been in the Van Cleve family for 76 years. Family-oriented operation, references and reservations required. It features riding, fishing, log-cabin accommodations and family-style meals. No credit cards accepted; no pets allowed; open June 23 to Labor Day. Contact the Van Cleves at Box 550 M, Big Timber, MT 59011; (406) 537-4404; fax: (406) 537-4593.

Lower Deer Creek Ranch, third-generation working cattle ranch. Full accommodations; unlimited riding; no credit cards accepted; pets allowed; open June 1 to September 30. Contact Remi and Susan Metcalf, Box 765, Big Timber, MT 59011; (406) 932-4572.

*Wild horses still roam the lowlands outside Yellowstone.*

Sweet Grass Ranch, 40 miles from Big Timber. This working cattle ranch has been family-operated for five generations. Unlimited riding, pack trips, fishing, rodeos and cookouts; no credit cards accepted; no pets allowed; open June 15 through Labor Day. Contact Bill and Shelly Carroccia, HC 87, Box 2161, Big Timber, MT 59011; (406) 537-4477, 537-4497 (winter); fax: (406) 537-4477; e-mail: sweetgrass@mcn.net website: http://www.mcn.net/~sweetgrass

### McLeod

Boulder River Ranch, 28 miles south of Big Timber. This working quarterhorse ranch has been family-operated since 1918. Featured are horseback riding program, fly fishing and hiking trails. No credit cards accepted; no pets allowed; open year-round, busiest July through August. Contact Steve and Jeane Aller, HC 59, Box 210, McLeod, MT 59052; (406) 932-6406 or (406) 932-6411; e-mail: boulderriver@mcn.net

Hawley Mountain Guest Ranch, 23 miles north of Yellowstone National Park and 42 miles south of Big Timber on Highway 298. The ranch has been in operation since 1976. Featured are horseback riding, fly fishing, river rafting, 4 x 4 trips and guided elk and deer hunts. No credit cards accepted; no pets allowed; arrive via 17 miles of gravel road; open June through September for summer guests, through November for hunting. Contact Ron Jarrell and Bryant Blewett, Box 4A, McLeod, MT 59052; (406) 932-5791.

**SUGGESTED DINING**

The Grand Hotel and Restaurant, 139 McLeod, Big Timber, MT; (406) 932-4459.

The Road Kill Bar and Cafe, 16 miles south of Big Timber on Montana 298, McLeod, MT; (406) 932-6174.

Prospector Pizza Plus, 121 McLeod, Big Timber, MT; (406) 932-4846.

**VISITOR INFORMATION & SERVICES**

The Sweet Grass Chamber of Commerce is off I-90 at Exit 367, PO Box 1012, Big Timber, MT 59011; (406) 932-5131. Visitors can enjoy a splendid view of the Crazy Mountains from the new log cabin Visitors Center.

While you're visiting the town's sights, you may park your RV at the Chamber of Commerce or fairly easily around town.

### MEDICAL SERVICES

Sweet Grass Health Care, 515 Hooper, Big Timber, MT; (406) 932-4012.

Pioneer Medical Center, 24-hour emergency room, pharmacy, 301 W. 7th, Big Timber, MT; (406) 932-5482.

Cole Drug Co., 136 McLeod, Big Timber, MT; (406) 932-5667.

### REPAIR & TOWING

Bob Faw Chevrolet & Towing (AAA), 326 McLeod, Big Timber, MT; (406) 932-5334.

Jerry's Conoco Service & Repairs, Jerry Hauge, Big Timber, MT; (406) 932-5183.

### VETERINARY SERVICES

Big Timber Veterinary Clinic, Dr. Langford, 407 E. 7th, Big Timber, MT; (406) 932-5205.

All Creatures Veterinary Service, Dr. Jim Felton, off I-90, Exit 370, Big Timber, MT; (406) 932-4324.

### GREYCLIFF

The Greycliff Prairie Dog Town State Park is a western enigma. The prairie dog was the long-standing enemy of both cattle and sheep ranchers, and about the only thing the two had in common. However, several government and private agencies have joined in the protection of this colony.

The location of the Greycliff Prairie Dog Town is 9 miles east of Big Timber on I-90 at the Greycliff Exit. The burrows of the black-tailed prairie dog provide a lesson in watching wildlife, and there are several interpretive signs. Bring along your camera, as the antics of the little critters can be quite amusing. The day-use area is open year-round, but from May to September, there is a $3 entrance fee per vehicle. There is a picnic area to enjoy; however, water and restrooms are available only at the rest area a few miles east. Protection of the prairie dog community is provided by the efforts of the Montana Departments of Transportation and Fish, Wildlife and Parks, and support from the Nature Conservancy. For further information, contact (406) 247-2940, or (406) 252-4654.

### REEDPOINT

Each Labor Day weekend, one of Montana's smallest towns becomes one of the most crowded. The annual sheep roundup, or Running of the Sheep, draws a huge crowd for the crazy sheep drive that runs through the middle of town. Stand back, but have no fear—these sheep aren't likely to trample you like the bulls of Madrid. You'll love the festive spirit of this event and will meet some of the nicest folks in Montana.

## CAMPGROUNDS & RV PARKS

▲ ***Best Shot for a Camp Spot***
Cedar Hills Campground, just off I-90, Exit 384, 5 S. Division, Reedpoint, MT 59069. 24 RV sites (10 pull-throughs), hook-ups, hot showers, laundry, propane; open year-round; (406) 326-2266.

## BED & BREAKFAST ESTABLISHMENTS

Hotel Montana, restored 1890s boarding house. Five rooms, each with private bath; period costumes available; credit cards accepted; no pets allowed. Contact Russ Schlievert, Box 356, 13 Division, Reedpoint, MT 59069; (406) 326-2288.

*Top: Sheep Festival at Reedpoint, Montana*
*Below: A sheep being shorn at the Sheep Festival*
DONNIE SEXTON/COURTESY TRAVEL MONTANA

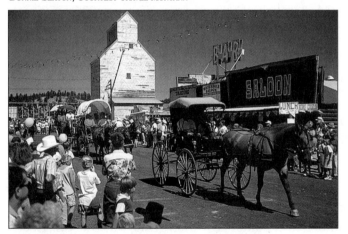

Buckin' Horse Bed & Breakfast/Cabin, off I-90, Exit 384, 3.6 miles dirt road on Bridge Creek Road. The inn has been operating since 1996. Genuine western atmosphere and decor; no credit cards accepted; pets conditional. Contact Rod and Janis Maclean, proprietors, HC 57, Box 521, Reedpoint, MT 59069; (406) 932-6537.

## GUEST RANCHES

Range Riders Ranch is on Bridger Creek Road. This is a fourth-generation working cattle ranch. Featured are scenic and historical trail rides (choose one- to six-hour rides), authentic cattle drives, overnight campouts, abundant wildlife, excellent horses and riding lessons. No credit cards accepted; pets with leashes allowed; open year-round; busiest in July, slowest September through October. Contact Terry and Wyoma Terland, HC 57, Box 519, Reedpoint, MT 59069; (406) 932-6538.

## FAVORITE DRIVE:
## BIG SKY COUNTRY TO THE MARTINSDALE RESERVOIR

The rugged Crazy Mountains lure you north of Big Timber, away from I-90 and the Yellowstone River Valley. Well-maintained U.S. 191 is narrow with little shoulder but provides an interesting drive. Follow U.S. 191 north about 20 miles to Melville, and then head west on the back road to Twodot. Melville was named for the arctic explorer, Lieutenant Melville. The town is the headquarters for the Cremer Stock Ranch, which breeds bucking horses and stock for rodeos. (Visit the new rodeo exhibit at Big Timber's Crazy Mountain Museum.)

West from Melville, the paved road gives way to gravel after about 12 miles but is in relatively good condition, and the peaceful scenery is worth the slower pace. Continue about 35 miles to Twodot, which is on the Mussellshell River. Twodot was named for "Two Dot" Wilson, a wizened cattleman whose thief-proof brand was near impossible to alter. The brand was two dots, one on the shoulder and one on the thigh. In 1900, the Montana Railroad reached Twodot; the weather-beaten station can still be seen along the tracks. Twodot is just off U.S. 12, which runs along the southern edge of the Judith Basin.

On U.S. 12, head west about 10 miles to Montana 294 and the turnoff to Martinsdale. There's good fishing for big trout, mostly rainbows, at Martinsdale Reservoir, and camping is available nearby. (There are private campgrounds at Martinsdale and public campgrounds north of White Sulphur Springs.) Montana 294 continues 27 miles and connects to U.S. 89. The trip onward is a nice drive through rolling ranchland.

# TWODOT TO HARLOWTON: U.S. 12

If you head east from Twodot toward Harlowton on Highway 12, you can swing around to Billings through some genuine Montana Big Sky Country. The rolling hills and ranchlands are typical of the state, as are the weather extremes. The eastern side of Montana gets hotter in summer and colder in winter. And without the Rockies to block the wind, it can rip across the prairie, bending flat everything from grass to tree.

Harlowton is about 23 miles east of Twodot. The town, settled in 1881, became a railroad town in 1900. Named for Richard Harlow, who built the "Jaw Bone" Milwaukee branch to Lewistown, Harlowton served as a division point on the Milwaukee Railroad. Sheep ranching, wheat growing and flour milling were extremely important to the area's origin. The Wheatland County Seat, Harlowton, with a population of about 1,100, remains well preserved. Main street's original stone buildings, cut from native quarries, have become a historic district.

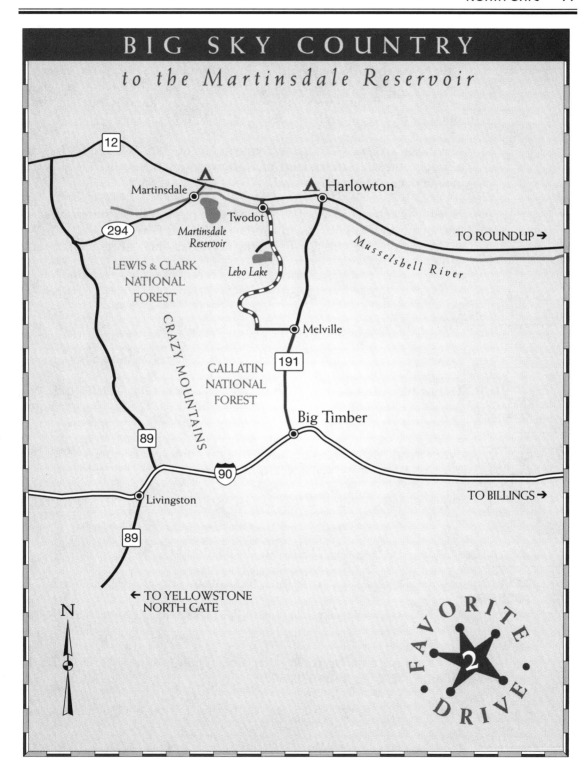

# BIG SKY COUNTRY
## to the Martinsdale Reservoir

12

Martinsdale

Harlowton

Twodot

294

Martinsdale
Reservoir

TO ROUNDUP →

Musselshell River

LEWIS & CLARK
NATIONAL
FOREST

Lebo Lake

CRAZY MOUNTAINS

Melville

191

GALLATIN
NATIONAL
FOREST

Big Timber

89

90

TO BILLINGS →

Livingston

89

← TO YELLOWSTONE
NORTH GATE

N

FAVORITE · DRIVE
2

## OVERNIGHTING

## CAMPGROUNDS & RV PARKS

Chief Joseph Park, west end of Harlowton on U.S. 12. 8 RV sites (no pull-throughs), electrical hook-ups only, no other services; playground and fishing pond on site; July 4th weekend is busiest time; open April 1 through November 30; (406) 632-5532.

Deadman's Basin—Montana Department of Fish, Wildlife and Parks Campground, 20 miles east of Harlowton on U.S. 12. RVs allowed, no services; open year-round.

Spring Creek—U.S. Forest Service Campground, 33 miles west of Harlowton on U.S. 12, then 4 miles north on Forest Road 274. RVs allowed (max. length 22 feet), no services; open summer through fall.

## SUGGESTED DINING

Broken Spur, east of Harlowton, Harlowton, MT; (406) 632-5500.

The Cornerstone, 11 N. Central, Harlowton, MT; (406) 632-4600.

Graves Hotel, 106 S. Central, Harlowton, MT; (406) 632-5855.

## VISITOR INFORMATION & SERVICES

Harlowton Chamber of Commerce, PO Box 694, Harlowton, MT 59036; (406) 632-4694; fax: (406) 632-5633.

## MEDICAL SERVICES

Wheatland Memorial Hospital, 24-hour emergency room, 530 3rd St. NW, Harlowton, MT; (406) 632-4351.

Blair Memorial Clinic, 1130 3rd St. NW, Harlowton, MT; (406) 632-4343.

Staley Drug Co., 22 S. Central, Harlowton, MT; (406) 632-4222.

## REPAIR & TOWING

Judith Gap Oil-Conoco, 302 High, Judith Gap, MT; (406) 473-2321.

Cliff's Wrecker Service, 24 hours, (AAA-rated), Billings, MT; 1-800-656-2337.

Hanser's Automotive & Wrecker Co., repairs, 430 S. Billings Blvd., Billings, MT; 1-800-345-1754.

## VETERINARY SERVICES

Holmes Veterinary Clinic, Dr. Catherine Parks, east of Harlowton, MT; (406) 632-5548.

# SECTION 3

# NORTHEAST GATE

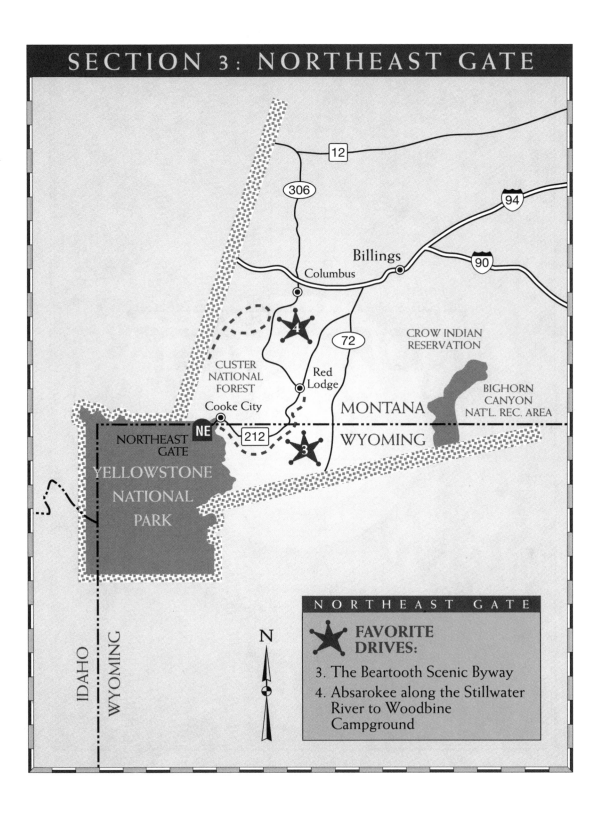

12

306

94

90

Billings

Columbus

4

72

CROW INDIAN
RESERVATION

CUSTER
NATIONAL
FOREST

Red
Lodge

BIGHORN
CANYON
NAT'L. REC. AREA

Cooke City

MONTANA

NE

212

WYOMING

NORTHEAST
GATE

3

YELLOWSTONE

NATIONAL

PARK

IDAHO

WYOMING

N

### NORTHEAST GATE

## FAVORITE DRIVES:

3. The Beartooth Scenic Byway

4. Absarokee along the Stillwater River to Woodbine Campground

# GENERAL OVERVIEW

Silver Gate and Cooke City are the first towns you'll pass as you exit Yellowstone's Northeast Gate. Ahead of you the highway divides, and you must choose between two incredibly beautiful and scenic highways. The magnificent Chief Joseph Scenic Byway on Wyoming 296 heads through the Sunlight Basin to Cody, Wyoming. The northern route puts you on the Beartooth Scenic Byway. Filled with breathtaking vistas high above timberline, the highway crosses the Beartooth Plateau and descends into Red Lodge, Montana, on U.S. 212. From there you can go northeast to I-90 and Billings, or you can head west following the rural roads through the Absaroka Mountains and come out at Columbus on I-90.

**SILVER GATE AND COOKE CITY**

Cooke City, named for Jay Cooke, Jr., began as a mining town in the 1870s. The son of a Northern Pacific financier, Cooke was primarily interested in the mining claims. The prospectors found gold, silver and lead, and the mines flourished for a time, but they were just too far back in the wilderness for the ore quality to pay off. The ore still remains untouched. A recent effort by a Canadian firm, Noranda, to open the Crown Butte Mine was unsuccessful after a furious battle. President Clinton finally stepped in and gave Noranda $65 million to settle its claim and keep the area pristine.

The early settlement earned its keep by being a trade center for goods shipped up the Yellowstone River through Red Lodge and then transported down to Cody, Wyoming. When the Beartooth Highway from Red Lodge opened in 1936, Cooke City suddenly became a tourist attraction. Today, the year-round population is only about 100 folks, but many more call it home in the summer. It's a quaint, rustic town that makes for an enjoyable quick stop to walk along the main street. The introduction of wolves into Yellowstone has created a mini-boom for Cooke City as wolf observers use the town as a base from which to dine and lodge.

The tiny town of Silver Gate is just four miles from Cooke City. It was established in 1937, named for Silver Mountain in the rugged Beartooth Range. If you're a trivia buff, here's a tidbit for you: It's impossible to get to either of these Montana towns without going through Wyoming—unless you can drop in via a parachute or hang glider.

**OUTDOOR RECREATION**

Guided fly fishing, scenic horseback trips and wildlife viewing are available through Beartooth Plateau Outfitters, Ronnie Wright, Box 1127, Main St., Cooke, City, MT 59020; 1-800-253-8545, or (406) 838-2328; and Skyline Guide Service, Box 1074, Cooke City, MT 59020; (406) 838-2380.

The Silver Gate area is famous for excellent snowmobiling. There are over 60 miles of groomed trails in the Gallatin National Forest. The Cooke City trail system also connects with 50 miles of groomed trails in Wyoming. Cooke City can be accessed only through Yellowstone's Mammoth entrance at Gardiner in the winter. Access to the Northeast Gate from Cody is closed to vehicular traffic because of heavy snow over the passes. The season runs Thanksgiving through mid-May. There is a shuttle service between Mammoth and Cooke City. For detailed trail information, contact the Gardiner Ranger District, Gallatin National Forest, Box 5, Gardiner, MT 59030; (406) 848-7375; or the Upper Yellowstone Snowmobile Club at Box 39, Silver Gate, MT 59081.

## RV CAUTION

Archaeology lovers will be intrigued by the "Grasshopper Glacier." The glacier has dark bands of grasshoppers that have been frozen within the ice for centuries. The migrating grasshoppers were caught in one of the harsh storms relatively common to the high-altitude area. Usually about August, enough snow has melted away that the dark band is visible. If you're pulling a high-clearance 4-wheel drive vehicle (necessary even to begin the journey up LuLu Pass—Goose Lake Road), then consider putting the side trip on your itinerary. You need to make a very strenuous hike to get to the glacier; don't attempt this climb unless you're in great shape, and do not even think about driving your RV in here.

## OVERNIGHTING

## CAMPGROUNDS & RV PARKS

Whispering Pines Cabins, 1 mile from the northeast entrance to Yellowstone on U.S. 212, Silver Gate, MT 59081. 6 RV sites, full hookups; features include horseback riding trails, fishing; open summers; (406) 838-2228.

Big Moose Resort, 3 miles east of Cooke City on U.S. 212, PO Box 1009, Cooke City, MT 59020. 6 RV sites; water and electric hookups only; credit cards accepted; open June 1 through September 30; (406) 838-2393.

Soda Butte—U.S. Forest Service Campground, 1 mile east of Cooke City on U.S. 212. RVs allowed (max. length 22 feet), no services; open July 1 through September 15.

Colter—U.S. Forest Service Campground, 2 miles east of Cooke City on U.S. 212. RVs allowed (max. length 22 feet), no services; open July 1 through September 15.

Chief Joseph—U.S. Forest Service Campground, 4 miles east of Cooke City on U.S. 212. RVs allowed (max. length 22 feet), no services; open July 1 through September 10.

Top of the World Store RV Park, U.S. 212 east of the junction between the Chief Joseph Scenic Byway (Wyoming 296) and Red Lodge. RV sites (no pull-throughs), hook-ups; open July 1 through September 15.

## BED & BREAKFAST ESTABLISHMENTS

Big Bear Lodge, 7 miles east of Yellowstone's northeast entrance on U.S. 212, 3 miles east of Cooke City. This lodge, with rustic log cabins, has been operating since 1995. Open year-round; busiest in winter, March and summer, slowest in November; credit cards accepted, no pets allowed. Contact Scott and Lisa Sanders, Box 1052, Cooke City, MT 59020; (406) 838-2267.

## GUEST RANCHES

Soda Butte Lodge, operating since 1969; open year-round; busiest in summer and winter, slowest October 15 through December and March 15 through May; credit cards accepted; pets additional charge. Contact RaeAnn and Andy Eckland, Box 1119, Cooke City, MT 59020; (406) 838-2251; 1-800-527-2251; fax: (406) 838-2253.

K Bar Z Guest Ranch & Outfitters, 24 miles from the Northeast Gate to Yellowstone on Wyoming 296. This guest ranch has been operating since 1989. Features include private cabins, hot tub and sauna, horseback riding, pack trips, hiking and fishing; in addition, there are two hunting camps in the Absakorka Wilderness. Open year-round; busiest July through August, slowest in April; credit cards accepted; pets conditional. Contact Dawna Barnett, Box 2167, Cody, WY 82414; (307) 587-4410; fax: (307) 527-4605.

**SUGGESTED DINING**   Joan & Bill's Family Restaurant, Main St., Cooke City, MT; (406) 838-2280.

Miners Saloon, Main St., Cooke City, MT; (406) 838-2214.

Pinetree Café, Main St., Cooke City, MT; (406) 838-2161.

Prospector Inn, Soda Butte Lodge, U.S. 212, Cooke City, MT; (406) 838 2251; 1-800-527-6462.

**VISITOR INFORMATION & SERVICES**

The combined Cooke City, Silver Gate and Colter Pass Chamber of Commerce is in the High Country Motel; write to PO Box 1071, Cooke City, MT 59020; (406) 838-2262; (406) 838-2495.

**MEDICAL SERVICES**

See Livingston, MT (page 68) or Mammoth, WY (page 57) in winter; Cody, WY (page 138) in summer.

**REPAIR & TOWING**

Bob Smith Repair & Towing, Cooke City, MT; (406) 333-9040.

Cooke City Exxon—Repair & Towing, Cooke City, MT; (406) 838-2244.

**VETERINARY SERVICES**

See Livingston, MT (page 68) or Mammoth, WY (page 57) in winter; Cody, WY (page 139) in summer.

# COOKE CITY TO RED LODGE: U.S. 212

Wyoming 296 joins this highway about 15 miles down the road and is described in the East Gate Section (see page 141).

Once you leave the Northeast Gate, you're in for a treat, whether you take the Beartooth Scenic Byway over to Red Lodge, Montana, or the Chief Joseph Scenic Highway down to Cody, Wyoming. The road from the gate winds up through dense pine and fir forests, eventually topping out on the Beartooth Plateau at an elevation of 10,947 feet. When you get to the Chief Joseph Highway Junction, you must remain on U.S. 212 to get to the Beartooths. To get to Cody, Wyoming, you can reverse your route after driving up and viewing the Beartooths, and drive down the Chief Joseph Highway (Wyoming 296), or go to Red Lodge, Montana, and then go back to Cody via a number of different routes.

## FAVORITE DRIVE:
## BEARTOOTH SCENIC BYWAY

The Beartooth Scenic Byway is a breathtaking passageway through alpine tundra above timberline. You'll see stunted trees and bushes trying to eke out an existence in a land that offers just a few weeks of growing season. Lakes and streams are everywhere, from roadside waters to remote lakes requiring a hike or an all-terrain vehicle.

U.S. 212 became one of 52 routes to receive the esteemed designation of a National Scenic Byway. The 65-mile drive from Cooke City to Red Lodge crosses the Beartooth Range at a summit of 10,947 feet; you truly feel you're at the "Top of the World." At the urging of a Red Lodge physician, J. C. F. Siegfriedt, and **Carbon County News** editor, O. H. P. Shelley, Congress authorized the construction of "approach highways" to national parks. After five years and a cost of $2.5 million, the Beartooth Highway officially opened in 1936.

Be sure to bring along plenty of film for the panoramic views, and maybe oxygen if you're a flatlander. Sunscreen and insect spray are essentials if you plan on a picnic or camping in one of the campgrounds. The Vista Point visitor area has an awesome overlook at the end of a short trail. It's worth the walk. The view down into Rock Creek Valley will take your breath away.

The highway winds around the snow-covered peaks, and you can enjoy alpine meadows blanketed with wildflowers and snowfields as late as July. Try to allow at least two to three hours for the trip, so that you can enjoy several stops along the way. Be aware that it can snow any time of the year here, so take the weather into account before you make the drive. If you need basic supplies, stop at the quaint "Top of the World" store located on the highway near Beartooth Lake. Don't be afraid of the big white dog that greets visitors; he looks dangerous but he's really friendly.

**RED LODGE**

The Red Lodge area was once part of the Crow Reservation. With increasing pressure to make the fertile lands available to white settlers, the reservation was considerably reduced in size by the Treaty of 1882. Founded in 1884, the town was first named Rocky Fork after the two small streams that join at Rock Creek. However, the settlement soon took on the name of Red Lodge. There are several tales relating how Red Lodge got its name, but no real proof to claim one over another. Many say that Red Lodge was named for the lodges of the Crow, richly decorated with the red clay found nearby. Others say it came about because there were so many "red man's" lodges about the area. Still another version holds that the town was named because of a stream flowing out of a giant outcropping of red rock shaped like a teepee. The Natives named the stream Red Lodge Creek. All these stories refer to the Crow and their indelible presence in the area.

# BEARTOOTH SCENIC BYWAY

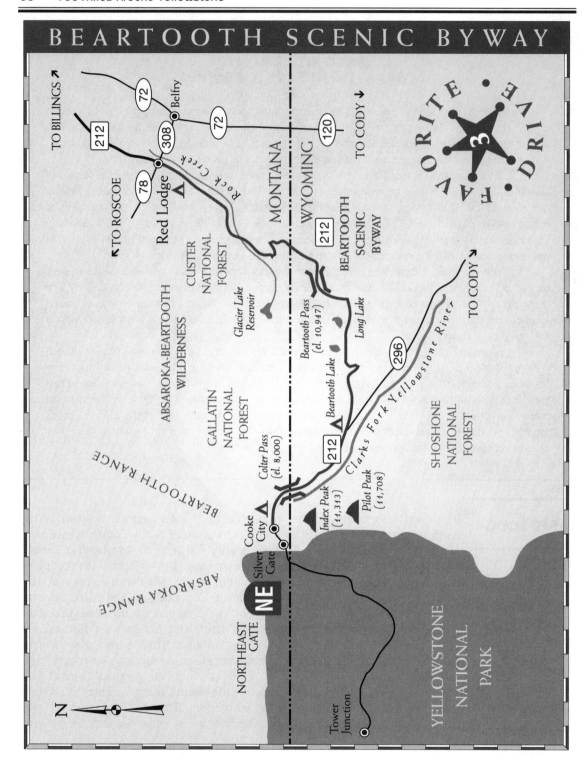

TO BILLINGS ↗

72

Belfry

72

212

308

120

TO CODY →

78

TO ROSCOE ↙

Red Lodge

Rock Creek

MONTANA

WYOMING

CUSTER NATIONAL FOREST

212

BEARTOOTH SCENIC BYWAY

FAVORITE DRIVE

3

Glacier Lake Reservoir

ABSAROKA-BEARTOOTH WILDERNESS

GALLATIN NATIONAL FOREST

Beartooth Pass (el. 10,947)

Long Lake

Beartooth Lake

296

Clarks Fork Yellowstone River

TO CODY →

Colter Pass (el. 8,000)

212

BEARTOOTH RANGE

SHOSHONE NATIONAL FOREST

Index Peak (11,313)

Pilot Peak (11,708)

Cooke City

Silver Gate

NE

NORTHEAST GATE

ABSAROKA RANGE

YELLOWSTONE NATIONAL PARK

Tower Junction

N

*Red Lodge, Montana, is a popular summer and winter destination.*

James "Yankee Jim" George, a gold prospector, discovered coal in the area in 1866. When the Northern Pacific Railroad came to Montana in the 1880s, powered by coal-hungry steam engines, the boom days of Red Lodge were born. Coal mining was the economic basis of the community for over 40 years. The town swelled to almost 6,000 residents; that's 4,000 more folks than inhabit the area today. By 1910, Carbon County produced more coal than anywhere else in the state. The town prospered financially, but suffered as the mine disasters claimed many lives. The biggest mine tragedy in Montana's history took place in 1943. An explosion at the Smith Mine trapped 74 men; all were killed. Many more died in the rescue attempt. The weathered cabins and sheds and tailing scars can still be seen, a reminder of the past.

*The Smith Mine disaster near Red Lodge took a huge human toll.*

Like everything, mining suffered during the Depression years. Many took to making illegal liquor to provide a living. Some, on the other hand, looked around and saw the incredible beauty of the area, men such as Dr. J. C. F. Siegfriedt, who was credited with the creation of the Beartooth Highway.

Golf and skiing round out the summer through winter activities, and there is always something fun to do. Snowfall averages 150 inches per year. It's no surprise that skiing is so popular. The 2,300 to 2,800 members of the Red Lodge community cater to travelers. A diverse array of cafes and restaurants, gift shops, art galleries and craft shops abound in the town. Following in the footsteps of Jackson, Wyoming, Red Lodge is seeking to balance maximum economic growth with minimizing environmental impact and preserving its historical flavor.

OUTDOOR
RECREATION

Beartooth–Red Lodge Elks Golf & Country Club has 9 holes. The public course is southwest of Red Lodge off Red Lodge Mountain Road. For more information or tee times, call (406) 446-1812; (406) 446-3938.

Red Lodge Mountain Golf Course is an 18-hole public course located beneath the Beartooth Mountains. Golf anytime from May to October, depending on the weather. The address is 828 Upper Continental Drive, PO Box 750, Red Lodge, MT 59068, or call (406) 446-3344; 1-800-514-3088.

As for fishing, practically every creek and stream in the Beartooths has trout, most of them brook trout that are easy to catch. Be aware that the highway runs through both Wyoming and Montana, so you'll need a license for the state you're fishing in. Beartooth Lake and the streams that run in and out of it are fine places to fish, offering good bank fishing if you don't have a boat. A campground at the lake allows close and easy access.

White-water river rafting adventures are an exhilarating way to view unsurpassed natural beauty. View the inspiring scenery from a perspective never experienced on pavement: Feel the water pull the raft, and feel the cold water splash your face. You may float down the rapids of either the Stillwater or Yellowstone River in craft handled expertly by professional guides. For your convenience, a couple of river rafting outfitters are included here; other companies are listed with the Chamber of Commerce. Adventure Whitewater, Inc. (AAA-rated) offers trips; contact them at Box 636, Red Lodge, MT, 59068; 1-800-897-3061. Full- and half-day rafting adventures on the Stillwater River are offered in oar, paddle or "row your own" boats. Beartooth White-water (AAA-rated) has full- and half-day rafting trips available on the Stillwater and Yellowstone Rivers. Check them out at PO Box 781, Red Lodge, MT 59068; (406) 446-3142.

Downhill skiing, for skiers of all ages, is popular at Red Lodge Mountain Ski Area. The ski area is 6 miles from

*Twin Lakes, among many lakes and ponds in the Beartooth Mountains*
COURTESY WYOMING TRAVEL COMMISSION

*Clark's Fork, one of Wyoming's finest, is born in the Beartooth Mountains.*
*COURTESY WYOMING BLM*

Red Lodge and a transport shuttle is available. The base elevation is 7,075 feet, rising to 9,146 feet. The longest run 2.5 miles, and there is a newly expanded 2,350 vertical drop. Average snowfall is 250 inches. For ski reports and/or vacation packages, call (406) 446-2610; 1-800-444-8977.

Another favorite winter activity, cross-country skiing, is found at Red Lodge Nordic Ski Area just 2 miles west of Red Lodge off Montana 78. The area is across from Red Lodge Mountain Golf Course. There are 15 km of groomed trails offered in the immediate area, and more than 30 miles of trails are available in all. For maps and information, contact TW Recreational Services, Inc., in Yellowstone National Park, WY 82190; (307) 344-7311.

## ATTRACTIONS

In the old Labor Temple, the Carbon County Museum houses colorful local history and many artifacts. One of the most interesting exhibits is the homestead cabin of John Garrison. His life became the basis for the Robert Redford movie *Jeremiah Johnson*. He was known as "Liver Eatin' Johnson" and supposedly killed a man and then ate his liver. The museum is at 1131 S. Broadway Ave., Red Lodge, MT; (406) 446-3914.

The Pollard Hotel is a member of the Historic Hotels of America. In 1893, the residents of Red Lodge celebrated the opening of the Spofford Hotel, which was also the town's first brick building. The posh hotel was built halfway between the train depot and the most densely populated area of town. The brick hotel was purchased in

1902 by Thomas F. Pollard, a hotel man who had moved over from Virginia City. The hotel was the center attraction of Red Lodge, and the center of Pollard family's life until it was sold in 1946. Many famous personalities stayed there, including Buffalo Bill Cody, Calamity Jane, Liver Eatin' Johnson, with even a few more cultured types like orator William Jennings Bryan and General Miles. The beautifully restored hotel, now owned by the Hotel Company of Red Lodge, forms the cornerstone of Red Lodge's historic district. You can enjoy a wonderful meal here and make it a starting place to tour the sights of the town.

The Pollard is at 2 N. Broadway, and there is RV parking within one block. From Broadway turn onto 11th Street and go past the hotel one block. You can park on 11th Street, or turn onto Platt Street and park in the parking lot on the left-hand side of the street (the Pollard owns the property). For additional information about the hotel, call 1-800-POLLARD.

A Self-guided Walking Tour has been prepared by the Carbon County Historical Society. The tour is good exercise and takes only 40 minutes to enjoy the historical flavor of the town. Buildings that hosted Calamity Jane and Buffalo Bill and the original 1889 railroad station are included. Most of the buildings in the central business district are on the National Register of Historic Places. Walking tour maps are available at the Red Lodge Area Chamber of Commerce.

The Festival of Nations, held the first full week of August, celebrates the ethnic and western history of the area. Activities include parades, demonstrations, exhibits, costumes, arts and crafts, excellent international cuisine and street dancing. The Festival received recognition by the New York *Times* and *Reader's Digest Almanac of Summer Stops*. In 1997, the event commemorated its 48th year. A schedule of daily events is available from the Red Lodge Chamber of Commerce.

The annual Home of Champions Rodeo has been held for more than 60 years. The July 2–4 event is sanctioned by the Professional Rodeo Cowboys Association and the Women's Professional Rodeo Association. All seven rodeo events are included. A gala parade precedes each day's rodeo. For more information, contact the Red Lodge Chamber of Commerce.

The Round Barn Restaurant and Dinner Theater, located 2 miles north of Red Lodge on U.S. 212, will lighten your spirits. Enjoy homecooked entrees with all the fixin's and presentations by talented performers. The theater is open seasonally. Call (406) 446-1197 for reservations and/or theater tickets.

The National Finals Ski Joring is a most unusual winter event. The craziest combination of western cowboy and European skier can be seen at this early March competition. Excitement mounts as teams of riders and skiers compete for the lucrative purse; in 1997 it was $7,000 for the Open Division alone. The action: A horse and rider pull a skier through a snow-packed, 250-yard course with 16 to 24 gates. Rider, horse and skier all hang on while barreling full-out across the snow to beat the clock. To win, the skier must cross the finish line in an upright position (we hope so) and have at least one ski on the ground (who knows where the other one is pointed). It's a hoot! Sponsored by the Red Lodge Ski-Joring Association, the winter event is held at the Red Lodge Rodeo Grounds.

The Annual Northern Rocky Mountain Winter Games are held in late February. Sponsored by the Montana Winter Sports Foundation, the contests are geared to all levels of athletes to provide competitive experience, and increase community involvement in winter sports. Events include alpine and cross-country skiing, snowshoe races, snowboarding, telemark skiing, ice hockey, the Montana Special Olympics and more. For more information, contact the Red Lodge Chamber of Commerce.

## OVERNIGHTING

### CAMPGROUNDS & RV PARKS

▲ ***Best Shot for a Camp Spot***
Red Lodge KOA, 4 miles north of Red Lodge on U.S. 212. 75 RV sites, hook-ups, dump station, hot showers, laundry, swimming pool, propane station, children's playground, pets on leash only; open summer, closed winter; (406) 446-2364.

Perry's RV Park & Campground, 2 miles south on U.S. 212. 30 RV sites, water and electric hook-ups only, dump station, hot showers, laundry; open May 25 to September 15; (406) 446-2722.

Basin—U.S. Forest Service Campground, 1 mile south of Red Lodge on U.S. 212, then 7 miles west on Forest Service Road 71. RVs allowed (max. length 30 feet), no services; open May 27 to September 5; reservations: 1-800-280-CAMP.

Cascade—U.S. Forest Service Campground, 2 miles south of Red Lodge on U.S. 212, then 10 miles west on Forest Service Road 71. RVs allowed (max. length 30 feet), no services; open May 27 to September 5; reservations: 1-800-280-CAMP.

Greenough Lake—U.S. Forest Service Campground, 12 miles southwest of Red Lodge on U.S. 212, then 1 mile southwest on Forest Service Road 421. RVs allowed (max. length 30 feet), no services; open May 27 to September 5; reservations: 1-800-280-CAMP.

Limber Pine—U.S. Forest Service Campground, 12 miles southwest of Red Lodge on U.S. 212, then 1 mile west on Forest Service Road 421. RVs allowed (max. length 35 feet), no services; open May 27 to September 5; reservations: 1-800-280-CAMP.

M–K—U.S. Forest Service Campground, 12 miles southwest of Red Lodge on U.S. 212, then 4 miles southwest on Forest Service Road 421. RVs allowed (max. length 16 feet), no services; open May 30 to September 5.

Palisades—U.S. Forest Service Campground, 1 mile west of Red Lodge on Forest Service Road 71, then 2 miles west on County and Forest Service Road 3010. RVs allowed (max. length 16 feet), no services; open June 15 to September 15.

Parkside—U.S. Forest Service Campground, 12 miles south of Red Lodge on U.S. 212, then 1 mile southwest on Forest Service Road 421. RVs allowed (max. length 30 feet), no services; open May 27 to September 5; reservations: 1-800-280-CAMP.

Sheridan—U.S. Forest Service Campground, 5 miles southwest of Red Lodge, then 2 miles southwest on Forest Service Road 379. RVs allowed (max. length 22 feet) no services; open May 26 to September 5; reservations: 1-800-280-CAMP.

## BED & BREAKFAST ESTABLISHMENTS

Inn on the Beartooth, Inc., western log building with a spectacular view of Beartooth Mountains located just 2 miles south of Red Lodge. This inn has been operating since 1995. Credit cards accepted, no pets allowed; open year-round, busiest in summer and December, slowest in spring and fall. Contact Robert and Jan Goehringer, 6648 U.S. 212 South, Box 1515, Red Lodge, MT 59068; (406) 446-3555; 1-888-222-7686.

Willows Inn, rooms and cottages in 1903 Victorian style. This inn has been operating since 1979. Credit cards accepted; no pets allowed; open year-round, busiest in summer, slowest October through November and April. Contact Kerry and Carolyn Boggio, PO Box 886, 224 S. Platt Ave., Red Lodge, MT 59068; (406) 446-3913.

The Wolves Den Bed & Breakfast, rural setting on Rock Creek. The establishment has been operating since 1994. No credit cards; no pets allowed; open year-round, busiest in June through August; slowest February through April. Contact Ron and Kathy Erdmann, Route 1, Box 1231, Red Lodge, MT 59068; (406) 446-1273.

## GUEST RANCHES

Rock Creek Resort, on Rock Creek at the foot of the Beartooth Mountains. This ranch has been operating since 1970. Credit cards accepted; no pets allowed; open year-round, busiest June through September, slowest October through May. Contact Dan Drobny, HC 49, Box 3500, U.S. 212 South, Red Lodge, MT 59068; (406) 446-1111; fax: (406) 446-3688; 1-800-667-1119; website: http://www.rcresort.com

**SUGGESTED DINING**

The Pollard, 2 N. Broadway, Red Lodge, MT; 1-800-POLLARD (see page 92).

Old Piney Dell, south of Red Lodge, MT; (406) 446-1111.

Bogart's, 11 S. Broadway, Red Lodge, MT; (406) 446-1784.

Round Barn, north of Red Lodge, MT; (406) 446-1197.

**VISITOR INFORMATION & SERVICES**

The Red Lodge Chamber of Commerce, 601 N. Broadway, Box 988, Red Lodge, MT 59068; (406) 446-1718; e-mail: redlodge@wtp.net website: http://www.net/redlodge

Montana Ski Reports and Travel Information, 1-800-VISIT MT, ext 3WG; (406) 444-2654.

The Red Lodge Shuttle Service offers local and area service to restaurants, shopping, the golf course, skiing, and other places. Contact them at PO Box 635, Red Lodge, MT 59068, or (406) 446-2257; 1-888-446-2191.

Custer National Forest, Beartooth Ranger District, (406) 446-2103.

**MEDICAL SERVICES**

Carbon County Memorial Hospital; 24-hour emergency room; 600 W. 21st St., Red Lodge, MT; (406) 446-2345.

Mountain View Medical Center, 24-hour answering service; across from Carbon County Memorial Hospital, 501 W. 20th St., Red Lodge, MT; (406) 446-3800.

The Red Lodge Clinic, 10 S. Oakes St., Red Lodge, MT; (406) 446-2412.

Beartooth IGA Pharmacy, on Broadway, Red Lodge, MT; open Monday through Friday, 9:30 A.M. to 9 P.M., Saturday, 9:30 A.M. to 6:30 P.M., and Sunday, 9:30 A.M. to 12 NOON; (406) 446-2684.

Red Lodge Drug, 101 S. Broadway, Red Lodge, MT; open Monday through Saturday, 8 A.M. to 5:30 P.M.; (406) 446-1017.

**REPAIR &
TOWING**

Horse Power Wagon Works—Towing & Repairs (AAA-rated), 24-hour service; Red Lodge, MT; (406) 446-1277.

**VETERINARY
SERVICES**

Red Lodge Veterinary Clinic, Dr. John Beug; located west of Red Lodge, MT; (406) 446-2815.

# WASHOE, BEARCREEK AND BELFRY: MONTANA 308

As you depart Red Lodge heading toward Washoe on Montana 308, you immediately climb up a 7.5 percent grade. However, the road is extremely steep only for about .3 mile, and then it winds down into Washoe. Another 8 miles puts you in Belfry, a town built on the junction of Montana 308 and 72. It is known as the home of the Bats, the school mascot, which is no surprise. Be sure to check out the creative faces on the town's fire hydrants. A small café offers wholesome meals, and a grocery store has basic supplies.

Washoe and Bearcreek were mining camps located within a few miles of Red Lodge on what is known as the East Bench. Washoe, founded in 1907, was named by the Anaconda Copper Mining Company after one of its Nevada mines. Bearcreek, established in 1905, was named for the many bears seen along the banks of the creek. Residents depended on area mines such as the Washoe, Brophy, Foster and Smith. Coal mining suffered a slowdown after the Depression and as the use of electricity, gasoline and diesel fuels

increased. After the Smith Mine disaster in 1943, the mines closed and the towns shriveled away. The past is buried deep, but the natural beauty of the area has brought about renewed interest for summer and rural residents as well as for tourism potential. An interpretive sign along the road describes the Smith Mine disaster.

*This rock structure is a typical landmark on a ridge. Most were erected by sheepherders.*

## Special Attraction

The Pig Races at the Bearcreek Saloon are the most unusual attraction in the area. Montana's own brand of racing—pig racing—has become a celebrated event in Bearcreek. It's so crazy you have to love it. Dreamed up by Bearcreek Saloon owners Bob "Pits" and Lynn DeArmond, the local races have attracted national television shows and movie actors such as Mel Gibson. A sports pool method of betting takes place, in which 50 percent of the money is given to a scholarship fund for local students. Races take place every summer weekend from Memorial Day to Labor Day at Bearcreek Downs, just behind the saloon.

# ROBERTS, BOYD AND COONEY RESERVOIR: U.S. 212

The main highway goes to I-90 and Billings. Another choice is to take Montana 78 to Roscoe, Absarokee and other communities.

Roberts is located on the banks of Rock Creek. It was established in 1896 at the Merritt railroad station. Most likely, it was named for W. Milnor Roberts, the chief engineer for the Northern Pacific Railroad. W. M. Roberts was the chief engineer responsible for construction of the rail line, working on the original survey teams in 1867 through to its completion in the 1880s.

The Boyd Post Office was named in 1909 for a settler named John Boyd. The rich land has ample irrigation water for ranching and farming, the primary occupation of most locals. The Cooney Dam turnoff is on U.S. 212 at Boyd. Free advice and fishing updates are offered by the Country Store & Gift Shop at the turnoff junction, or call (406) 962-3318. However, they don't sell fishing licenses so be sure to purchase one in advance.

There's plenty of camping at Cooney State Park, which is open year-round. The 289-acre Cooney Reservoir recreation area lies a few miles west of Boyd on a county road. The administration of Governor Frank Cooney built the flood control dam, and the lake provides some great fishing. There is a designated recreation center with boat ramp and picnic grounds. This is the closest public campground to Billings that has restroom facilities, water and showers (open May 1 to September 30 only). The 75 camping sites are scattered along the shore in five groups. Marshall Cove has the most trees.

Joliet was another town that grew up under the influence of the Northern Pacific Railroad. Shipping the locally grown agricultural products was critical to the area's welfare, and the railroads were the key. As in the other small towns along this route, the local industry is geared to ranching and farming, though many new homes are being constructed—not surprising due to the proximity of the Red Lodge ski area.

## OVERNIGHTING

### CAMPGROUNDS & RV PARKS

Cooney—Montana Department of Fish, Wildlife and Parks Campground, 22 miles southwest of Laurel, at Milepost 90, go west 8 miles on County Road. 75 campsites, RVs allowed, drinking water and shower facilities (May 1 to September 30), boat launch; open year-round; information: summer (406) 445-2326; winter (406) 252-4654.

# COLUMBUS, ABSAROKEE, AND ROSCOE: MONTANA 78

You can take this route—Montana 78—from Red Lodge, driving north, or start at Columbus, heading south, depending on your ultimate destination. Columbus is on I-90, which runs across most of Montana connecting several major cities.

## COLUMBUS

The original residents of Columbus had almost as hard a time settling on the location for their town as they did settling on its name. The first name chosen was Eagle's Nest, and the town was about 2 miles west of its current location. Then Sheep Dip, a Native trading stop referred to by the type of whiskey served up, became the center of attention. In 1882, Northern Pacific built a railroad station, and the tracks were laid through the area before the town was built, based on the ultimatum of the railroad bosses. However, the chosen name, Stillwater, caused confusion with Stillwater, Minnesota. Once again, the name had to be changed. The town's final name, Columbus, may have been named for the great explorer.

Columbus is the county seat of Stillwater County. Located along the banks of the Stillwater River, the town was established as a shipping center, and remains so today. At one time the sandstone quarry was a viable economic resource. The state capital in Helena was built from stone produced here. Today, ranch and farm country surround the town of about 1,700 residents.

## OUTDOOR RECREATION

As you head south on Montana 78, there are several fishing access points on the Stillwater River between Columbus and Absarokee. The Fireman's Point Fishing Access is down a good gravel road; cross two bridges to the fishing access sign. There is no camping at this area, which is less than 2 miles from Columbus. The Swinging Bridge Fishing Access is down a bumpy road, but it's adequate for RVs. The river is about 1 mile in from the highway.

There are several secluded, unimproved camping sites with lots of trees and vegetation, a cozy spot.

**RV CAUTION**: The third access, closest to Absarokee on Montana 78, is not for RVs. The White Bird Fishing Access is very narrow and too cramped for an RV. There's very limited room to turn around at the access point, which is a half-mile from the paved highway.

Golfers will enjoy the Stillwater Golf Recreation Club. The location is near the Yellowstone River and the airport on 3rd Avenue and Montana 78. Call for information, (406) 322-4298.

Get out and about, and float the Yellowstone River. Upper Yellowstone Adventures, Inc., offers canoe or raft trips, lasting a half or full day. Their outfit is 3 miles east of Columbus on Route 10, House #1438. Call 1-888-BOAT-FLT for details.

For bird-watching, be sure to check out the refuges and lakes north of Columbus. Take Route 306 north to Rapelje (named for a general manager and vice-president of Northern Pacific Railroad), and then head east. Big Lake and the Hailstone and Halfbreed National Wildlife Refuges offer good birding spring, summer and fall. There are wildlife viewing sites, and literature is available at the Hailstone Refuge. Authorities recommend you check with the refuge manager regarding accessibility, management activities, fees and weather conditions before making the trip out to the refuge. Management activities may include shifting viewing areas to protect nesting sites. Information is available from Hailstone NWR, PO Box 110, Lewistown, MT 59457.

## ATTRACTIONS

The Museum of the Beartooths, open seasonally (406) 322-4588, has interesting artifacts of the Rosebud River Crow. There is a fascinating display of Northern Pacific Railroad memorabilia that gives a unique view of the local history. Look for the red Northern Pacific caboose at the corner of 5th and 5th North.

## OVERNIGHTING

### CAMPGROUNDS & RV PARKS

Itch-Kep-Pe Park, south of Columbus on Montana 78 just north of the Yellowstone River bridge. 49 campsites, RVs allowed, no services; open April 1 through October 31.

## SUGGESTED DINING

Branding Iron Cafe, 1036 E. Pike, Columbus, MT; (406) 322-4690.

Busy Bee Cafe, 434 Pike Ave., Columbus, MT; (406) 322-5468.

Stillwater Sandwich Co., 912 E. Pike, Columbus, MT; (406) 322-4658.

**VISITOR INFORMATION & SERVICES**

The area Chamber of Commerce is in Columbus, Montana; open seasonally; (406) 322-4505.

Cooney State Park at Cooney Reservoir, open year-round; information: summer (406) 425-1185; winter (406) 247-2940.

**MEDICAL SERVICES**

Stillwater Community Hospital, 24-hour service, 44 W. 4th Ave. N., Columbus, MT; (406) 322-5316.

Matovich IGA Pharmacy, 133 N. 5th, Columbus, MT; open Monday through Friday, 9:30 A.M. to 5:30 P.M., and Saturday, 9:30 A.M. to 12:30 P.M.; (406) 322 5652.

**REPAIR & TOWING**

Hanson Auto Body, 24-hour towing, 324 E. Pike Ave., Columbus, MT; 1-800-272-8879; (406) 322-5730, or after hours, 1-800-272-8879, or (406) 322-5973.

**VETERINARY SERVICES**

The Cloverleaf Veterinary Services, N. Frontage Rd., Columbus, MT; (406) 322-4581.

**ABSAROKEE**

The town of Absarokee (ab-SOR-kee) was originally within the borders of the Crow Reservation and bears a Native name of the clan. The Crow are said to be from the Great Lakes area, descendants of the Hidasta Tribe of the Sioux. In the Hidasta language, the word *Absarokee* is formed from two words, *absa*, meaning "large-beaked bird," and *rokee*, for "children." "Children of the large-beaked bird" was interpreted as Crow and became the white man's name for the tribe. The Crow call themselves the *Asaloga* in their tongue, and the translation to "Children of the large-beaked bird" is the same.

The Broken Horn Stampede, in mid-June (13–15), is the area's top rodeo and is held in Absarokee.

# ABSAROKEE AND VICINITY: MONTANA 419, MONTANA 420

On the south side of Absarokee, Montana 78 splits in two directions, then splits again. The southwest road, Montana 420, leads to Nye and follows along the Stillwater River, one of our favorite drives. The southeast road, Montana 419, heads to Fishtail on West Rosebud Creek, or Montana 78 leads to East Rosebud Lake. Whichever way you go, there's fishing, hiking and camping all along in the mountains of the Custer National Forest and nearby Absaroka-Beartooth Wilderness.

**FISHTAIL**

In Fishtail, the Rosebud Isle Fishing Access is on West Rosebud Creek. The narrow, half-mile-long road winds through the trees, but it's adequate for medium-sized RVs. There are nice sites along the creek. Fishing is very good most of the summer.

Fishtail's name is not what you think—the town wasn't named after the finny creature we love to catch. Instead, it was named for a Mr. Fishtail, a man who lived in the area when the post office was established in 1901. There are some who disagree and claim the name comes from a rock formation shaped like a fishtail. Either way, it's a fitting name for a Montana town where angling is a favorite pastime.

If you're hungry here, the Cowboy Bar and Supper Club serves up a hearty meal; it's 4 miles from Fishtail on Montana 419; (406) 328-4288.

# DEAN TO MYSTIC LAKE: MONTANA 419

Continue along Montana 419 toward Dean and experience one of Montana's prettiest rural roads. For a few short miles, the road is newly paved and in excellent condition. The West Rosebud Forest Access goes up to Mystic Lake. The dirt road is in reasonable shape; there are a few washboard sections and potholes, but in general it's OK. The aspen groves and open meadows eventually give way to ponderosa forest.

**RV CAUTION**: The Pine Grove Picnic Area is not for RVs. The picnic spot is about 9 miles outside of Fishtail, and it's too tight for even a small RV to turn around. Head on another mile or so to the Pine Grove Campground. The location across the creek is nice, and the spot has ample, pull-through RV sites.

You'll notice the huge power lines parallel to the road the last few miles up to the lake. Mystic Lake Dam generates hydroelectric power under the Montana Power Company's Mystic Lake Hydroelectric Project. The dam itself is above Emerald Lake. The Emerald Lake Campground is on the shores of a small, pleasant lake of the same name. The unimproved campsites are well suited for large RVs.

Mystic Lake, at 2,339 feet, is a long finger-like lake fed by West Rosebud Creek. The trip from the trailhead above Emerald Lake is about 2 miles.

*All sorts of wild plants decorate the western landscape.*

# NYE: MONTANA 419

From Dean to Nye, there's still pavement on Montana 419, but it's marred with the familiar potholes of most backcountry mountain roads. The history of Nye is like that of many mining boom towns, but this one had an unusual glitch. Jack Nye was a miner who discovered a huge section of copper-bearing ore that was 630 feet wide. Nye and his companions, the Hedges brothers, traced the ore for 15 miles across the Stillwater River. The announcement of this colossal rich find started a claim run, and the race was off and running. The mining camp was named Nye City at first. By 1884, when the Stillwater Mining Company had incorporated and built a smelter, a future similar to that of Butte's was planned. It was not to be. Government surveyors determined that Nye City was located on Native lands. Many of the mining operations were halted by 1889. Of course, that was a long time ago, and the boundaries of the lands have changed. The Mouat Mines operate in the Nye area.

At Nye, the Buffalo Jump Fishing Access is only 100 yards from the creek, and there are a few small campsites. As you continue south, watch out for lots of traffic on the road between 5 P.M. and 6 P.M., as the workers head home.

A couple of miles past the mine near Nye will put you in the Woodbine Campground. The campground is one of our favorite camp spots in this area. There is great fishing access to the Stillwater River. Small brook trout, averaging 10 inches, are common. This is also a trailhead site. If you're an avid hiker in better-than-average condition, follow the trail, which leads up to some stunning views.

The Woodbine Campground sits on a sidehill at the base of the towering crags and peaks of the Granite Range. Majestic peaks, such as Cathedral Point, Twin Peaks, Mount Hague, Mount Wood and Pyramid Mountain, shoulder up to Granite Peak, Montana's highest point at 12,799 feet. These mountains are within the borders of the Absaroka-Beartooth Wilderness. In total, there are 28 peaks over 12,000 feet in this wilderness section that adds nearly 1 million acres to the Greater Yellowstone Ecosystem. The wilderness is paradise for hikers, anglers and horseback riders. There are almost 1,000 alpine lakes and more than 900 miles of hiking trails.

## OVERNIGHTING

## CAMPGROUNDS & RV PARKS

Woodbine—U.S. Forest Service Campground, 8 miles southwest of Nye on Montana 419. RVs allowed (max. length 30 feet), no services; open June 15 through September 15.

# NYE TO ABSAROKEE: MONTANA 420 TO MONTANA 78

## FAVORITE DRIVE:
## STILLWATER RIVER

When you're returning from the Woodbine Campground, an alternative route back to Absarokee follows the Stillwater River. The well-maintained road winds down the canyon beside the river. The cliff walls have some very interesting rock formations, and the scenery is beautiful. The multitude of homes situated on the riverbanks attests to the area's popularity.

The Moraine Fishing Access offers limited camping, and the road might be slick when wet. It's better to pull off at the Castle Rock Fishing Access, where there are several sites along the grassy area just .3 of a mile from the main road. Watch for mule deer and whitetails in the area. The Cliff Swallow Fishing Access is the nearest site to Absarokee. After traveling through the canyon walls, the openness of these grass knolls is uplifting. This area, just 50 yards off the highway, offers camping, fishing and wheelchair access.

**ROSCOE**  The settlement of Roscoe started out as Morris, named after one of the area's first families. Unfortunately, postal workers frequently confused Morris with Norris and misdirected the mail. Imagine that! To remedy this problem, the Postal Service directed the town's postmistress, Mrs. Morris, to select a new name. In honor of her favorite horse, Mrs. Morris named the town Roscoe in 1905.

**SUGGESTED DINING**  One of the best things about Roscoe is the Grizzly Bar (406) 328-6789. Folks travel many miles, even up from Wyoming, to enjoy the great steaks and burgers. The ranchlands spreading out on both sides of the road have lots of deer. Keep a wary eye for these fence-jumpers, especially when traveling at dawn and dusk.

**LUTHER**  From Red Lodge northwest on Montana 78, the countryside is rolling grasslands. The dirt side loop to Luther can become a slick mudslide when wet. The small community, founded in 1907 by the Luther family, is situated among big ranches and grain silos. It's a pretty and serene drive as long as the weather's good.

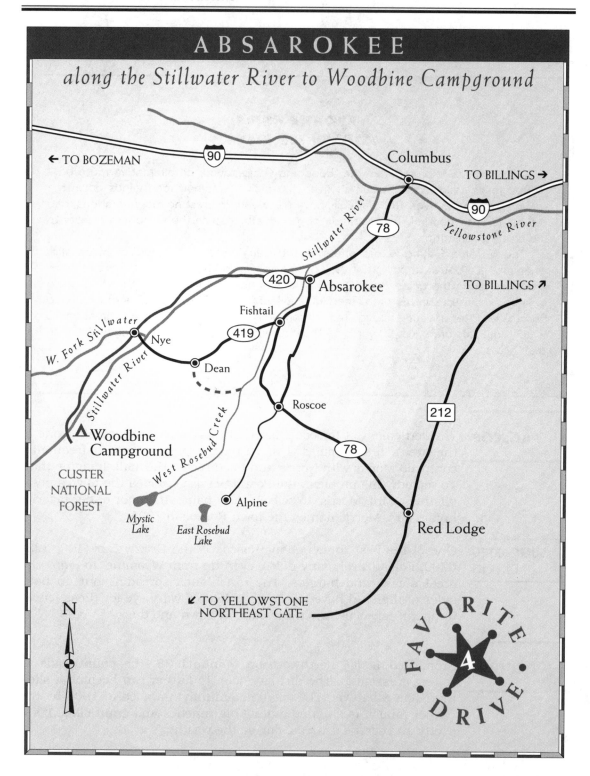

# ABSAROKEE
## along the Stillwater River to Woodbine Campground

← TO BOZEMAN

90

Columbus

TO BILLINGS →

90

Yellowstone River

Stillwater River

78

420

Absarokee

TO BILLINGS ↗

Fishtail

419

W. Fork Stillwater

Nye

Dean

Stillwater River

Roscoe

212

78

West Rosebud Creek

▲ Woodbine
Campground

CUSTER
NATIONAL
FOREST

Mystic
Lake

East Rosebud
Lake

Alpine

Red Lodge

N

↙ TO YELLOWSTONE
NORTHEAST GATE

FAVORITE · DRIVE

4

## ALPINE AND EAST ROSEBUD LAKE

Following along the back roads through Roscoe, a turn to the south will lead you up to Alpine and East Rosebud Lake. This was once one of the prettiest drives in Custer National Forest. Although quaking aspen line the road for the first 11 miles, the road itself is not pretty. In fact, it's in miserable shape with potholes and a washboard surface. Beyond that, a dreadful forest fire burned through the East Rosebud Lake area in 1996. Luckily, forest fires usually burn in a mosaic pattern. In many places, the river bottom was spared, and wildlife will be able to flourish in the new grass-covered open country. The burned landscape is eerie. The pristine water of Rosebud Creek rushes down through the blackened, lifeless trees. Wildflowers, like purple fireweed and Indian paintbrush, are crowded innocently around the charred, fallen timber, creating a strange contrast of life and death.

If you've the keen interest to see nature at work, and the stamina to forge ahead on this road, you'll arrive at Alpine and East Rosebud Lake. Named by the Branger family from Switzerland, the Alpine Post Office was open from 1914 to 1953, except for the war years 1943–45. The Brangers ran a hotel overlooking the lake that is surrounded by the rugged Beartooth Mountains. The East Rosebud Campground and trailhead are located above the resort, providing a view of the lake area. Again, fair warning: *This is a terrible road.* We recommend against taking it unless you really want to drive back in to this high mountain lake.

The settlement of Alpine is currently being rebuilt. Signs of construction are everywhere. In fact, the construction continues throughout the creek drainage. The miserable roads are in part due to the heavy equipment and delivery trucks. In time, the roads will be regraded. And, in a lot more time, the 1996 fire will become a faded memory.

## OVERNIGHTING

### CAMPGROUNDS & RV PARKS

**Rosebud Creek to East Rosebud Lake and Alpine**
East Rosebud Lake—U.S. Forest Service Campground, 12 miles south of Roscoe on County and Forest Service Road 177. RVs allowed (max. length 16 feet), no services; open May 27 through September 5.

Jimmy Joe—U.S. Forest Service Campground, 9 miles south of Roscoe on County and Forest Service Road 177. RVs allowed (max. length 16 feet), no services; normally open May 27 through September 5.

### West Rosebud Creek toward Mystic Lake

Pine Grove—U.S. Forest Service Campground, 1 mile west of Fishtail on Montana 419, then 6 miles southwest on Montana 425, 8 miles south on Forest Service Road 72. RVs allowed (max. length 30 feet), no services; open May 27 through September 15.

Emerald Lake—U.S. Forest Service Campground, 1 mile west of Fishtail on Montana 419, then 6 miles southwest on Montana 425, 12 miles south on Forest Service Road 72. RVs allowed (max. length 30 feet), no services; open May 27 through September 5.

## BED & BREAKFAST ESTABLISHMENTS

### Absarokee

Abigail Inn, log home with Victorian decor. The inn has been operating since 1994. Open year-round; busiest in summer, slowest in winter; credit cards accepted; no pets allowed. Contact Jan Olson, Box 636, Absarokee, MT 59001; (406) 328-6592.

The Magpie's Nest, N. Stillwater Rd. Open year-round; busiest July through September, slowest December through February; no credit cards accepted; no pets allowed. Contact Jack Ross, RR 1, Box 2818, Absarokee, MT 59001; (406) 328-4925.

## GUEST RANCHES

### Roscoe

Lazy E-L Ranch Corporation, 4.5 miles from Roscoe on E. Rosebud Rd. This 3,000-acre working cattle ranch has been a family operation for over 100 years. Featured are horseback riding and moving cattle, hunting, hiking and fishing, with 5 miles of private river. No credit cards accepted; no pets allowed; open May 15 through September 15. Contact Julie Childs, Box 36, Roscoe, MT 59071; (406) 328-6830; fax: (406) 328-6857;
website: http://www.imt.net/~lazyel/

Slow Elk Trails Inc., west of Red Lodge off Montana 78. Features cattle drives, western trail rides and wagon rides. Open year-round; busiest June through August; (406) 446-4179, 446-3926 (home); fax: (406) 446-3926.

### Absarokee

The Stoney Lonesome Ranch, on Bridger Creek Rd. (15 miles of gravel road). This working cattle ranch has been in operation since 1967. Families welcome; open May through September; no credit cards accepted; no pets allowed. Contact Corkey and Clarice Hedrick, Box 37, Absarokee, MT 59001; (406) 932-4452; fax: (406) 932-4452.

**VISITOR INFORMATION & SERVICES**

For visitor information, see Columbus (page 100).

**MEDICAL SERVICES**

Absarokee Medical Clinic, 55 N. Montana, Absarokee, MT; open Monday through Friday, 8 A.M. to 5 P.M.; (406) 328- 4497.

Absarokee Drug, Absarokee, MT; open Monday through Friday, 9 A.M. to 5 P.M.; (406) 328-4867.

**REPAIR & TOWING**

Hanson Auto Body, 24-hour towing service, 324 E. Pike Ave., Columbus, MT; 1-800-272-8879; (406) 322-5973.

**VETERINARY SERVICES**

Stillwater Veterinary Clinic, Dr. Bill Routen, Absarokee, MT; (406) 328-4159.

Valley Veterinary Service, Dr. Leatha Perry, Absarokee, MT; (406) 328-4527.

## The Legend of the Stillwater River

The Stillwater River races and roars down the canyons from its headwaters in Wyoming to merge with the Yellowstone River at Columbus. The river's incongruous name stems from a Native legend, a tale of lovers lost. Many braves sought the hand of the fair maiden Weeluna (Little Moon), but Nemidji won her heart. Before the wedding could take place, the braves departed to hunt for wild game. During their absence, food became very scarce. Weeluna herself led the young women of the tribe out in search of food. The girls were successful and returned with elk and moose. Weeluna, weak and overcome with exhaustion from the trip, passed away before Nemidji returned. The tribe prepared her body in the traditional manner by placing it in the branches of a tree. When Nemidji came home, a fierce storm blew her body into the raging waters of the river. To save her body, Nemidji jumped into the forceful current but was swept away and drowned. After the storm had passed, the river's path had been changed. At a point where once the waters had rushed straight through, a cove had been created and the stream slowed to a riffle. To honor Weeluna and Nemidji, the Natives named this the "Hallowed Place" or Stillwater.

# ROCKVALE, LAUREL AND BILLINGS: U.S. 212/310

Rockvale is a main junction, connecting Red Lodge, Cody, Lovell and other southern communities to I-90 and Billings. The section from Rockvale to Laurel runs through farm country. If you happen to pass by in the summer, stop at one of the farms that advertise fresh vegetables along the highway and treat yourself, especially to the unbelievable corn, which is available in mid-August.

## OVERNIGHTING

### CAMPGROUNDS & RV PARKS

Rockcreek Campground, at the junction of U.S. Highways 212 and 310. 24 RV sites, water and electric hook-ups only, dump station, hot showers and laundry; open April 15 to October 15; (406) 962-3459.

## LAUREL

Nobody's quite sure how the town of Laurel got its name, but this small town bears the brunt of the region's prosperity. The Northern Pacific, Chicago, Burlington and Quincy Railroads made Laurel a central hub; rail lines cris-cross through the area. The Cenex oil refinery, on the south side of town, dominates the skyline. Unfortunately, the smell in the air identifies the site even when the skyline is dark. Prosperity has its price. Fortunately, travel just a few blocks away, and you'd never know the industry is there. The true character and history of Laurel lie to the north.

The Nez Perce, led by Chief Joseph, crossed the Yellowstone River at Laurel in their flight from the Army after the 1877 Battle of the Big Hole. The Crow had refused to give asylum, so the Nez Perce fled toward Canada. They held off the Army at the Battle of Canyon Creek, fought just 7 miles north of Laurel. The Chief Joseph-Sturgis Battlefield Monument pays tribute to the battle in which the Army reportedly lost three men, and the Nez Perce claimed three wounded. The Friends of Canyon Creek Battlefield, Inc., are working to preserve and interpret the site. A Nez Perce trail brochure and map are available from BLM offices.

Laurel currently has about 6,500 residents. Many commute to Billings for employment; however, farming and related services, such as railway shipping, are a main force in the town's livelihood.

*Wildflowers are abundant in the country 100 miles around Yellowstone.*

**OUTDOOR RECREATION**

The Laurel Golf Club, an 18-hole course, is west of Laurel. The course is rated in the top ten in Montana; lots of water and challenging play. It's a private course, but reciprocal golf is available to card-carrying USGA-affiliated club members. Call for tee times at least one week in advance, (406) 628-4504.

**ATTRACTIONS**

Laurel is host to two fun celebrations; one held on July 4th, the other in October. Reputedly, Montana's biggest Fourth of July Fireworks Display is put on at Laurel. The free fireworks show is spectacular, and the entire community turns out to celebrate.

Similar to Germany's Oktoberfest, Laurel's three-day festival, the Laurel Herbstfest, features ethnic food, music and dancing. The celebration is made authentic by the area's many residents who are of German descent. It is held in late September at the Horse Palace, 2 miles east of Laurel via I-90, Exit 437. Contact: Laurel Herbstfest, Box 1192, Laurel, MT 59044; (406) 628-7852.

**OVERNIGHTING**

### CAMPGROUNDS & RV PARKS

▲ *Best Shot for a Camp Spot*
Pelican RV Park, off I-90, Exit 437. 40 RV sites (40 pull-throughs), full hook-ups, dump station, showers, laundry and store; 24-hour restaurant, propane; open year-round; busiest spring to Christmas, slowest in February; (406) 628-4324; fax: (406) 628-8442.

Riverside Park—U.S. Forest Service Campground, off I-90, Exit 434 to U.S. 212. 100 sites, RVs allowed (max. length 32 feet), 7 sites have drinking water and electrical services; showers and boat-launch ramp for 2-wheel drive; open year-round; reservations: (406) 628-2491.

### BED & BREAKFAST ESTABLISHMENTS

Riverside Bed & Breakfast, operating since 1991. Features include watching llamas and fly fishing the Yellowstone River; open year-round; busiest May through September, slowest January through May; credit cards accepted; no pets allowed. Contact Lynn and Nancy Perey, 2231 Thiel Rd., Laurel, MT 59044; (406) 628-7890; 1-800-768-1580; e-mail: riversidebb@cw2.com

**SUGGESTED DINING**

Side Car Restaurant, 216 1st Ave. S., Laurel, MT; (406) 628-4030.

The Owl Junction, 203 E. Main, Laurel, MT; (406) 628-4966.

Elk River, 119 E. Main, Laurel MT; (406) 628-4800.

**VISITOR INFORMATION & SERVICES**

The Laurel Chamber of Commerce is in the *Laurel Outlook* Newspaper Building at 415 E. Main, PO Box 395, Laurel, MT 59044; (406) 628-8105. Unfortunately, it's difficult to park at the chamber offices; however, parking lots are nearby.

The Bureau of Land Management has information on the Nez Perce Trail. Brochures and maps are available at BLM, 111 Gary Owen Rd., Miles City, MT 59301.

**MEDICAL SERVICES**

Laurel Medical Center, 1035 1st Ave., Laurel, MT; (406) 628-6311.

Gene's Pharmacy, 111 E. Main, Laurel, MT; open Monday through Saturday, 9 A.M. to 5:30 P.M.; (406) 628-7217.

**REPAIR & TOWING**

Modern Auto Towing & Repair, 24-hour service, 601 E. Main, Laurel, MT; (406) 628-7145; (406) 628-6396 or, after hours: (406) 628-4511.

**VETERINARY SERVICES**

Beartooth Veterinary Clinic, Dr. Krayton Kerns, 419 E. Main St., Laurel, MT; (406) 628-4309.

**PARK CITY**

If you head west out of Laurel toward Bozeman, you'll pass by the town of Park City. Laurel owes its fate to the bull-headed homesteaders who established this community in 1892. The group of settlers were from green-wooded Wisconsin and planted a grove of trees on the barren land. Later when the railroad built a station, officials of the Northern Pacific wanted to christen the station, and rename the town Rimrock. The settlers refused and kept on using the name Park City. Indignant about the settler's stubbornness, the officials moved the site of the intended railyards to Laurel. The trees are still growing in Park City's city park. Rail lines grew in Laurel.

**BILLINGS**

This comparatively big city serves as the western cornerstone to Montana's "Custer Country." Begin your exploration with historical sites such as Canyon Creek Battlefield on the Nez Perce Trail (National Park Trails System), the Pictograph Cave, the Crow Reservation, Chief Plenty Coups Park, Pompey's Pillar and Big Horn Canyon before you move on to the Little Bighorn Battlefield National Monument.

Montana is the fourth-largest state in the United States, and Billings is its largest city. In fact, Billings boasts it's the largest city north of Denver, west of Minneapolis and east of Spokane. All boasting aside, keep in mind that "big" is a relative term. Montana is definitely Big Sky Country, but her "big" city is anything but a towering concrete jungle, massive traffic jams or multilane highways. Although there are several buildings that require an elevator, the downtown center is pleasant rather than intimidating.

Billings is indeed the dominant service center for the greater Northern Plains area. It was founded in 1882 as a railroad trade center. The tradition as a major trade and shipping center continues today.

Over 10,000 years ago, the first inhabitants discovered the rich valley of

*Pompeys Pillar, near Billings*
DONNIE SEXTON/COURTESY TRAVEL MONTANA

the Yellowstone River and protective shelter of the rimrocks that rise 400 feet above the valley. Through the ages, several tribes—the Shoshone, Crow, Blackfeet and Sioux—hunted along the river and across the rich grassy plain. The various tribes hotly contested for rights to the area's hunting.

Continuous pressure by more and more white homesteaders was also felt in the valley. In 1877, the first settlers established the town of Coulson, a few miles south of present-day Billings. Coulson's residents expected to rake in the dough from the coming railroad and bustling trade business. When the Minnesota and Montana Improvement Company came through, seeking rights for the Northern Pacific Railroad, the Coulsonites tried to cash in. Instead, they found themselves left with a ghost town. The Northern Pacific refused the Coulsonites' high price.

In 1882, a new townsite was platted and post office opened. The railroad's Montana headquarters was named after Frederick Billings, the president of Northern Pacific Railroad from 1879 to

*Billings,
Montana*

1881. Billings had been instrumental in obtaining financial assistance and planning for the railway. His plan to fund construction by offering $100 in stock for each $100 bond sold generated $2.5 million. Later, as construction costs to cross the mountains proved even more expensive than estimated, Billings raised another million dollars. His keen financial sense led to prosperity and growth of the railroad and for the entire region. The rail system took over what once was the domain of the Yellowstone River, transporting settlers, cattle, agricultural products and, eventually, coal.

Today, the Billings area is home to approximately 100,000 residents. In addition to its traditional ranching, agriculture and energy base, the medical services sector has taken on tremendous importance, serving the entire region. Montana State University and two colleges add an educational mix to the city's development.

**OUTDOOR RECREATION**

There are several golf courses in the Billings area, both public and private. Certain private courses allow limited public play. The Circle Inn Golf Links is a 9-hole course; (406) 248-4202. Briarwood Country Club is a full 18-hole course at 3429 Briarwood Blvd., Billings, MT. This private course allows limited public play; call for tee times and information: (406) 248-2702. The Par-3 Exchange City Golf Course is a public course located on Central Avenue at 19th St. W., Billings, MT; (406) 652-2553. Lake Hills Golf Club, located near Lake Elmo State Park has 18 holes; call for more information: (406) 252-9244. The Peter Yegen, Jr., Golf Club is an 18-hole course at 3400 Grand Ave., Billings, MT; (406) 656-8099. The Pryor Creek Golf Course is a private course that allows limited public play; call for details: (406) 256-0626.

Lake Elmo State Park is located just north of Billings in Billings Heights. This 64-acre reservoir offers many water sports: swimming, sailboarding, nonmotorized and electric-powered boating and fishing. The shallow lake, 16 feet at the deepest spot, holds largemouth bass, channel catfish, yellow perch and black crappie. No pets are allowed, not even on a leash. Open year-round for day-use only. An entrance fee is charged Memorial Day through Labor Day. Annual passport is $15; individual fee of $1 per adult and 50 cents for children under 11. The address is 2400 Lake Elmo Dr., Billings, MT. More information is available at (406) 247-2940.

**ATTRACTIONS**  Pictograph Cave State Park is located 7 miles southeast of Billings. To go there, drive southeast of Billings on I-90, take the Lockwood Exit (452), then turn south on Coburn Road, follow the pavement for 3 miles, then another 3 miles of gravel road.

The caves were discovered by white explorers in the 1800s. Since then, the caves and artifacts contained inside have undergone everything from mild interest (1930s), to vandalism and apathy (1940–50s), to a revered status. The caves have been protected as a National Historic Landmark since 1964 and were made a state park in 1969. Over 30,000 artifacts were unearthed and 106 pictographs found on one wall alone. Get some exercise and walk in along the quarter-mile paved trail (very steep in some places), which leads to the cave homes. For over 10,000 years, the caves were occupied by prehistoric hunters and a long succession of inhabitants. Interpretive panels offer instruction on the way to Pictograph, Ghost and Middle Caves. Remember to bring binoculars to help in viewing the more distant pictographs. The park is open 8:00 A.M. to 8:00 P.M., 7 days a week, from mid-April to mid-October. Entrance fee $3 per carload or $15 annual passport; (406) 245-0227 summer; (406) 247-2940 winter.

Step into the past through the doors of the Peter Yegen, Jr., Yellowstone County Museum. It is housed in an authentic log cabin built in 1893. The story of settling this wild territory is told in the excellent dioramas, paintings and photographs. The permanent collection also includes the last steam engine to operate in Billings, a chuckwagon, western artifacts, pioneer tools, firearms and Native American artifacts on display in the 5,000 square feet of exhibit area. Hours: Monday through Friday, 10:30 A.M. to 5:00 P.M., Sunday, 2:00 P.M. to 5:00 P.M. Admission is free. The museum is located on the Rimrocks near Billings' Logan International Airport. (406) 256-6811.

At the Visitor Center, the Cattle Drive Monument welcomes Billings' visitors and stands in tribute to the Great Montana Centennial Cattle Drive of 1989. The impressive bronze sculptures are of a cowboy on horseback herding two longhorn steers. This artwork is among a group of five sculptures commemorating western heritage along 27th Street from I-94, Exit 450, to the airport, called the Avenue of Sculptures. The Chamber of Commerce and Visitor Center are at 815 S. 27th St. (off I-90, Exit 450), Billings, MT 59107; (406) 245-4111; 1-800-735-2635.

While you're up at the airport, take a drive along Black Otter Trail. Winding around the Rimrocks' ridge, the trail offers a scenic view of Billings. The sandstone rimrocks, which rise 400 feet above the Yellowstone Valley floor, have always been the master landmark of the region. Black Otter Trail is named for Chief Otter, a Crow buried on the rugged trail after dying in a battle with the Sioux.

The Black Otter Trail begins on U.S. 10 in East Billings and leads to a vantage point of five grand mountain ranges: the Crazies and Snowies in the northwest, the Big Horns in the southeast, the Pryors in the west and farther southwest, the Beartooths.

All that's left of Coulson, the valley's first town, are the tombstones of its settlers at Boothill Cemetery. Founded in 1876, the small community was built near the place where the Northern Pacific bridge now spans the Yellowstone River.

The Sacrifice Cliffs can be seen to the west of Billings in the distance across the Yellowstone River. The Native legend about the cliffs adds meaning beyond their beauty. Here is one version of the story.

The white man was not the only enemy of the Native people; smallpox proved an insufferable foe. Death came without the glory of battle to many warriors and wiped out their families. A legend describes the tragic events of a Crow village. Two young braves returned to their village to find it decimated by smallpox. Their brother, the village chief, and the maidens they had courted were among the fallen. Overcome with grief, they mounted the best pony and rode double through the village, singing songs of days past. They rode up the cliff and along the ridge, continuing their songs. Then, the two braves blindfolded the pony and rode off the 200-foot cliff, hoping to appease the gods and stop the sickness by sacrificing their lives. And so, the cliffs were named.

The Moss Mansion is at 914 Division Street in Billings. This stately and somewhat ostentatious home was once owned by Preston B. Moss, one of Montana's wealthiest men. The three-story mansion, completed in 1903, remains authentic to the turn-of-the-century period with the original furnishings. Moss engaged New York City architect H. J. Hardenbergh, designer of the Waldorf Astoria and Plaza Hotel, for the project. The Moss Mansion is open for tours year-round; admission is charged. Call for the special exhibits schedule: (406) 256-5100.

Visit over 20 other building sites on a Historic District Walking Tour. Travel along Montana Avenue from North 22nd to North 26th Streets. The Northern Pacific Depot, undergoing major restoration, will be the center highlight of the tour when complete. A detailed historic guide is available at the Chamber of Commerce.

Outstanding interactive exhibits detailing settlement of the Yellowstone Valley from 1880 to 1940 can be found at the Western Heritage Center. The museum's permanent displays include videos, photographs and an oral history of the pioneers, even an early dude ranch. The museum also describes the settlement's impact on Native Crow and Northern Cheyenne tribes. The center is located at 2822 Montana Ave. in Billings; or call (406) 256-6809. Open year-round, Tuesday through Saturday, 10 A.M. to 5 P.M., Sunday, 1 P.M. to 5 P.M., and admission is free.

If you've been on the road too long, stop and enjoy some culture. The Alberta Bair Theater for the Performing Arts hosts over 30 organizations annually, such as the Billings Symphony Orchestra, Community Concerts, Fox Committee for the Performing Arts, Billings Studio Theatre and local college and public school performances. Schedule of performances and tickets are available at the ABT box office, MetraPark and Bob's and Denny's SuperValu. The ABT is the first facility within 500 miles to offer the technical requirements for full-scale productions; it is truly first-class. The ABT ticket office hours are: Monday through Saturday 10 A.M. to 5:30 P.M. Write to ABT at Broadway and 3rd Ave. N., Billings, MT 59101, for advance schedules, or call (406) 256-6052.

Pompeys Pillar Recreation Area is the site of a National Historic Landmark. "Wm. Clark, July 25, 1806" is inscribed in the soft sandstone of the towering rock. This inscription, carved beside older Native pictographs, is the only physical evidence that remains of the Lewis and Clark Expedition. Captain William Clark noticed the huge rock as the party was floating down the Yellowstone River. Clark named the rock after Sacajawea's young son, Baptiste, whom he

*A sunset near Billings, Montana, typical of most in the Rockies*

fondly called "Little Pomp" or "Little Chief." He carved his name and the date upon the rock and called it "Pompey's Tower." The Landmark and Visitor Center, (406) 238-1540, are off I-94, 28 miles east of Billings; follow highway signs. The nearby town, Pompeys Pillar, is named after Pompey's Tower. The U.S. Bureau of Reclamation has a year-round camping area at Anita Reservoir, 4 miles south of I-94 via the Pompey's Pillar Exit. The camping area is acceptable for picnics and boating, but no sites are available for RVs.

ZooMontana is a 70-acre wildlife park providing natural habitat for its occupants; it is definitely not your typical zoo. Getting rave reviews these days is the young pair of eastern grey wolves delivered to the park in December 1997. According to the *Billings Gazette*, ZooMontana Director Bill Torgerson believes the pair gives the zoo a start on its goal of having a small pack of wolves. "We have room for four to six animals, a small pack," said Torgerson. If you haven't had any luck seeing wolves in Yellowstone, then visit this wildlife park for a firsthand view. The park also offers tours of an early 1900s Montana homestead ranch. ZooMontana, located at 2100 S. Shiloh Rd., Billings, MT, is open year-round, weather permitting. Summer hours are 10 A.M. to 5 P.M., 7 days a week, winter hours 10 A.M. to 4 P.M. on weekdays only. Tours are given a various times, inquire on site, or call ahead: (406) 652-8100.

The Montana State Fair, held at MetraPark every August, is Montana's largest statewide event. If you're here in August, there are country western music stars, carnival rides, exhibits and competitions, a rodeo and horse racing to enjoy. The MetraPark is also the site of many concerts and expositions. Contact MetraPark, PO Box 2514, Billings, MT 59103, or call (406) 256-2400; 1-800-366-8538 for a current schedule.

The Yellowstone Art Museum, featuring contemporary art, celebrated its opening in January 1998. If you're a fan of contemporary art, this is a good place to visit in Billings. Better still, there's a convenient RV-size parking lot for the museum at 401 N. 27th St., Billings, MT. The facility is closed Monday, and open Tuesday, Wednesday, Friday and Saturday, 11 A.M. to 5 P.M.; Thursday, 11 A.M. to 8 P.M., and Sunday, noon to 5 P.M. For more information, call (406) 256-6804.

## OVERNIGHTING

### CAMPGROUNDS & RV PARKS

▲ ***Best Shot for a Camp Spot***
Big Sky Campground, off I-90, Exit 446. 54 pull-through RV sites (29 full hook-ups, 25 water and electric sites); 23 tent sites, sewer hook-ups, dump station, showers and laundry; open year-round; busiest May 30 through September 1; (406) 259-4110.

▲ *Best Shot for a Camp Spot*
Billings Metro KOA, off I-90, Exit 450, then south to Garden Ave.,
turn right; 547 Garden Ave., Billings, MT 59101. 185 RV sites, full
hook-ups, dump station, showers and laundry; mini-golf, playground, pool, BBQ and spa available; open April 15 through October 15; (406) 252-3104; 1-800-562-8546.

Eastwood Estates, off I-90, Exit 452, .5 mile on U.S. 87 East, then go
.4 mile east. 20 RV sites, full hook-ups, no dump station, showers and
laundry; open year-round; very busy in summer; (406) 245-7733.

▲ *Best Shot for a Camp Spot*
Trailer Village, off I-90, Exit 447, then 6 blocks north on S. Billings
Blvd. 40 RV sites, full hook-ups, dump station, showers, laundry
and playground; no large dogs; open year-round; busiest May 1
through September 30, slowest November 1 through March 30;
(406) 248-8685.

## BED & BREAKFAST ESTABLISHMENTS

Charter House, operating since 1995; open May through September; no credit cards accepted; pets conditional. Contact Gene
Reichert, 21 Nightingale Dr., Billings, MT 59101; (406) 252-0733;
1-800-447-4370; fax: (406) 252-3530;
e-mail: GReich911@aol.com

The Josephine Bed & Breakfast, historic home within walking distance of downtown shopping. Operating since 1992; open year-
round; busiest June through September. Contact Douglas and
Becky Taylor; 514 N. 29th, Billings, MT 59101; (406) 248-5898; 1-
800-552-5898; e-mail: josephine@imt.net
website: http://mt-adnet.com/josephine

Pine Hills Place Bed & Breakfast, four-bedroom cabin in pine-cov-
ered hills. Operating since 1987; open year-round; busiest April
through May, slowest December through January. Contact manager, 4424 Pinehill Dr., Billings, MT 59101; (406) 252-2288, 252-
0313, 259-5132; fax: (406) 256-7582.

Sanderson Inn, operating since 1991; open year-round; busiest
July through August, slowest December through January; no credit
cards accepted; no pets allowed, but can be boarded at nearby veterinarian's facility. Contact Margaret Sanderson, 2038 S. 56th St.
W., Billings, MT 59101; (406) 656-3388.

**SUGGESTED DINING**

*RV parking may be difficult at the restaurants listed below.*
Casey's Golden Pheasant, 109 N. Broadway, Billings, MT; (406) 256-5200.

Pug Mahon's, 3011 1st Avenue N., Billings, MT; (406) 259-4190.

Montana Brewery, 113 N. Broadway, Billings, MT; (406) 252-9357.

Jakes, 2701 1st Avenue N., Billings, MT; (406) 256-8485.

*RV parking is accessible in adjacent parking lots of the restaurants listed below.*
Applebee's Neighborhood Grill & Bar, 740 S. 24 W., Billings, MT; (406) 655-0255.

CJ's Restaurant, 25th St. W. and Central Ave., Billings, MT; (406) 656-1400.

Dos Machos, 24th St. W. and Phyllis Lane, Billings, MT; (406) 652-2020.

Olive Garden, 2201 Grant Rd., Billings, MT; (406) 652-1395.

**VISITOR INFORMATION & SERVICES**

The combined Chamber of Commerce and Visitor Center, 815 S. 27th St. (off I-90 Exit 450), PO Box 31177, Billings, MT 59107; (406) 245-4111; 1-800-735-2635; fax: (406) 245-7333.

Unfortunately, Billings is like most cities in that it's difficult to park an RV in the downtown area. There is limited street parking, much of it metered, and no RV parking lots or areas. However, there is plenty of parking at the event center and the MetraPark, as well as on the street behind the Chamber of Commerce. Inquire at the Visitor Center for information on parking at the sights you intend to visit.

Bureau of Land Management, Resource Area Office, 810 E. Main, Billings, MT 59105; (406) 238-1540.

Montana Department of Fish, Wildlife and Parks, Region 5 Headquarters, Billings, MT; (406) 247-2940.

Custer National Forest Headquarters, 1310 Main St., PO Box 50760, Billings, MT 59105; (406) 248-9885.

**MEDICAL SERVICES**

St. Vincent Hospital at 1233 N. 30th St., Billings, MT; (406) 657-7070.

Deaconess Medical Center at 2800 10th Ave. N., Billings, MT; (406) 657-4000.

**REPAIR & TOWING**

Hanser's Automotive, Wrecker & Repairs, 430 S. Billing Blvd., Billings, MT; 1-800-345-1754.

Billings RV Repair, 24 hours, 7416 Danford Rd., Billings, MT; (406) 652-6339.

**VETERINARY SERVICES**

Laurel East Veterinary, Dr. Don Werner, 1310 Allendale Rd., I-90, Exit 437, Billings, MT; (406) 259-7942.

*Fireweed commonly appears just after a forest fire burns through an area.*

# SECTION 4

# EAST
# GATE

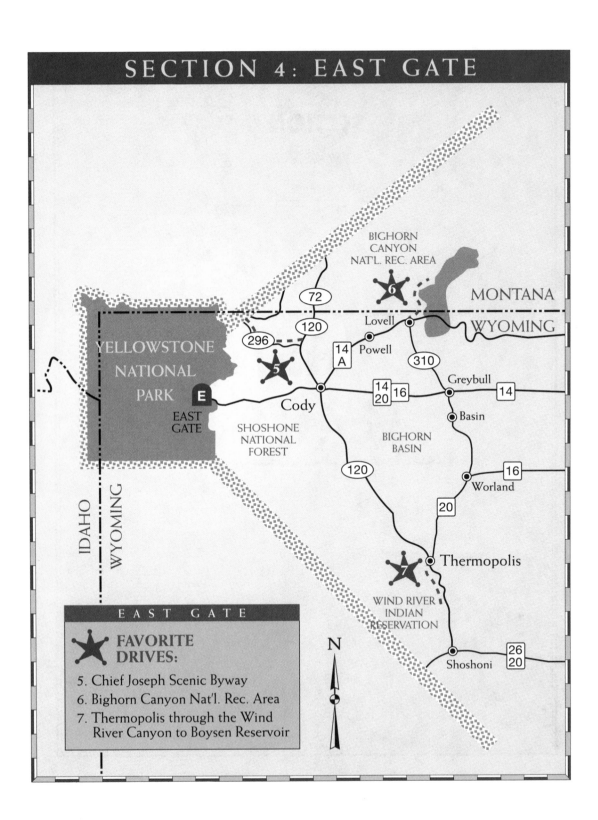

# SECTION 4: EAST GATE

BIGHORN CANYON NAT'L. REC. AREA

MONTANA

WYOMING

72

120

296

Lovell

14 A

Powell

310

Greybull

14

YELLOWSTONE NATIONAL PARK

E

EAST GATE

Cody

14 20

16

Basin

SHOSHONE NATIONAL FOREST

BIGHORN BASIN

120

16

Worland

20

IDAHO

WYOMING

Thermopolis

7

WIND RIVER INDIAN RESERVATION

Shoshoni

26 20

## EAST GATE

### FAVORITE DRIVES:

5. Chief Joseph Scenic Byway
6. Bighorn Canyon Nat'l. Rec. Area
7. Thermopolis through the Wind River Canyon to Boysen Reservoir

N

# GENERAL OVERVIEW

After exiting Yellowstone at the East Gate, you have no choice but to follow the highway to Cody, 54 miles down the road. Once there you have four major options. You can go north on Wyoming 120 to Clark, then continue into Montana through Belfry, Bridger, Laurel and Billings. You may also turn onto the magnificent Chief Joseph Highway 17 miles from Cody and head for the Beartooth Highway or back into Yellowstone at Cooke City. The next option from Cody is to take U.S. 14 to Powell and Lovell, and ascend the very steep grade up into the Bighorn Mountains. You can avoid this grade and take U.S. 14/16/20 out of Cody to Greybull 57 miles away, and head up into the Bighorns via Shell on Wyoming 14. At Greybull you can also turn south on U.S. 16/20 and go to Basin and Worland, taking yet another route, U.S. 16 up into the Bighorns via Ten Sleep. Finally, you can leave Cody on Wyoming 120, traveling south to Meeteetse, Thermopolis and Shoshoni.

# EAST GATE TO CODY: U.S. 14/16/20

The road from the East Gate to Cody has many names: the North Fork Highway, U.S. 14/16/20, the Yellowstone Highway, and most recently, the Buffalo Bill Cody Scenic Byway. Don't be confused; they all refer to the same two-lane paved road. Keep this in mind if you ask a local for directions; it can be quite misleading. The road meanders through the Shoshone National Forest along the North Fork of the Shoshone River and through the Wapiti Valley. The Shoshone Forest, by the way, was the first in the National Forest system, established by President Benjamin Harrison in 1891. The ranger station at Wapiti (which means elk) is also the first in the nation, constructed in 1903.

The 6-mile stretch from the East Gate past Pahaska Tepee is an ideal place to see grizzlies from the highway. The bears may be there from May through September, but most often, in the spring. Inquire at Pahaska Tepee for information on recent bear sightings. Pahaska Tepee is one of the first of many guest ranches in the long canyon to Wapiti. At Pahaska, you can see Buffalo Bill's original hunting lodge (where we were married in 1992, incidentally). The name *Pahaska*, or "Long hair," was a Native name given to Buffalo Bill.

*Portrait of William F. "Buffalo Bill" Cody, about 1895*
COURTESY PARK COUNTY TRAVEL COUNCIL

If you camp or hike in the canyon, beware of the possibility of seeing grizzly bears. Carry a can of bear spray. You'll follow the Shoshone River through the canyon. It offers outstanding fishing when the water is clear. See page 126 for detailed information. Before you reach the end of the canyon, you will see intriguing dark red volcanic rock formations on the north side of the highway. This area is called Holy City, and you can stop at the parking area to take some memorable photographs. As you leave the canyon and enter the Wapiti Valley, stop at the Red Barn store and tell Chet we said hi. Here you can get the best, cheapest gas in the county and plenty of local information. Outside the store, look to the southwest and you'll see a strange landmark—a pagoda-like structure that sits on a ridge. No, it's not an Oriental building or a mine shaft, but the dream of an engineer who was tragically killed when he fell off one of the many roofs.

## Shoshone River

John Colter originally named this waterway the "Stinking River," after its odorous nature. He left the Lewis and Clark Expedition in 1806 to continue exploring the new territory. Colter was the first white man to journey into the northwestern portion of present-day Wyoming, and he discovered the river while traveling alone in the winter. The river's name was changed to Shoshone River in the early 1900s.

**CODY**   The town of Cody was named after the great western showman, Buffalo Bill Cody. Known for his Wild West shows, Buffalo Bill had a most remarkable life. His many careers included Army scout, Pony Express rider, guide, Native fighter, and of course, buffalo hunter. Buffalo Bill's exploits influenced the entire nation's, and Europe's, view of the "Wild West." Above all, Cody was a great showman. His many escapades, somewhat embellished, were made famous by the articles and novels of New Yorker Ned Buntline. By the 1890s, his Wild West Shows were at a peak, renowned on two continents, and earning Buffalo Bill more than a million dollars per year.

Buffalo Bill guided expeditions through the Bighorn Basin and along the Shoshone River during the 1870s. He was greatly impressed with the possibilities of the area, so much so that he

*Shoshone River, next to Buffalo Bill Cody Scenic Byway, near Cody*
COURTESY PARK COUNTY TRAVEL COUNCIL

returned 15 years later and joined a development group. In 1895, George T. Beck of Sheridan, banker Horace Alger and Cody formed the Shoshone Land and Irrigation Company. Beck and Alger saw the importance to the project of a well-known name, especially to attract willing homesteaders. The two decided to name their town Cody, and Buffalo Bill, who had wanted the same, was rightly pleased.

The original townsite, called Richland, was actually near DeMaris Springs, a short distance west of town at the mouth of the canyon. The mineral springs were the namesake of Colter's Hell, according to modern historians. Others believed Colter's Hell was actually Yellowstone National Park.

The Shoshone Land and Irrigation Company was responsible for initiating the Buffalo Bill Dam project that subsequently backed up a reservoir of the same name. The company was unsuccessful, but the seeds for the irrigation project were planted. Eventually the U.S. Bureau of Reclamation funded Wyoming's first federal project and completed the dam in 1910. Cody is given much credit for development and promotion of the project. In fact, farmland he owned on the Irma Flat and near Marquette ended up under water. The dam, initially named the Shoshone Dam, was renamed the Buffalo Bill Dam, and the irrigation water and electric power it provided were fundamental in securing the community's future.

The beautiful scenery, abundance of wildlife and proximity to Yellowstone National Park were key elements that had once attracted Buffalo Bill. Today, these same things attract visitors from around the world. The town of Cody is a veteran when it comes to the tourist trade. It is the only town to claim two entrances to Yellowstone National Park, the traditional 54 miles to the East Gate and also via the northeast entrance, 81 miles away. Both routes offer drives through incredibly beautiful country. The East Gate is reached through the North Fork Highway along the Shoshone River that was recently designated the Buffalo Bill Cody Scenic Byway. The northeast entrance, via the Chief Joseph Scenic Highway, offers panoramic views from on top of the world.

Today, Cody still maintains a western lifestyle despite the influx of new residents and developments. Its 8,000 permanent citizens are often addressed by strangers who say, "You're from Cody? What a beautiful place!"

## OUTDOOR RECREATION

The Olive Glen Golf & Country Club is a championship 18-hole course, par 72. In addition to golf, the club has swimming, tennis courts, driving range and practice facility. Visitors are welcome. The club is at 802 Meadow Lane, Cody, WY 82414; (307) 587-5551; (307) 587-3508.

The Cody area is perfect for all anglers with great fishing at Buffalo Bill Reservoir, the Shoshone River, Newton Lakes and many trout streams. Explore on your own, or seek out the experts; it's fun either way. The following are some of Cody's fly-shops and sporting goods outlets where you can gear up or contact guide services. Scott Aune, Aune's Absaroka Angler, 754 Yellowstone Ave. (307) 587-5015, offers guided trips, clothing and instruction. Tim Wade's North Fork Anglers has guided trips, fishing hot spots, flies and clothing. Wade's shop is at 1438 Sheridan Ave., (307) 527-7274. Yellowstone Troutfitters Fly Shop and Guide Service offers professionally guided trips and rental equipment from the shop at 239A Yellowstone Ave., (307) 587-8240. Rocky Mountain Discount Sports at 1820 17th St., across from Albertson's, offers a full selection of fishing tackle and gear. There's more; just check with the Chamber of Commerce.

River rafting adventures are an exhilarating way for all ages to enjoy the scenery and wildlife. Cody has many companies offering trips down the North Fork of the Shoshone River. Wyoming River Trips, one of Cody's first outfits, has two locations in town; call (307) 587-6661, or 1-800-586-6661. River Runners is another one of the oldest companies; call (307) 527-7238; 1-800-535-RAFT. Red Canyon River Trips, (307) 587-6988, offers excursions; and other companies are listed with the Chamber of Commerce.

Surprisingly, the small town of Cody has 17 public parks; all offer a respite from the road and an easy mode of exercise. Our favorite is the Beck Lake Park and Recreation Area. The area has picnic facilities, hiking and biking trails, lakes stocked with fish and piers that are accessible to the disabled. The lakes are also a great place to view 80 species of native waterfowl. Beck Lake is visible from U.S. 14/16/20 on the south side of Cody. You can reach the park by turning west onto Meadow Lane, then turning south on 14th Street. Another important park is the Vietnam Veterans Memorial Park built in memory of Wyoming individuals lost in the war. The memorial is similar in design to the national monument in Washington, D.C. The park is on the south end of Cody just off U.S. 14/16/20. Complete details of all Cody parks are available from the City of Cody Parks Department, (307) 527-7511, or through the Cody Country Chamber of Commerce.

*Holy City, in the North Fork of the Shoshone River, near Cody, Wyoming*

**ATTRACTIONS**

Without a doubt, the Buffalo Bill Historical Center is a place you must visit during your stay in Cody. For many, the BBHC is the primary reason for coming to Cody. It is the largest western heritage museum in the world with over 250,000 visitors each year.

Four major museums are within the Buffalo Bill Historical Center. The Buffalo Bill Museum, the Plains Indian Museum, the Cody Firearms Museum and the Whitney Gallery of Western Art are contained in the BBHC's 150,000 square feet of interior space. Open year-round, the facility is dedicated to the history of art, technology and material culture of the American West. The BBHC is very RV accessible and has a huge parking lot; even so, there are some busy times when the lot is full. The Historical Center is open, year-round with varying hours, June through September, 7 A.M. to 8 P.M. daily; October, 8 A.M. to 5 P.M. daily; November through March, 10 A.M. to 2 P.M., Thursday through Monday; April, 10 A.M. to 5 P.M., daily; and May, 8 A.M. to 8 P.M. daily. For information, call (307) 587-4771; 1-800-227-8483.

*Above and Below:*
*The Buffalo Bill*
*Historical Center*
COURTESY PARK COUNTY
TRAVEL COUNCIL

Old Trail Town & Museum of the Old West is a collection of some of the most significant old buildings in the west, including the Meeteetse River Saloon, Butch Cassidy's Hole-in-the-Wall cabin and the remains of several famous Wyoming cowboys like John "Jeremiah Liver

*Old Trail Town in Cody includes 23*
*authentic western-style buildings.*
COURTESY PARK COUNTY TRAVEL COUNCIL

Eatin'" Johnson. The founders, Bob and Terry Edgar, are well known and respected for their knowledge of western history. Stroll along the frontier boardwalk and witness what Cody might have looked like to the original founders. Old Trail Town is open from mid-May to mid-September, 8 A.M. to 7 P.M. There is a small admission fee to view the town, which is on the West Yellowstone Highway east of the Rodeo Grounds. For more information, call (307) 587-5302.

A visit out west isn't complete without taking in a rodeo, and there's none better than the Cody Nite Rodeo. This rodeo is on every night from June 1 through August 31, beginning at 8:30 P.M. The Cody Nite Rodeo has been entertaining visitors since 1938 and is included on the championship circuit. Cody is the rodeo capital of the world, and this event offers the very best of Buffalo Bill's Wild West. There are clowns, special events for kids, and the grandstands are covered for your comfort. Cody Nite Rodeo runs almost continuously until the Grand Finale on Labor Day. Cody Nite Rodeo is produced by the Jim Ivory Rodeo Company; (307) 587-2992; 1-800-207-0744. Website: http://www.comp-unltd.com/~rodeo/rodeo.html

The special Fourth of July celebration brings on the Stampede Rodeo, July 1–4. With a purse of $240,000, this competition is the highest-paying July 4th rodeo in the world. And that means top talent and tough stock. Information and reservations can be obtained through the Cody Stampede office, PO Box 1327, Cody, WY 82414; (307) 587-5155.

There are also two other rodeos, the Senior Pro Rodeo and the Northwest College Trapper Stampede, both held at the end of the season in September.

Rodeo tickets are available at the ticket booth wagon in City Park, or at the gate after 7 P.M. All rodeos are held at Stampede Park located on the west end of Cody on the Yellowstone Highway, U.S. 14/16/20. Be sure to take in the excitement.

The Irma Hotel is one of the featured buildings of the mile-long Cody Historic Walking Tour. Built by Buffalo Bill Cody in 1902, the hotel was named for his daughter. Many downtown buildings were made from native sandstone mined in a quarry that's now under water at Buffalo Bill Reservoir. The complete tour, brochures and maps are available at the Cody Chamber.

*The Irma Hotel, a famous landmark in Cody*
COURTESY PARK COUNTY TRAVEL COUNCIL

The Wyoming Territory Miniature Village and Museum is the largest miniature village of its kind. The exhibits depict historical scenes from the 1600s through the 1800s, using thousands of miniature figures, models and antique trains. There are displays of authentic artifacts, Native American weapons and period clothing in the museum. The complex is at 142 W. Yellowstone, Cody, WY 82414; (307) 587-5362. The hours are 8 A.M. to 8 P.M. daily, mid-May through mid-September.

The Mormons played a significant part in the history of Wyoming. These pioneers blazed the trails and then worked tirelessly to conquer the arid soil and barren land. The Cody Mural, painted in 1951 on the domed ceiling of the LDS Church by Edward Grigware, depicts the events. The mural is in the Cody Mural and Visitors Center, LDS Church, 17th St. and Wyoming Ave., Cody, WY 82414; (307) 587-3290.

If you're tired of the driver's seat, try Yellowstone Tours. The owner, Bob Richard, is a Cody native who knows the area and his history. You can relax and get the inside story on a tour with Powder River Trailways, PO Box 1013, Cody, WY 82414. Call Bob at (307) 527-6316.

Cody's summer calendar is filled with special events every week. So, no matter when you visit, there's always something special to see and do. A small selection is shown below, but be sure to check with the Chamber of Commerce for a complete list and current dates.

In the summer the Buffalo Bill Historical Center sponsors two events. Regional Native American dancing, crafts and food are the best at the Annual Plains Indian Powwow, in June. Watching the colorful traditional dances is an excellent way to gain appreciation of the Native Americans of the west. The Annual Frontier Festival, in July, is a turn-of-the-century celebration of crafts, entertainment, food, games and skills.

The biggest annual event in Cody is the Fourth of July Celebration and the Annual Cody Stampede. There are parades, rodeos, entertainment, an artisan/craft show, barn dance and fireworks. The celebration continues a tradition started in 1919.

The Winchester Gun Show, also held in July at the Cody High School, features over 250 displays of collectible firearms and products representing western history (90 percent are dedicated to Winchester products). The Winchester Arms Collectors Association has over 4,000 members, and the show generates national interest.

Summer's end signals the time for the Buffalo Bill Celebrity Shootout where celebrities join locals in shooting competitions. The August event is held at the Cody Shooting Complex located north of town off Wyoming 120.

*Wapiti
Campground
west of Cody*

Buffalo Bill State Park is indeed named for the "Wild West" showman, Colonel William F. "Buffalo Bill" Cody. But there's more than just showmanship behind Buffalo Bill's contribution to the reservoir. The irrigation needs, promotion of agricultural development and initial damming of the river were directly influenced by Cody. Even some of the land within the state park was once owned by him. The completion of the Buffalo Bill Dam secured the future of Cody and the surrounding eastern farm and ranchlands.

The Buffalo Bill Dam, which blocked the Shoshone River at the mouth of Shoshone Canyon, was completed in 1910 after five years of work by the U.S. Bureau of Reclamation. The 325-foot-high dam cost $929,658, and was the highest in the world at that time. In 1993, another 25 feet was added to the crest after the completion of an eight-year construction project. The project included building two new power plants below the dam. The reservoir has a 40-mile shoreline; water now covers 8,500 acres with a water storage capacity of about 650,000 acre-feet. Irrigation and drinking water for Cody are supplied by the reservoir.

The reservoir is loaded with rainbow trout, and plenty of lake trout and cutthroat trout make fishing popular. There are several boat ramps, and fishing from shore is also quite lucrative. The southern side of the reservoir, accessed from the South Fork Road, Wyoming 291, offers fishing access and boat ramps at the Bartlett Lane area, but no camping.

The lake is surrounded by mountains of the Absaroka Range and the view from the campsites on the north shore, the North Shore Bay campground, is quite stunning. However, this area can be somewhat windy at times. There is another campground farther west called the North Fork campground that has pleasant campsites along the river. The two campgrounds constitute our choice for a Best Shot for a Camp Spot in the Buffalo Bill State Park. They aren't full even on the Fourth of July weekend.

The Buffalo Bill Dam Visitor Center is located on U.S. 14/16/20 at the northeast end of the reservoir just before the tunnel. The new facility has excellent exhibits and displays on the history of the dam, and for those with vertigo, a gripping look straight down into the canyon bottom 400 feet below. You can also walk out across the top of the dam and gain a unique view of the canyon. The Visitor Center is open May 1 through September 30, 8 A.M. to 8 P.M. daily, with limited winter access. The park headquarters has more information; call (307) 587-9227. The Buffalo Bill Dam Visitor Center's mailing address is 1002 Sheridan Ave., Cody, WY 82414; (307) 527-6076.

## CAMPGROUNDS & RV PARKS

**OVERNIGHTING**

Absaroka Bay RV Park, 2001 U.S. Hwy. 14/16/20, Cody, WY, 1 mile west of airport next to Burger King. 99 RV sites (80 pull-throughs), hook-ups, showers, laundry and some services; open May 15 through September 15; busiest June 15 through July 15; (307) 527-7440; 1-800-557-7440.

Camp Cody RV Park, 415 Yellowstone Ave., Cody, WY. 63 RV sites (no pull-throughs), hook-ups and some services, open year-round; (307) 587-9730.

Cody KOA, 5561 Greybull Hwy., U.S. 14/16/20, Cody, WY. 150 RV sites (60 pull-throughs), hook-ups and some services; features include pool, horses, free rodeo shuttle and shady view of peaks; open May 1 through October 1; busiest June 15 through July 15; (307) 587-2369; 1-800-932-5267; fax: (307) 587-2369.

Elk Valley Inn, 20 miles west of Cody on North Fork Hwy., U.S. 14/16/20. RV sites available (no pull-throughs), hook-ups and some services; open April 1 to October 30; (307) 587-4149.

▲ *Best Shot for a Camp Spot*
Gateway Campground, 203 Yellowstone Ave., Cody, WY. 74 RV sites (12 pull-throughs), hook-ups and some services; open April 1 through October 1; busiest on July 4th holiday; (307) 587-2561.

▲ *Best Shot for a Camp Spot*
Parkway RV Campground, 132 W. Yellowstone Ave., Cody, WY. 25 RV sites (8 pull-throughs), full hook-ups and some services; open year-round; busiest June through August, slowest January; need reservations on July 4th weekend; (307) 527-5927.

Ponderosa Campground, along Yellowstone Hwy., 1815 8th Ave., Cody, WY. 135 RV sites (25 pull-throughs), full hook-ups and some services; open May 1 through October 15; busiest July through August; reservations accepted; (307) 587-9203.

River's View RV Park, 109 W. Yellowstone Ave., Cody, WY. 5 RV sites (no pull-throughs), hook-ups and some services; open year-round; (307) 587-6074; fax: (307) 587-8644.

▲ *Best Shot for a Camp Spot*
7K Motel & RV Park, 232 W. Yellowstone Ave., Cody, WY. 39 RV sites (2 pull-throughs), full hook-ups and some services; open May 1 through September 1; (307) 587-5890; 1-800-223-9204.

▲ *Best Shot for a Camp Spot*
Yellowstone Valley Inn RV Park, 19 miles west of Cody on Shoshone River, 3324 North Fork Hwy., Cody, WY. 120 RV sites (80 pull-throughs), hook-ups and some services; restaurant on site is open 7 days a week, 7 A.M. to 7 P.M.; campground and inn are open year-round; busiest June through August; (307) 587-3961; 1-800-705-7703.

Deer Creek—U.S. Forest Service Campground, 47 miles southwest of Cody on Wyoming 291 (South Fork Road). 7 RV sites (no pull-throughs), no hook-ups or services; open year-round.

▲ *Best Shot for a Camp Spot*
Buffalo Bill State Park—Wyoming State Park, 9 miles west of Cody on U.S. 14/16/20, the Yellowstone Highway. Campgrounds are located on lakefront or river with beautiful views. RV sites with pull-throughs, no hook-ups, has dump station, some services; open May 1 through October 1; there are always campsites here regardless of season, even July 4th weekend; (307) 587-9227.

Big Game—U.S. Forest Service Campground, 28 miles west of Cody on U.S. 14/16/20, the Yellowstone Highway. 16 RV sites (no pull-throughs), no hook-ups or services; open May 15 through September 30.

Wapiti—U.S. Forest Service Campground 29 miles west of Cody on U.S. 14/16/20, the Yellowstone Highway. RV sites (no pull-throughs), no hook-ups or services; open May 15 through October 30.

Elk Fork—U.S. Forest Service Campground, 29 miles west of Cody on U.S. 14/16/20, the Yellowstone Highway. 13 RV sites, (no pull-throughs), no hook-ups or services; open May 15 through October 30.

Clearwater—U.S. Forest Service Campground, 31 miles west of Cody on U.S. 14/16/20, the Yellowstone Highway. 32 RV sites (no pull-throughs), no hook-ups or services; open May 15 through September 30.

Rex Hale—U.S. Forest Service Campground, 36 miles west of Cody on U.S. 14/16/20, the Yellowstone Highway. 8 RV sites (no pull-throughs); no hook-ups or services; open May 15 through September 30.

Newton Creek—U.S. Forest Service Campground, 37 miles west of Cody on U.S. 14/16/20, the Yellowstone Highway. 31 RV sites (no pull-throughs), no hook-ups or services; open May 15 through September 30.

Eagle Creek—U.S. Forest Service Campground, 44 miles west of Cody on U.S. 14/16/20, the Yellowstone Highway. 20 RV sites (no pull-throughs), no hook-ups or services; open May 15 through October 30.

Sleeping Giant—U.S. Forest Service Campground, 47 miles west of Cody on U.S. 14/16/20, the Yellowstone Highway. 6 RV sites (no pull-throughs), no hook-ups or services; open May 15 through October 30.

Three Mile—U.S. Forest Service Campground, 48 miles west of Cody on U.S. 14/16/20, the Yellowstone Highway. RV sites (no pull-throughs) no hook-ups or services; open May 15 through October 30.

Pahaska—U.S. Forest Service Campground, 49 miles west of Cody on U.S. 14/16/20, the Yellowstone Highway. 24 RV sites (no pull-throughs), no hook-ups or services; open May 15 through September 30.

Top of the World Store RV Park, U.S. 212 east of the junction between the Chief Joseph Scenic Byway, Wyoming 296, and Red Lodge. RV sites available (no pull-throughs), hook-ups; open July 1 through September 15.

## BED & BREAKFAST ESTABLISHMENTS

Buffalo Bill's Cody House, historic home. Open year-round; busiest May through October, slowest January through February; credit cards accepted, no pets allowed. Contact Nancy Short, 101 Robertson St., Cody, WY 82414; (307) 587-2528; fax: (307) 765-4794.

Casual Cove Bed & Breakfast, 1908 historic home operating since 1994. Open year-round; busiest June through September, slowest October through May; credit cards accepted; no pets allowed. Contact Jean B. Dyer, 1431 Salisbury Ave., Cody, WY 82414; (307) 587-3622.

Cody Guest Houses, private historic lodging; choose from eight distinctive properties. The lodging firm has been operating since 1989. Open year-round; busiest June through August, slowest November through March; credit cards accepted; no pets allowed. Contact Kathy and Daren Singer, 1401 Rumsey Ave., Cody, WY 82414; (307) 587-6000; 1-800-587-6560; fax: (307) 587-8048.

Parson's Pillow Bed & Breakfast, 1902 historic home and the first church built in Cody. The establishment has been operating since 1991. Open year-round; busiest June through September, slowest November through March; credit cards accepted; no pets allowed. Contact Lee and Elly Larabee, 1202 14th St., Cody, WY 82414; (307) 587-2382; 1-800-377-2348.

Rockwell Ranch Bed & Breakfast, ranch house located 5 miles east of Cody. The bed & breakfast has been operating since 1994. Open April through October; credit cards accepted; no pets allowed. Contact George and Barbara Rockwell, 43 Judy Hill Lane, Cody, WY 82414; (307) 587-8223.

The Mayor's Inn, historic inn built in 1908 by Cody's first mayor. The inn has been operating since 1997. Open year-round; equipped with an intimate in-room spa; credit cards accepted; no pets allowed. Contact Daren and Kathy Singer, 1413 Rumsey, Cody, WY 82414; 1-800-587-6560; fax: (307) 587-8048. Website: http://www.wtp.net/cghouses

Wind Chimes Cottage Bed & Breakfast, historic home. Open year-round; busiest June through September 15, slowest rest of year; credit cards accepted; no pets allowed. Contact Hardy and Sylvia Stucki, 1501 Beck Ave., Cody, WY 82414; (307) 527-5310; 1-800-241-5310.

Kinkade Guest Kabin, modern log cabin in the shade of Green Creek. Opened for business in 1996; open seasonally, small to mid-sized RVs only; credit cards accepted; pets on leash allowed. Contact Becky or Martha Kinkade, 87 Green Creek Rd., Wapiti, WY 82450; (307) 587-5905.

Lockhart Bed & Breakfast, historic home currently undergoing an ownership change. Contact 109 W. Yellowstone, Cody, WY 82414; (307) 587-6074.

## GUEST RANCHES

Pahaska Tepee Resort, Buffalo Bill's original Hunting Lodge built in 1901. The lodge is listed on the National Register of Historic Places. Pahaska Tepee is located 2 miles east of Yellowstone National Park's East Gate on U.S. 14/16/20. Open December 15 through March, and May 10 through October; credit cards accepted; no pets allowed. Contact Bob Coe, owner, or John Helms, manager, 183 Yellowstone Hwy., Cody, WY 82414; (307) 527-7701; 1-800-628-7791; fax: (307) 527-4019.

*Pahaska Teepee Guest Ranch, near east gate of Yellowstone National Park*

Rimrock Dude Ranch, operating since 1956. Gary and Dede Fales hosted President George Bush on a wilderness backcountry trip, complete with Secret Service agents and all sorts of interesting complications. What better reference could you have? The ranch features beautiful scenery, horseback riding, campfire dinners, fishing, billiards, ping-pong, square dances and big-game hunting. Open year-round; busiest June through August, slowest March through April; credit cards accepted; no pets allowed. Contact Gary and Dede Fales, 2728 North Fork Hwy., Cody, WY 82414; (307) 587-3970; fax: (307) 527-5014; e-mail: rimrock@wyoming.com website: http://www.rimrockranch.com

Goff Creek Lodge, 8 miles east of Yellowstone National Park's East Gate on U.S. 14/16/20. This lodge has been operating since the 1950s. Features include guided trail rides, hiking, hunting, fishing and snowmobile rides. Open year-round; busiest June through September, slowest November through December and April; credit cards accepted; pets allowed. Contact Valerie or Rick Merrill, PO Box 155, 955 E. Yellowstone Hwy., Cody, WY 82414; (307) 587-3753; 1-800-859-3985; e-mail: goffcreek.com

Bill Cody Ranch, east of Yellowstone National Park's East Gate on U.S. 14/16/20, 25 miles from Cody. This ranch has been operating since 1925. Wilderness horseback riding featured. Open May through September; credit cards accepted; no pets allowed. Contact John and Jamie Parsons, 2604 Yellowstone Hwy., Cody, WY 82414; (307) 587-6271.

Blackwater Lodge, 12 miles east of Yellowstone National Park's East Gate on Hwy. 14/16/20. This lodge has been operating since 1993. Features include wilderness trail rides, lawn games, fishing and pack trips. Open June through September 20; no pets allowed. Contact Debbie Carlton, 1516 North Fork Hwy., Cody, WY 82414; (307) 587-5201.

Red Pole Ranch, on the North Fork of the Shoshone River 9 miles east of Yellowstone National Park. The ranch is at the west end of Buffalo Bill Reservoir, accessible by crossing the bridge to Sheep Mountain. Contact Don Schmalz, Box 175, Cody, WY 82414; (307) 587-5929.

Shoshone Lodge, 4 miles east of Yellowstone National Park's East Gate on U.S. 14/16/20. This lodge has been operating since 1948. Features include horseback riding, fishing, cookouts, square dancing, pack trips and big-game hunting. Open May through November; credit cards accepted; pets allowed. Contact Elizabeth Woodruff or Keith Dahlem, 349 Yellowstone Hwy., Cody, WY 82414; (307) 587-4044; fax: (307) 587-2681.

Absaroka Mountain Lodge, 12 miles east of Yellowstone National Park's East Gate on U.S. 14/16/20. For information, contact Absaroka Mountain Lodge, 1231 E. Yellowstone Hwy., Wapiti, WY 82450; (307) 587-3963.

Breteche Creek Ranch, rustic educational guest ranch featuring creative writing, ornithology, geology, western history and horsemanship; naturalist on staff. The ranch is located 25 miles west of Cody on the North Fork Hwy., U.S. 14/16/20, then south on County Rd. 6FU. Call for appointment to visit. Operating since 1991; open June 15 through September 15; no credit cards accepted; pets allowed. Contact Bo Polk, Box 596, 250 Rd. 6FU, Cody, WY 82414; (307) 587-3844; fax: (307) 527-7032.

Double Diamond X Ranch, 34 miles southwest of Cody on the South Fork of the Shoshone River. This family-style ranch has been operating since 1988. Features include horseback riding, fishing, pack trips, photography, square dancing and kids programs. Open year-round; busiest June through September; credit cards accepted; no pets allowed. Contact Russ and Patsy Fraser, 3453 South Fork Rd., Cody, WY 82414; (307) 527-6276; 1-800-833-7262; fax: (307) 587-2708; e-mail: beverly @wave.park.wy.us Website: http://www.wave.park.wy.us\~beverly\ddx.html

Flying T Ranch, 16 miles southwest of Cody in the South Fork Valley. This working cattle ranch has been operating since 1987. Open May through October; pets allowed; no credit cards accepted. Contact Robert and Nanette Till, 1557 South Fork Rd., Cody, WY 82414; (307) 587-2666.

Castle Rock Ranch, 17 miles southwest of Cody on Wyoming 291 in the South Fork Valley. This adult/family adventure center has been operating since 1993. Features include pool, private accommodations with bath, western and Native American decor and winter pack trips to Yellowstone. Open June through September. Contact Dereck and Gina McGovern, 412 Road 6NS, Cody, WY 82414; (307) 587-2076.

Hidden Valley Ranch, 17 miles southwest of Cody on Wyoming 291. This guest ranch has been operating since 1979. Features include fishing, wilderness pack trips, horseback riding, hiking, swimming and big-game hunting; guests also may participate in ranch work. No minimum stay; open May through November; credit cards accepted; pets by permission. Contact Duaine Hagen, Hidden Valley Ranch, 153 Hidden Valley Rd., Cody, WY 82414; (307) 587-5090; 1-800-894-7262; fax: (307) 587-5265.

Hunter Peak Ranch, 58 miles northwest of Cody on the Chief Joseph Scenic Byway. This ranch has been operating since 1949. Features include horseback riding, pack trips, fishing, hiking, hunting, cross-country skiing, snowshoeing and snowmobiling. Open year-round; busiest July through August, slowest in spring; pets allowed; credit cards accepted. Contact Louis and Shelley Cary, Box 1731, Cody, WY 82414; (307) 587-3711.
Website: http://www.nezperce.com/ranchhp.html

7D Ranch, in Sunlight Valley, 50 miles northwest of Cody. Features include daily horseback rides, great fishing, big-game hunts and excellent family-style meals. Reservations by week; pack trips by pre-arrangement. Contact Manager, 7D Ranch, Box 100, Cody, WY 82414; (307) 587-9885; (307) 587-3997.

Squaw Creek Ranch, in the Clark's Fork River Valley, 56 miles northwest of Cody on the Chief Joseph Scenic Byway. Features include trail rides, fishing, summer pack trips, educational programs, fall hunting, snowmobiling and trips to Yellowstone. Open year-round; busiest in July and hunting season, slowest in January. Contact Tim and Geri Hockhalter, 4059 Crandall Rd., Painter Rt., Box 2513, Cody, WY 82414; (307) 587-5249; 1-800-348-8947.
Website: http://w3.trip.com/~gerih/

## SUGGESTED DINING

Maxwell's, 937 Sheridan, Cody, WY;  (307) 527-7749.

La Comida, 1385 Sheridan, Cody, WY; (307)587-9556.

Franca's, 1421 Rumsey Ave., Cody, WY; (307) 587-5354.

Stephan's Restaurant, 1367 Sheridan Ave., Cody, WY; (307) 587-8511.

Sunset House, 1651 8th St., Cody, WY; (307) 587-2257.

The Yellowstone Valley Inn, 3324 Yellowstone National Park Hwy., Cody, WY; (307) 587-3961.

Wapiti Lodge & Steak House, 18 miles west of Cody on Yellowstone Hwy., Cody, WY; (307) 587-6659.

## VISITOR INFORMATION & SERVICES

The Cody Country Chamber of Commerce is housed in a log building along with the Cody Country Art League and the Shoshone Recreation District. The log structure, once owned by Cody Mayor Paul Stock, is listed on the National Register of Historic Places. The building is at the west end of Sheridan Avenue, where it bends around to the south, and the area is known as the Paul Stock Park. City Park is across the street. Visitor hours are Memorial Day through Labor Day, Monday through Saturday, 8 A.M. to 7 P.M., Sunday, 10 A.M. to 3 P.M.; winter, Monday through Friday, 8 A.M. to 5 P.M.

Cody Country Chamber of Commerce, PO Box 2777, 836 Sheridan, Cody, WY 82414; (307) 587-2777; e-mail: cody@codychamber.org

Highway information and construction schedules are available through the Chamber of Commerce, (307) 587-2777.

## MEDICAL SERVICES

West Park Hospital, 24-hour emergency room, full-service medical center, 707 Sheridan Ave., Cody, WY; (307) 527-7501; 1-800-645-9447.

## REPAIR & TOWING

Child Towing & Recovery, 24-hour service, 2517 Frank Ct., Cody, WY 82414; call 1-800-NEED-TOW; (307) 527-7018.

Collision Towing & Auto Body, 24-hour service, 2933 Big Horn Ave., Cody, WY 82414; 1-800-400-5365; (307) 527-7788.

M & P Auto Repair & RV, 5739 Greybull Hwy., Cody, WY 82414; (307) 527-7389.

Yellowstone RV Center, 124 W. Yellowstone Ave., Cody, WY 82414; (307) 587-3305.

**VETERINARY SERVICES** Cody Veterinary Hospital, Dr. Dave Pendray, Dr. Scott Moore and Dr. Steve Sekerak, 5524 Greybull Hwy., Cody, WY 82414; (307) 587-3151; pager 587-9043, #3350.

Chadwick Veterinary Hospital, Dr. Lynne Chadwick, 3008 Big Horn Ave., Cody, WY 82414; (307) 527-7213; 1-800-469-7213.

**Cody to Powell, Lovell: U.S. 14-A—see page 144.**
**Cody to Greybull: U.S. 14/16/20—see page 155.**
**Cody to Thermopolis: Wyoming 120—see page 167.**

# CODY TO MONTANA: WYOMING 120

As you head north from Cody on Wyoming 120, the highway moves along a natural division between rolling hills and sagebrush country on the west, and badlands, sparse vegetation and high-desert country on the east. The junction with Wyoming 296, the Chief Joseph Scenic Byway, is about 17 miles north of Cody. This scenic route deserves your attention and time; for more, see page 141.

Wyoming 120 continues on toward the Montana border through country that is excellent for wildlife viewing. Mule deer and whitetail deer are often seen feeding in the valley bottoms and agricultural fields, and antelope can be observed to the east on the sagebrush-dotted badlands. Where the highway first crosses the Clark's Fork of the Yellowstone River, about 30 miles north of Cody, there is a fishing access point on the north side of the bridge. If the water's clear, it's a good place to wet your line. The river, under federal environmental protection, has been designated Wyoming's only Wild and Scenic River because the Clark's Fork of the Yellowstone is the state's only undammed river.

The Edelweiss Stop is next, providing gas, supplies, cafe and a tavern. This area was along the Nez Perce Trail. According to a sign erected by the local Boy Scout troop, "In 1877 the Nez Perce Indians of Idaho, led by Chief Joseph, fled the US Army. They crossed the Clark's River near this point (Edelweiss) while trying to outrun the soldiers to Canada." There is a junction at Edelweiss that heads west to the community of Clark, and you can enjoy good fishing for trout and whitefish in the river.

Back on Wyoming 120, just north of Edelweiss, there is a turnoff to Powell (Wyoming 294), which leads back to U.S. 14-A and the Bighorn Canyon National Recreation Area. The route straight north on Wyoming 120 takes you to Montana through lots of farmland—wheat, sugar beets, barley and the best local sweet corn around. Stop at a roadside stand and enjoy the fresh produce. At Belfry, Montana, the road splits. Red Lodge is 15 miles west on Montana 308, or you can wind through Belfry and keep on toward Bridger.

At the state border, the highway numbers change; Wyoming 120 becomes Montana 72. Just before Bridger, Montana 72 connects into U.S. 310 from Lovell, Wyoming, and offers another route back to the Bighorn Recreation Area. The Crow Indian Reservation is to the east in the Pryor Mountains, and a visit to Chief Plenty Coups Memorial Park is a unique side trip; see more on page 143. From Bridger north, U.S. 310 moves along the Clark's Fork of the Yellowstone River through lush farmland and ends up at Billings.

*Ranching in Buffalo Bill's country, near Cody*
COURTESY PARK COUNTY TRAVEL COUNCIL

# FAVORITE DRIVE:
# CHIEF JOSEPH SCENIC BYWAY

About 17 miles north of Cody, Wyoming 296 takes off west from the main highway, Wyoming 120. The side road heads over the Chief Joseph Scenic Byway through the Shoshone National Forest and is truly one of the most beautiful drives around.

The byway honors Chief Joseph and the Nez Perce who hastily scrambled down the Clark's Fork of the Yellowstone River in their desperate attempt to flee the U.S. Army. In the fall of 1877, the Nez Perce band followed a well-worn wildlife migration route into the Bighorn Basin on their long passage to escape, but would later give up with Chief Joseph making the most legendary surrender speech of all time (see page 46).

About 1995, the highway project to pave the entire route was completed, making the drive accessible to all types of vehicles, or at least those with good brakes. At first, the highway winds through rolling ranchlands and sagebrush-covered hills, and slowly begins to climb into the Absaroka and Beartooth Mountains. The road becomes steeper, continuing up Dead Indian Pass, one of the last sections to be paved. Near the pass summit at 8,060 feet, there is an overlook into Sunlight Basin, and the panoramic view is awesome. Next, the highway makes a series of switchbacks down the pass and then stretches out as it crosses the basin. There are many hiking trails and wilderness climbs for athletic types, and the Forest Service can provide detailed information on where to go and precautions to take. The area also has many campgrounds; for overnighting information, see the Cody section, page 131.

The beautiful scenery continues as you approach a small-looking bridge with a rest area on the east. This is a good place to stop, as you are about to cross Wyoming's highest bridge over Sunlight Creek. The gorge here is narrow, rugged and very deep. Many folks like to walk out on the bridge for a better look down the canyon. If you're afraid of heights, be careful here! Sunlight Creek flows into the Clark's Fork of the Yellowstone River, which has cut a deep gorge into the basin floor with canyon walls 1,200 feet high.

The highway follows the Clark's Fork of the Yellowstone River and climbs out of the basin passing the Crandall area and Ranger Station. As it winds up through the forest, the peaks and crags of the Beartooths form an impressive ring along the skyline. The Chief Joseph Scenic Byway merges into U.S. 212, where you can go west to Yellowstone National Park's northeast entrance at Cooke City or east to Red Lodge via the Beartooth Scenic Byway.

# CHIEF JOSEPH SCENIC BYWAY

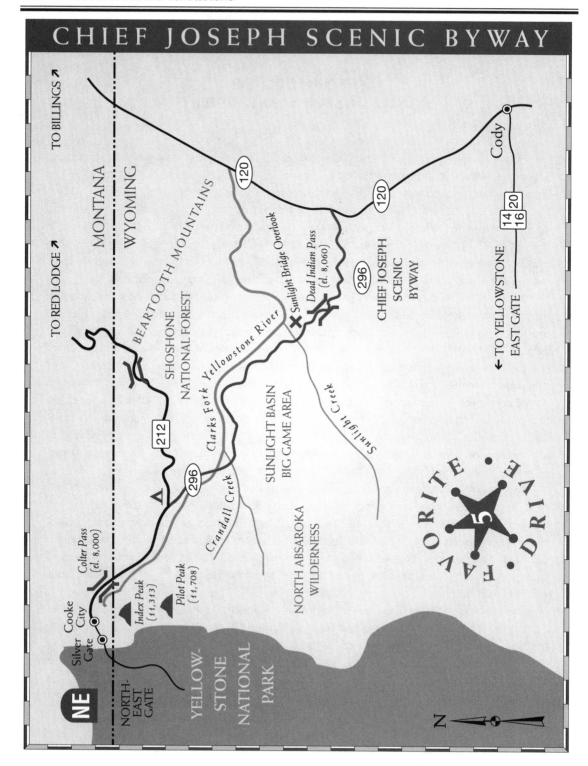

TO BILLINGS

TO RED LODGE

MONTANA

WYOMING

120

120

Cody

14
16
20

← TO YELLOWSTONE EAST GATE

BEARTOOTH MOUNTAINS

SHOSHONE NATIONAL FOREST

Sunlight Bridge Overlook

Dead Indian Pass
(el. 8,060)

296

CHIEF JOSEPH SCENIC BYWAY

Clarks Fork Yellowstone River

Sunlight Creek

212

296

SUNLIGHT BASIN BIG GAME AREA

Crandall Creek

Colter Pass
(el. 8,000)

Index Peak
(11,313)

Pilot Peak
(11,708)

NORTH ABSAROKA WILDERNESS

Cooke City

Silver Gate

NORTH-EAST GATE

YELLOW-STONE NATIONAL PARK

NE

FAVORITE DRIVE 5

N

# Chief Plenty Coups Memorial Park

Chief Plenty Coups was the last chief of the Crow. His philosophy and vision for his people are explained at the Visitor Center along with many interesting educational exhibits about the culture of the Crow People. The log home of Plenty Coups, the Chief's gravesite and his historic store have been preserved at the park. The Visitor Center is dedicated exclusively to the Crow. Covering 195 acres, the park is also the site of the Medicine Spring and a day-use picnic ground area.

Located 35 miles south of Billings, the park is open 8 A.M. to 8 P.M. from May 1 to September 30. The Visitor Center is open daily 10 A.M. to 5 P.M. Fees are $15 annual passport, $3 per carload or walk-in fee of 50 cents per person; call (406) 252-1289.

There are four possible routes to take to the park. The two roads from Billings are common, the route from Edgar is a pleasant adventure, and the fourth road, from a turnoff south of Bridger, can be a nightmare. The primary route is from Billings; get off I-90 at Exit 447, go south on Montana 416 following signs to Pryor, and go 1 mile west of Pryor.

If you're coming north out of Cody, you can get to Chief Plenty Coups Memorial State Park by turning east at Edgar onto an improved gravel road that is good year-round. This 16-mile backcountry route travels through rolling sagebrush hills and grassy ranchland. In view are the Pryor Mountains, which spread along the eastern horizon. Best of all, there's a wave and a smile from every car you pass. There's a gas station and convenience store in Pryor, open 8 A.M. to 5 P.M. except Sunday.

## RV CAUTION

Be sure to head all the way up to Edgar as you travel north from Cody. The first route to Chief Plenty Coups State Park cuts east off of U.S. 310 south of Bridger. On the Montana state map, this backcountry road looks just like the one from Edgar, and the signs read Pryor Mountain Road and National Forest Access. What begins as a well-signed, improved gravel road treks across the Indian Reservation and deteriorates into a one-lane, bumpy dirt road, with unmarked junctions. On top of that, if a summer rain-storm blows in, as they often can in the late afternoon, the dirt road will turn to a muddy quagmire. The reservation is not a place to get stuck or run out of gas. That's not because the locals are hostile. They are some of the friendliest folks around; there just aren't very many of them. You can drive for hours and never see another car.

# CODY TO POWELL, LOVELL, AND THE BIGHORN MOUNTAINS: U.S. 14-A

U.S. 14-A, the alternate route across the Bighorn Mountains was named the Medicine Wheel Passage. A National Scenic Byway, the road from Cody through Powell and Lovell takes you through the Bighorn Basin's ranch and agricultural communities that helped to establish Buffalo Bill's Yellowstone Country. Farther east lies the spectacular Bighorn Canyon National Recreation Area and Yellowtail Reservoir. Be sure to take in both before you head on up the Bighorns toward the ancient Medicine Wheel (see page 154), located on the west face of the mountain range.

**RV CAUTION:** U.S. 14-A from Lovell up into the Bighorn Mountains winds around tight curves and is extremely steep, with an 8- to 10-percent grade. It's not uncommon for vehicles to overheat when making this climb; be sure your coolant system is in tip-top shape. If you're coming down the grade, use low gear and "feather" your brakes lightly.

## HEART MOUNTAIN

Heart Mountain dominates the sky east of Cody, and travelers heading north or south can judge their distance by the mountain's distinctive crown. Heart Mountain is a geological puzzle. About 45 million years ago, the limestone mountain broke away from the Rockies and slid 25 miles on a detachment fault to the present site. The top section of the mountain is older than the base. No adequate explanation exists for this phenomenon.

Although it has little resemblance to a heart, it supposedly got the name because its two summits are vaguely shaped like a valentine. In retrospect, the name may have been most inappropriate. A Japanese detention camp was built on its slopes in 1942; after that, the sweetheart-valentine image just doesn't seem deserved.

After the bombing of Pearl Harbor in 1941, many people believed the Pacific Coast was vulnerable and that security of our shores would be improved if Japanese-Americans were moved inland. President Roosevelt established the War Relocation Authority to accomplish the task of moving 110,442 persons from Washington, Oregon, California and Arizona.

One of ten remote relocation centers constructed to confine the Japanese-Americans was built just east of Heart Mountain. Constructed in just 62 days, the relocation center became the third-largest city in Wyoming. In total, 11,000 persons of all ages were

*Heart Mountain,*
*near Cody,*
*Wyoming*
COURTESY
WYOMING *BLM*

imprisoned at the bleak desert camp in 465 tarpaper barracks. The army-type camp was surrounded by barbed-wire fence and had nine guard towers equipped with machine guns and searchlights. Wyoming's western hospitality was replaced with wartime prejudice and paranoia. The alarmists became excessively vocal, the fair-minded more silent.

Two-thirds of the Japanese evacuees at the Heart Mountain Relocation Center were American-born, United States citizens. Out of the Heart Mountain group, over 900 Japanese men joined the U.S. Army; 20 were killed in action. Eventually, Wyoming people eased their resentment toward the Japanese and became more considerate, but not enough to want them to stay after the war. In 1943, the evacuees were barred from voting or owning property in the state. The Japanese, however, had little regard for Wyoming, and by 1950, only 450 Japanese remained in the state.

The site today is surrounded by farmland, and the remnants of what few buildings remain crumble more with each passing winter. The relocation camp itself is on public land about 15 miles from Cody on Wyoming 14-A, heading east toward Powell. A nonprofit group, the Heart Mountain Relocation Center Memorial Association, is working to preserve the site and open a visitor center and museum. Interested parties may contact them at Heart Mountain Relocation Center Memorial Association, Box 774, Ralston, WY 82424.

# CODY TO POWELL, FRANNIE, BYRON, AND COWLEY: U.S. 14-A

This highway runs through ranch and farmland, following the Shoshone Heart Mountain Canal that carries water from Buffalo Bill Reservoir to the agricultural areas of the Bighorn Basin. Barley is a major crop here, much of it contracted by large breweries. Sugar beets are also a primary crop.

**POWELL**

The town of Powell was originally known as Camp Coulter. The Shoshone Reclamation Project established the site as its headquarters during the 1890s, and the town incorporated in 1910. The dual purpose of the huge reclamation project was to store water from the Shoshone River, and then move it across the basin to the Powell area. This was Wyoming's first reclamation project under the 1902 Newlands Act, federal funding aimed toward permanent settlement of the wild and arid west.

Several years before, Colonel William F. Cody (Buffalo Bill himself) and his partners had attempted a similar project as the Shoshone Land and Irrigation Company. However, their dreams did not materialize. The project failed, and the German colonists recruited to homestead the land abandoned the area in September 1896. The water rights held by Cody and his partners were later developed by the Shoshone Reclamation Project, which successfully completed the Buffalo Bill Dam in 1910.

Camp Coulter, the project's first town, was later named Powell after Major John Wesley Powell (1834–1902). Powell had fought hard for development of land and water use systems in the western desert regions. A one-armed veteran of the Civil War, this indomitable man had organized many scientific expeditions with the U.S. Geological Survey and became its director in 1881. He is best known for exploring the Colorado River drainage system, navigating the Green River Canyon and the Grand Canyon.

Successful implementation of Powell's conservation dreams was not accomplished until the year of his death, 1902. At that time, President Theodore Roosevelt established the U.S. Bureau of Reclamation.

Powell was declared an "All-American City" in 1994. Today, Powell's economy is still largely based on agriculture, along with oil production, ranching and the community college. The primary crops are sugar beets, barley and dry beans. Northwest College is part of Wyoming's community college network. There are over 2,000 students and 250 full- and part-time faculty in Powell. One final trivia fact: W. Edwards Deming, the father of Statistical Process Control, is Powell's most famous son.

## OUTDOOR RECREATION AND ATTRACTIONS

The Powell Country Club has an 18-hole course at 600 Hwy. 114, Powell, WY 82435; (307) 754-7259. Other recreation in town includes tennis courts, softball and baseball fields, and horseshoe pits. The small town has 11 city parks and 12 baseball fields.

The 23-year-old Homesteaders Museum is devoted to the history of homesteaders in the Shoshone Valley. The log-home structure dates back to the 1930s and houses displays of the early days in Powell. Outside there are many antique pieces of equipment used by the pioneers. There is also an incredible rock and fossil collection on display. The free museum is just off U.S. 14-A on First and Clark Street; there's plenty of room along the street to park an RV. The museum is open seasonally; from October to May on Friday and Saturday from 10 A.M. to 5 P.M.; from June through September, Tuesday through Friday, 1 P.M. to 5 P.M. For more information, contact Homesteaders Museum, PO Box 54, Powell, WY 82435; (307) 754-9481.

There is a walking tour of Powell, including its most historic buildings. The downtown area makes for a pleasant stroll through middle America, and the shops have some interesting items.

The Park County Fairgrounds are in Powell. Many concerts, seasonal events and the Park County Fair are featured. For more information, contact the Powell Valley Chamber of Commerce.

## OVERNIGHTING

### CAMPGROUNDS & RV PARKS

▲ *Best Shot for a Camp Spot*
Homesteader Park, east of Powell on U.S. 14-A. 25 RV sites (no pull-throughs), no hook-ups; dump station, some services; open April 5 to October 31.

▲ *Best Shot for a Camp Spot*
Park County Fairgrounds. 130 RV sites (no pull-throughs), hook-ups and some services; open May 1 to September 1; (307) 754-5421; fax: (307) 754-5947.

### BED & BREAKFAST ESTABLISHMENTS

I Can Rest Bed & Breakfast, country farm home located on paved road. Tours and wagon rides are offered. Some credit cards accepted; outdoor kennels for pets; open year-round; busiest from June through August, slowest in December and January. Contact Luanne and Eric Loloff, 1095 Mountain Vista Rd., Powell, WY 82435; (307) 754-4178; fax: (307) 754-8017.

## SUGGESTED DINING

Hamilton Steak House, 201 Hamilton, Powell, WY; (307) 754-5703.

Skyline Café, 141 E. Coulter, Powell, WY; (307) 754-8052.

Lamplighter, 234 E. 1st, Powell, WY; (307) 754-2226.

China Town, 151 E. Coulter, Powell, WY; (307) 754-7924.

## VISITOR INFORMATION & SERVICES

Powell Valley Chamber of Commerce, 114 S. Day, PO Box 814, Powell, WY 82435; (307) 754-3494; 1-800-325-4278; fax: (307) 754-3483; website: http://wyod@aol.com

## MEDICAL SERVICES

Powell Hospital, 24-hour emergency room, 777 Ave. H, Powell, WY; (307) 754-2267.

Skyline Drug, 235 N. Bent, Powell, WY; open Monday through Saturday, 8 A.M. to 5:30 P.M.; (307) 754-2622.

## REPAIR & TOWING

Bob's Auto & Towing, 613 E. Coulter Ave., Powell, WY 82435; (307) 754-9880.

Arrowhead RV Sales, Service & Parts, 938 Alan Rd., Powell, WY 82435; Monday through Saturday, 8 A.M. to 6 P.M.; (307) 754-0272.

Western Collision Auto Body Repair & Paint, 590 S. Bent, Powell, WY; (307) 754-3554.

## VETERINARY SERVICES

Heart Mountain Animal Health, Teri Ann Oursler, DVM, 256 S. Douglas, Powell, WY 82435; (307) 754-9393.

Powell Veterinary Services, Gene Bischoff and Lyle Bischoff, 522 S. Division, Powell, WY 82435; (307) 754-3034, or residence after hours, 754-4137.

*In the winter, plenty of snow piles up in and around Yellowstone National Park.*

# FRANNIE, BYRON, COWLEY AND LOVELL:
# U.S. 14-A, WYOMING 114

**FRANNIE**

Frannie, located just two miles from the Montana border, is touted as the "Biggest Little Town in Wyoming." As you travel north on U.S. 789, Park County is on the left and Big Horn County on the right.

In 1894, the Postal Service gave William "Jack" Morris permission to open a post office, which he named after his six-year-old little girl, Frannie. It is said she was an accomplished equestrian and once rode with Buffalo Bill's Wild West show.

The town was incorporated in 1954. Frannie's economy is based on the oil industry, agriculture and limestone. The lime quarry is located 10 miles north in the Pryor Mountains, and the drying plant is just 1 mile north of Frannie. Lime is used in refining sugar beets into sugar, and also used in scrubbers to enhance air quality and water purification. The population of the small community was 148 when taken for the 1990 U.S. Census.

**VISITOR INFORMATION & SERVICES**

Frannie Town Hall, PO Box 72, Frannie, WY 82423; (307) 664-2323.

**BYRON**

The town of Byron was named after Byron Sessions, the construction manager for the Sidon Canal built by the Big Horn Colonization Company. Settled in 1900 by the Mormons, the town, with 470 residents, is mostly an agricultural community. However, natural gas wells, first developed in 1906, and oil have also played a part in the area's economic growth.

**COWLEY**

Cowley is an agricultural community of about 500 people today. The town was started in 1900 by Mormon families preparing the way for the Burlington and Northern Railroads. The families lived in tents until the railroad reached sufficient progress to allow families time to build real homes. The town was dedicated as a townsite in 1901 by Abraham O. Woodruff of the Church of the Latter Day Saints. In the past, oil development spurred growth, but it was short-lived and now accounts for only a small portion of the farming community's livelihood. Cowley's biggest celebration occurs in July; Pioneer Days honor the past.

**LOVELL**

The town of Lovell (LOVE-ul) is named for Henry Clay Lovell, an enterprising man with know-how, experience and little else to fund his way. In 1882, he teamed up with Anthony L. Mason, a financier, to form the largest ranch in the eastern Bighorn Basin. The cattle were ranged from Ten Sleep to Lovell, and pushed up the Bighorns for summer grazing. The ranch headquarters were located near the junction of the Bighorn River and today's Highway U.S. 14-A. A cow camp was set up at Willow Creek, just east of the Lovell townsite. The historic ML Ranch had 25,000 to 30,000 head of cattle at its height. When Mason died in 1892, the partnership ended. Lovell kept the deeded land, restocked the ranch and ran it until his death in 1902.

Like many of the small towns in the Bighorn Basin, farming is a common livelihood. The area was settled mostly by Mormons, who built irrigation systems to provide water to their farms under Abraham Woodruff's Big Horn Colonization Company. Sugar beets are a main crop and the Western Sugar factory, built in 1916, is an important employer today. Oil fields and two bentonite plants (used in making drywall board) also provide viable employment.

Scandal tore through the quiet little town in 1983 when a prominent local doctor was brought to trial for raping or molesting dozens of his patients. For 25 years, the women were too intimidated to speak up at the outrage; the few who had were branded as liars. Finally, under alleged political pressure from as high up as the governor's office (under Governor Herschler), Dr. John Story was brought up on multiple rape charges. He was convicted and sentenced to 20 years in the state penitentiary. A fascinating book by Jack Olson, *Doc*, details the sordid story of Wyoming's recent history.

The physician's actions are in stark contrast to the otherwise friendly family town that serves as the gateway to the Bighorn Canyon, Yellowtail Wildlife Habitat, Pryor Mountain Wild Horse Range and the mysterious Medicine Wheel in the Bighorn Mountains. Base your opinion on the fine folks who live in Lovell today.

## OUTDOOR RECREATION

The Foster Gulch Golf Course is open to the public. Play a round at 925 Lane 13, Lovell, WY; (307) 548-2445.

Lovell is a gateway of its own, providing access to enjoy scenic and historic attractions, fishing, camping and water sports programs at several nearby areas. The areas listed below are described in greater detail at the end of this section. The Bighorn Canyon and Bighorn Lake are a popular fishing and water sports area (see page 152). The Yellowtail Wildlife Habitat offers fishing, hiking and seasonal wildlife photography opportunities (see page 152). View wild horses at the Pryor Mountain Wild Horse Range (see page 154), and visit the sacred Medicine Wheel Archaeological Site (see page 154).

## OVERNIGHTING

### CAMPGROUNDS & RV PARKS

Camp Big Horn RV Park, on Main Street at the east end of Lovell. 18 RV sites (no pull-throughs), hook-ups and some services; open year-round; (307) 548-2725; fax: (307) 548-7479.

Bald Mountain—U.S. Forest Service Campground, 33 miles east of Lovell on U.S. 14-A. 15 RV sites (no pull-throughs), no hook-ups or services; open June 15 to October 31.

Horseshoe Bend—National Park Service Campground, 2 miles east of Lovell on U.S. 14-A to junction at Wyoming 37, then 14 miles north. 128 RV sites (no pull-throughs), no hook-ups or services; open year-round.

Porcupine—U.S. Forest Service Campground, 33 miles east of Lovell on U.S. 14-A, then 1.6 miles north on Forest Service Road 13. 16 RV sites (no pull-throughs), no hook-ups or services; open June 15 to October 31.

Barry's Landing—National Park Service Campground, 27 miles north of Lovell on Wyoming 37. 9 camping sites, RVs allowed, no services, boat-launch access for 2-wheel drive with trailer; open year-round.

### GUEST RANCHES

Schively Ranch, working guest ranch under current operation since 1979. Features rides with cowboys on the 55-mile spring and fall cattle drives. Small RVs allowed, pick-up service available; credit cards accepted; no pets allowed; open mid-April through mid-November. Contact Joe and Iris Bassett, 1062 Road 15, Lovell, WY 82431; (307) 548-6688; fax: (307) 548-2322.

**SUGGESTED DINING**

Big Horn, 605 W. Main, Basin, WY; (307) 548-6811.

**VISITOR INFORMATION**

Lovell Area Chamber of Commerce, PO Box 295, 287 E. Main, Lovell, WY 82431; (307) 548-7552.

**MEDICAL SERVICES**

North Big Horn Hospital, 24-hour emergency room (walk-in clinic), 1115 Lane 12, Basin, WY; (307) 548-2771.

Lovell Drug Co., 164 E. Main, Lovell, WY; open Monday through Friday, 8:30 A.M. to 6 P.M.; (307) 548-7231.

**REPAIR & TOWING**

Burnham Towing & Auto Salvage, 1047 Rd. 13, Lovell, WY; (307) 548-2468.

Midway Motors, 24-hour service, 1785 U.S. 310, Lovell, WY; (307) 548-7522, after hours, 548-7533.

**VETERINARY SERVICES**

Lovell Veterinary Service, 1220 Rd. 11, Lovell, WY; (307) 548-2452, after hours, 548-7553.

# FAVORITE DRIVE:
# THE BIGHORN CANYON NATIONAL RECREATION AREA

Bighorn Canyon National Recreation Area was established in 1966. The multipurpose area was intended for recreation; to utilize renewable natural resources (including hunting and grazing); to preserve the scenic, scientific, and historic resources; and to administer land and water use in the surrounding area. The area is administered by the National Park Service.

The construction of Yellowtail Dam began on May 10, 1961. Over five years later, on December 22, 1966, the 525-foot-high dam was completed. The dam spans 1,480 feet along its crest and backs up water for 71 miles to form the lake. The filling of Bighorn Lake in 1967 was one of the most significant events in the history of the canyon area.

The Crow Indian Reservation shares two-thirds of its boundary with Bighorn Canyon National Recreation Area. At one time, the reservation encompassed 38 million acres; today it covers 2.5 million acres, less than one-tenth the original size. The history of the Crow is intertwined with this territory, their beloved homeland. They defended it against the Sioux and Cheyenne, and shared camp in friendship with the whites when Fort Smith was first established. Many of the place names at the recreation area are Crow in origin; names like the Bighorn River, Frozen Leg, Pretty Eagle, and, of course, Yellowtail. The Crow still carry on their traditions, and the Crow Fair, which takes place in August at Crow Agency, is an annual reunion and reaffirmation of the Crow way of life.

The Yellowtail Dam Visitor Center in Fort Smith, at the north end of the area, is just 2 miles from Yellowtail Dam. On the south end, the Bighorn Canyon Visitor Center is just east of Lovell. There is no direct route connecting the north and south ends of the recreation area.

Interesting sights include Pryor Mountain Wild Horse Range, set up in 1968 by the Secretary of the Interior to preserve the wild horse herds; Yellowtail Wildlife Habitat, administered by Wyoming Game and Fish Department; and, of course, the spectacular canyon itself (there's a great view from the Devil's Canyon Overlook). The Yellowtail Wildlife Habitat is an upland game bird and waterfowl habitat unit. The area offers fishing, hiking and seasonal wildlife photography opportunities. There are also four historic ranches within the park and 32 historic buildings.

Fishing is excellent on both the Bighorn River and Bighorn Lake. Trout fishing on the Bighorn River is blue-ribbon quality with predominantly brown trout, but rainbows are also present. Year-round fishing on the lake offers walleye, yellow perch, crappie, catfish, ling, as well as brown and rainbow trout.

In 1997 entrance fees of $5 per vehicle per day were charged for the first time. Annual passes are also available. The fees are designed to provide revenues for maintenance work and improvements.

## VISITOR INFORMATION
Bighorn Canyon Visitor Center, 20 U.S. Hwy. 14-A East, Lovell, WY 82431;
open daily, 8:15 A.M. to 5 P.M.; (307) 548-2251
Yellowtail Dam Visitor Center on Montana 313, Fort Smith, MT; PO Box 548, Yellowtail, MT 59035;
open May through Labor Day; (406) 666-3234
Park Headquarters, Bighorn Canyon NRA, PO Box 458, Fort Smith, MT 59035; (406) 666-2412
Horseshoe Bend Ranger Station, entrance to Horseshoe Bend Campground; (307) 548-7236

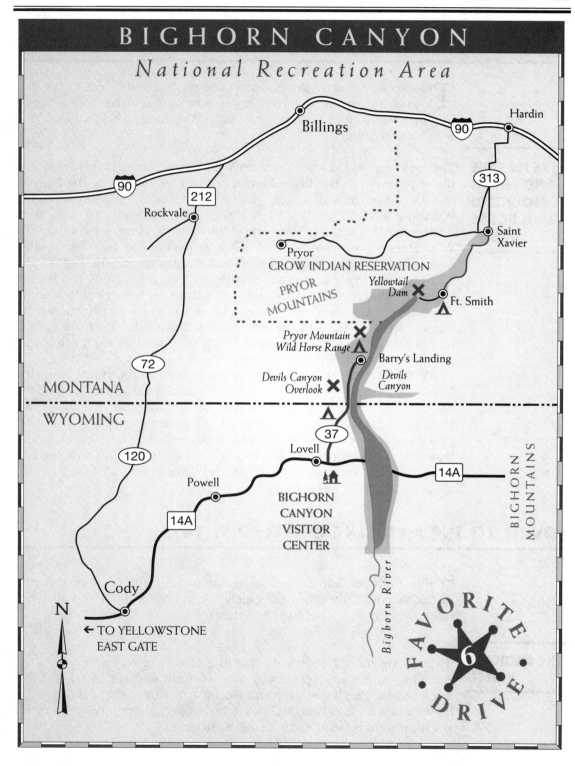

# BIGHORN CANYON
## National Recreation Area

Billings

Hardin

90

90

313

212

Rockvale

Saint Xavier

Pryor

CROW INDIAN RESERVATION

*PRYOR MOUNTAINS*

*Yellowtail Dam* ✕

Ft. Smith ⛺

Pryor Mountain Wild Horse Range ✕

⛺

72

Barry's Landing

*Devils Canyon*

Devils Canyon Overlook ✕

MONTANA

WYOMING

⛺

37

120

Lovell

Powell

🏠🏠

14A

BIGHORN CANYON VISITOR CENTER

14A

BIGHORN MOUNTAINS

Cody

N

← TO YELLOWSTONE EAST GATE

*Bighorn River*

★ FAVORITE DRIVE 6

## LOVELL TO PRYOR MOUNTAIN: WYOMING 37

This area is mostly dry country; the road travels west of the Yellowtail Reservoir. On your right, you can see the snow-capped Bighorn Mountains that range in both Wyoming and Montana. (See RV Caution below.)

**THE ICE CAVE AND PRYOR MOUNTAIN WILD HORSE RANGE**

The Ice Cave and Pryor Mountain Wild Horse Range is a federal wild horse preserve in the Pryor Mountains, administered by the Bureau of Land Management (BLM). Some horses may be seen from the Wyoming side. Take U.S. 14-A about 2.5 miles east of Lovell, turn north onto Wyoming 37 and travel 25 miles to Barry's Landing. The Wild Horse Protection Act of 1968 required the BLM to protect horses on the open range and establish quotas for the herds. The 100-year-old Pryor Mountain herd was given a quota of 100 horses by land managers in compliance with the new law. Horses wander the range in bands of from two or three up to about fifteen. Winter snows force the herd to the lower elevations for feed. In the spring, mares drop their foals. Stallions begin to challenge each other and gather bands usually in late May.

**RV CAUTION:** Another route into the wild horse range from the Montana side also leads to the Ice Cave and Wild Horse Range. The Ice Cave is noted for impressive ice formations and crystals. However, the fair-weather roads are not advisable for RVs. It is important to obtain detailed maps and a current weather report before traveling this back route; the roads are rough and the end reaches near the Wild Horse Range are 4-wheel drive only.

## LOVELL TO THE MEDICINE WHEEL: U.S. 14-A

This highway leaves the bottomlands and climbs high into the Bighorns. This is an extremely steep grade of 10 percent with tight switchbacks. Use good judgment.

**THE MEDICINE WHEEL**

If you're up for a 1-mile walk, put the Medicine Wheel on your stop list. The sacred site spreads across a windy plateau at 10,000 feet in elevation. You'll feel atop the world. A breathtaking landmark, it may make you breathless, if not light-headed as well. (Watch out for strenuous exercise at such a high altitude.)

*Medicine Wheel
in the Bighorn
Mountains, near
Lovell, Wyoming*
Courtesy Wyoming
Division of tourism

The Medicine Wheel is considered a source of spiritual and religious power to Native Americans. Limestone rocks are arranged in the shape of a wheel, an 80-foot-diameter circle with 28 "spokes." The stones are piled in such a way that they point to the rising of key stars on the summer solstice. These cairns also have other significant attributes that indicate an understanding of stellar alignments. Whether the wheel was built as a guide for astronomical understanding, or built along stellar lines to increase the sacred powers, are sides of an argument that continues today. The archaeologists and astronomists will have to figure it out.

Located in the Bighorn National Forest, the Medicine Wheel is administered by the U.S. Forest Service. To get there, turn off U.S. 14-A about 34 miles east of Lovell near the Bald Mountain Campground; watch for the sign that reads, "Medicine Wheel Archaeological Site."

**VISITOR
INFORMATION
& SERVICES**

Medicine Wheel Ranger District, Bighorn National Forest Office, 604 E. Main, Lovell, WY 82431; (307) 548-6541.

# CODY TO EMBLEM, BURLINGTON, OTTO, GREYBULL AND SHELL: U.S. 14/16/20

This highway takes you across miles of desert, barren sagebrush land that is mostly federal land. Though it looks sterile, you'll see plenty of antelope if you look closely, and if you park your vehicle and take a walk, you'll spot all sorts of wildlife activity. Imagine how tough the early pioneers had to be to eke an existence out of this waterless land.

**EMBLEM**

Both the state and federal government sought settlers to occupy the vast territory of Wyoming. Like much of the Bighorn Basin, water was the key. The federal government's Carey Act, named for Wyoming Senator Joseph Carey, provided that desert land be donated to the state once the land was irrigated, occupied and cultivated by settlers.

Water was diverted from the Greybull River to the Germania Bench by S. L. Wiley's Big Horn Basin Development Company. The canal, completed in 1902, was the state's first successful Carey Act Project. Wiley attracted some 600 German immigrants from Illinois and Iowa to occupy the land.

Until World War I, the German community and surrounding area were known as Germania and Germania Bench. Wyoming, which was staunchly patriotic, turned a watchful eye toward German aliens during the war years. German books were set ablaze at nearby Greybull and a few other towns. French replaced German in high school curricula. By 1918 the state librarian, Agnes Wright, had removed all German propaganda, books on explosives and neutrality, in cooperation with the government. Because of sentiments like these, brought out by the war, the name Germania was changed to Emblem. The name, Emblem, was selected for the American flag. The Germans wanted a new home.

Both Burlington and Otto are reached by turning off U.S. 14/16/20 onto Wyoming 30 just before Emblem. This is all farm country.

## BURLINGTON

The once-desert area, covered with sagebrush and sand, was settled in the 1890s. David P. Woodruff claimed a homestead and settled on the Wood River. A few hundred Mormon families followed and settled along the Greybull River, naming their town Burlington.

In keeping with their religion's decree to farm the land, they dug a ditch to carry water to the dry soil. The Mormon families worked with resolve to build an irrigation system that would become known as the Bench Canal. The canal was started in 1893 and completed in 1907, without government assistance.

Today, Burlington's economy is based solely on agriculture. Most residents live on farms surrounding the town. The major crops are sugar beets, barley, corn and hay. The town was recently incorporated in 1984.

## OTTO

Otto was named for German Count Otto Franc von Lichtenstein, the first big cattle rancher to settle in Bighorn Basin. Otto was the original owner of the huge Pitchfork Ranch, located west of Meeteetse, and settled there in 1878. He came out west from New York, drove a herd of cattle across the Owl Creek Mountains from Idaho, and established his ranch in the Bighorn Basin. The baron, who went by the name Otto Franc, opened the first U.S. post office on his ranch in 1882. Otto was well known for extending a helping hand to legitimate homesteaders, especially those settling along the Greybull River at Burlington, Germania (Emblem) and, of course, Otto.

## GREYBULL

The town of Greybull and the Greybull River both carry the name of an albino or gray bison bull who roamed the area. The albino bison, depicted on pictographs at the sandstone bluffs along the river, was held sacred by the Native tribes of the region.

Greybull is a farming and ranching community with a railroad background. The area was settled by cattlemen in the 1880s and 1890s. Farmers, predominantly members of the Church of Jesus Christ of Latter-Day Saints (Mormons), followed the cattlemen. The railroad's completion in 1909–10 and development of oil and gas exploration further spurred settlement of the area.

Today the community boasts a population of 2,000. In addition to two refineries, the area is also a center for bentonite production.

## OUTDOOR RECREATION AND ATTRACTIONS

Wide-open spaces are made for golfers. Greybull folks go to the Midway Golf Club, an 18-hole course north of Basin; (307) 568-2255.

An interesting site is the Old Stone Schoolhouse, built in 1903. The school building, 7 miles east of Greybull on U.S. 14, is listed on the National Register of Historic Places. It was the first nonlog community building to be built and was used as a school until the early 1950s. After that the town continued to use the building for town meetings until the 1970s. It has recently been renovated in keeping with its historical style. The Stone Schoolhouse can be reached at (307) 765-4384.

Near Greybull, along U.S. 14/16/20, is the South Big Horn County Airport. Many World War II planes, such as the PB4Y-2s, are here. The facility is home to the Hawkins & Powers Aviation firm, which operates a fire-retardant bomber/tanker service. Hawkins & Powers is one of the oldest aerial fire-fighting companies in the world. Their fleet of airplanes and helicopters is impressive, along with their contingent of over 40 pilots.

The Museum of Flight and Aerial Fire Fighting boasts a nationally renowned collection of World War II planes. Bombers, helicopters and the world's largest air tanker, the KC-97, are included. The museum is open in summer Monday to Friday, 8 A.M. to 6 P.M., Saturday and Sunday, 10 A.M. to 6 P.M., and weekdays, 8 A.M. to 5 P.M. in winter. For more information, contact Hawkins & Powers Aviation, Inc., Greybull Airport, 2441 Hwy. 20, Greybull, WY 82426; (307) 765-4482.

Interesting archeological and geological exhibits are on display at the Greybull Museum at 325 Greybull Ave. The museum is open at varying times depending on the season: June through Labor Day, weekdays, 10 A.M. to 8 P.M., Saturday 10 A.M. to 6 P.M.; September through October, weekdays, 1 P.M. to 5 P.M.; November through March, Monday, Wednesday, and Friday, 1 P.M. to 4 P.M., April through May, weekdays, 1 P.M. to 5 P.M.; (307) 765-2444.

A fun festival of the west is held in Greybull during the "Days of '49" Celebration. The annual event is held the second week of June. The Chamber of Commerce has dates and details.

## CAMPGROUNDS & RV PARKS

**OVERNIGHTING**

▲ *Best Shot for a Camp Spot*
Green Oasis Campground, on U.S. 14/16/20 at 12th Ave. N. 16 RV sites (9 pull-throughs), hook-ups and some services; open May 15 to September 30. Contact the Green Oasis Campground, 540 N. 12th Ave., Greybull, WY 82426; (307) 765-2856.

▲ *Best Shot for a Camp Spot*
Greybull KOA, 4 blocks north of U.S. 14 or 4 blocks east of U.S. 16/20. 62 RV sites (16 pull-throughs, 30 with full hook-ups, 32 with water and electric hook-ups), tables and grills, dump station, cable TV; large heated pool; open May 1 to October 15. Contact Bob and Marilyn Patterson, KOA, 333 N. 2nd, PO Box 387, Greybull, WY 82426; (307) 765-2555.

## GUEST RANCHES

The Hideout & Filtner Ranch, working cattle ranch established in 1906. Under current operation since 1982, the ranch offers authentic working cowboy adventures. Credit cards accepted; no pets allowed; open year-round; busiest from April through October, slowest from November through April. Contact David and Paula Filtner, 3208 Beaver Creek Rd., Greybull, WY 82426; (307) 765-2080; 1-800-354-8637.

**SUGGESTED DINING**

Lisa's Cafe, 200 Greybull St., Greybull, WY; (307) 765-4765.

Wheel's Inn Restaurant & Gift Shop, 1336 N. 6th, Greybull, WY; (307) 765-2456.

**VISITOR INFORMATION & SERVICES**

Greybull Chamber of Commerce, 333 Greybull Ave., Greybull, WY 82426; open May through October, 9:30 A.M. to 12:30 P.M., 1:30 P.M. to 4:30 P.M.; November through April, 10 A.M. to 12 P.M., 2 P.M. to 4 P.M.; (307) 765-2100.

Paintrock Ranger Station, U.S. Forest Service, 1220 N. 8th St., Greybull, WY 82425; (307) 765-4435.

**MEDICAL SERVICES**

For hospitals, see Cody (page 138) or Worland (page 166).

Big Horn Drug Store, 513 Greybull Ave., Greybull, WY; open Monday through Friday, 8:30 A.M. to 5:30 P.M., and Saturday, 8:30 A.M. to 4 P.M.; (307) 755-4601, after hours 765-4678.

| | |
|---|---|
| **REPAIR & TOWING** | Rich's Towing & Auto Repair (AAA-rated), 24-hour service, 1000 N. 6th, Greybull, WY; (307) 765-4767; 1-800-871-4767. |
| **VETERINARY SERVICES** | See Cody (page 139) or Worland (page 167). |

# GREYBULL EAST TO SHELL: U.S. 14/16/20, OR SOUTH TO WORLAND: U.S. 16/20

You can head across ranchlands to the quaint little community of Shell, or turn south and head to Worland and Kirby through Basin. This is farm and ranch country, and the road travels next to the Bighorn River for the entire distance. If you're heading east through Shell, be advised the grade over the Bighorns is steep, though the highway is in excellent shape.

**SHELL**  A favored place by geologists, Shell takes its name from the invertebrate fossil shells common in the area. Ranching and farming are still the mainstays of the Shell area. The drive along U.S. 14 into the Bighorn Mountains is spectacular. Shell Canyon is a Scenic Byway and along the beautiful drive you can find many educational signs describing the age of the rock layers. The highway winds along Shell Creek, up, or down depending on your direction, through a beautiful canyon, changing in elevation from 4,210 to 9,003 feet as you climb to the top of the Bighorn Mountain Range. The Visitor Center has a lookout over the 120-foot Shell Falls, and information on the incredible geology exposed throughout the canyon. It's worth the stop.

There are also major dinosaur digs in the Shell area, and 4-wheel drive is recommended to reach them. Twelve large Jurassic Era sauropods have been excavated on the dig sites since 1934. The dinosaur bed dig sites are located 10 miles north of Shell on BLM land and are open to the public. Once again, if you're towing that 4-wheel-drive unit, now's the time for it.

**OVERNIGHTING**             **CAMPGROUNDS & RV PARKS**

Granite Creek Trailer Park—U.S. Forest Service Campground, 15 miles northeast of Shell on U.S. 14, then north on Forest Service Road 255. 26 RV sites (no pull-throughs), no hook-ups or services; open June 1 to October 31.

Cabin Creek Trailer Park—U.S. Forest Service Campground, 15 miles northeast of Shell on U.S. 14, then south on Forest Service Road 251. 26 RV sites (no pull-throughs), no hook-ups or services; open June 1 to October 31.

Ranger Creek—U.S. Forest Service Campground, 15 miles northeast of Shell on U.S. 14, then 2 miles on Forest Service Road 251. 10 RV sites (no pull-throughs), no hook-ups or services; open May 30 to October 31.

Shell Creek—U.S. Forest Service Campground, 15 miles northeast of Shell on U.S. 14, then 1 mile south on Forest Service Road 251. 11 RV sites (no pull-throughs), no hook-ups or services; open May 30 to October 31.

## BED & BREAKFAST ESTABLISHMENTS

Trapper's Rest Bed & Breakfast, cabin and tipi accommodations. The establishment has been under current operation since 1995. Some credit cards accepted; open year-round. Contact H. Jade Smith, 4351 Trapper Creek Rd., Box 166, Shell, WY 82441; (307) 765-9239.

## GUEST RANCHES

Kedesh Ranch, working guest ranch located 4 miles east of Shell on U.S. 14. There is access for small and medium-sized RVs. The ranch has been under current operation since 1988. Credit cards accepted; no pets allowed. Contact Chuck and Gail Lander, 1940 U.S. 14, Shell, WY 82441; (307) 765-2791.

Mayland Ranch Recreation & Snowshoe Lodge, on Snowshoe Pass in the Bighorn Mountains off the main highway on gravel road. Under current operation since 1993; credit cards accepted; pets are allowed; open year-round; busiest in winter, slowest in spring. Contact Martin and Diana Mayland, Box 215, 3226 Highline Dr., Shell, WY 82441; (307) 765-2669; (307) 568-2960.

Shell Creek Guest Ranch, under current operation since 1993. Credit cards accepted; pets are allowed; open year-round; busiest from May through October, slowest from November through April. Contact Bruce and Keiko Keller, 1710 Hwy. 14, Shell, WY 82441; (307) 765-2420; fax: (307) 765-2442.

| | |
|---|---|
| **SUGGESTED DINING** | Wagon Wheel Lodge, U.S. 14, Shell, WY; (307) 765-2561. |
| **VISITOR INFORMATION & SERVICES** | See Greybull (page 158). |

**RV CAUTION: State-designated Wyoming Backway: Red Gulch Road/Alkali Road**

Don't be tempted to take the back road from Shell to Hyattville. The Backway route, named Red Gulch Road/Alkali Road, traverses very colorful badlands and canyons along the foothills of the Bighorn Mountains. Although the area is rich in scenery and archaeological finds, the road is definitely not for an RV. Wyoming backcountry roads can be deceiving. The surface of this road looks almost like concrete. You'd never want to have to dig fenceposts along it for a living. But the least amount of rain makes the road impassable. The clay soil overlaying shale has a high content of bentonite. An otherwise valuable mineral, bentonite is a unique colloidal clay. *Coll* stems from the Greek word *koll*, and means "glue." Get it? If that doesn't quell your wandering spirit for off-road adventure, then take along some good hiking boots—and lunch. You'll have to wait for the road to dry before you can walk out.

**BASIN AND VICINITY**

Basin was settled as a farming and ranching community. The most notable point in its history occurred in 1896 when it won the honor of being chosen as the county seat for Big Horn County. Many Wyoming communities contested for status as the county seat. Basin battled it out in the press with the town of Otto, and eventually Cody, which entered the race at the tail end. The editors of the two newspapers, cowboy journalist Joe Magill of the *Basin City Herald* and New York editor Tom Dagget of the *Otto Courier*, voiced the benefits and attitudes of each town. In the end, it was said that Basin, the underdog, won the race because Cody pulled votes away from Otto.

As a county seat, Basin was able to pull through the lean times when many small communities like Otto and Manderson withered. Today, the county business along with the relatively new state retirement center provide a basis for commerce for Basin's population of 1,200. However, there is no comparison to Cody in size. Eventually Cody won the Park County seat, which encompassed much of the land included in Big Horn County in 1896.

The most impressive building in Basin is the brick courthouse. In 1909, the trial that sealed the end of the violent range wars took place inside its hallowed walls. Bitter feuds were waged for 20 years between cattle and sheep interests, because of the competition for sparse forage and water as well as a personal distaste for each other's herds. The feuds came to a head when seven cattlemen were brought to trial for the murders of three sheep ranchers. The attack on the sheep camp near Ten Sleep was made at night. Two men were murdered in their beds. The story goes that the third sheep rancher was shot as he came out of the wagon with hands held high above his head. Wyoming citizens had had enough; the cattlemen's violence had gone too far. Although the cattlemen hired the F. Lee Bailey of their day, the legal battle was less than expected. The first trial, for first-degree murder, ended quickly with a guilty verdict. Witnesses testified that Albert Brink had shot the sheep man as he emerged from the wagon. Brink's appeal resulted in a guilty verdict and life imprisonment. The remaining six men plea-bargained for lesser sentences. The success of the prosecutors sent a clear message, and the violence pretty much ceased in Wyoming. Unfortunately, the range wars continued until the 1920s in other states.

**OUTDOOR RECREATION AND ATTRACTIONS**

The Midway Golf Club, an 18-hole course north of Basin is open to the public. The address is 4053 Golf Course Rd., Basin, WY; (307) 568-2255.

The Big Horn County Fair and Bean Festival is held in August. Stop in and share the bounty of ranch life, plus great food and western entertainment. For specific dates and information, contact the Big Horn County Fair Board Office, Fairgrounds, Basin, WY 82410; (307) 568-2968.

**OVERNIGHTING**

### BED & BREAKFAST ESTABLISHMENTS

Harmony Ranch Cottage, 2.5 miles east of Manderson; the last three-quarter mile is dirt road. The farmhouse has cooking facilities and three guest rooms. No credit cards; pets and children welcome; open year-round; busiest from September through March, slowest in summer. Contact Nancy and John Joyce, 182 Hwy. 31, PO Box 25; Manderson, WY 82432; (307) 568-2514.

### GUEST RANCHES

Bighorn Rodeo Ranch, western working guest ranch located 1 mile off paved road. Lodging accommodations are in log cabins. Credit cards accepted; open year-round; busiest from May through August, slowest in winter. Contact Bill and Diana Butler, Box 834, 480 Road $12\frac{1}{2}$, Basin, WY 82410; (307) 762-3535; fax: (307) 762-3444.

| | |
|---|---|
| **SUGGESTED DINING** | Outpost Supper Club & Lounge, 115 N. 4th, Basin, WY; (307) 568-2134. |
| | Big B, 602 S. 4th, Basin, WY; (307) 568-2246. |
| **VISITOR INFORMATION & SERVICES** | For visitor information, see Worland (page 166). |
| **MEDICAL SERVICES** | Big Horn Clinic, 509 W. B Street, Basin, WY 82410; (307) 568-2499. |
| | Midway Medical Clinic, 388 S. U.S. 20, Basin, WY; open Monday through Friday, 9 A.M. to 5 P.M.; (307) 568-3311. |
| **REPAIR & TOWING** | Rick's Towing and Auto Repair, 1000 N. 6th St., Greybull, WY 82410; (307) 765-4767; after hours, (307) 765-2755. |
| **VETERINARY SERVICES** | Graham Veterinary Hospital, Timothy Graham, DVM, 314 W. E, Basin, WY 82410; (307) 568-9305; after hours, (307) 568-2967. |

# MANDERSON TO HYATTVILLE: WYOMING 31

**HYATTVILLE**

This peaceful ranching community gets its name from Sam Hyatt, the area's first postmaster back in 1886. Hyatt moved over the Bighorns from Buffalo to operate the post office. Mail was delivered once a month from Fort Washakie, 175 miles to the west.

Some of the residents of the small community of Hyattville are descendants of a colorful character in the pages of Wyoming history. In the mid-1800s, Asa Mercer persuaded a group of New York women to become the first mail-order brides. The women agreed to sail around the continent to become brides of pioneer men settling in Washington State. The unusual method of acquiring one's bride received national attention. Mercer and his new bride, a woman from the group, settled in Washington. There he helped establish the University of Washington and served as its first president. He then moved to Cheyenne to publish the *North Western Live Stock Journal.*

In 1894 he published *Banditti of the Plains*, a story of the Johnson County Invasion, which took place just two years before. His book told the tale of the bloody war between the big cattlemen who owned giant ranches and the small cattlemen. Sides were drawn

*It's not uncommon to see a flock of sheep being driven along a Wyoming highway.*

between the big Wyoming Stock Growers' Association and the new Northern Wyoming Farmers and Stock Growers' Association. The war culminated in 1892 when U.S. cavalry troops put an end to a siege between the big cattlemen's invaders and the Johnson County cattlemen. Because Asa Mercer told it straight and did not defend the big cattlemen in his new book, he fell from grace with the powerful ranchers. He had to flee Cheyenne after a fire burnt out his office and sent his new book up in flames. At last, Mercer settled in Hyattville where his descendants still remain.

Hyattville was originally known as Paintrock, named for the petroglyphs at Medicine Lodge Creek about 6 miles to the north. Even the rough cowboys and settlers recognized the importance of the ancient rock paintings (*pictographs*) and carvings (*petroglyphs*) found along the red cliff wall. Researchers have uncovered over 60 cultural levels, thousands of artifacts and several burial sites at the ancient campground, considered one of the most important archaeological sites in the world. The initial discovery in 1971 uncovered artifacts such as pottery, glass beads, tools and quartzite projectiles dating back 8,300 years. Subsequent discoveries have unearthed 10,000 years of history at the site.

The early dwellers were described by archaeologist George Frison as having an average lifespan of 30 to 35 years. He explained that their lifespan was short because they prepared much of their roots, grass and seed diet by grinding it with sandstone tools called *metates*. The grit left by the sandstone eventually wore away their teeth, and thus, their ability to eat. Without nutrition, they succumbed to an early death.

Drawn to the area because of the protection provided by the 750-foot-long cliff, ancient tribes found good water, shade in summer and quartzite for toolmaking. In more recent times, the Crow and Shoshone lived in the area. Today, preserved as a state park, the area along Paintrock Creek offers a secure and comfortable campsite, as it has for centuries.

The Medicine Lodge State Archaeological Site State Park is 6 miles northeast of Hyattville. From Hyattville go north and turn right onto Cold Springs Road, then go 4 miles and turn left at the sign to Medicine Lodge, then 1.5 miles up the gravel road to the park. The site is open May through early November. **RV CAUTION:** Before entering the area, check with the Bighorn National Forest Service Ranger District Office in Greybull for road conditions, current maps and additional information, as many of the roads in the area become 4-wheel drive only; (307) 765-4435.

## WORLAND

Worland is at the junction of Fifteen Mile Creek and the Bighorn River. The town was founded because of the area's agricultural potential and grew up under the influence of the plow. The town is now surrounded by irrigated farmlands.

Charlie "Dad" Worland homesteaded the site in 1900. Although a farmer by trade, he first opened a stage station and saloon to make his living. The agricultural potential was there, but water was needed. In 1905, Worland convinced engineers of the Hanover Canals Company to found a townsite near his homestead. The Hanover Canal is still used, along with many others, to provide water to farms in the Bighorn Basin. Several different crops were tried by farmers through the years: emmer wheat (made into cereal), alfalfa and sugar beet. Cattle and sheep ranching became important. The main cash crop became the sugar beet, attracting many settlers, particularly German and Ukrainian farmers.

A sugar beet factory, begun in 1916, was completed in 1918 after a delay during World War I. In 1920 it became the Holly Sugar Company. Today, it is Wyoming's oldest sugar-processing mill and currently supports 15,000 acres of sugar beets.

Worland became the Washakie County Seat. Like many western towns, Worland had its boom times. In 1917, oil was discovered in the Hidden Dome field. The oil was pumped out, and the boom times faded. However, the demand for sugar beets grew, and over the years the farmers expanded to other crops, to sheep and cattle ranching, and to feedlot operations. In the 1990s, barley crops were produced under contract to both the Coors and Anheuser-Busch breweries.

Today, even though there are 5,700 residents, Worland still has a stage-stop feel. It's a good place to rest and take shelter from the wide-open country around it.

### Charlie "Dad" Worland

Charlie "Dad" Worland, a tree-seedling peddler from Missouri, saw his future in the long growing season, good soil and hot summer temperatures in Wyoming. In 1900 he claimed a homestead at the mouth of Fifteen Mile Creek. Worland took advantage of the location that was on the stage route between Thermopolis and Basin. He opened a stage station and saloon. As timber was scarce, he built his establishment by digging a cave into the riverbank and extending log walls out front. The saloon was fittingly known as the "Hole-in-the-Wall." A. G. Rupp came along and built a general supply store in the same riverbank cave manner, and the settlement began to grow. Notorious outlaw Butch Cassidy was known to pass through the town. As the story goes, Rupp first met Cassidy as he gazed upon a poster tacked on the general store wall. The poster offered a $5,000 reward for George Leroy Parker, alias Butch Cassidy, dead or alive. The picture wasn't a real good likeness, and when Cassidy commented on that fact, Rupp agreed and promptly followed the outlaw's request to take it down.

**ATTRACTIONS**

The Washakie County Museum and Cultural Center is inside the LDS church. Exhibits and displays feature Native American artifacts, ranch equipment, cowboy gear, and an interesting geology and fossil collection. The museum is at 1115 Obie Sue Ave., in Worland; (307) 347-4102.

Near the Washakie County Court House at 10th and Big Horn Avenue, there is a fountain that is fed by a 4,330-foot-deep artesian well. The well is 23 miles north of Worland and flows at 14,000 gallons per minute. Incredibly, there is sufficient pressure to push water the entire 23 miles to Worland.

August is fair time and Worland makes no exception. The Washakie County Fair is held at the Washakie County Fairground, 602 Fifteen Mile Rd., Worland, WY 82401. For specific dates, call (307) 347-8989.

**OVERNIGHTING**

**CAMPGROUNDS & RV PARKS**

Worland Cowboy Campground, 2401 Big Horn Avenue #3 (just 1 mile east of Junction of U.S. 16 and U.S. 20 South); open April to October; (307) 347-2329.

**SUGGESTED DINING**

Ram's Horn Café, 629 Big Horn, Worland, WY; (307) 347-6351.

The Office Lounge & Restaurant, 1515 Big Horn, Worland, WY; (307) 347-8171.

Antone's Supper Club, 973 Hwy. 16, Worland, WY; (307) 347-9261.

Harry's Steak House, 1620 Big Horn, Worland, WY; (307) 347-9261.

**VISITOR INFORMATION & SERVICES**

Worland Chamber of Commerce, 120 N. 10th St., Worland, WY; (307) 347-3226.

While you're visiting the town's sights, you may park your RV at the Washakie County Court House parking lot. Unfortunately, there is only limited street parking available at the Chamber of Commerce offices.

Bighorn National Forest, Ten Sleep Ranger Station, 2009 Big Horn Ave., Worland, WY; (307) 347-8291.

**MEDICAL SERVICES**

Washakie Memorial Hospital, 24-hour emergency room, 400 S. 15th, Worland, WY 82401; (307) 347-3221.

Graham's Family Pharmacy, 719 Big Horn, Worland, WY; open Monday through Friday, 8:30 A.M. to 5:30 P.M., and Saturday, 8 A.M. to noon; (307) 347-2851; after hours, Robert Horne's residence (307) 347-4569.

Ricker Pharmacy, 738 Big Horn, Worland, WY; (307) 347-2282; after hours, call Felix Mercado's residence (307) 347-4507.

**REPAIR & TOWING**

Washakie Garage, 1054 U.S. 20 North, Worland, WY 82401; (307) 347-4156; after hours (307) 347-4507.

**VETERINARY SERVICES**

Cloud Peak Veterinary Services, P.C., Dan R. Miller, DVM, 801 N. 10th, Worland, WY 82401; (307) 347-2781.

**KIRBY**

In 1878 the first settlement on the Bridger Trail was claimed by Kris Kirby, a cowboy from Texas. The small town that sits on the Bighorn River was named for Kirby along with a tributary creek. The stage route from Thermopolis to Casper followed Kirby Creek, and outlaws from the "Hole-in-the-Wall" gang often met along its banks. If you continue 12 miles down the road, you'll come to Thermopolis.

# CODY, MEETEETSE AND THERMOPOLIS: WYOMING 120

This highway winds gradually through a combination of ranch and grassland, and, once past Meeteetse, is almost all sagebrush and juniper trees in rocky terrain. Though you can't see much of it from the highway, this country holds several oil-producing areas.

**MEETEETSE**

The wooden sidewalks and hitching rails symbolize the past of this small western cowtown. The early history of this town is preserved in its old buildings, and more by the manner of its residents. In 1904, the population of Meeteetse grew to 400; today the population is roughly the same.

The site was originally claimed as a homestead by a blacksmith, William McNally, in August 1883. It cost McNally $6 to file the claim. After two years, McNally sold out for $2,500 to Anna W. Thomas (What a profit on that investment!). Anna and her husband surveyed the townsite in 1896, and the town was established on the south side of the Greybull River. Local residents took to using the name of a post office that had been operating on the north side of the river, Meeteetse.

Meeteetse, (pronounced ma-TEET-see), comes from a Shoshone word with various meanings, such as the "meeting place," "near-by place," "long way from water," and "place of rest." According to L. G. Phelps of the Pitchfork Ranch, the word meant the "meeting place" and how it was pronounced, in short syllables or long and slow, indicated the distance to the meeting site.

The town was situated at the junction of the main route north to Billings and east from Pitchfork (today's State Highways 120 and 290). In its heyday, the area was the center of activity for the Greybull River country and several big cattle ranches. The way of the ranchers strongly influenced the town.

The largest and most prominent ranch, the Pitchfork, was founded on the Greybull River in 1878 by German Count Otto Franc von Lichtenstein. Known in Wyoming as Otto Franc, he became one of the great cattle barons of the area as well as a notable big-game hunter. The Lichtenstein ranch became known for its brand, the Pitchfork.

Franc often battled cattle and horse rustlers, including George Leroy Parker, better known as the notorious outlaw Butch Cassidy. Although acquitted at a trial in Lander, Cassidy was convicted on a second complaint by prosecutor Bill Simpson. The distinguished Wyoming family of former Governor Milward and Senator Alan Simpson are descendants of the successful attorney. Butch Cassidy prospered in a life of crime after serving his two-year jail term, and claimed Otto Franc drove him to it.

Relentless in fighting outlaws, Franc welcomed legitimate home-steaders, especially the Mormons who settled along the Greybull River Valley. The town of Otto is named after him. After Franc died in 1903, the ranch was sold to Louis Graham Phelps, a wealthy cat-tleman and land baron.

Through the years the ranch shrank and then in 1972 expanded again as descendants purchased holdings to increase the ranch to close to its original size. In 1978, the Phelps family celebrated the centennial of the 250,000-acre ranch. Passed down through the female line, the Pitchfork is operated by the Phelps family to this day. However, that may change in the near future since the ranch is now up for sale.

One of the most notable eras at the Pitchfork was during the 1930s, when it was run by Eugene Phelps with his sister Frances and brother-in-law, Charles Belden. A nationally acclaimed photographer, Charlie Belden's work depicted the vanishing cowboy's life. His work is on display at the museum in Cody as well as other places in the state.

A historic building, the Meeteetse Mercantile, was built in 1899. The old bank building, which now houses the Meeteetse Museum, was spared by Butch Cassidy, who wouldn't rob the bank where his friends kept their dough.

**OUTDOOR RECREATION AND ATTRACTIONS**

If you're feeling energetic or looking for a great place to take a horseback ride, Meeteetse is the spot. The Anderson Lodge was built in 1903 by A. A. Anderson, the organizer and first superintendent of the Forest Service (Forest Reserve). Anderson, a famous portrait painter, used the lodge as an artist's studio. The two-story lodge has been restored and is listed on the National Register of Historic Places. A fascinating page from history, the Anderson Lodge is only accessible by hiking or horseback riding up Vick Creek Trail 5.5 miles. Ask at the Meeteetse Visitor Information Center for details.

There are three museums in Meeteetse. The Meeteetse Bank Museum at 1033 Park Avenue is open May 15 to September 30, Monday to Saturday, 10 A.M. to 5 P.M.; Sunday, 1 P.M. to 4 P.M. The Hall Museum has interesting collections of historic photographs, ranching and cowboy gear and pioneer memorabilia. The Hall Museum is at 942 Mondell Street; open May 15 to September 30, Monday to Saturday, 10 A.M. to 5 P.M.; Sunday, 1 P.M. to 4 P.M. Both museums offer tours by request, (307) 868-2423. The Charles J. Belden Museum-Western Photography is open May 15 to September 30, daily from 9 A.M. to 5 P.M. The museum features 1930s–40s photographs taken by famous photographer Charles Belden on the Pitchfork Ranch. The beautiful photographs depict ranch life and the western cowboy.

Meeteetse is well known for its Labor Day Weekend Celebration. The celebration was first organized in 1912 by Josh Dean, who barbecued a whole beef in a pit. It took two to three days cooking time to have the beef ready to serve on Labor Day. Thousands came from all over the Bighorn Basin to enjoy the free meal and festivities. Today, the traditional barbecue continues, although prepared in a more modern way. There's a rodeo, a parade, games for kids, music, an arts and crafts and collectibles show, a shutterbug show, a tug-of-war, open house at the three museums, a ferret race and dancing.

**OVERNIGHTING**

## CAMPGROUNDS & RV PARKS

Oasis Campground, on north side of the bridge at Meeteetse. RV sites available (no pull-throughs), full hook-ups; open year-round. Contact Oasis Campground, PO Box 86, 1702 State St., Meeteetse, WY 82433; (307) 868-2551; fax: 868-2687; 1-888-568-2570.

Brown Mountain—U.S. Forest Service Campground, 6 miles southwest of Meeteetse on Wyoming 290, then 15.8 miles southwest on County Road, 3.2 miles west on Forest Service Road. 6 RV sites (no pull-throughs), no hook-ups or services; open May 31 to November 15.

Jack Creek—U.S. Forest Service Campground, 11 miles west of Meeteetse on Wyoming 290, then 15.3 miles west on Forest Service Road 208. 7 RV sites (no pull-throughs), no hook-ups or services; open year-round.

Wood River—U.S. Forest Service Campground, 6 miles southwest of Meeteetse on Wyoming 290, then 15.8 miles southwest on County Road, 3 miles west on Forest Service Road 200. 5 RV sites (no pull-throughs), no hook-ups or services; open June 1 to November 15.

## BED & BREAKFAST ESTABLISHMENTS

Doc Bennett Bed & Breakfast, historic home under current operation since 1995. Reservations suggested; no credit cards accepted; pets allowed; open year-round; busiest in September through November, slowest in April and May. Contact Janet Griffith, 2005 Warren, PO Box 403, Meeteetse, WY 82433; (307) 868-2486.

Broken Spoke Bed & Breakfast, in operation since 1994. Credit cards accepted; no pets; open year-round. Contact Shirley Peterson, 1943 State St., Meeteetse, WY 82433; (307) 868-2362.

Ranch At Meeteetse Bed & Breakfast, 28 miles southwest of Cody. The ranch is a working cattle ranch. Activities include riding, roping, swimming and relaxing. Contact Linda Bilyeu, 544 Lower Greybull River Rd., Meeteetse, WY 82433; (307) 868-9266; 1-800-868-9266.

**SUGGESTED DINING**

Broken Spoke, 1943 State St., Meeteetse, WY; (307) 868-2362.

**VISITOR INFORMATION & SERVICES**

Meeteetse Tourist Information Center, 1033 Park Ave., PO Box 509, Meeteetse, WY 82433; open May 15 through September 30, Tuesday through Saturday, 9 A.M. to 5 P.M.; October 1 through May 14, Monday, Tuesday and Friday, 9 A.M. to 5 P.M.; (307) 868-2423.

**MEDICAL SERVICES**

Meeteetse Medical Clinic, 1909 Franklin, Meeteetse, WY; open Wednesdays from 9 A.M. to noon; (307) 686-2504.

**VETERINARY SERVICES**

Gould Veterinary Clinic, Bill Gould, DVM, 123 Pitchfork Rd., Meeteetse, WY; (307) 868-2440 (day or night).

## The Black-Footed Ferret

The only known colony of black-footed ferrets was found on the Pitchfork Ranch in 1981. The animal had been listed as an endangered species in 1967, and many researchers thought it extinct. Wildlife researchers believed the newly found Pitchfork colony was in danger from an outbreak of canine distemper, and so moved them to the Sybille Canyon Research Station near Laramie. A captive-breeding program was begun by the Wyoming Game and Fish Department. Fundraising efforts were undertaken. Among them was a painting done by Wyoming artist Vivi Crandall, who donated all the proceeds to the ferret program. The funds collected were substantial.

In 1991 the first captive raised ferrets were released in the Medicine Bow and Shirley Basin areas. The prairie dog is the ferret's chief food source. Plague epidemics and rancher killings have reduced the prairie dogs, which in turn makes it more difficult for the ferrets. Although the survival rate has been poor, the ferrets are making a slow recovery.

**THERMOPOLIS**  Thermopolis, home of the world's largest hot springs, was named in 1894 by Dr. Julius A. Schuelke, a German physician. Unlike most common names in Wyoming, the sophisticated name is derived from the Latin word *thermae* for heat and the Greek word *polis* for city, meaning the "City of Hot Springs." Dr. Schuelke visited the area to obtain water samples for analysis in the 1890s. Shortly after that, the U.S. Government began its campaign to regain this area from the Wind River Indian Reservation.

Although the Shoshone and Arapaho tribes shared the reservation, the Thermopolis area belonged to Chief Washakie and his Shoshone. Long revered as a sacred area, the Shoshone believed the Great Spirit had led them through the Wind River Canyon to the hot springs. The mineral springs were called *Bah-que-wana*, or "Smoking Water," by the Shoshone, who believed the waters had healing qualities.

In 1896, the government completed a treaty with the Shoshone and Arapaho, acquiring 10 square miles around the Big Springs area for $60,000—a bargain. Shoshone Chief Washakie ceded the area only on the condition that some of the waters be kept free and open to all people forever, and that a campground be reserved for the Natives. "I, Washakie, chief of Shoshone, freely give to the great white father these waters, beloved by my people; that all may receive that great blessing of bodily health in the bathing," stated Washakie. To comply with these terms, the U.S. Government gave 1 square mile of land, including the hot springs, to the State of

Wyoming. Wyoming then established the Hot Springs State Park, and a public bathhouse. To date, despite a 1974 request by park officials to charge a fee, lawmakers have provided that the park is still free and open to the use of all people.

Thermopolis is a pleasant tourism center with a population of 3,800.

## OUTDOOR RECREATION AND ATTRACTIONS

Anglers will want to purchase a Wyoming fishing license and a Wind River Indian Reservation permit in Thermopolis in order to enjoy the excellent fishing in the Bighorn River, Wind River Canyon and Boysen State Park (see page 178). The Chamber of Commerce can provide information on fishing guides in the area.

Golfers can enjoy a round of golf at the #15 Legion Golf Course & Pro Shop. The 9-hole course is on Airport Road. Call for tee times; (307) 864-5294.

At the foot of Monument Hill, Big Springs boils up from an unknown depth at a temperature of 135 degrees Fahrenheit and flows at approximately 3.6 million gallons per day. Believed to be the largest hot springs in the world, the blue-green waters flow out into several ponds and then cascade down mineral terraces into the Bighorn River. Created over thousands of years, the Big Horn Hot Springs Terraces are chiefly composed of lime and gypsum, a mineral compound known as travertine. The beautiful mauve and gold coloring of the travertine is due to the many species of algae that thrive in the warm waters of Big Horn Spring. As the algae dies, the color disappears, leaving only the white travertine.

*Hot springs at Thermopolis, among the biggest in the country*

*The hot springs in Thermopolis*

Many visitors walk the path across the travertine ledges and between the ponds, sampling the mineral-rich water. The short walk leads to the Swinging Bridge. Originally built in 1916, it was condemned in 1984; restoration efforts completed the new bridge in 1992. Be sure to cross the swaying bridge for a scenic view of the terraces—marvelous colors and mounded shapes that sparkle as the water falls down to the smooth flowing waters of the Bighorn River.

The rich mineral waters have made Thermopolis, and Hot Springs State Park, a popular place for many decades. Today it is known as the best place to "soak, swim or slide." Indoor and outdoor water slides are offered by two privately operated pools. The Hot Springs Water Park is open 7 days a week, 9 A.M. to 9 P.M.; (307) 864-9250. The Star Plunge also has slides and pools; call (307) 864-3771. The State of Wyoming operates a free bathhouse at Hot Springs State Park. The bathhouse is open Monday through Saturday, 8 A.M. to 6 P.M.; Sunday and holidays, noon to 6 P.M. Many other hot mineral water pools for soaking may be found in town.

The Holiday Inn at Hot Springs State Park, (307) 864-3131, hosts Wyoming's largest wildlife display with animals from around the world. The state park is also home to about 15 bison, who freely roam the Buffalo Pasture located on the east side of the park.

The Wyoming Dinosaur Center is within minutes of Hot Springs State Park. The road signs from the park make it easy to find. The large museum complex, completed in 1995, has excellent displays and educational exhibits, plus guided tours are offered to actual dinosaur excavation sites. On the nearby Black Butte Ranch, the skeleton of a brachiosaur has been unearthed, and crews are currently working on a camarasaur, a herbivorous dinosaur. Just visit, or "dig-for-a-day" (fee required). Contact the dinosaur center at 1-800-455-DINO, or (307) 864-2997.

Among the exhibits featured at the Hot Springs County Historical Museum is the cherrywood bar from the Hole-in-the-Wall Saloon where Butch Cassidy and members of the infamous outlaw gang stopped to wet their whistle. Other displays include local and Native American artifacts, and scenes depicting frontier life. The museum features a fun family night with the Little Broadway Theater. The presentation of "Oils Well That Ends Well" is melodrama comedy at its best. Join the entertainment every night except Sunday. The Hot Springs County Historical Museum is at 700 Broadway, Thermopolis, WY.

The area surrounding Thermopolis is rich with interesting scenery and Native American culture. Legend Rock Petroglyph Site, about 25 miles northwest of Thermopolis, is Wyoming's most impressive petroglyph area with 283 pictures dating back 2,000 years. The petroglyphs are carved on sandstone cliffs in the foothills of the Owl Creek Mountains. Archaeologists think the rock art was associated with shamanism and ritual healing. The area is located on Cottonwood Creek Road near the remote Hamilton Dome oil fields. A quarter-mile hike is required after driving over about 8 miles of gravel roads. A descriptive guide map and specific directions (a good idea) are available at the Hot Springs State Park office in Thermopolis. It is also possible to obtain a key to drive in closer to the site for those who may have difficulty hiking the hill. However, it is not advisable to drive the last quarter-mile with an RV.

To reach the site, go north on Wyoming 120 to the Hamilton Dome Road turnoff (Wyoming 170); after 5 miles turn right onto the gravel Cottonwood Creek Road. Continue 2 miles to the second cattle guard and follow the road a short distance to a parking area in front of a gate. Then walk down the hill to the cliffs.

**RV CAUTION:** These roads are fair-weather dirt/gravel roads. Heed the warning and only visit this site if there's no prediction of rain.

As you're traveling the Hamilton Dome area, avoid visiting Anchor Dam, which lies farther west of Legend Rock. There's not much point in jarring your back bouncing over several additional miles of gravel to see a dam that won't hold water. The dam, finished in 1960, turned out to be a costly engineering faux pas. The lake bed rests above porous limestone that leaches the water away.

The month of August is a great time to visit Thermopolis. The Gift of the Waters Pageant is put on by Shoshone from the Wind River Reservation and local residents. The pageant features performances that celebrate the gift of the hot springs from the Shoshone and Arapaho to the federal government. Tipi camps are set up by Natives from the Wind River Reservation who assist in the performances.

Another fun August event is the Outlaw Trail Ride. Participants ride the escape trail of Butch Cassidy, the Sundance Kid and the Wild Bunch for a fee. Cover over 100 miles and experience the west astride the original horsepower. Contact: Outlaw Trail, Inc., Box 1046, Thermopolis, WY 82443; (307) 864-2287.

## CAMPGROUNDS & RV PARKS

▲ *Best Shot for a Camp Spot*
Country Campin', 5 miles north of Thermopolis on East Sunnyside Lane, North U.S. 20, Thermopolis, WY 82443. 40 RV sites (pull-throughs), full hook-ups and some services; open April 1 to November 1; features include guided fishing and horseback riding. Contact Country Campin' at (307) 864-2416; 1-800-609-2244; e-mail: camp@trib.com

Eagle RV Park, 204 South U.S. 20, Thermopolis, WY 82443. 45 RV sites (23 pull-throughs), hook-ups and some services; swimming pool; open year-round; (307) 864-5262.

Fountain of Youth RV Park, 250 North U.S. 20. 52 RV sites (pull-throughs), hook-ups and some services; features a large mineral pool; open March 1 to October 31. Send inquiries to PO Box 711, Thermopolis, WY 82443; (307) 864-3265.

Grandview Trailer Park, 122 South U.S. 20. 21 RV sites (pull-throughs), no hook-ups; dump station and some services available; open May 1 to October 15. Send inquiries to Box 139, U.S. 20 South, Thermopolis, WY 82443; (307) 864-3463.

M/K RV Park, 720 Shoshoni, Thermopolis, WY 82443. 10 RV sites (no pull-throughs), hook-ups and some services; open April 15 to October 15; (307) 864-2778.

Latchstring RV Park, 204 South U.S. 20, Thermopolis, WY 82443; (307) 864-5262.

New RV Park, 113 N. 2nd St., Thermopolis, WY 82443. 15 RV sites (no pull-throughs), hook-ups and water; open April 1 to November 1; (307) 864-3926.

## BED & BREAKFAST ESTABLISHMENTS

Broadway Inn Bed & Breakfast, a historic hotel built in 1903, is located in the downtown area. Reservations suggested; some credit cards accepted; pets allowed; no alcohol or smoking allowed. Contact Judith Harvey, owner, or Debbie Bryant, manager, 342 Broadway, Thermopolis, WY 82443; (307) 864-2636; 1-888-821-9759.

Faye's Bed & Breakfast, country home under current operation since 1993. Reservations suggested; some credit cards accepted; pets allowed; open year-round. Contact Faye Hoffman, 1020 Arapahoe, Thermopolis, WY 82443; (307) 864-5166; (307) 864-3733.

Out West Bed & Breakfast, historic home built in 1908; under current operation since 1994. Reservations suggested; some credit cards accepted; open year-round; busiest June through August, slowest from December through February. Contact Arlen N. Miller and Wes Baker, 1344 Broadway, Thermopolis, WY 82443; (307) 864-2700.

## GUEST RANCHES

High Island Guest Ranch, working cattle ranch under current operation since 1994. Their slogan is, "Live the life of a cowboy for a week." Open June through September; no pets allowed. Contact Frank Robbins, Box 71, 3081 Upper Cottonwood Creek Rd., Hamilton Dome, WY 82427; (307) 867-2374; fax: (307) 867-2314.

Sanford Ranch, working cattle ranch under current operation since 1989. Credit cards accepted; pets allowed; open May through October. Contact Norman and Jerry Sanford, Box 191, Luceren Rd., Thermopolis, WY 82443; (307) 864-3575.

**SUGGESTED DINING**

Safari Club at the Holiday Inn, 115 E. Park, Thermopolis, WY; (307) 864-3131.

Pumpernicks Family Restaurant, 512 Broadway, Thermopolis, WY; (307) 864-5151.

Upper Crust Bakery & Coffee House, 517 Broadway, Thermopolis, WY; (307) 864-3665.

*Boysen Reservoir, near Shoshoni, Wyoming*
COURTESY WYOMING
DIVISION OF TOURISM

**VISITOR INFORMATION & SERVICES**

Thermopolis Chamber of Commerce, Tourist Information, 700 Broadway, PO Box 786, Thermopolis, WY 82443; 1-800-786-6772 (1-800-SUN-N-SPA).

Hot Springs County Memorial Hospital, 150 E. Arapahoe, Thermopolis, WY; (307) 864-3784; 1-800-788-9459.

**MEDICAL SERVICES**

Basin Clinic Family Practice, 827 S. 6th, Thermopolis, WY; (307) 864-2351.

Vicklund Pharmacy, 621 Richards, Thermopolis, WY; open Monday through Friday, 8:30 A.M. to 5:30 P.M., and Saturday, 9 A.M. to 2 P.M.; (307) 864-22369; 1-800-287-2369.

Corner Drug, 444 Broadway, Thermopolis, WY; open Monday through Friday, 8:30 A.M. to 5:30 P.M., and Saturday, 9 A.M. to 3 P.M.; (307) 864-3784.

**REPAIR & TOWING**

Auto & RV Specialties, 144 N. 6th, Thermopolis, WY; (307) 864-3681.

Auto Tech, 321 Buffalo Creek Secondary, Thermopolis, WY; (307) 864-2113.

**VETERINARY SERVICES**

Hot Springs Veterinary Clinic, 827 S. 6th, Thermopolis, WY; (307) 864-5553.

*The authors' Jayco travel trailer in the Wind River Canyon near Thermopolis*

# THERMOPOLIS TO SHOSHONI: U.S. 20

## FAVORITE DRIVE:
## WIND RIVER CANYON

This route runs through the Wind River Canyon, a spectacularly beautiful winding drive that leads to Boysen State Park, just 20 minutes south of Thermopolis. The highway follows the Wind River, which cuts through the rock, exposing geological layers representing 2.7 billion years of history. A special permit is required from the Wind River Indian Reservation to fish in the excellent waters of the Wind River. See page 231 for details on fishing this river. Boysen Reservoir is at the southern end of the canyon, and U.S. 20 basically follows along the reservoir to the town of Shoshoni, where U.S. 20 merges with U.S. 26.

## BOYSEN STATE PARK

Boysen State Park is 18 miles south of Thermopolis on U.S 20, just beyond the beautiful Wind River Canyon. Boysen Dam is 220 feet high by 1,143 feet long. The dam was built to control floods, provide irrigation and supply electricity. It was named for Asmuss Boysen, a Danish emigrant who built the first dam in 1903. Boysen wanted electricity for his mining camps on nearby Copper Mountain. Unfortunately, Boysen's dam flooded the railroad tunnels and had to be destroyed. Another dam was built in 1948.

The reservoir holds 36,480 acre feet of water and offers great fishing. Many state records have been set here. Rainbow and brown trout, walleye, large-mouth bass, black crappie, yellow perch, ling and catfish are among the species available. Fishing is best mid-June to mid-August, except when the weather is extremely hot. Facilities include boat ramps, cabins and campgrounds. Nearby Boysen Lake Marina has docking facilities and necessities; open April 15 to October 1; (307) 876-2772.

## OVERNIGHTING

### CAMPGROUNDS & RV PARKS

▲ *Best Shot for a Camp Spot*
Boysen State Park Campground, on U.S. 20/26 at the south end of Wind River Canyon. RV sites and pull-throughs are available, no hook-ups or services; open May 1 to October 1; (307) 876-2796.

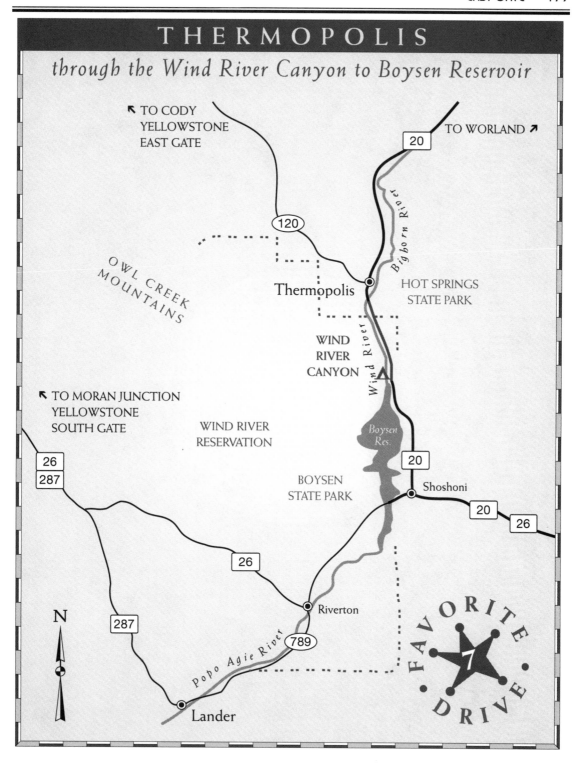

# THERMOPOLIS
## *through the Wind River Canyon to Boysen Reservoir*

↖ TO CODY
YELLOWSTONE
EAST GATE

TO WORLAND ↗

20

120

Bighorn River

OWL CREEK MOUNTAINS

Thermopolis

HOT SPRINGS
STATE PARK

WIND
RIVER
CANYON

Wind River

↖ TO MORAN JUNCTION
YELLOWSTONE
SOUTH GATE

WIND RIVER
RESERVATION

Boysen Res.

26
287

20

BOYSEN
STATE PARK

Shoshoni

20

20

26

26

N

287

Riverton

789

Popo Agie River

Lander

FAVORITE

7

DRIVE

# SECTION 5

# SOUTH GATE

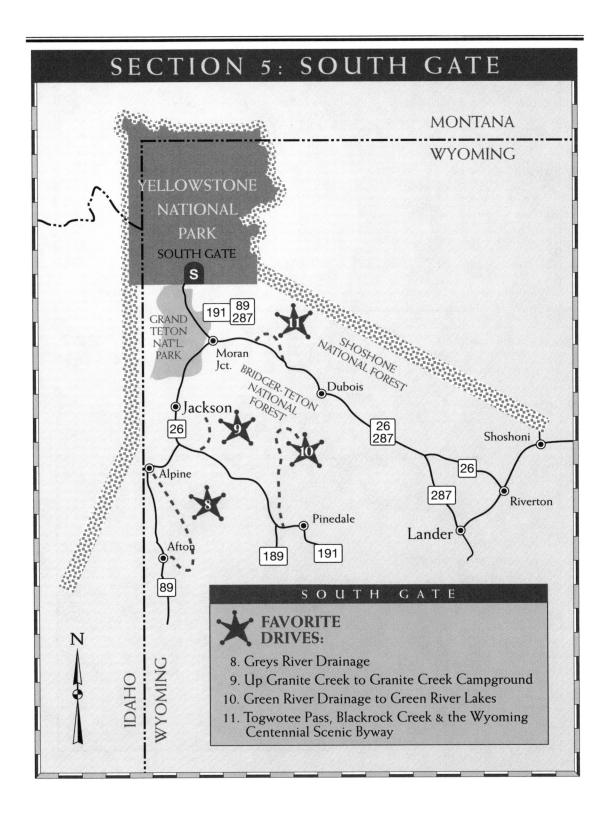

# SECTION 5: SOUTH GATE

MONTANA

WYOMING

YELLOWSTONE
NATIONAL
PARK

SOUTH GATE

**S**

191  89 287

GRAND
TETON
NAT'L.
PARK

Moran
Jct.

SHOSHONE
NATIONAL
FOREST

11

BRIDGER-TETON
NATIONAL
FOREST

Dubois

Jackson

26

9

10

26
287

Shoshoni

26

Alpine

287

Riverton

8

Lander

Afton

Pinedale

189    191

89

N

IDAHO    WYOMING

## SOUTH GATE

### FAVORITE DRIVES:

8. Greys River Drainage
9. Up Granite Creek to Granite Creek Campground
10. Green River Drainage to Green River Lakes
11. Togwotee Pass, Blackrock Creek & the Wyoming
    Centennial Scenic Byway

# GENERAL OVERVIEW

Once you exit Yellowstone from the South Gate, you follow the John D. Rockefeller Memorial Parkway past Jackson Lake to Moran Junction. This is decision time, because you have a choice of continuing to Jackson by driving south on U.S. 191, or heading southeast on U.S. 26 toward Dubois, Lander and Riverton. Both routes offer plenty of splendid sights and activities. If you opt to head for Jackson, you can then continue south to Hoback Junction from there turning southwest and taking in the sights along the Snake River toward Alpine, or turning southeast at Hoback Junction and heading for Pinedale, Big Piney, and ultimately to I-80 at Rock Springs or Green River. You can also choose to head west out of Jackson, taking in Teton Village and then motoring over Teton Pass and down into Idaho, where you'll lay eyes on some of the prettiest rolling grain country in the west.

# GRAND TETON NATIONAL PARK, MORAN JUNCTION, JACKSON HOLE, HOBACK JUNCTION, STAR VALLEY AND SODA SPRINGS: U.S. 89/191/287

### South Gate to Moran Junction: U.S. 89/191/287

*The Tetons, one of the most photographed mountain ranges in the country*
COURTESY WYOMING DIVISION OF TOURISM

When you leave Yellowstone at the South Gate, you'll continue on the John D. Rockefeller Memorial Parkway, which looks much like what you've seen in Yellowstone—plenty of mountains, forests and streams throughout. The roadway was dedicated in 1972, honoring Rockefeller's generous donations to the creation of Grand Teton National Park. After a few minutes' travel down this excellent roadway, you'll enter Grand Teton National Park. (By the way, the fee you pay to get into Yellowstone is also good for Teton Park, and vice versa.) Soon you'll begin to see the Grand Tetons off to the west, and, if you're like most travelers, you'll want a better look. To do so, you have two choices. Once you pass Jackson Lake to the west, you can take the Jenny Lake Road, or drive a few more miles and head south on U.S. 191 from Moran Junction. The Jenny Lake Road and U.S. 191 meet up again at Moose. Note: To follow U.S. 26/287 to Dubois, Lander and Riverton, see page 220.

### Moran Junction to Jackson: U.S. 26/89/191

A few miles past Moran Junction will put you in Jenny Lake, where a paved loop road takes you to the lake's shores, offering a nifty view of the Tetons. There's also a very nice bicycle trail if you're hauling one or two on your RV and want some exercise in a lovely scenic area.

*The Tetons look down on lovely Jenny Lake.*

Though you'll no doubt be uplifted by the awesome panorama, you might conversely be a bit saddened to learn some of the area's history that revolved around Richard Leigh. Typical of many of the early trappers who helped settle the west, Leigh had know-how and courage and was just too plain stubborn to give up and go back east.

The Shoshone called him the "Beaver," an apt name for the English-born fur trapper with oversized front teeth. Richard Leigh, known by his fellow trappers as "Beaver Dick," began trapping in the valley about 1840. In 1872 he guided Dr. F. V. Hayden and the U.S. Geological Survey team through the Jackson Hole area. The surveyors came to respect him enormously and named Leigh Lake for him, and Jenny Lake for his wife, a Shoshone.

Jenny and Beaver Dick had four children with one more on the way when tragedy struck in the cold winter of 1876. The family contracted smallpox shortly after Christmas. Jenny, the newborn babe, and all four children died. Leigh, who recovered from the sickness, buried his family in Jackson Hole. He never returned to his old home, saying it was bad luck. It was bad even for some of his cows that had sought refuge in the old empty cabin; they got trapped when the wind blew the door shut and starved to death.

Years later, Beaver Dick moved to the mouth of the canyon on what is now Leigh Creek. He married a Bannock woman, Susan Tadpole, and raised another family. Beaver Dick died in 1899.

*Mount Moran, in the Teton Range, and the Snake River*
COURTESY WYOMING DIVISION OF TOURISM

## MOOSE

Despite the great name, there's not much going on at Moose, which is just down the highway from Jenny Lake. You'll see a couple of nice stores with gifts, outdoor gear and a few groceries.

**RV CAUTION:** On your map you'll see a road that goes from Moose to Teton Village. Do not take this road, because RVs are banned. You will be stopped and asked to turn around! This task is not easily accomplished, because there's not much of a spot to make the turn. Evidently the road is too windy for oversized vehicles and travel trailers. Instead, take the main drag, U.S. 191, down into Jackson. This, of course, is the same road that you can take at Moran Junction if you opt not to go to Jenny Lake, and it's definitely the road to take if you're in a hurry. You can still stop at several places to photograph the Grand Tetons.

Moose, the headquarters for Grand Teton National Park, has an interesting history. In the old days, the only way to cross the Snake River between Wilson and Moran was at Menor's Ferry (pronounced MEE-ners). William Menor, the first settler west of the Snake River, claimed his homestead in 1894. Menor ran the ferry until 1918 when he sold it to Maude Noble. Maude continued the ferry until 1927 when a new bridge put him out of business.

Grand Teton National Park was founded in 1929 to preserve and protect the land of the Teton Range. The park indeed protected the mountains, but not the rich Snake River Valley. A project to include protection for the bottomlands was begun in 1923 by a group of locals dismayed at changes caused by the influx of Yellowstone tourism. The group's efforts were aimed at purchasing the surrounding ranches and donating them to the park preserve. John D. Rockefeller, Jr., and his Foundation were persuaded to spearhead the project, and land was purchased under the name of the Snake River Land Company. Over the course of the next 27 years, a battle raged between those in favor of the park and preservation, and those seeking growth, forest grazing and expansion of commerce. Eventually, in 1943, President Franklin D. Roosevelt stepped in and created the Jackson Hole National Monument that set aside an additional 130,000 acres of Forest Service land and 32,000 acres donated by the Roosevelt Foundation. (The President needed congressional approval to

*Teton Village and ski area, west of Jackson Hole*

*The Teton Range provides a spectacular backdrop for RVing in the Grand Teton National Park area.*
COURTESY JACKSON HOLE CHAMBER OF COMMERCE

establish a national park, but not a national monument.) The controversy erupted, but years later, in September 1950, when all the dust settled, the expanded Grand Teton National Park was finalized. It encompasses 500 square miles, including the Teton Range, Jackson Lake, Jenny Lake and the Snake River bottom.

Along the Snake River you'll see the lovely Chapel of the Transfiguration, built in 1925. The Grand Teton is framed in the window behind the altar of this Protestant church, creating a most impressive, beautiful sight. A trail leads from the church to the original Menor's cabin and a replica of the ferry. Not surprisingly, plenty of weddings occur in the chapel each year. You can be sure these marriages are a trifle different from those performed in Las Vegas!

## KELLY

A few miles south of Moose, you can take a nice little detour to Kelly. Like Jenny Lake, this area also has tragedy written into its history. The Gros Ventre (GROW-vont) Range east of Kelly was known for its unstable conditions. The Gros Ventre tribe stayed away from the canyon and claimed they could hear the earth rumbling at night. In 1895 the first homesteader, Billy Bierers, heard the rumblings on Sheep Mountain and concurred. "Anywhere on that slope, if I lay my ear to the ground, I can hear the water tricklin' and runnin' underneath," Bierers said. "If we have a wet enough spring, that whole mountain is gonna let loose and slide."

On June 23, 1925, with a wet spring and continuous heavy rains, the north end of the mountain indeed gave way and slid into the canyon, fulfilling Billy's prophecy. Slide Lake was suddenly formed. The citizens of Kelly didn't completely trust the naturally formed earthen dam, and two years later, on May 18, 1927, their fears were realized. The dam broke loose, spewing forth a tumultuous 15-foot wall of water that raced through town. Six people drowned, and Kelly was devastated. The little town has been rebuilt, but the scars of the slide still mar Sheep Mountain.

## JACKSON HOLE

Notice as you're traveling toward Jackson that the area is actually a big valley ringed by mountains. Mountain men commonly called land features like this hole, thus the name Jackson Hole.

It was in 1806 that John Colter scouted this rugged country. Colter was the first white man to travel this land and is credited with discovering Yellowstone National Park. On the return trip with the Lewis and Clark Expedition, Colter was given permission to take a side trip south with some fur trappers. Eventually, he ended up in the Jackson Hole area, leading another group of trappers under Manuel Lisa. It was on this adventure that Colter traveled through Jackson Hole and on up into Yellowstone. Upon his return, he described the scenic mountains, abundant wildlife and boiling, steaming ground. Most easterners, including Washington politicians, branded him a liar, but later they learned that he indeed was telling the truth. The Yellowstone area was nicknamed Colter's Hell, but modern historians now claim that Yellowstone was really not his "hell." The name describes a hot spring just outside Cody, Wyoming.

The two owners of the Rocky Mountain Fur Company, David E. Jackson and William Sublette, explored the area in 1829. Sublette coined the name "Jackson's Big Hole" for the area along the upper Snake River, and "Jackson's Little Hole" for the region along the Hoback River. The stunning, jagged mountains that form the west side of the hole were named "Les Trois Tetons" by French-Canadian trappers in the early 1800s. Eventually the name for the valley was modified to Jackson Hole. The possessive form was dropped because there were just too many lewd jokes. Folks couldn't resist a snicker or two as they talked about Jackson's Hole and "Les Trois Tetons." (The French words literally mean the "Three Tits." As you can imagine, French tourists must get a kick out of this name.)

The Jackson Hole Valley is flanked by two major mountain ranges. The impressive Teton Range on the west reaches 13,772 feet high at the summit of the Grand Teton. The peaks closest to it are the Middle and South Teton. To the north is Mount Moran with an elevation of 12,605 feet. The eastern flank of the valley is formed by the Gros Ventre Range, meaning "Big Belly."

Jackson Hole remained mostly vacant after the fur trade dwindled around 1845. The Hayden survey parties, sent by the federal government in the 1870s, brought attention to the area once again, especially through photographs taken by William H. Jackson, and drawings and paintings by artist Thomas Moran. Eager homesteaders arrived in 1884, and cattle ranches were quickly established.

Although often used interchangeably, "Jackson Hole" refers to the valley, and "Jackson" to the town (population 5,900). The valley is 60 miles long and up to 20 miles wide. The towns and communities of the valley are Jackson, Wilson, Teton Village, Moose, Kelly and Jenny Lake. The population of Teton County was 11,173 in 1990. The community hosts the 2 million plus visitors that annually travel through the South Gate of Yellowstone National Park.

*Jackson Chamber of Commerce office, just north of town*

As you near Jackson from the north, you'll drive by the National Elk Refuge on your left. If you're a summer visitor, you probably won't see any elk, since the refuge was established to feed enormous numbers of elk in the winter. As many as 10,000 animals winter here, making it the largest concentration of elk in the world. If you happen to be in the area in the fall or winter when elk are present, be sure to take a trip to the herds via a horse-drawn wagon; you'll see the animals up front and close. For information on this fascinating refuge, stop in at Jackson's Chamber of Commerce.

Though all of the larger cities described in this book have chambers of commerce, Jackson's gets our vote as the best of them all. That's saying a mouthful, but this chamber, with its unique dirt roof that grows grass, and location right alongside waterfowl-filled marshes next to the elk refuge, must be seen by every traveler interested in Jackson Hole. There's much to do in this valley, and the chamber has fascinating exhibits, along with an art gallery featuring work of local artists. Be aware that, although there's a large parking lot, you might have a bit of difficulty maneuvering your RV when the town is crowded during the peak summer season. Our suggestion is to get there as early in the morning as possible.

## JACKSON

Ah, Jackson, Wyoming—the town some people love to hate. Depending on your perspective, you'll get along nicely in Jackson, enjoying its exquisite shops and ski-town atmosphere, or you'll be glad to drive past it and get on down the road. Jackson is so unlike the rest of the state that some Wyomingites would prefer that it quietly go away. Others are proud of its existence, and visit it every chance they get. Let's describe it this way. If you're interested in a cowpoke town where life is slow and easy, and most locals have real horse manure on their boot soles, don't look for it in Jackson (though there are indeed nearby working ranches and authentic cowboys). But if you want superb dining, world-class art galleries, exciting nightlife and the chance to bump into longtime resident Harrison Ford or other famous celebrities, then hang out in Jackson. Be aware that the streets are very narrow, the crowds are very large and RV parking is extremely limited. Basically, one area is reserved for RV parking, the Home Ranch Town Parking Lot. Located one block south of the town square, it's paved, free and has a restroom. There's no overnight parking. If this is full, there's an overflow area a block east of the town square on Deloney Street. You can also park around the Lutheran Church and the elementary school.

Historians claim that Jackson originally went by the name of Marysvale for the first postmistress, Mary White. But in 1897, the wife of a local banker, Grace Miller, bought some land and planned the actual town site. The town of Jackson was then named for the fur trader David Jackson. Later, keeping true to form with Wyoming's position as the "Equality State," Jackson was governed by women. The 1920 town council and members were all women, as was the town marshal, and Grace Miller was the mayor. The gals remained in office until 1923, performing their duties admirably.

The Jackson area originated as a ranching community, and plenty of cattle ranches remain. However, it's a touch more difficult to notice them among the elaborate homes of wealthy families, ski resorts and condominiums. Jackson has bent to the constant pressure of tourism and all its trappings, even though it's well disguised by the western motif and rustic wood required by zoning laws. Without question, the area offers more art, fine dining, nightlife and culture than the rest of Wyoming. Activities include climbing, hiking, ballooning, gliding, biking, skiing, rafting, kayaking, horseback riding, hunting and fishing. Of course, Jackson is a full-service resort community.

At the south end of Jackson, you can drive south to Hoback Junction. Or, you may turn west and head over Teton Pass into Idaho, going through Wilson and making a stop at Teton Village, site of a popular ski area.

*View of the Tetons; the elk range is located nearby.*

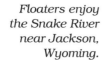

## JACKSON HOLE

*Floaters enjoy the Snake River near Jackson, Wyoming.*

## OUTDOOR RECREATION

Golfers take note! The Jackson Hole Golf and Tennis Club, with an 18-hole course, is 8 miles north of Jackson off U.S. 89 at the Gros Ventre Junction. *Golf Digest* rates the club among the top ten resort courses in the nation. For information, call (307) 733-3111. The Teton Pines Resort, designed by Arnold Palmer, also offers 18 holes. Contact Teton Pines at 3450 N. Clubhouse Dr., Jackson, WY 83001; (307) 733-1005; 1-800-238-2223.

Sensational is the best way to describe fly fishing in the area. A Wyoming fishing license and Conservation Stamp are required. Equipment, guides and water condition information are available from the Jack Dennis Outdoor Shop, 50 E. Broadway (across from the Town Square), Jackson, WY 83001; (307) 733-3270. The staff at High Country Flies will also suit your needs; they are at 165 N. Center St., Jackson, WY 83001; (307) 733-7210.

Ballooning is an interesting way to get out and about, and the view is unique. The Wyoming Balloon Company, $515\frac{1}{2}$ N. Cache, Jackson, WY 83001; (307) 739-0900, has the details.

Biking is an easy way to get around in Jackson and vicinity. There are lots of paved roads and reasonably easy access to Moose, Wilson and Grand Teton National Park. The more athletic bikers will find the off-road trails a challenge. Hoback Sports, Teton Cyclery (by Jackson Town Square), Adventure Sports and Wilson Backcountry Sports all have rentals and trail maps.

Mountaineering is billed as the ultimate Jackson experience, and why not? The Tetons are spectacular, so to stand atop could be nothing less. Two respected and internationally known schools are based in Jackson. Exum Mountain Guides, established in 1931, offers guided climbs to the summit of Grand Teton. They are at PO Box 56, Moose, WY 83012; (307) 733-2297. Jackson Hole Mountain Guides and Climbing School, 165 N. Glenwood St., Jackson, WY 83001; (307) 733-4979, offers guided trips in the Tetons and surrounding mountains.

Tours offer a relaxing alternative to navigating through crowds of travelers and lines of cars. Many Jackson companies offer new ways to experience the Tetons and Yellowstone. There are bike tours; narrated vehicle tours sharing history, scenery, geology and wildlife; winter tours by horse-drawn sleigh; fishing floats; snowmobiles; pack trips; horseback riding; and wagon trains. There's no better way to spend a day or to have an unforgettable experience in the vast beauty of Jackson Hole. The Jackson Hole Visitor Center has complete information; the following are a selection of tour companies.

Wagons West, owned and operated by Peterson-Madsen Outfitters, offers covered wagon treks in the Tetons. Reservations can be made through PO Box 1156, Afton, WY 83110; 1-800-447-4711; (307) 886-9693. Guests travel on an authentic replica of a pioneer covered-wagon train used by the early settlers. The cookouts, campfire singing and old-timer's yarns are most enjoyable.

Winter wildlife tours of Grand Teton National Park are the specialty of Callowishus Park Touring Company, (307) 733-9521. The tour includes a horse-drawn sleigh ride into the elk refuge, park history and geology.

Tours West, PO Box 6950, Jackson, WY 83002; (307) 734-8311, has a variety of packages for folks to ride in comfort in a conversion van with personal guide. The individually designed vehicle tours fit specific interests.

Jackson's Hole Adventure, PO Box 2407, Jackson, WY 83001; 1-800-392-3165, or, in Alpine, (307) 654-7849, uses a Chevrolet Lumina APV with sunroof and tinted windows on customized van tours. Guides share legends and lore of the first settlers while traveling through some inspiring scenery.

The most amazing winter activity is dog sledding. The Jackson Hole Iditarod offers four-passenger dog-sled trips. For more information, contact them at 1-800-554-7388. Different excursion packages are also available from the following: Cowboy Village at Togwotee, 1-800-543-2847; Geyser Creek Dog Sled Adventures, 1-800-531-MUSH; Grand Targhee Resort, 1-800-TARGHEE; and Washakie Outfitting, (307) 733-3602.

Winter skiing in Jackson Hole is coveted worldwide by ski enthusiasts. The deep powder, narrow chutes, greatest continuous vertical rises in the United States, and a combined 2,500 acres of skiable slopes make the area a winter paradise. For complete details, contact the following resorts: Jackson Hole Ski Resort, 7658 Tweewinot, Teton Village, WY 83025; (307) 733-2292; (307) 733-4005; 1-800-443-6931. Grand Targhee Resort, Hill Rd., Alta, WY 83422; (307) 353-2300; 1-800-827-4433. Snow King Resort, 100 E. Snow King, Jackson, WY 83001; (307) 733-5200; 1-800-522-7669.

Cross-country skiing is equally popular. Information on trails may be obtained from the following: National Park Service, Grand Teton National Park, (307) 739-3300. U.S. Forest Service, 340 N. Cache, Jackson, WY 83001 (307) 739-5500. Grand Targhee, with 12 km of groomed trails, (307) 353-2304. Jackson Hole Nordic Center, 7658 Teewinot, Teton Village, WY 83001 (307) 733-2629. Teton Pines Cross Country Skiing Center, with 13 km of groomed trails, (307) 733-1995. Spring Creek Resort, with 14 km of groomed trails open to non-guests for a fee, 1800 N. Spirit Dance Rd., Jackson, WY 83001 (307) 733-1004.

## ATTRACTIONS

The Wyoming Information Center is combined with the Jackson Hole Visitors Council and Chamber of Commerce. The location is three blocks north of the Town Square at 532 N. Cache, PO Box E, Jackson, WY 83001. Visiting the center is a must, any time of year. Make your first stop the superb information center, then decide where to go next. There's room to park an RV in the adjacent parking lot, but come early in the day.

The Home Ranch Town Parking Lot, at the intersection of Gill Avenue and North Cache Street, is the place to park your RV while visiting the sights of Jackson. The Town Square is two blocks south.

The Town Square is exciting during the nightly "Wild West Shoot Outs" held at 6:00 P.M. The Town Square is centrally located at the intersection of Broadway and Cache Streets. Heroes and villains shoot it out western-style in the street-theater duel. Expert pistol drawing and sharpshooting will amaze you. The Town Square, with its four elk antler arches, is the most prominent point of reference in Jackson. Because of Jackson's tourism focus, more art galleries, gift shops, saloons and restaurants than you can see in a week are within walking distance of the square.

The National Wildlife Art Museum is at 110 N. Center St., Jackson, WY, (307) 733-5771. The permanent collection includes over 1,300 paintings and sculptures featuring every major wildlife artist, including Conrad Schwiering, Carl Rungius, Ernest Thompson and Charles M. Russell. The remarkable building, located just 3 miles north of Jackson on U.S. 89, overlooks the National Elk Refuge.

*Rolling grain fields in the lovely farm country of the Teton Valley, west of Jackson, Wyoming*

A quaint museum with an emphasis on local history from prehistoric to present-day is the Jackson Hole Museum. Information on walking tours of the historic downtown buildings is available. A small fee is charged. The location of this museum is 105 N. Glenwood, Jackson, WY, (307) 733-2414.

More exhibits and history are at the Teton County Historical Center, 105 Mercell Ave. Jackson, WY, (307) 733-9605. The center is also an excellent research facility for the true history buff. Old books and photo archives are plentiful. There's a good collection of mountain men and fur trader wares and artifacts, Native American beads and rotating exhibits.

Art galleries are everywhere you look. Jackson Hole proudly represents fine western, wildlife, abstract and southwestern paintings, photography, sculpture, pottery, hand-crafted furniture, weavings and exquisite Native American art collections, rugs and handmade jewelry. There are close to 50 art galleries in Jackson Hole, half of which belong to the Art Gallery Association. For more information, contact the Chamber of Commerce.

The Grand Teton Music Festival in Teton Village is composed of a series of concerts held from July through August. The festivals, which began in the early 1960s, are considered some of the premier summer concerts in the country. If you're not in town when a concert is scheduled, drop in for a look at one of the Festival Orchestra's rehearsals. Concerts and rehearsals are held in the Walk Festival Hall; for tickets and information, call (307) 733-3050.

The Aerial Tram is a fun way to enjoy the view, and the only easy way to climb to the top of Rendezvous Mountain. The trip takes just ten minutes and gives you a chance to take some stunning photographs. The Aerial Tram is in Teton Village and part of the development complex at the Jackson Hole Ski and Summer Resort. The tram runs from May through September, but there are lots of activities in Teton Village year-round. The best way to learn about them is from the Guest Service Center, which is open daily from 9 A.M. to 5 P.M. For information, call (307) 739-2753.

The National Elk Refuge and Elk Refuge Visitor Center is located 2 miles north of Jackson, (307) 733-9212. The 25,000-acre refuge is at a natural winter feeding ground that scientists believe elk have used for 500 years. You must visit the area in fall, winter or early spring to see elk here. If you're in the area the second Saturday in May, plan on spending that day in town and watch the amazing annual antler auction. Elk shed their antlers each year, and the antlers are highly valued as aphrodisiacs by Orientals, as well as for home furnishings such as lamps, candelabras and all sorts of lovely decorations. Boy Scouts gather the antlers from the refuge grounds, and the auction proceeds go to community fund-raising programs and charities. Make no mistake, this is a big deal. Upward of $100,000 and more is spent at the auction; one or two high bidders normally buy most of the antlers.

## OVERNIGHTING

## CAMPGROUNDS & RV PARKS

▲ *Best Shot for a Camp Spot*
Crystal Creek—U.S. Forest Service Campground, 13 miles east of Kelly on Forest Service Road. 6 RV sites and restrooms; open June 5 through October 30; reservations accepted, 1-800-280 2267.

▲ *Best Shot for a Camp Spot*
Red Hills—U.S. Forest Service Campground, 13 miles east of Kelly on Forest Service Road. 5 RV sites and restrooms; open June 5 through October 30; reservations accepted, 1-800-280 2267.

▲ *Best Shot for a Camp Spot*
Granite Creek Campground—U.S. Forest Service Campground, on U.S. 189/191, 11 miles southeast of Hoback Junction. See Overnighting section for Bondurant, WY (page 210).

*Campers enjoy the solitude along Granite Creek near Jackson, Wyoming.*

Astoria Hot Springs, 3 miles south of Hoback Junction on U.S. 89, 12500 S. U.S. 89, Jackson, WY. 50 RV sites, hook-ups, dump station, restrooms, hot showers and laundry; hot springs mineral pool; open May 1 through August 31; (307) 733-2659.

Elk Country Inn & RV Park, 480 W. Pearl St., Jackson, WY 83001. 12 RV sites (no pull-throughs), hook-ups, dump station, restrooms, hot showers and laundry; open May 1 through October 1; (307) 733-2364.

Flagg Ranch Village, 2 miles south of Yellowstone on U.S. 89/287, PO Box 187, Jackson, WY 83001. 170 RV sites (pull-throughs), hook-ups, dump station, restrooms, hot showers and laundry; open May 15 through October 15; (307) 543-2861.

Lone Eagle, 17 miles south of Jackson on U.S. 189/191, Star Rt. Box 45-C, Jackson, WY 83001. 50 RV sites, hook-ups, restrooms, hot showers, pool and laundry; open May 1 to September 30; (307) 733-1090; 1-800-321-3800; fax: (307) 733-5042.

Snake River Park KOA, 1 mile north of Hoback Junction, 9705 S. U.S. 89, Jackson, WY 83001. 57 sites (50 pull-throughs), hook-ups, dump station, restrooms, hot showers, cabins and tent sites; pets allowed in campground, not cabins; open April 1 through October 6; (307) 733-7078; 1-800-562-1878; fax: (307) 733-0412.

Virginian Lodge RV Park, 750 Broadway, Jackson, WY 83001. 105 RV sites, hook-ups, dump stations, restrooms, hot showers, pool, laundry and rec-room; open May 1 through October 5; (307) 733-7189.

Wagon Wheel Campground, 5 blocks north of Town Square, 525 N. Cache, Jackson, WY 83001. 35 RV sites, dump station, hot showers and laundry; open year-round; (307) 733 2357.

Signal Mountain—National Park Service Campground, 2 miles southwest of Teton Park Road, or 5 miles northwest of Moran on U.S. 89/287. 80 RV sites (no pull-throughs), no services except dump station; open May 15 to September 30.

Gros Ventre—National Park Service Campground, 2 miles southwest of Kelly on Gros Ventre Road. RV sites (no pull-throughs), no services except dump station; open May 1 to October 10.

Atherton Creek—U.S. Forest Service Campground, 7 miles east of Kelly on Forest Service Road. 13 RV sites, no services, restrooms; open June 5 through October 30.

Curtis Canyon—U.S. Forest Service Campground, 6 miles east of Jackson from Elk Refuge entrance to Curtis Canyon, 3 miles east. Open June 5 through September 10.

Hatchet—U.S. Forest Service Campground, 8 miles east of Moran Junction on U.S. 26/287. 9 RV sites; open June 25 through September 10.

Snake River—National Park Service Campground, 25 miles north of Moran on U.S. 89/287. 24 RV sites (no pull-throughs), no services; open June 15 to September 15.

## BED & BREAKFAST ESTABLISHMENTS

Don't Fence Me Inn, a mountain log lodge, operating since 1995; open year-round; busiest in summer, slowest spring and fall; credit cards accepted; no pets allowed. Contact Maureen Mackay, Box 25170, 2350 N. Moose-Wilson Rd., Jackson Hole, WY 83001; (307) 733-7979.

The Huff House Inn, a historic home, operating since 1993; open year-round; busiest in summer, slowest fall and spring; credit cards accepted; no pets allowed. Contact Jackie and Weldon Richardson, Box 1189, 240 E. Deloney, Jackson, WY 83001; (307) 739-9091.

Moose Meadows Bed & Breakfast, ranch home, 1 RV hook-up, operating since 1990; open year-round; busiest June 15 through October 1; credit cards accepted; no pets allowed. Contact Juli James, Box 371, 1225 Green Lane, Wilson, WY 83014; (307) 733-9510.

Nowlin Creek Inn, guest rooms each with private bath and hot tub; operating since 1992; open year-round; busiest in summer, slowest November through April; credit cards accepted; no pets allowed. Contact Susan Nowlin, Box 2766, 660 E. Broadway, Jackson, WY 83001; (307) 733 0882; 1-800-533-0882.

The Painted Porch, 1901 country farmhouse, operating since 1990; credit cards accepted; no pets or smoking allowed; children six and older welcome. Contact Matt and Martha MacEachern, Box 6955, 3755 N. Moose-Wilson Rd., Jackson, WY 83002; (307) 733-1564, 733-1981.

The Sassy Moose Inn, country inn operating since 1991, open year-round; busiest June through September, slowest in April; credit cards accepted; pets allowed; no smoking. Contact Polly Kelley, 3895 Miles Rd., Jackson, WY 83001; (307) 733-1277; 1-800-356-1277; fax: (307) 839-0793.

Sundance Inn Bed & Breakfast, 1950s town inn, operating since 1986; busiest June through September, slowest April through November; credit cards accepted; no pets allowed. Contact Amy and Case Morton, PO Box I, 135 W. Broadway, Jackson, WY 83001; (307) 733-3443.

A Teton Tree House, mountain lodge; open year-round; busiest May through October, slowest April and November; credit cards accepted, no pets or smoking allowed. Contact Denny Becker, PO Box 550, Wilson, WY 83014; (307) 733-3233; fax: (307) 733-0713.

Teton View Bed & Breakfast, country home; seasonal operation. Contact John and Joann Engelhart, PO Box 652, 2136 Coyote Loop, Wilson, WY 83014; (307) 733-7954.

Twin Trees Bed & Breakfast, town home, operating since 1990; open year-round; busiest June through September, slowest April and November; credit cards accepted; no pets or smoking allowed; children 15 and older welcome. Contact Patricia A. Martin, PO Box 7533, 575 S. Willow, Jackson, WY 83002; (307) 739-9737; 1-800-728-7337.

The Wildflower Inn, mountain lodge with private bath and hot tub, operating since 1988; open year-round; busiest in summer, slowest April and November; credit cards accepted; no pets allowed. Contact Manager, PO Box 11000, 3725 Teton Village Rd., Jackson, WY 83002; (307) 733-4710; fax: (307) 739-0914.

## GUEST RANCHES

Goosewing Ranch & High Mountain Adventure, 30 miles northeast of Jackson in the Gros Ventre Wilderness. This ranch has been in operation since 1995. Featured are horseback riding, pack trips, cookouts, fly fishing and a kids' program; winter activities include snowmobiling, cross-country skiing and dog sledding. Seasonal: summer season July 1 through September 15; RV accessible in summer; winter access by snowmobile only, 20 miles; credit cards accepted; no pets allowed. Contact Francois Corrand, Box 7760, Jackson, WY 83003; (307) 733-6127; 1-888-733-5251; fax: (307) 733-1405.

Spotted Horse Ranch, 17 miles south of Jackson off U.S. 189/191 on the Hoback River. This ranch has been operating since 1958.

Featured are fishing, float trips, cookouts and horseback riding. Open June 1 through November 1 and winter; busiest July through August, slowest June and September; credit cards accepted; pets allowed. Contact Dick and Dian Bess, PO Box 43, Jackson, WY 83001; (307) 733-2097; (307) 733-3712.

*Palisades Reservoir, south of Jackson*

Twin Creek Cabins, 5 miles northeast of Jackson near the National Elk Refuge. Featured are hiking with a full view of the Grand Teton Range, fishing and recreation area for kids under 12. Open May 15 through October 1. Contact Christopher and Susan Johansson; Box 697, Jackson, WY  83001; (307) 733-3927.

Moose Creek Ranch, 18 miles west of Jackson. This family-oriented guest ranch has been in operation since 1989. Featured are a great riding program, float trips, heated pool, hot tub, fishing and cookouts. Open year-round; busiest June through September, slowest May and October; credit cards accepted; no pets allowed. Contact Kelly and Roxann Van Orden, PO Box 3108, Jackson, WY  83001; 1-800-676-0075; (208) 787-2784.

Red Rock Ranch, 30 miles northeast from Jackson on the Gros Ventre River, has been operating since 1975. This working cattle ranch with cattle drives features a heated swimming pool, fishing, cookout rides, game room and special riding program for kids six and older. Open June through September; no credit cards accepted; no pets allowed. Contact Dave and Deborah MacKenzie, owners, or Chris and Trish Martin, managers, PO Box 38, Kelly, WY  83011; (307) 733-6288; (307) 733-6287.

Lost Creek Ranch, 8 miles north of Moose. Featured are a magnificent view of the Tetons, heated pool, hot tub, skeet range, tennis courts, horses, float trips, hiking and a full-service spa and fitness center. Open May through September; credit cards accepted. Contact Bev Halpin, PO  Box 95, Moose, WY  83012; (307) 733-0945.

Gros Ventre River Ranch, 18 miles northeast of Jackson. This ranch has been operating since 1987. Featured are a view of the Tetons, fly fishing, horseback riding, hiking, mountain biking, pack trips, cookouts, ski touring and snowmobiling. Open year-round, except April and November; no credit cards accepted; no pets allowed. Contact Karl and Tina Beber, 18 Gros Ventre Rd., Moose, WY 83012; (307) 733-4138; fax: (307) 733-4272.

Cowboy Village Resort at Togwotee, on U.S. 26/287, between Dubois and Moran Junction. Featured are horseback riding, buggy rides, pack trips, fly fishing, mountain biking, hiking and naturalist programs for the kids; winter offers snowmobile rentals and tours, cross-country skiing and dog sledding. Open year-round, except April and November; credit cards accepted; no pets allowed. Contact Manager, PO Box 91, Moran, WY  83013; (307) 543-2847; 1-800-543-2847; fax: (307) 543-2391.

*Granite Creek area, near Jackson*

Heart Six Ranch, 35 miles north of Jackson overlooking the Buffalo River and the Teton Mountains. This guest ranch has been operating since 1977. Featured are a children's program and youth Wrangler, horseback riding, fishing, cookouts, pack trips, biking, photography, float trips, evening entertainment and a hot tub. Open year-round; busiest June through September; snowmobiling and hunting in season; credit cards accepted; no pets allowed. Restaurant is open to the public on Friday through Sunday. Contact Brian Harris, owner, Joe and Karen Dowdy, managers, Box 70, Moran, WY 83013; (307) 543-2496.

Turpin Meadow Ranch, 40 miles north of Jackson on the Buffalo River. This ranch has been operating since 1992. Featured are horseback riding, pack trips, fishing, cookouts, evening entertainment, snowmobiling and hunting. Open year-round; busiest in summer, slowest April through May; credit cards accepted; pets allowed. Contact the Castango Family, Box 379, Moran, WY 83013; (307) 543-2496; 1-800-743-2496.

Diamond D Ranch & Outfitters, 12 miles east of Moran Junction. This ranch has been operating since 1972. Featured are pack trips, fishing trips, big-game hunting in the fall, snowmobiling and cross-country skiing; guides available. Offers RV camping with full hook-ups; open year-round; busiest May 15 through October, slowest December 15 through April; credit cards accepted; no pets allowed. Contact Rod and Rae Doty, PO Box 211, Moran, WY 83013; (307) 543-2479.

Box K Ranch, in Moran, 1 mile off U.S. 287. This ranch has been operating since 1967. Open June 20 through August for horseback trips into remote areas of the Teton Wilderness and Yellowstone National Park for fishing. Fall big-game hunting season is from October 1 until season's end. Credit cards accepted; no pets allowed. Contact Walter M. Korn; Box K Ranch, Moran, WY 83013; (307) 543-2407.

R Lazy S Ranch, 1 mile north of Teton Village. This ranch has been operating since 1990. It features a fishing and riding program for adults and children; open June 15 through September; no credit cards accepted; no pets allowed. Contact Clair McConaughy, manager, Box 308, Teton Village, WY 83025; (307) 733-2655.

**SUGGESTED DINING**

Jackson has an enormous assortment of eating places; see the Jackson Hole Dining Guide from the Chamber of Commerce.

The Snake River Grill, 84 E. Broadway, Jackson, WY; (307) 733-0557.

Nani's, 3 blocks from Broadway on Glenwood, Jackson, WY; (307) 733-3888.

Off Broadway, King St. off Broadway, Jackson, WY; (307) 733-9777.

Gouloff's, 3600 N. Moose-Wilson Rd., Jackson, WY; (307) 733-1886.

Nora's Fish Creek Inn, Hwy. W, Wilson, WY; (307) 733-8288.

The Range, 225 N. Cache, Jackson, WY; (307) 733 5481.

**VISITOR INFORMATION & SERVICES**

Jenny Lake Visitor Center, Jenny Lake, Wyoming, (307) 739-9259.

Moose-Grand Teton National Park Headquarters and Visitor Center, (307) 739-3300.

Bridger-Teton National Forest Visitor Center, (307) 739-5500.

Jackson Hole Visitors Council and Chamber of Commerce and the Wyoming State Information Center, 3 blocks north of the Town Square, 532 N. Cache, PO Box E, Jackson, WY 83001; (307) 733-3316; 1-800-443-6931; or Jackson Hole Visitors Council, 1-800-782-0011. You can park your RV at the Jackson Hole Visitors Center while you're there. The Home Ranch Town Parking Lot, at the intersection of Gill Avenue and North Cache Street, is the place to park your RV while visiting the sights of Jackson. The Town Square is 2 blocks south.

**MEDICAL SERVICES**

Saint John's Hospital, 24-hour emergency room, 625 E. Broadway, Jackson, WY; (307) 733-3636.

Instant Care, 545 W. Broadway, Jackson, WY; open Monday through Saturday from 9 A.M. to 8 P.M., and Sunday from 9 A.M. to 7 P.M.; (307) 733-7003.

Emer-a-Care, 974 W. Broadway, Jackson, WY; open Monday through Friday from 9 A.M. to 5 P.M.; (307) 733-8002.

The Stone Pharmacy, 830 Broadway, Jackson, WY; open Monday through Saturday, 8 A.M. to 7 P.M., and Sunday, 9 A.M. to 5 P.M.; (307) 733-6222.

Albertson's Pharmacy, 520 W. Broadway, Jackson, WY; Monday through Friday, 9 A.M. to 9 P.M., Saturday, 9 A.M. to 7 P.M., and Sunday, 10 A.M. to 4 P.M.; (307) 733-9223.

**REPAIR & TOWING**

Brown's Towing, 24 hours, 4040 S. Pub Place, 3 miles south of Jackson on U.S. 89, Jackson, WY; (307) 733-6239.

AAA Best Towing in Jackson, call (307) 739-2378 (739-BEST).

Teton Towing, (307) 733-1943.

Wyoming Adventures (RV repairs), 1050 S. U.S. 89, Jackson, WY; open Monday through Friday, 8 A.M. to 5 P.M.; (307) 733-2300.

**VETERINARY SERVICES**

Spring Creek Animal Hospital, Dr. M. J. Forman and Dr. Daniel Forman, 1035 W. Broadway, Jackson, WY 83001; (307) 733-9223.

# JACKSON TO HOBACK JUNCTION: U.S. 191

There are a couple of options at Jackson. You can choose to head west on Wyoming 22 to Wilson, and then over Teton Pass into Idaho, or continue south to Hoback Junction. If you head west to Idaho, the route takes the Teton Scenic Byway over Teton Pass, which is one of our favorite drives. **RV CAUTION:** Be aware that both sides of Teton Pass are very steep in places, often having grades up to 10 percent. Be sure your RV is in top condition to tackle this road.

From Jackson on U.S. 191, you have a short 12-mile drive that runs through one of Jackson's newly established communities, taking you to Hoback Junction where you must make a big driving decision. At the junction, you can either head southwest on U.S. 26/89, which takes you to Alpine and then down into Star Valley as well as to Idaho destinations, or turn southeast at Hoback Junction on U.S. 189/191, which takes you down to Pinedale or Big Piney, and then to I-80 at either Green River or Rock Springs, depending on the route you choose. For U.S. 189/191 route information to Pinedale and Big Piney, see page 208.

# HOBACK JUNCTION TO ALPINE: U.S. 26/89

This 23-mile section runs alongside the Snake River, which attracts thousands of visitors who challenge the river in rafts or kayaks. Plenty of white-water companies in and around the Jackson area will take you down the river in a raft. If you just want to observe, there are lots of turnouts along the highway that will accommodate RVs. The route also has plenty of Forest Service campgrounds, but you need to arrive early, since many are full by noon during peak season. As a matter of interest, this route takes you across a spot that slid away during the spring of 1997. A huge landslide carried much of the highway down to the river below, and the road was closed for many weeks, much to the dismay of visitors, as well as Jackson merchants.

**ALPINE**    Just a stone's throw from the Idaho border, Alpine was established in 1899 as the site of a ferry crossing for the Snake River. By 1912, the surrounding area was claimed by homesteaders, and the town developed around the ferry site. Settlers used the ferry to cross the Snake River until the first steel bridge was completed in 1914. The old bridge spanned from Wyoming on the west to Idaho on the east, and the town of Alpine spread across both states. In 1941 the U.S. Bureau of Reclamation was authorized to build the Palisades Dam. The resulting reservoir flooded over the original site of Alpine. A year later, the old steel bridge and the entire town moved east into Wyoming. Today, the settlement of 180 residents is a crossroads for travelers along U.S. 26/89. There are several restaurants and motels, and ample public campgrounds are available on nearby Palisades Reservoir and up into the Greys River area on Greys River Loop Road. For information on Palisades Reservoir and Idaho destinations, see page 355.

# ALPINE THROUGH STAR VALLEY: U.S. 89

This route winds through several small communities. The region's claims to fame are a very good cheese factory in Thayne and a massive arch in Afton made of elk antlers. Our 100 miles ends at Smoot at the south end of Star Valley. Continue down the highway to I-80. If you like early corporate American history, be sure to stop in Kemmerer and visit the original J. C. Penney store, commonly called the "mother store." Fossil Butte National Monument is just west of Kemmerer on U.S. 30.

## FAVORITE DRIVE:
## GREYS RIVER

If you're in an adventuresome spirit and the roads aren't wet, you can take a beautiful drive along the Greys River via Forest Road 10138. This dirt and gravel road runs some 70 miles through the Bridger-Teton National Forest, roughly paralleling U.S. 89 through Star Valley. RV Caution: The road accommodates two-way traffic throughout much of its length, although there are some very narrow spots and ruts on the southern end.

There are several campgrounds, and trout fishing is available throughout on the river that courses close to the road. On the north end, the road begins near Alpine and runs south until it connects with Forest Service Road 10072, then it turns west and joins up with U.S. 89. Expect to see moose along the route amid sensational mountain scenery.

**STAR VALLEY** The upper Star Valley begins at the junction of Highways 89 and 26 just north of Alpine. Known as the "Little Switzerland of America," the valley is flanked on the west by the Caribou Mountains and Webster Range, and on the east by the Salt Range. The Salt River forms a valley between the rugged mountains. Salt deposits and saline springs, found along the banks of the river, generated its name, but the water of the Salt River is not salty. This area is predominantly dairy and farming country.

As early as 1812, the Astorians trapped beaver in the streams, and the Shoshone were known to spend summers in the valley. Before 1870, descriptions of the rich grasses and abundant wildlife were found in Shoshone teachings. However, the major influx of settlers began in the late 1870s when Brigham Young sent church members to colonize the region. Mormon Apostle Moses Thatcher and Bishop William Preston first came to the valley in 1877. By 1879 they were given appointments by the Mormon Church to establish settlements.

The Mormon emigrants were seeking freedom from religious harassment, which had increased dramatically in 1882 when Congress passed the Edmunds Anti-Polygamy Act. Idaho authorities actively enforced the law. On the other hand, Wyoming sought to populate the area, welcoming large families. Personal questions were kept to a minimum. Today, a majority of the area's inhabitants are members of the Church of Jesus Christ of Latter-Day Saints (LDS)—the name by which Mormons prefer to be called.

# GREYS RIVER DRAINAGE

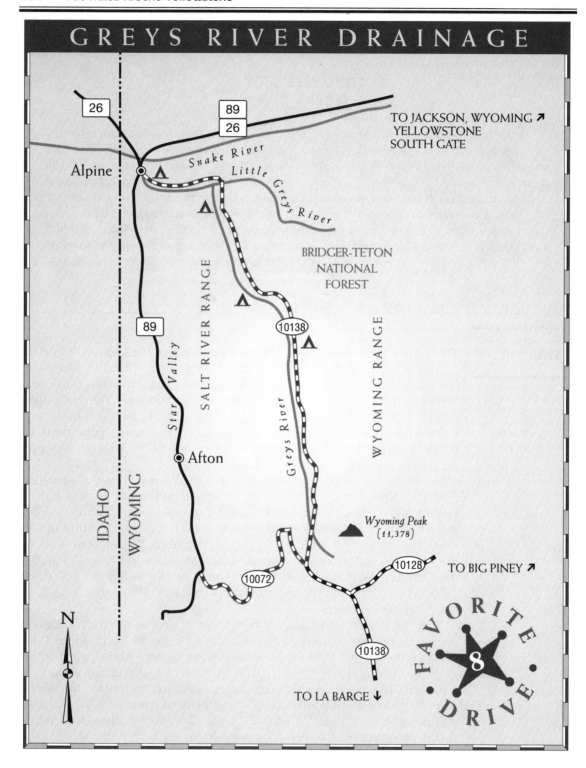

26

89
26

TO JACKSON, WYOMING ↗
YELLOWSTONE
SOUTH GATE

*Snake River*

Alpine

*Little Greys River*

BRIDGER-TETON
NATIONAL
FOREST

SALT RIVER RANGE

WYOMING RANGE

89

*Star Valley*

10138

*Greys River*

Afton

IDAHO

WYOMING

*Wyoming Peak*
*(11,378)*

10128

TO BIG PINEY ↗

10072

N

10138

TO LA BARGE ↓

FAVORITE
8
DRIVE

There are three versions regarding the origin of the name Star Valley. One is that Moses Thatcher named his new home "because it is the star of all valleys." Another version states that because the first few winters were so harsh and the new settlers had insufficient food, they dubbed it "Starved Valley." Later, as the settlement expanded and conditions improved, they shortened the name to Star Valley. Finally, a third version credits a group of cowboys for naming it as they sat beneath the star-filled sky and saw the five peaks at the east end of the valley, which resemble the points of a star.

Star Valley grew famous for producing cheese, especially Swiss and Italian varieties. Dairy farming is still the principal industry. In 1889 the first creamery opened in Afton. Through the years up to 11 cheese factories were in operation throughout the area. Between 1932 and 1937, 1 million pounds of Swiss cheese alone were produced. In 1993, with modern production methods, one single factory produced 1.5 million pounds of cheese. The industry has passed its peak, but Star Valley still produces more milk than any other region in Wyoming and is well known for its dairy products. A trip down the valley should include a stop for cheese. The factory in Thayne is a good place to shop.

## FREEDOM

From Freedom you have the option to continue through the Star Valley, or you can head west on Idaho 34 and take the lovely Pioneer Historic Byway to Soda Springs; see page 183.

Freedom lies just a couple of miles off U.S. 89 and has a unique history. It's the oldest settlement in Star Valley and was founded in 1879 by a group of Mormons following the Apostles Thatcher and Rich. The town, which lies on the state line between Idaho and Wyoming, got its name because the group was seeking to escape prosecution for polygamy. When they arrived at the site, one member of the group, Arthur Clark, proclaimed, "Here we shall find freedom." This was indeed the case. When Idaho prosecutors later brought action against polygamists living in Idaho, citizens escaped arrest by merely stepping across the street to the Wyoming side of town. Idaho authorities were enforcing the Edmunds Anti-Polygamy Act of 1882, but Wyoming sheriffs didn't follow suit. These days Freedom is a small community with a population of about 100. The town is most known for a small gun manufacturer named Freedom Arms. The factory makes handguns, including the powerful .454 Casull, the "World's Most Powerful Hand Gun."

*A beautiful sunset over the Teton Range, with the Snake River in the foreground*
PETE SALOUTOS/
COURTESY WYOMING
DIVISION OF TOURISM

**THAYNE**

Thayne is a small community just south of the Freedom turnoff. If you'd like to buy a chunk of great cheese, pay a visit to the cheese factory on the east side of the highway. Cutter races were invented here in the 1920s. They were started by dairy farmers racing each other to the local creamery to avoid waiting in line once there. The horses pull chariots over frozen pastures at breakneck speeds. The world record is 21.8 seconds for a quarter-mile run. Races are now held in seven states, with the "world finals" taking place in Pocatello, Idaho. Races take place between December and February.

**AFTON**

Settled in the late 1870s, Afton was founded by Moses Thatcher, an LDS (Mormon) apostle. The town was named after a stream from a British song, "Flow gently, sweet Afton, Among thy green braes." The mail service began in 1880 when a regular route was established to Afton from Montpelier, Idaho.

Afton is now the primary and largest town of Star Valley with a population of 1,487. It serves as the marketing center for the dairy and farm products of the area, as well as the site of the sawmill factory for timber harvested in the nearby forests.

**OUTDOOR RECREATION**

Golfers will enjoy a quick round at the 9-hole course in Freedom. The Valli-Vu Golf Course, south of Freedom on U.S. 89, (307) 886-3338, is open to the public. The Star Valley Ranch Resort has an 18-hole course. Go 3 miles north of Thayne on U.S. 89, then turn right on Vista Drive for 5 miles; (307) 883-2454.

Winter skiers enjoy downhill skiing at Snowshoe Hollow Ski Area. For information, call (307) 886-9831.

In June, don't miss the Mountain Days in Alpine. This is an event that includes Native American dancing and crafts, live music, knife and tomahawk competitions, and authentic mountain men.

If you're touring in the winter, check out the Elk Feeding Ground, located 1 mile south of Alpine on U.S. 89. Not as large as the Jackson herd, this one has more than 1,000 elk in the area. See them best in the morning when they're fed.

*Motorists in Afton, Wyoming, pass under the elk arch made of thousands of antlers.*

The Elk Antler Arch was built in 1958. The 18-foot-high arch contains 3,011 antlers, worth more than $300,000, and is no doubt the most photographed spot in town.

The Pioneer Museum is of special interest to women. The Daughters of Utah Pioneers have prepared several exhibits containing tools, a weaving loom and spinning wheel used by early settlers. Located at 46 5th Ave., Afton, WY.

The Periodic Spring is the largest of three similar phenomena in the world. Water pours out of a cliff for 18 minutes, and then shuts off for about an equal amount of time. During the dry season, a spring fills an underground chamber until it overflows, the chamber empties, and then takes time to refill and begin the process anew. During the runoff season in spring, the water flows constantly. Periodic Spring is located in Swift Creek Canyon, 6 miles out of town (go out on Second Avenue), and then three-quarters of a mile along a hiking trail.

## OVERNIGHTING

### CAMPGROUNDS & RV PARKS

**Alpine**

Elbow—U.S. Forest Service Campground, 14 miles east of Alpine on U.S. 89. Some RV sites (no pull-throughs), no services; open June 10 to September 10.

Forest Park—U.S. Forest Service Campground, 37 miles southeast of Alpine on U.S. 89. 13 RV sites (no pull-throughs), no services; open May 27 to October 31.

Lynx Creek—U.S. Forest Service Campground, 13 miles southeast of Alpine on U.S. 89. 14 RV sites (no pull-throughs), no services; open May 27 to October 31.

Moose Flat—U.S. Forest Service Campground, 19 miles southeast of Alpine on U.S. 89. 10 RV sites (no pull-throughs), no services; open May 27 to October 31.

Murphy Creek—U.S. Forest Service Campground, 12 miles southeast of Alpine on U.S. 89. 10 RV sites (no pull-throughs), no services; open May 27 to October 31.

Station Creek—U.S. Forest Service Campground, 11 miles east of Alpine on U.S. 89. 15 RV sites (no pull-throughs), no services; open June 10 to September 10.

### Freedom

Cabin Creek—U.S. Forest Service Campground, 16 miles east of Alpine on U.S. 89. 10 RV sites (no pull-throughs), no services; open May 27 to October 31.

### Afton

Swift Creek—U.S. Forest Service Campground, 2 miles east of Afton (take 2nd Ave.) on County and Forest Service Road. 13 RV sites (no pull-throughs), no services; open May 27 to October 31.

### Thayne
▲ *Best Shot for a Camp Spot*
Flat Creek RV Park, quarter-mile south of Thayne on U.S. 89. 20 RV sites (1 pull-through), full hook-ups, bathhouse, laundry and cabins; open year-round; (307) 883-2231.

## GUEST RANCHES

Tincup Mountain Guest Ranch, on Idaho 34, 3 miles west of Freedom. This ranch has been operating since 1968. Featured are horseback riding, pack trips and overnight hunting trips. Open May through November. Contact David Haderlie, PO Box 175, Hwy. 34, #5336, Freedom, WY 83120; (307) 873-2368; 1-800-253-2368.

**VISITOR INFORMATION & SERVICES**

Afton Visitor Center (summer only) is at Second and Washington Streets, Afton, WY; (307) 886-3156; 1-800-426-8833.

# HOBACK JUNCTION TO BIG PINEY AND PINEDALE: U.S. 189/191

When you take this route from Hoback Junction, you'll travel about 53 miles to Daniel, where the routes divide, one going to Big Piney, the other to Pinedale. As you leave the Hoback, you'll find a fine highway, running through Hoback Canyon and then through lovely forest regions and willow bottoms. As soon as you leave the Bridger National Forest, as noted by a highway sign, you begin to enter more arid country, with plenty of sagebrush as well as ranches.

## FAVORITE DRIVE: GRANITE CREEK

You might want to take a detour and drive the dirt road up Granite Creek, which is about a 15-minute drive from Hoback Junction. This is Forest Service Road 30500, which can be slippery when wet. Do not take this road during extensive rainy periods. It can also be bumpy, depending on how long ago it was graded. A check with the Forest Service, (307) 739-5500, will get you updated information. Granite Creek Campground, 9 miles up the road, is seldom full, offering a camp spot during the peak tourist season. A big attraction here is Granite Hot Springs, a short distance above the campground. A concessionaire charges a fee to swim in this beautiful natural spa, but be sure to check with the Forest Service to determine if the springs are open. As another bonus, you can enjoy some undisturbed fishing for trout and whitefish in Granite Creek, which flows close to the road.

## BONDURANT

In the early 1900s, Benjamin Franklin Bondurant settled in the valley with his wife, Sarah. They established a post office, store and dude ranch. The ranch, one of the first of its kind in Wyoming, was in operation for about 20 years. The community now has a population of 100.

A humorous event occurred during a religious service conducted by Reverend Samuel Parker, who crossed South Pass in 1835. On August 23 of that same year, he preached the first Protestant sermon in Wyoming on the riverbank near Bondurant. As the story goes, he faced stiff competition from a herd of buffalo, and his hungry "congregation," mostly trappers such as Jim Bridger, Jedediah Smith and Kit Carson, dashed off before the final benediction. It's interesting to note that rugged mountain men such as that legendary trio took the time to attend a church service. Maybe they had some help from above getting out of the skirmishes they always seemed to be involved in.

*Wind River Mountain Range, near Pinedale, Wyoming*

## OVERNIGHTING

### CAMPGROUNDS & RV PARKS

Smiling S Motel & RV Park, U.S. 189/191, Bondurant, WY. 7 RV sites (no pull-throughs), some services; open May 15 through September 30; (307) 733-3457.

▲ *Best Shot for a Camp Spot*
Granite Creek—U.S. Forest Service Campground, 10 miles northwest of Bondurant on US 191/189, then 9 miles northeast on Forest Service Road. 52 RV sites (no pull-throughs), no services except drinking water; open June 25 through September 10.

Hoback—U.S. Forest Service Campground, 14 miles northwest of Bondurant on U.S. 191/189. 14 RV sites (no pull-throughs), no services except drinking water; open June 5 through September 10.

Kozy—U.S. Forest Service Campground, 7 miles west of Bondurant on U.S. 191/189. 8 RV sites (no pull-throughs), no services; open June 1 through September 5.

---

### FAVORITE DRIVE: GREEN RIVER LAKES

As you continue down U.S. 189/191, you come to a major junction just before Daniel. Turn east toward Pinedale on U.S. 191, go 5 miles, and then turn north on Wyoming 352, which takes you up the beautiful Green River drainage and ultimately to Green River Lakes. There's a log building store at Cora, but you might miss it if you don't look quickly enough. If you're willing to drive the 50 miles to the end of the road, and we sincerely recommend it, you'll arrive at Green River Lakes and a cozy campground (see page 217). The long drive is well worth it in terms of scenery, wildlife and outstanding fishing. Trout abound in the river, which offers a variety of runs, riffles, pools—in short, every imaginable kind of water you can fish. Don't be surprised to see moose wallowing about in the valley bottom, deer and elk in the surrounding forests and a fine assortment of birds.

---

## CORA

This tiny town holds just a few people, but practically every Wyomingite has heard of it, perhaps because it's the gateway to the headwaters of the Green River. In the heart of cattle country, Cora hosts a wonderful roundup called the "Green River Drift," where cowboys sort out over 7,500 cattle brought down from the summer forest range. If you want to really relive the past, this is an authentic cattle roundup, one of the biggest in the west. Make sure you have lots of film, because you'll want to show these photos to your family back home.

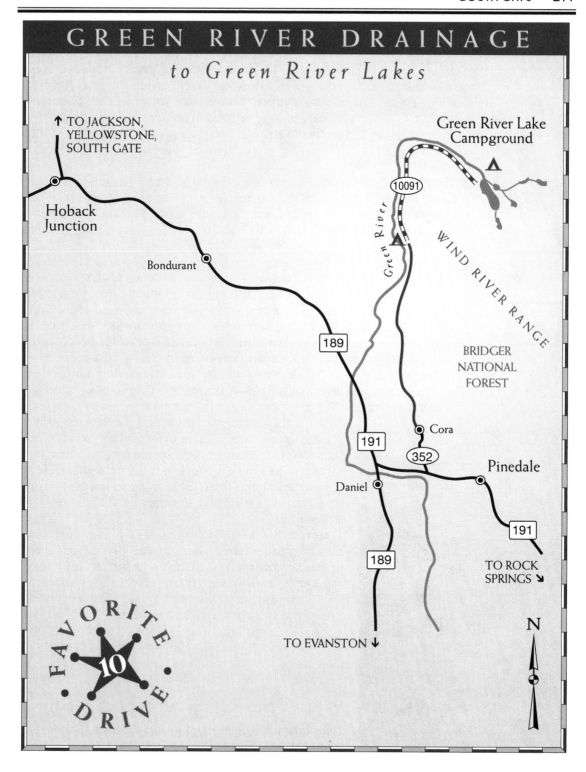

# GREEN RIVER DRAINAGE
## to Green River Lakes

↑ TO JACKSON, YELLOWSTONE, SOUTH GATE

Hoback Junction

Bondurant

Green River Lake Campground

10091

Green River

WIND RIVER RANGE

BRIDGER NATIONAL FOREST

189

191

Cora

352

Pinedale

Daniel

191

TO ROCK SPRINGS ↘

189

TO EVANSTON ↓

FAVORITE 10 DRIVE

N

**GUEST RANCHES**

Green River Guest Ranch, 15 miles north of Cora on paved road. This ranch has been operated as a dude ranch by the Reintses since 1993. Open year-round; busiest in August and February, slowest in April and November; credit cards accepted; pets allowed. Contact Darlene Reints, PO Box 176, Hwy. 352, Cora, WY 82925; (307) 367-2314.

Lozier's Box R Ranch, 12 miles northeast of Cora. This is a working guest ranch. Open late May through mid-September; credit cards accepted; no pets allowed. Contact Lozier's Box R Ranch, Cora, WY 82925; (307) 367-2291; (307) 367-6260.

**MERNA**

Drive to Merna via Wyoming 354 just a mile or so north of Daniel. This road is okay when it's dry but might be slick during extensive rains. It also may have some potholes. The post office in Merna was built in 1900 at the site of abandoned Fort Bonneville. In 1832 the U.S. Army gave Captain Benjamin Bonneville permission to scout out the west. Leading an expedition of more than 100 men, Bonneville reached the Green River Valley in July of that same year. With fur trapping and trading as a mainstay, Bonneville's aim was to compete with other trapping companies and eventually gain control of the territory. Intended as a permanent trading post rather than a temporary rendezvous site, Captain Bonneville established the fort in a strategic location. Unfortunately, extremely harsh winter weather forced him to abandon the camp. The fort was dubbed Bonneville's Folly or Fort Nonsense.

Merna is still surrounded by ranches, but much smaller ones than in the old days. Developers are breaking up the big ranches and turning them into summer "ranchettes" for modern-day commuters, which is, unfortunately, becoming too common in the west.

*Cows take up residence at this unfurnished apartment near Pinedale, Wyoming.*

**DANIEL**

This little community was named for Thomas P. Daniel, the town's first postmaster in 1900. It is also the site of a memorial to the Jesuit missionary who said Wyoming's first Roman Catholic Mass. On July 5, 1840, Father Pierre De Smet recited the Holy Mass to French trappers and Natives attending a mountain man rendezvous. The Mass was given from atop a grassy bench overlooking the valley where Horse Creek joins the Green River and where Daniel is now located.

In 1925, a monument was erected to commemorate "La Prairie de la Messe" and the memory of Father De Smet. The memorial can be found just past the Daniel Cemetery.

**OVERNIGHTING**

### CAMPGROUNDS & RV PARKS

Warren Bridge—U.S. Bureau of Land Management Campground, 24 miles north of Pinedale on U.S. 187/189. No services or drinking water; open June 1 to October 31.

Harper's Park & RV, 23 E. 2nd St., Box 4478, Marbleton, WY. 15 RV sites (some pull-throughs), all services except showers; open year-round.

(More overnighting services are listed in the Pinedale section.)

### GUEST RANCHES

David Ranch, 90 miles south of Jackson; follow U.S. 191 to Daniel, then take Siems Road (gravel). The ranch was established as a guest ranch in 1985. Featured are real western experiences on a working cattle ranch; adults only. Open May 25 through October 25; no credit cards accepted; pets allowed. Contact Melvin and Toni David, PO Box 5, 145 Siems Rd., Daniel, WY 83115; (307) 859-8228; fax: (307) 367-2864.

**BIG PINEY**

In November 1879, Hugh McKay and Daniel Budd were driving a herd of 750 cattle from Nevada through Wyoming headed for market on the Union Pacific Railroad line in southern Wyoming. Winter set in hard, and the pair decided to hole up along the Green River. The cattle survived surprisingly well, convincing McKay and Budd that cattle could make it through the tough, windy winters in good condition. Both partners eventually settled around Big Piney. McKay kept to ranching and Budd established a homestead, which became the town site of Big Piney.

# The Rendezvous

Early trappers, fur traders and mountain men had periodic meetings to market their pelts, stock up on supplies, barter for needed items and to raise a bit of hell. Native Americans also attended the affairs, eager to join in the trading and games. At several, there were even as many Natives in attendance as whites. Some of those get-togethers were noteworthy events; a few ended in serious fistfights and fatal skirmishes that left some participants dead. The annual rendezvous were held for a period of 16 years from 1825 to 1840. More of these great gatherings took place on Horse Creek not far from modern-day Pinedale than any other single location.

Famous mountain men participated in the rendezvous, such as Jim Bridger, Jedediah Smith, Kit Carson and Captain Benjamin Bonneville. Others, such as Father Pierre De Smet, and Narcissa Whitman and Eliza Spalding (the first white women to cross America in 1836), attended the events as well. The nearby town of Daniel is the site of two historical markers honoring Father De Smet and the two brave pioneer women.

Typically, one of the leaders would designate a time and place for a meeting, such as at the fork of a major river on or about a certain date. With luck, many of the trappers and traders would show up, minus those killed by hostile Natives, a grizzly bear or a fall off a cliff. The last four rendezvous were sponsored by the American Fur Trading Company.

Today you can find a modern-day rendezvous to visit practically every week of the summer and fall. The state tourism or local chamber of commerce offices will have a calendar of events listing the rendezvous' date and place. Most participants will be wearing buckskin clothing that many make themselves, and they'll be camped in tipis, also called lodges. They'll be eating out of huge black pots hanging over a fire, and they're some of the most interesting folks you've ever met. But don't let the clothing and customs fool you. The disguises hide regular citizens such as doctors, lawyers, bankers, the clergy—all sorts of people who enjoy reliving the past in a nearly authentic way.

You'll also see plenty of items for sale, such as beadwork, tanned hides, elk ivory jewelry, homemade tools, clothing and a huge variety of other items. If you're a good negotiator, you'll probably be able to haggle over prices and work out a bargain. You may also see a woman sitting at a spinning wheel, making yarn from raw wool that she carefully guides off a spindle, while using her feet to depress the treadle. A man may be sitting in front of his lodge, chipping a piece of flint into the shape of an arrowhead.

Many contests are held. You may watch a tomahawk-throwing event, a tobacco-spitting contest, a muzzleloader tournament, a venison stew-cooking contest, and other challenges that duplicate the real thing from years gone by.

Here's a tip: Some of these rendezvous are so popular that you may have to park a half-mile away. Try to get there as early in the day as possible, and be sure to park your RV where you can maneuver it easily when other vehicles crowd in.

As an old cattle town of the 1870s, and a more recent oil boom-town of the 1970s, Big Piney's main distinction is that of being cold, very cold, a lot of the time. In the 1930s, Big Piney had the coldest year-round average temperature in the nation, prompting meteorologists to choose the town as an official government weather-station site.

The weather patterns haven't changed much, but Main Street is pretty well boarded up these days, even though the population is about 450. The rural areas have fared much better, and attractive homes can be found.

## OVERNIGHTING

### CAMPGROUNDS & RV PARKS

Middle Piney Lake—U.S. Forest Service Campground, 25 miles west of Big Piney on Wyoming 350 (Middle Piney Road) and Forest Service Road 10024. 6 RV sites (no pull-throughs), no services except drinking water; open July 1 through September 30.

Sacajawea—U.S. Forest Service Campground, 22 miles west of Big Piney on Wyoming 350 (Middle Piney Road) and Forest Service Road 10024. 26 RV sites, no pull-throughs; no services except drinking water; open June 15 through September 30.

### GUEST RANCHES

C. K. Hunting & Fishing Camp, 45 miles from Big Piney (28 miles on gravel and dirt road). The camp has been under current operation since 1985. Open June through September 10; no credit cards accepted; pets allowed. Contact Darrell Copeland, Box 458, North Cottonwood Creek Rd., Big Piney, WY 83113; (307) 276-3723; fax: (307) 276-3471.

*Cattle being driven down a road outside Pinedale, Wyoming*

## PINEDALE

Native Americans traveled through this area on hunting expeditions for buffalo and elk. In the 1800s, mountain men came along, and the fur trade formed the basis for more extensive exploration. The Green River area was favored by the Rocky Mountain fur trade, and six rendezvous were held nearby on the Upper Green River in the 1830s. Today, Pinedale boasts that it's the "Mountain Man's Base Camp for Adventure."

Mountain men, however, kept on the move and didn't linger too long in one place. The first permanent residents were the cattle ranchers who began arriving in 1878. Bob Graham settled on Pine Creek and opened a post office in 1899. The town became official in 1912 and won the designation as Sublette County Seat in 1921.

Cattle ranching is still an important part of the economy, and Pinedale houses government offices for Sublette County, the U.S. Forest Service, Wyoming Game and Fish, and the BLM. Tourism is also becoming more important to the 1,200 residents and is growing fast. Especially picturesque is Fremont Lake, located just 4 miles from Pinedale. The lake is the second-largest natural lake in Wyoming and is popular for boating, fishing and camping.

## OUTDOOR RECREATION AND ATTRACTIONS

Rendezvous Meadows golf course is open to the public. Call for tee times, (307) 367-4252.

The Museum of the Mountain Man, open May 1 to October 1, has exhibits on fur trade, Plains tribes, early exploration and settlement history. The museum sponsors special events like the Green River Rendezvous Pageant. This reenactment of the trader's annual gathering puts you in the saddle. There's a bundle of activities like blackpowder shootouts, authentic costumes and tools for trappin' and tannin', historical demonstrations, crafts, cowboy poetry and a parade. The pageant, one of Wyoming's oldest, is held the second Saturday in July. The museum has all the information, PO Box 909, 700 E. Hennick St., Pinedale, WY 82941; (307) 367-4101; fax: (307) 367-6768.

## OVERNIGHTING

### CAMPGROUNDS & RV PARKS

Lakeside Lodge Resort & Marina, 4 miles north of Pinedale on south shore of Fremont Lake. 20 RV sites (no pull-throughs), hook-ups and some services; open May 15 through November 1; (307) 367-2221.

Pinedale Campgrounds, 204 S. Jackson, Pinedale, WY. 24 RV sites (no pull-throughs), hook-ups and some services; open May 25 through October 15; (307) 367-4555.

Fremont Lake—U.S. Forest Service Campground, 3 miles northeast of Pinedale on County Road, then 4 miles northeast on Forest Service Road 111. 54 RV sites (no pull-throughs), no services except drinking water; open May 25 through September 10.

Green River Lake—U.S. Forest Service Campground, 25 miles north of Pinedale on Wyoming 352, then 31 miles north on Forest Service Road 091. 36 RV sites (no pull-throughs), no services except drinking water; open June 15 through September 10.

Half Moon—U.S. Forest Service Campground, 3 miles northeast of Pinedale on County Road, then 5 miles northeast on Forest Service Road 134. 18 RV sites (no pull-throughs), no services; open June 1 through September 10.

Narrows—U.S. Forest Service Campground, 21 miles north of Pinedale on Wyoming 352, then 5 miles east on County Road, 3 miles east on Forest Service Road 107. 19 RV sites (no pull-throughs), no services except drinking water; open June 1 through September 10.

New Fork Lakes—U.S. Forest Service Campground, 21 miles north of Pinedale on Wyoming 352, then 5 miles east on County Road, 3 miles southeast on Forest Service Road 107. 15 RV sites (no pull-throughs), no services except drinking water; open June 1 through September 10.

Scab Creek—U.S. Bureau of Land Management Campground, 20 miles southeast of Pinedale on Wyoming 353, then north 10 miles on County Road. 10 RV sites (no pull-throughs), no services except drinking water; open June 1 through October 31.

Trails End—U.S. Forest Service Campground, 3 miles northeast of Pinedale on County Road, then 11 miles northeast on Forest Service Road 134. 8 RV sites (no pull-throughs), no services except drinking water; open June 25 through September 10.

Whiskey Grove—U.S. Forest Service Campground, 36 miles north of Pinedale on Wyoming 352 and Forest Service Road 091, then 095. 9 RV sites (no pull-throughs), no services except drinking water; open June 15 through September 10.

Boulder Lake—U.S. Forest Service Campground, 3 miles east of Boulder on Wyoming 353, then 10 miles north on Boulder Lake Road. 20 RV sites (no pull-throughs), no services; open June 1 through October 15.

Wind River View Campground, 8889 Hwy. 191, Boulder, WY. 22 RV sites (no pull-throughs), full services; open May 15 through September 30; (307) 537-5453.

## BED & BREAKFAST ESTABLISHMENTS

The Chambers House Bed & Breakfast, historic home built of logs and stone in 1920s, originally used as a schoolhouse; credit cards accepted; well-behaved dogs allowed, but no cats; open year-round; busiest in summer, slowest in November and December. Contact Antonette Chambers Noble, Box 753, 111 W. Magnolia St., Pinedale, WY 82941; (307) 367-2168; 1-800-567-2168; fax: (307) 367-4209.

Pole Creek Ranch Bed & Breakfast, ranch house with lakeside lodge, tipi and hot tub; located on paved road, except last quarter-mile is dirt. Operated by the Smiths since 1993; no credit cards accepted; open year-round; busiest June through September, slowest October through May. Contact Dexter and Carole Smith, 244 Pole Creek Rd., Pinedale, WY 82941; (307) 367-4433.

## GUEST RANCHES

Flying A Ranch, 50 miles south of Jackson, 7 miles from highway on gravel road. Private cabins have been under current operation since 1988; open June 15 through October 15; no credit cards accepted; no pets allowed. Contact Debbie Hanson or Keith Dagel, Rt. 1, Box 7, Pinedale, WY 82941; 1-800-678-6543; (307) 367-2385.

DC Bar Guest Ranch, 30 miles north of Pinedale (last 5 miles on dirt road), adjacent to Bridger-Teton National Forest. Experience the west at this historic ranch while staying in individual cabins. Under current operation since 1982; open year-round; busiest June through October, slowest November through April; credit cards accepted; no pets allowed. Contact Tim Singewald, Box 561, Pinedale, WY 82941; (307) 367-2268; 1-888-803-7316; website: http://www.bwo.com

Fort William Recreation Area, in the Wind River Range. Contact Lynn or Wendy Robertson, Box 1081, 308 Fall Creek Rd., Pinedale, WY 82941; (307) 367-4670.

Boulder Lake Lodge, 12 miles from U.S. 191 and Boulder on gravel road. Under current operation since 1981; open year-round; busiest in July and August, slowest May and October; no credit cards accepted; no pets allowed. Contact Kim Bright, PO Box 1100, 48 Bridger Dr., Pinedale, WY 82941; (307) 537-5400.

Elk Ridge Lodge, 30 miles north of Pinedale on Wyoming 352 (gravel road to lodge); under current operation since 1988; open year-round, except April; busiest in summer and winter snow months, slowest in November; no credit cards accepted; no pets allowed. Contact Terry Reach, PO Box 705, 125 Rock Creek Rd., Pinedale, WY 82941; (307) 367-2553.

Half Moon Lake Guest Ranch, working cattle ranch; new owners in 1998; has RV sites. Contact Half Moon Lake, Box 983, Pinedale, WY 82941; (307) 367-6373 or (208) 788-9800.

Big Sandy Lodge, in Bridger-Teton National Forest, 44 miles north-east of Boulder (25 miles on gravel road). The lodge was established in 1929 and has been under current operation since 1982. Open June through October; no credit cards accepted. Contact Bernie and Connie Kelly, Box 223, 1050 Big Sandy Opening Rd., Boulder, WY 82923; (307) 332-6782.

**SUGGESTED DINING**

Della Rose, 120 E. Pine, Pinedale, WY; (307) 367-2810.

McGregor's Pub, 21 N. Franklin, Pinedale, WY; (307) 367-4443.

Stockman's Steak & Pub, 117 W. Pine, Pinedale, WY; (307) 367-4563.

Elk Country Barbeque, 709 W. Pine, Pinedale, WY; (307) 367-2252.

**VISITOR INFORMATION & SERVICES**

Pinedale Chamber of Commerce at PO Box 176, 32 E. Pine, Pinedale, WY 82941; open Monday through Friday 9 A.M. to 5 P.M., summer; Monday through Friday, 1 P.M. to 5 P.M., winter; (307) 367-2242.

While you're visiting the town's sights, you may park your RV at the Chamber of Commerce, or fairly easily around town.

**MEDICAL SERVICES**

Pinedale Clinic, 619 E. Hennick, Pinedale, WY; open Monday through Friday, 9 A.M. to 5 P.M., and Saturday, 9 A.M. to 12 NOON; (307) 367-4133.

Pinedale Drug, 341 E. Pine, Pinedale, WY; open Monday through Friday, 9 A.M. to 5:30 P.M., and Saturday, 9 A.M. to 12 NOON; (307) 367-4451; after hours, (307) 367-4429.

| | |
|---|---|
| **REPAIR & TOWING** | Belreal Body Shop, 24-hour service, 219 E. Mill, Pinedale, WY; (307) 367-6331. |
| **VETERINARY SERVICES** | Animal Clinic of Pinedale, Dr. Brent Dean, 43 S. Madison, Pinedale, WY; (307) 367-4752. |

# MORAN JUNCTION: U.S. 26/287

The official southern gate to Yellowstone National Park, Moran Junction was named after the artist Thomas Moran. Along with photographer William Henry Jackson, Moran helped bring to the public's attention the splendor, and even more, the reality of Yellowstone. All too astounding for eastern city-slickers to believe, previous descriptions of the area given by explorers were thought to be the exaggerations of western "liars." John Colter, the first white explorer to enter Yellowstone Country from the southern route in 1807–8, was branded a liar for his tales of steaming ground and boiling mud waterfalls.

Thomas Moran journeyed through Jackson Hole and the southern park area in 1871 with Dr. Ferdinand V. Hayden and his government expedition. In 1872, spurred by the proof shown by Moran's etchings and paintings and Jackson's photographs, Congress created Yellowstone National Park.

One of the grand peaks of the Teton Range, 12,605-foot Mount Moran is named after the famous painter. Some of Moran's watercolors may be seen at the Horace Albright Visitor Center at Mammoth Springs in Yellowstone National Park.

# MORAN JUNCTION TO DUBOIS, RIVERTON, AND LANDER: U.S. 26/287

| | |
|---|---|
| **OVERNIGHTING** | **CAMPGROUNDS & RV PARKS** |

▲ *Best Shot for a Camp Spot*
Grand Teton Park KOA, 1 mile east of Grand Teton National Park, Box 92, Moran Junction, WY. 185 RV sites (70 pull-throughs), hook-ups, dump station, hot showers, hot tub, playground, store and snack bar; open year-round; (307) 543-2483.

## FAVORITE DRIVE:
## TOGWOTEE PASS: BLACKROCK CREEK &
## THE WYOMING CENTENNIAL

This is a nicely paved highway that draws you upward through evergreen forests, and along the Buffalo Fork and Blackrock Creek drainages. The road ascends gradually until you top out at Togwotee Pass (pronounced Toe-ga-tee), placing you at 9,658 feet on the Continental Divide. From here, the streams and creeks flow eastward to the Yellowstone River, eventually ending up in the Gulf of Mexico. Togwotee Pass has been used for thousands of years by Native Americans as a natural pass from the Yellowstone mountainous regions to the plains. It's also a favorite grizzly bear hangout. There are probably more grizzly bear-cattle conflicts on nearby ranches here than anywhere else in the Greater Yellowstone Area. Don't be surprised to see snow on the pass in late June or early July.

Togwotee Pass crosses the Continental Divide at a height of 9,658 feet, and then descends along Blackrock Creek, eventually winding into Dubois. The pass was named after the leader of the Sheepeater tribe, a branch of the Shoshone; Togwotee was a sub-chief of Chief Washakie. Togwotee guided a U.S. exploratory expedition of this pass in 1873, and reportedly guided President Chester A. Arthur on his tour to Yellowstone in 1883. The pass is designated as a Wyoming Scenic Byway.

As you come to Dubois, you'll leave the high-country forests and enter sagebrush. The Wind River flows parallel to the highway; you can easily spot it by following the line of willows and cottonwood trees. As you continue into Dubois and drive out of it, you'll notice more arid land characterized by sagebrush. Soon you enter the Wind River Indian Reservation, which has the distinction of being the only reservation in Wyoming. Lander and Riverton are at the end of our 100-mile circle. The highway out of Lander will take you over famous South Pass, where the Oregon Trail crossed the backbone of the Rockies; the Riverton route carries you to Casper and down into Cheyenne and Denver.

Colter Bay RV Park, 10 miles north of Moran Junction on U.S. 89/287, PO Box 240, Moran Junction, WY. RV sites (no pull-throughs), hook-ups, dump station, hot showers; open May 15 through September 30; 1-800-628-9988; fax: (307) 543-3143.

Colter Bay—National Park Service Campground, 2 miles off U.S. 89/287, and 8 miles north of Moran. 112 RV sites (no pull-throughs), hook-ups, dump station, hot showers; open May 15 through October 4.

Jenny Lake—National Park Service Campground, 8 miles north of Moose on Teton Park Road. No services; open May 15 through September 15.

# TOGWOTEE PASS

## *Blackrock Creek & the Wyoming Centennial Scenic Byway*

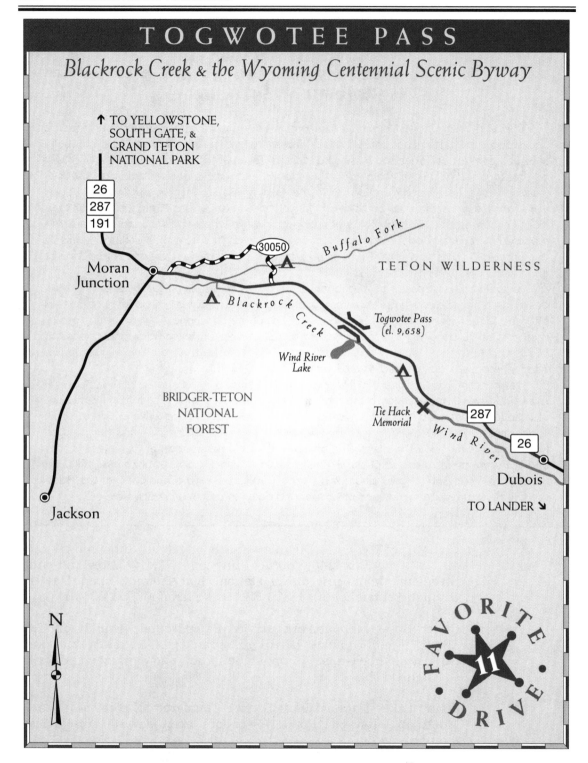

↑ TO YELLOWSTONE,
SOUTH GATE, &
GRAND TETON
NATIONAL PARK

26
287
191

Moran
Junction

30050

*Buffalo Fork*

TETON WILDERNESS

*Blackrock  Creek*

Togwotee Pass
(el. 9,658)

Wind River
Lake

BRIDGER-TETON
NATIONAL
FOREST

Tie Hack
Memorial

*Wind  River*

287

26

Jackson

Dubois

TO LANDER ↘

N

FAVORITE · DRIVE ·

11

Lizard Creek—National Park Service Campground, 18 miles north of Moran Junction on U.S. 89/287. 60 RV sites (no pull-throughs), no services; open June 15 through September 1.

Hatchet—U.S. Forest Service Campground, 8 miles east of Moran Junction on U.S. 26/287. 9 RV sites (no pull-throughs), no services; open June 25 through September 10.

## BED & BREAKFAST ESTABLISHMENTS

The Inn at Buffalo Fork, rural country home; operated since 1993; credit cards accepted; no pets allowed; open January through October. Contact Eugene and Jeannie Ferrin, PO Box 311, 18200 E. Hwy. 28, Moran, WY 83013; (307) 543-2010; fax: (307) 543-0935.

## GUEST RANCHES

Flagg Ranch, 2 miles from the South Gate of Yellowstone National Park on the Snake River; Box 187, Moran, WY 83013; (307) 543-2861; 1-800-443-2311; fax: (307) 543-2356.

## The Tie Hackers

In 1914 the timber trade boomed. Vast numbers of railroad ties were needed to supply the expanding Chicago and Northwestern Railroads. A new era was born—that of the professional "Tie Hack"—and it continued until the 1950s.

The predominately Scandinavian immigrants used a simple hand tool, the tie hack, to carve a timber into railroad ties that measured an exact 7 inches wide. The work was extremely hard, and the men were rough, brawling fighters whose feats of strength were unbelievable. Besides the physical requirement, the skill of these woodsmen was renowned. Over the years 10 million ties were made; approximately 40 million board-feet of lumber were harvested. But, as the railroads faded, so too, passed the tie hacker's trade. In 1946, the Wyoming Tie and Timber Company erected a monument in recognition of their great feats. At the Hack Memorial, a state historical marker on U.S. 26/287, stands the 14-foot limestone statue of a rugged lumberjack, square-jawed and broad-shouldered, stoutly facing his harsh way of life.

## DUBOIS

Situated in what is now known as the Upper Wind River Valley, the Dubois region's settlement began in the late 1800s. Fur trappers, traders and explorers passed through the area, but the Fort Bridger Treaty in 1863, which created the Wind River Indian Reservation, helped establish the area and encouraged settlement in the upper valley.

The Shoshone, Bannock, Gros Ventre, Arapaho, Crow, Flathead and Nez Perce tribes all used the Dubois-Union Pass area as a corridor during hunting expeditions. Union Pass (elevation 9,210 feet) crosses the Continental Divide and marks the separation of waters flowing to the Mississippi, Columbia and Colorado Rivers.

John Jacob Astor and his followers were famous as the first white men, besides John Colter, to enter western Wyoming. Astor's attempt to establish a foothold in the fur trade, which was dominated by the Hudson's Bay Company, was foiled when Fort Astoria was ceded to the British in the War of 1812. His men abandoned Washington and returned to New York, once again across western Wyoming. The return group, led by Astorian Robert Stuart, is said to have passed through the Dubois area. A state historical marker on U.S. 26/287 notes the passage of the Astorians in 1811–12.

The town of Dubois ("Dew-boys") was named after an Idaho senator by the U.S. Postal Service. The government agency suggested the senator's name after rejecting the original name submitted on the application, "Never Sweat."

Rich in scenery, the mountainous region surrounding the town is heavily forested with lodgepole pine and thick willow bottoms, broken open by lush grassy meadows. Abundant with wildlife, the area is perfect habitat for moose and elk. Early settlers depended on the forest. Ranching, fur trapping and timber harvesting were the fundamental occupations.

In the early 1900s, dude ranches became popular in Wyoming. By the 1920s the number of ranches catering to tourists who wanted to experience western living was on the increase. Ranches in the Dubois area were among the first to participate in this new trade. After the vacuum left by the shutdown of the timber industry in the late 1980s, local citizens focused again on tourism. There has been a strong resurgence in "guest ranching," as it's known today; the term dude is a bit crude for today's sophisticated tourist. The town of 900 residents now places a lot of reliance on out-of-town visitors.

*Ranchland close to the Wind River Mountains near Dubois, Wyoming*
COURTESY WYOMING DIVISION OF TOURISM

## OUTDOOR RECREATION

Golfers enjoy the Antelope Hills 9-hole course on the western end of town. Call for tee times, (307) 455-2888.

Wintertime brings snowmobilers by the dozens. The surrounding mountains are extremely popular, with hundreds of miles of trails. Cross-country skiers like the peace and quiet of trails where snowmobiles are prohibited. Other winter activities include dog sledding and snowshoeing. Many of the trails for all these winter sports are via the Continental Divide Trail, which has more than 250 miles of groomed trails in the upper Wind River country. More trails are in the Togwotee Pass direction to the west. Local shops have equipment to rent and can provide specific trail information. Contact the Dubois Chamber of Commerce, (307) 455-2556.

*Rocky red foothills in the Wind River country near Dubois, Wyoming*

## ATTRACTIONS

The Wind River Historical Center and Dubois Museum and Visitor Center are at 909 W. Ramshorn, Dubois, WY; (307) 455-2284. There is no charge to view the exhibits featuring various Native American artifacts, natural history, pioneer settings and a collection of petrified wood. The museum is open May through September, Monday through Saturday, 10 A.M. to 5 P.M.; and Sunday, noon to 5 P.M.

The National Bighorn Sheep Center, finished in 1993, is in Dubois next to the museum. The center offers educational and interpretive displays about this Rocky Mountain wild sheep and is open daily in the summer. The largest herd of bighorn sheep in the lower 48 states, 900 to 1,000, winters at Whiskey Basin because of mild winters, Chinook winds and lack of deep snow. Tours to the winter range on Whiskey Mountain are also available. The mountain, easily viewed from town, got its name during Prohibition days from the many whiskey stills secreted on the slopes. For more information, write to PO Box 1435, Dubois, WY 82513; or call 1-888-209-2795.

Dubois has several weekend festivals throughout the year. In February the Sno-Katters Fun Days are held on Presidents' Weekend. The Dubois Pack Horse Races take place over Memorial Day Weekend. June brings the Wind River Reunion/Little Fawn Rendezvous; this Father's Day Weekend is loads of fun. The Whiskey Mountain Buckskinners Rendezvous takes place during the second weekend of August. The end of the year brings about the Bighorn Sheep Safari on the first weekend of December.

## OVERNIGHTING

### CAMPGROUNDS & RV PARKS

▲ *Best Shot for a Camp Spot*
Circle-Up Camper Court, at the center of town on U.S. 287, PO Box 1520, Dubois, WY 82513. 80 RV sites (20 pull-throughs), full hook-ups; swimming pool; open May 15 through December 15; (307) 455-2238.

Diamond Bar E Ranch Campground, 15 miles west of Dubois. 18 RV sites, some services; open June through October.

Pinnacle Buttes Lodge & Campground, 3577 W. Hwy. 26, Dubois, WY 82513. 15 RV sites, hook-ups and some services; open year-round; (307) 455-2506; fax: (307) 455-3874.

Brooks Lake—U.S. Forest Service Campground, 23 miles west of Dubois on U.S. 287, then 5 miles north on Forest Service Road. 14 RV sites, no services; open late June through September.

Double Cabin—U.S. Forest Service Campground, 29 miles north of Dubois on Forest Service Road 285. 15 RV sites (max. length 16 feet), some services; open June through September.

Falls—U.S. Forest Service Campground, 25 miles west of Dubois on U.S. 287. 46 RV sites, no services or drinking water; open June through October.

Horse Creek—U.S. Forest Service Campground, 12 miles north of Dubois on Forest Service Road. 9 RV sites, no services or drinking water; open June through October.

Pinnacles—U.S. Forest Service Campground, 23 miles northwest of Dubois on U.S. 26/287, then 15 miles on Forest Service Road 515. 21 RV sites, some services; open late June through early September.

### BED & BREAKFAST ESTABLISHMENTS

Geyser Creek Bed & Breakfast, ranch home; credit cards accepted. Contact Norina and Clayton Shields, 151 Bald Mountain Rd., Dubois, WY 82513; (307) 455-2702.

Jakey's Fork Homestead, country home; operated since 1991; credit cards accepted; no pets; open year-round, busiest in summer, not in spring. Contact Justin and Irene Bridges, Box 635, Fish Hatchery Rd., Dubois, WY 82513; (307) 455-2769.

Ramsview Bed & Breakfast, ranch house; no credit cards accepted; well-behaved pets; open May 15 through October 15; busiest in July and August, slowest in May and September. Contact Leota and Bernard Didier, Box 761, 10 Warm Springs, Dubois, WY 82513; (307) 455-3615.

The Stone House Bed & Breakfast, historic home built in 1947; only small RV access; no credit cards accepted; seasonal. Contact Grace Whalen, PO Box 1446, 207 S. 1st St., Dubois, WY 82513; (307) 455-2555.

Wapiti Ridge Ranch Bed & Breakfast, mountain lodge 17 miles from Dubois on main highway; most credit cards accepted; no pets or smoking allowed; open year-round; busiest in July and February, slowest April through May, November to December. Contact Pat Dantzier, 3915 U.S. 26, Dubois, WY 82513; (307) 455-2219; 1-800-927-4844; fax: (307) 2219; e-mail: wapitiridgeb-b@wyoming.com

## GUEST RANCHES

Bitterroot Ranch, 26 miles northeast of Dubois, via gravel/dirt road. This working horse ranch has been operating since 1971. Featured are quality horseback riding; major credit cards accepted; no pets allowed; open May through September. Contact Bayard or Meloena Fox, Hwy. 27/286, Dubois, WY 82513; 1-800-545-0019.

Brooks Lake Lodge, in Shoshone National Forest along Continental Divide 24 miles west of Dubois; access by snowmobile in winter; credit cards accepted; no pets allowed; open year-round. Contact Barbara Carlsberg, 458 Brooks Lake Rd., Dubois, WY 82513; (307) 455-2121.

MacKenzie Highland Ranch, guest ranch for independent living; travel half-mile on dirt road. This ranch has been owned and operated since 1953; 10 RV sites, full services; credit cards accepted; pets welcome; open year-round except April; busiest season is July. Contact MacKenzie Highland Ranch, 3945 U.S. Hwy. 26, Dubois, WY; (307) 455-3415; fax: (307) 455-2208.

**SUGGESTED DINING**

Dunloggin Cafe, 305 S. 1st St., Dubois, WY 82513; (307) 455-2445.

The Timbers, 1408 Warm Springs Dr., Dubois, WY 82513; (307) 455-3670.

*This seemingly barren badlands area near Dubois has a beauty of its own.*

**VISITOR INFORMATION & SERVICES**

Dubois Chamber of Commerce, PO Box 632, 616 W. Ramshorn St., Dubois, WY 82513; open May through August, daily, 8 A.M. to 7 P.M., September through April, Monday through Friday, 8 A.M. to 12 P.M., 1 P.M. to 4 P.M.; (307) 455-2556. While you're visiting, you may park at the Chamber of Commerce.

U.S. Forest Service Ranger Station, 209 E. Ramshorn, Dubois, WY, 82513; (307) 455-2466.

**MEDICAL SERVICES**

Dubois Medical Clinic & Pharmacy, 706 McKem, Dubois, WY; open Monday, Tuesday, Friday, 8:30 A.M. to 4:30 P.M., and Wednesday, 8 A.M. to 12 NOON; (307) 455-2516.

**REPAIR & TOWING**

Bill's Conoco Station, 219 Ramshorn, Dubois, WY; (307) 455-2770.

**VETERINARY SERVICES**

Dubois Veterinary Clinic, Dr. Waldron, 408 W. Ramshorn, Dubois, WY; (307) 455-3434; after hours, (307) 455-2728.

## WIND RIVER INDIAN RESERVATION

This sprawling reservation takes in the towns of Crowheart, Fort Washakie, Ethete and Arapahoe, among others.

*A Native American powwow on the Wind River Reservation*
COURTESY WYOMING DIVISION OF TOURISM

## CROWHEART

The small village, basically just a country store, carries the same name as the butte that dominates the nearby landscape. Cattle ranches along the Wind River surround the area.

The name Crowheart Butte carries within it a testimony to Chief Washakie, his bravery and the respect he earned from his people. In 1866, the Shoshone and their allies, the Bannock, engaged in battle with the Crow over disputed hunting rights. Hunting lands granted to the Shoshone in the 1863 Treaty of Fort Bridger had also been given to the Crow via the Fort Laramie Treaty of 1851. A fierce and bloody battle ensued for four days, at which point a bargain between the two dominant chiefs was made, winner-take-all. Chief Washakie of the Shoshone would fight Chief Big Robber of the Crow in a single combat to be held atop the butte. Legend has it that Washakie killed the Crow chief and then ate his heart. This story, passed through the ages, inspired awe in listeners because Washakie's savagery and crude strength made him a leader to be feared. Less gruesome, mitigated versions claim he cut out the heart and displayed it on the end of his lance. Later when asked, Washakie neither denied nor affirmed the tale. He said, "When a man is in battle and his blood runs hot, he sometimes does things that he is sorry for afterwards."

Crowheart Butte is still used as a spiritual place and for vision quests by members of the tribe, but, it is illegal for non-Natives to climb the butte. It's also said that those who do, do not come back.

## OVERNIGHTING

### GUEST RANCHES

Early Guest Ranch, on the Wind River inside the Wind River Indian Reservation boundaries. Contact Ruth and Wayne Campbell, 7374 U.S. 26, Crowheart, WY 82512; (307) 455-4055; 1-800-532-4055; (307) 455-2414.

## FORT WASHAKIE

The Shoshone and Arapaho tribal councils and the Bureau of Indian Affairs are currently headquartered at Fort Washakie. The former home of Chief Washakie, the town began as a U.S. Army camp. As of 1997, the population includes 2,501 enrolled Shoshone and 4,564 enrolled Arapaho.

Chief Washakie's Shoshone treated the white men as friends, and for the most part, did not make war against the white settlers and trappers. Meant as a reward, in 1863 the first of five treaties with the Shoshone conferred to them the fertile lands of the Wind River Basin. The lands included the valley of the Popo Agie River (pronounced "Po-poshia"), and extended to the Wyoming-Utah border. Although the Shoshone agreed to remain on the reservation, other tribes kept no such agreements. The Arapaho and Sioux, traditional enemies of the Shoshone, continued raids against both the Shoshone and the whites. Illegal white settlers, coveting the rich Popo Agie lands, pushed the Shoshone north.

At the Treaty of Fort Bridger in 1868, General Augur established the Wind River Reservation. The boundaries became the Owl Creek and Wind River Mountains, the Wind River and the Popo Agie River. Originally the Bannock tribe was included, but they later chose to settle in Idaho. Camp Augur was established in 1869 to protect agency families and the Shoshone from Arapaho and Sioux warriors who still raided fiercely. In 1870 it was renamed Camp Brown, and in 1871, the camp was moved 16 miles northwest to its current location. In 1878, it was renamed Fort Washakie, in honor of the Shoshone Chief.

By 1877, most Plains tribes were placed on reservations. However, at the onset of winter in 1877, the Northern Arapaho tribe still had no home. Despite the fact that the Arapaho tribe was the traditional enemy of the Shoshone, Chief Washakie submitted to the government's request and allowed them to spend the winter on the Wind River Reservation. The government administration changed hands over the winter, and promises to find a home for the Northern Arapaho were forgotten. Washakie repeatedly demanded that the Arapaho, his traditional enemies, be removed, but the government turned a deaf ear. The temporary winter kindness became a permanent solution.

The Wind River Reservation was reduced in size in 1872, 1896 and 1905. In 1939 the Shoshone were successful in the U.S. Court of Claims. The award netted the tribe about $4 million. In subsequent years, other awards were made to both the Shoshone and Arapaho.

Francis E. Warren, a powerful Republican Senator from 1895 through 1929, was chairman of the Senate Military Affairs Committee. Referred to in the press as a "pork barrel" politician, Warren favored the presence of a large army in Wyoming. Troops were kept at Cheyenne, Sheridan and Fort Washakie until 1909.

The Wind River Indian Reservation has rich lands and is indeed rewarding. There is abundant wildlife, beautiful scenery and excellent fishing for cutthroat, golden, rainbow, brook, brown and lake trout. A special license is required for non-reservation residents, but the fishing is some of the best in Wyoming. Ranching is the predominant occupation. Other natural resources include oil, gas and agriculture, especially hay, alfalfa, barley and oats.

**OUTDOOR RECREATION AND ATTRACTIONS**

Fishing in the Wind River is outstanding. A special permit from the Wind Indian Reservation is required, available in surrounding towns. See the chapter on fishing for details (page 22).

The Chief Washakie Graveyard is a revered site. Washakie (pronounced "Wau-sik-he") was born about 1800, and died February 20, 1900. The Native legend says that Chief Washakie's mother was a Shoshone, and his father was a Flathead. His upbringing was left to his mother, and he was devoted to her his entire life. Chief Washakie was long noted as a friend of the white man. The Washakie memorial inscription testifies to this: "Always loyal to the government and his white brothers. A wise ruler." The graveyard is west of town on South Fork Road.

Sacajawea's Cemetery is close to Chief Washakie's; follow the South Fork Road and veer left at the "Y" and left again at the log church. Sacajawea was the Shoshone guide and wife of Toussaint Charbonneau, both members of the Lewis and Clark Expedition. Wyoming's version of her gravesite at the Wind River Reservation is disputed. Most historians and scholars concur that Sacajawea's grave is in South Dakota. However, the Wyoming cemetery has a grand headstone. John Baptiste, one of her sons, is buried alongside, and other descendants are also in the cemetery.

Native American arts and crafts are available at Warm Valley Arts & Crafts, on north fork of U.S. 287, Fort Washakie; open Monday through Saturday, 8 A.M. to 4 P.M.; call (307) 332-7330. Crafts are also available at the Wind River Trading Co., which is next to Hines General Store.

The Shoshone Episcopal Mission was established in 1883 by the Reverend John Roberts. The Welsh missionary was known as the "White Robe." During his stay at the mission, the boarding school for Native girls was built in 1891. The location of the historic mission is 1.5 miles southwest of Fort Washakie on Trout Creek Road.

In June, the Treaty Day Celebration is held, as well as the Fort Washakie-Eastern Shoshone Powwow and Rodeo. The three-day event is open to the public; activities include a reenactment of the treaty signing with the federal government, traditional dances, rodeo, crafts and great food.

## ETHETE

Ethete (EEE-thuh-tee) is the main Arapaho community on the reservation. It was established in 1887 by the Reverend John Roberts, who asked Chief Sharp Nose for permission to build the mission. Chief Sharp Nose answered by saying *ethete*, meaning "good."

At one time, St. Michael's Episcopal Mission was the principal school for Arapaho children. The school building is now used mainly as a community center. Most other buildings there were completed between 1910 and 1917 under Bishop Nathaniel Thomas. The church, "Our Father's House," is one of the most outstanding buildings, a low log structure with many Native American motifs, and a picture window behind the altar facing the Wind River Mountains. Similar to the Chapel of the Transfiguration at Moose in Jackson Hole, the altar and celebration of God through a window view of the beautiful Wind River Mountains is especially fitting to the Arapaho.

At the mission, be sure to visit the Arapaho Cultural Museum, which is open Monday through Friday, 8 A.M. to 5 P.M., and Saturday from 10 A.M. to 3 P.M. The exhibits are very well done, and the beadwork display is most impressive. The summer months are community celebration time. In mid-June, the Ethete Community Powwow is held. In July the Annual Ethete Celebration and Northern Arapaho Sun Dance ceremony (no cameras) are held at Ethete Powwow grounds.

## ARAPAHOE

The town came into being when the age-old animosity between the Shoshone and Arapaho again surfaced. The Arapaho began the subagency community in order to handle distribution of annuities without sneers from the Shoshone at Fort Washakie.

## ST. STEPHENS

St. Stephens is the site of an old Catholic mission that was started in 1884. The mission was founded by Father John Jutz with the permission of Arapaho Chief Black Coal. The Jesuits and nuns ran a school for boys and girls, and also began a tradition of preserving the Native arts and crafts. The older mission buildings are based on grand Victorian and early twentieth-century architectural style, and contrast sharply to the newer reservation and agency buildings. The tradition of Native arts and crafts is continued at the museum and North American Indian Heritage Center. The location of the mission is on Wyoming 138, about 8 miles from Arapahoe. More information is available from the Wind River Rendezvous Magazine, PO Box 278, St. Stephens, WY 82524, or the North American Indian Heritage Center, (307) 856-4330.

## VISITOR INFORMATION & SERVICES

The Shoshone Cultural and Resource Center is an information and heritage center. The facility is the White House on the BIA Compound, Fort Washakie, WY; (307) 332-9106.

## LANDER

Frederick West Lander was the man who engineered the major road from South Pass and spent the winter of 1857-58 in the nearby Popo Agie Valley. Lander negotiated with Shoshone Chief Washakie for a right-of-way along his road, the "Lander Cutoff." In 1869 the Army established Camp Augur, later named Camp Brown. In 1875 the town was named for Lander and later became the Fremont County Seat.

Lander is built along the Popo Agie River. The Crow name, Popo Agie, means "Beginning of the Waters." It is the Crow's description of the bubbling spring from which flows the Middle Fork of the Popo Agie River. The river disappears into a cave at the "Sinks" and reappears a half-mile away at a spring called the "Rise." Originally the river was completely aboveground, but over time it sank into the soft limestone ground and formed an underground cave. The geological wonder is located at Sinks Canyon State Park.

Oil was a main resource for the area. First discovered in 1824, oil was not developed until 1884, when the first oil well drilled in Wyoming was completed near Lander. The Dallas Dome wells produced for more than a century. Mining was big from 1960 to 1983. The Columbia-Geneva iron mine in Atlantic City employed hundreds of workers. Today, the primary occupations are in government, ranching and tourism-related industries.

Fremont County is known as the "Land of the Trails" because of its proximity to South Pass, where the migration of 350,000 pioneers marked the land forever. The pass is now known as part of the Oregon Trail. Today, the area is a center for outdoor enthusiasts with hiking, fishing and hunting abundant in the surrounding forests and wilderness. The population is about 7,500. Lander is also a center for environmental and conservation groups. The National Outdoors Leadership School (NOLS), Wyoming Outdoor Council and the Nature Conservancy are all headquartered in Lander.

*Red Canyon, near Lander, Wyoming*
COURTESY
WYOMING TRAVEL
COMMISSION

**OUTDOOR RECREATION AND ATTRACTIONS**

The Lander Golf & Country Club is available for those who miss the green. The course is at Capitol Hill Ave. and Buena Vista Dr., (307) 332-4653.

The Pioneer Museum at 630 Lincoln St., Lander, WY 82520, (307) 332-4137, has interesting local history and artifacts. The small museum has a section dedicated to the One-Shot Antelope Hunt, an annual celebrity hunt held in Lander. From June to September 15, the hours are Monday through Friday, 10 A.M. to 6 P.M., weekends, 1 P.M. to 4 P.M. The rest of the year the weekday hours are 1 P.M. to 5 P.M., and on Saturday from 1 P.M. to 4 P.M.

Wyoming is rich in Native American heritage, and that's particularly true in this region that lies so close to the Wind River Indian Reservation. During the summer, Native American Cultural Presentations are held every Wednesday at the Lander Chamber of Commerce building. The presentations begin at 7:30 P.M. Contact the chamber for the summer schedule.

Special events held in the summer pay note to the Native American heritage and mountain men days. In June the Popo Agie Rendezvous is held, a reenactment of the mountain men's annual gatherings to trade and celebrate. The Pioneer Days, Northern Arapahoe Nation Powwow and Lander Valley Powwow events take place in July. Contact the Chamber of Commerce for specific dates of these annual events.

Sinks Canyon State Park is worth a side trip if you have the time. The Popo Agie River disappears into a cave and remains underground until it reappears at the "Rise." Sinks Canyon, along Wyoming 131, begins at the Loop Road, a major trail into the Wind River Mountains. The 60-mile trip ends in Atlantic City and there are many sights, campgrounds, lakes and wildlife along the way.

**OVERNIGHTING**

## CAMPGROUNDS & RV PARKS

▲ *Best Shot for a Camp Spot*
Sleeping Bear RV Park Campground, east of Lander on Wyoming 789, 715 E. Main, Dubois, WY 82513. 21 RV sites (21 pull-throughs), full hook-ups, laundry and showers; open year-round; 1-888-SLP-BEAR; e-mail: cdem@rmisp.com
Website: http://rimsp.com/sleepingbear

Hart Ranch Hideout RV Park & Campground, 8 miles southeast of Lander at the junction of Wyoming 28 and Wyoming and U.S. Hwys. 789/287. 56 RV sites (56 pull-throughs), hook-ups and some services; open year-round; (307) 332-3836; 1-800-914-9226.

Holiday Lodge Campground, 210 McFarland Dr., Lander, WY 82520. 2 RV sites, hook-ups, some services; open May 1 through October 1; (307) 332-2511; 1-800-624-1974; (307) 332-2256.

K-Bar Ranch, 8 miles southeast of Lander at the junction of Wyoming 28 and Wyoming 789. 68 RV sites (no pull-throughs), hook-ups and some services; open February 1 through November 30; (307) 332-3836.

Lander City Park, 405 Fremont St., Lander, WY 82520. 7 RV sites (no pull-throughs), no services; open May 1 through September 30; (307) 332-4647.

Maverick Mobile Home Park, 1104 N. 2nd St., Lander, WY 82520. 60 RV sites, (some pull-throughs), full services; open April 1 through September 30; (307) 332-3142.

Ray Lake Campground & Cafe, 39 Ray Lake Rd., Lander, WY 82520. 15 RV sites (no pull-throughs), hook-ups and some services; open May 1 through September 30; (307) 332-9333.

▲ *Best Shot for a Camp Spot*
Rocky Acres Campground, 5700 U.S. 287, Lander, WY 82520. 13 RV sites (12 pull-throughs), hook-ups and some services; open May 1 through September 30;  (307) 332-6953.

Atlantic City—U.S. Bureau of Land Management Campground, 25 miles south of Lander on Wyoming 28, Atlantic City Road. A few RV sites (no pull-throughs), no hook-ups or services; open June 1 through October 31.

Big Atlantic Gulch—U.S. Bureau of Land Management Campground, 25 miles south of Lander on Wyoming 28, Minder's Delight Road. Some RV sites (no pull-throughs), no services; open June 1 through October 31.

Dickinson Creek—U.S. Forest Service Campground, 34 miles northwest of Lander. 6 RV sites (no pull-throughs), no services; open June 20 through September 15.

Fiddlers Campground—U.S. Forest Service Campground, 18 miles southwest of Lander. Some RV sites (no pull-throughs), no services; open June 30 through September 15.

Fiddler's Lake—U.S. Forest Service Campground, 25 miles southwest of Lander. 13 RV sites (no pull-throughs), no services; open July 1 through September 30.

Louis Lake—U.S. Forest Service Campground, 30 miles southwest of Lander. 9 RV sites (no pull-throughs), no services; open July 1 through September 30.

Popo Agie—U.S. Forest Service Campground, 28 miles southwestof Lander. 1 RV site (not a pull-through), no services; open July 2 through September 30.

Sinks Canyon—U.S. Forest Service Campground, 11 miles south of Lander. 9 RV sites (no pull-throughs), no services; open May 1 through October 31.

Sinks Canyon State Park, 6 miles southwest of Lander on Wyoming 131. Some RV sites (pull-throughs), no services; open May 1 through November 1.

Worthen Meadows—U.S. Forest Service Campground, 18 miles southwest of Lander. 20 RV sites (no pull-throughs) no services; open July 1 through September 30.

## BED & BREAKFAST ESTABLISHMENTS

Blue Spruce Inn Bed & Breakfast; elegant inn built in 1920; some credit cards accepted; no pets allowed; open year-round; busiest in June through September, slowest November to March. Contact Marvin and JoAnne Brown, 677 S. 3rd St., Lander, WY 82520; (307) 332-8253; 1-888-503-3311.
Website: http://www.rmisp.com/bluespruce

The Bunk House Bed & Breakfast, historic, renovated barn; operated since 1994; most credit cards accepted; pets allowed. Contact Therese and Scott Woodruff, 2024 Mortimore Lane, Lander, WY 82520; (307) 332-5624; 1-800-582-5262; fax: (307) 332-5624.

Edna's Bed & Breakfast, ranch home located 5 miles northwest of Lander on main road; operated since 1987; no credit cards accepted; pets allowed. Contact Edna Whiter, 53 North Fork Rd., Lander, WY 82520; (307) 332-3175.

Outlaw Bed & Breakfast-Wunder Ranches, Inc.; rustic mountain cabins located 4 miles from Lander; operated since 1994; no credit cards; no pets; open year-round; busiest July and August, slowest November through January. Contact Beverly Wunder, 2415 Squaw Creek Rd., Lander, WY 82520; (307) 332-9655.

Piece of Cake Bed & Breakfast, separate guest cabins; operated since 1996; credit cards accepted; pets allowed; open year-round; busiest in summer, slowest in fall and winter. Contact Sarah and David Love, 2343 Baldwin Creek Rd., Lander, WY 82520; (307) 332-7608; fax: (307) 332-7608.

Whispering Winds Bed & Breakfast, historic home built in 1902; some credit cards accepted; no pets or smoking allowed; open year-round; busiest in summer, slowest October through May. Contact Arlene Ingle, 695 Canyon St., Lander, WY 82520; (307) 332-9735.

## GUEST RANCHES

Allen's Diamond Four Ranch, accommodations in remote cabins. This working horse ranch in the Wind River Range has operated since 1978. No credit cards accepted; no pets allowed; open June through October; busiest in July and August. Contact Jim and Mary Allen, Box 243, Lander, WY 82520; (307) 332-2995; fax: (307) 332-7902.

Black Mountain Ranch, large guest house accommodates visitors on ranch located 10 miles from Lander; travel 3 miles on gravel road. The ranch has been operating since 1986. No credit cards accepted; no pets; open May through November 1; busiest June and July. Contact Dan or Rosie Ratigan, 548 North Fork Rd., Lander, WY 82520; (307) 332-6442.

The Resort at Louis Lake, 60-year-old resort with cabin on lake; located at 1811 Louis Lake Road (last 9 miles are on dirt road). Current operators have owned it since 1995; popular for snowmobiling in winter along Continental Divide. No credit cards accepted; pets allowed; open year-round; busiest June through October, slowest January through March. Contact Vera and Steve Faerber, 8032 Lauderdale Rd., Lander, WY 82520; (307) 332-5549; 1-888-422-2246.

Three Quarter Circle Ranch, working cattle ranch covers 35,000 acres; located on Twin Creek Road; call for directions. No credit cards accepted; no pets; open May through October. Contact Jim Allen or Tony Malmberg, PO Box 243, Lander, WY 82520; (307) 332-2995; fax: (307) 332-7902.

Rock Shop Inn, guest ranch has RV hook-ups; located 35 miles southwest of Lander on South Pass. The ranch also has separate guest cabins; credit cards accepted; pets allowed; open year-round; busiest in winter, slowest in November. Contact Chuck Reed, 4260 Hwy. 28, South Pass, Lander, WY 82520; (307) 332-7396.

## SUGGESTED DINING

The Maverick, 808 Main St., Lander, WY; (307) 332-4868.

JB Sausage & Smokehouse, 628 Main St., Lander, WY; (307) 332-2065.

Sweet Water Grill, on Main St., Lander, WY; (307) 332-7388.

The Hitching Rack, half mile south of Lander on U.S. 287, Lander, WY; (307) 332-4322.

Club El Toro and Svilar's Restaurant in Hudson, see page 239.

## VISITOR INFORMATION & SERVICES

The Lander Chamber of Commerce, 160 N. 1st St., Lander, WY 82520; 1-800-433-0662; (307) 332-3892. While you're visiting the town's sights, you may park your RV at the chamber, and there are picnic tables available for your use. The chamber also offers an informative, self-guided adventure driving tour on a cassette tape for rent for $6, or for purchase for $12.

## MEDICAL SERVICES

Lander Valley Medical Center, 24-hour emergency room, 1320 Bishop Randall Dr., Lander, WY; (307) 332-4420.

Corner Drug, 300 Main St., Lander, WY; open Monday through Friday, 9 A.M. to 7 P.M., and Saturday, 9 A.M. to 5 P.M.; (307) 332-2270; after hours, (307) 332-9597.

## REPAIR & TOWING

Landerson Sinclair, 24-hour towing; (307) 332-0453.

L S P Auto-RV repair, 24 hours; (307) 332-9830.

## VETERINARY SERVICES

Wind River Veterinary, 108 Tweed Lane, Lander, WY; open Monday through Friday, 8 A.M. to 5 P.M., Saturday, 9 A.M. to noon; (307) 332-5512.

# HUDSON, RIVERTON AND SHOSHONI: WYOMING 789, U.S. 26

At Lander you can continue south on Wyoming 28 and head over South Pass, getting a splendid view of the Oregon Trail where actual wagon-wheel ruts are still easily seen. Another option is to head southeast on U.S. 287 to Rawlins via Jeffrey City. Another choice is to drive east on Wyoming 789 to Hudson and Riverton, continuing to Shoshoni, and then to Casper, to pick up I-25.

**HUDSON**

In 1890, George Rogers and his wife Emma Hudson Rogers homesteaded on the site that is now Hudson. In 1909 when the town incorporated, it was originally called Rogersville. Unfortunately, Wyoming already had a town called Rogersville. At the request of the U.S. Postal Service, the name was changed to Hudson after Emma's father, John G. Hudson, a legislator who helped bring in the railroad.

Hudson was primarily a railroad and mining town. At its peak in the 1920s, the town population was 1,500, and estimates of surrounding coal mining camps skyrocketed to about 10,000. Demand for coal declined with the development of diesel and natural gas. In 1941, the last coal mine closed.

Today Hudson is pretty sparse with a population of 392. The town's highlight is two very competitive restaurants on its main street. The two dining establishments are both run by Yugoslavian families of very different political views. Svilar's, founded in the 1920s, is staunchly Republican, while Club El Toro, owned by the Vinich family, tends to be liberal. John Vinich was a Democratic state senator. The food is good at both restaurants, but only Club El Toro accepts credit cards. You may notice this fact by the not-so-subtle, 3-foot "Mastercard-Visa" sign on the El Toro entry door.

**RIVERTON**

The 1830 and 1838 mountain man rendezvous were held along the banks of the Wind River, where it converges with the Little Wind, the Popo Agie and the Little Popo Agie. Later in 1905 when the Shoshone and Arapaho relinquished 1.3 million acres of land to white settlers, a "tent city" was formed where the rivers merge. By 1906, homesteaders sought to fulfill the promise of a rich farming paradise. Irrigation water was needed. Diversion Dam, which holds enough water for 100,000 acres, was completed in 1923. The dam is 650 feet high. Agriculture remains one of the primary mainstays for the town. Mining played a part in its history, but most mines closed down in the 1980s.

*Foxtail grass picks up late sun near Lander, Wyoming.*

Riverton is surrounded by the Wind River Indian Reservation. The city, with a population of 9,200, is the largest in the region. Its growth is due to petroleum and uranium development and continued strength in agriculture.

**OUTDOOR RECREATION AND ATTRACTIONS**

Native American Powwows are colorful dance ceremonies. The rhythm of the performance is set by the drummers, who chant a song that speaks of ancient days. Some presentations are made by professionals, while others are made by locals. Regardless of the performers, the traditional movements are captivating.

The most popular seasonal events in Riverton are listed below. The Wild West Winter Carnival is held in February, the United Tribes Powwow in May, and the Shoshone Treaty Days and Powwow in June. However, the folks in Riverton really celebrate in July. Be there to see the famous 1838 Mountain Man Rendezvous and Riverton Rendezvous and Balloon Rally that features a living encampment with 125 camps, good food, dancing, campfires and games of skill. There is also the Riverton Rendezvous Rodeo and the Arapaho Powwow. Things slow down only a little in August until the Fremont County Fair and Rodeo opens. October is special with the Cowboy Poetry Gathering. Contact the Riverton Chamber of Commerce for specific dates and details about these and many other special events in the area.

**OVERNIGHTING**

**CAMPGROUNDS & RV PARKS**

▲ *Best Shot for a Camp Spot*
Owl Creek Campground, 5 miles from Riverton on U.S. 26 East. 19 RV sites (19 pull-throughs), 7 full hook-ups, 10 electric and water hook-ups, some services; open May 15 to September 15; (307) 856-2869.

▲ *Best Shot for a Camp Spot*
Rudy's Camper Court; one-half block off U.S. 26 North on Roosevelt Ave., Riverton, WY 82501. 21 RV sites (10 pull-throughs), full hook-ups; open year-round; (307) 856-9764.

Riverton RV Park, 1618 E. Park, Riverton, WY 82501. 60 RV sites (some pull-throughs), hook-ups and some services; open year-round; (307) 856-3913; 1-800-528-3913; fax: (307) 856-9559.

*Wild sunflowers dot the landscape near Riverton, Wyoming.*

## BED & BREAKFAST ESTABLISHMENTS

Cottonwood Ranch Bed & Breakfast, farm home operated as inn since 1987; the butte behind house has artifacts; no credit cards accepted; outside pets allowed; open year-round; busiest July to August, slowest in January and February. Contact Judith and Earl Anglen; 951 Missouri Valley Rd. (Hwy. 134), Riverton, WY 82501; (307) 856-3064.

## GUEST RANCHES

Strathkay Wranglers Ranch, working ranch operated for guests since 1992; no credit cards accepted; pets are allowed; open March through November; busiest in May. Contact Howard W. and Sally Fern Davidson, 189 Young Rd., Riverton, WY 82501; (307) 856-2194; fax: (307) 856-2194.

**SUGGESTED DINING**

Broker, 203 E. Main, Riverton, WY; (307) 856-0554.

Bull, 1100 W. Main, Riverton, WY; (307) 856-4728.

Trailhead, 832 N. Federal, Riverton, WY; (307) 856-7990.

Depot, 110 S. 1st, Riverton, WY; (307) 856-2221.

**VISITOR INFORMATION & SERVICES**

Riverton Chamber of Commerce, 101 S. 1st St., Riverton, WY 82501; (307) 856-4801.

The Wind River Visitors Council, PO Box 1449, Riverton, WY 82501; 1-800-645-6233.

**MEDICAL SERVICES**

Columbus Riverton Memorial Hospital, 24-hour emergency room, 2100 W. Sunset, Riverton, WY; (307) 856-4161.

Western Family Care, 1620 Riverview, Riverton, WY; (307) 856-6591.

A & A Temple Drug, 523 N. Federal, Riverton, WY (307) 856-3668.

Smith's Pharmacy, 1200 W. Main, Riverton, WY (307) 856-4931.

**REPAIR & TOWING**

Bob's Hilltop Sinclair, RV repairs, 912 W. Main, Riverton, WY; (307) 856-1414.

Riverton RV Sales & Service, RV repairs, 1420 S. Federal, Riverton, WY; (307) 856-6010.

McDonald Body Shop & Towing, 601 W. Adams, Riverton, WY; 1-800-859-2590.

**VETERINARY SERVICES**

See Lander Services (page 238).

*Indian Paintbrush is seen throughout Yellowstone country and is the Wyoming state flower.*

## SHOSHONI

Located just 1 mile east of the Wind River Indian Reservation, the town of Shoshoni is named for a Native word that means "Little Snow." Note the different spelling of the word Shoshoni as compared to Shoshone, the latter translated to mean "stinking water." In 1904 the Pioneer Townsite Company founded the town that boomed into a tent city of over 2,000 inhabitants within one year. Building materials were scarce and had to be brought 100 miles by wagon from Casper. The growing mining town was destroyed by fires in 1907 and 1908, and thereafter, brick became the preferred material. Today, the small community has a population of about 500.

## OUTDOOR RECREATION

Boysen State Park, located 14 miles north of Shoshoni on U.S. 20, is the entrance to the beautiful Wind River Canyon. Boysen Reservoir holds 36,480 acre feet of water and offers great fishing; many state records have been set here. Rainbow and brown trout, walleye, largemouth bass, black crappie and yellow perch are among the species available. Facilities include boat ramps, marinas, cabins and camping and trailer parks.

Rockhounds will want to trek up to Copper Mountain, located 13 miles north of Shoshoni. The area is excellent for hunting petrified wood, agate, tourmaline, quartz, and Native American artifacts and arrowheads.

## ATTRACTIONS

The Yellowstone Drug Store is world famous for malts and shakes. Join the tradition and stop in for a delicious break.

In May, Shoshoni's Memorial Day Annual State Championship Old Time Fiddle Contest is worth a visit. Call the Chamber of Commerce for details.

## OVERNIGHTING

### CAMPGROUNDS & RV PARKS

Boysen State Park, on U.S. 20 and U.S. 26 at the south end of the Wind River Canyon. RV sites and pull-throughs available, no hook-ups or services; open May 1 through October 1; (307) 876-2796.

Boysen Lake Marina, 13 miles north of Shoshoni on U.S. 20 at Boysen Lake. RV sites available (no pull-throughs), hook-ups and some services; open December 1 through October 1; (307) 876-2772.

## VISITOR INFORMATION & SERVICES

Shoshoni Chamber of Commerce, PO Box 324, Shoshoni, WY 82649; (307) 876-2561.

**MEDICAL SERVICES**

See Riverton Services (page 242).

**REPAIR & TOWING**

Trail Town Supply, 107 W. 2nd, Shoshoni, WY; (307) 876-2561.

Greasy Ranch, 206 W. Main St., Shoshoni, WY; (307) 876-2770.

**VETERINARY SERVICES**

Dr. James Briddle, on Wyoming 789 (between Riverton and Shoshoni), Shoshoni, WY; (307) 856-0550.

*The Tetons provide spectacular scenery for visitors to 100 miles around Yellowstone.*

# SECTION 6

# WEST GATE

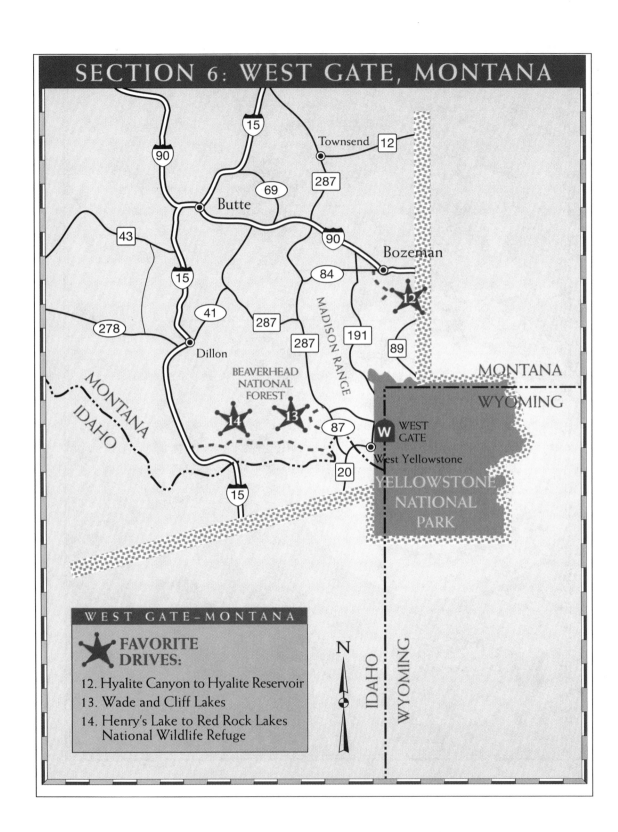

# SECTION 6: WEST GATE, MONTANA

15

Townsend 12

90

287

69

Butte

43

90

Bozeman

15

84

12

41

287

MADISON RANGE

278

287

191

Dillon

287

89

MONTANA

WYOMING

BEAVERHEAD
NATIONAL
FOREST

14

13

87

WEST
GATE

MONTANA

IDAHO

West Yellowstone

20

YELLOWSTONE
NATIONAL
PARK

15

## WEST GATE—MONTANA

### FAVORITE DRIVES:

12. Hyalite Canyon to Hyalite Reservoir
13. Wade and Cliff Lakes
14. Henry's Lake to Red Rock Lakes
    National Wildlife Refuge

N

IDAHO

WYOMING

# GENERAL OVERVIEW

Once you exit the park at the West Gate, you have three options, two of which take you north, the other south. The south route, U.S. 20, heads west out of West Yellowstone and then cuts south through Island Park and then to Ashton, Rexburg and Idaho Falls, hooking up with I-15. From Ashton, a nice drive takes you through Driggs and Victor, and back around to Jackson via Teton Pass. The two northerly routes out of the West Gate take you to Bozeman on U.S. 191 through the gorgeous Gallatin Canyon and Big Sky, or to Ennis, Norris, Twin Bridges and Butte on either U.S. 287, Montana 87 or Montana 287.

## WEST YELLOWSTONE

The West Gate is right at the edge of West Yellowstone, Montana, whose claim to fame just might be its notoriety as one of the coldest spots in the lower 48 states. Locals know it simply as "West," and are brave souls who are fond of deep snow and extreme cold temperatures. The town is best known for its snowmobile friendly access and activities and always seems to draw plenty of tourists, no matter what the season. It's no surprise that West Yellowstone has been called the "Snowmobile Capital of the World." Between the Big Sky Ski Area just up the highway and the snowmobile market, the place jumps all winter. Of course, its close proximity to the park creates plenty of summer business. Spring fishing and fall hunting bring in even more travelers.

West Yellowstone became an official entrance in 1907 when the Oregon Short Line completed the branch railway to the community. Union Pacific began operating a passenger train from Ashton, Idaho, in 1909. By 1915, cars were streaming down the highway from Bozeman, bringing eager tourists. The town grew up as a gateway to the park and today is Yellowstone National Park's busiest entry. It was incorporated in 1966.

## OUTDOOR RECREATION

Blue-ribbon trout streams galore—the Yellowstone, Madison, Gibbon, Firehole and Henry's Fork Rivers—and many outstanding lakes, make this premier fishing country. West Yellowstone has the folks who know how. The following list has a few of the area's many fly shops, outfitters and guide services. Bud Lilly's Trout Shop at 39 Madison Avenue is the oldest shop. Guided trips, fishing gear and outdoor clothing are offered. Stop in or call for details, 1-800-854-9559. Bob Jacklin's Outfitters at 105 Yellowstone Avenue has fly-fishing instruction and schools as well as guides and gear, (406) 646-7336. The Madison River Fly Shop, at 117 Canyon Street, provides guide services, and the shop carries tackle, custom flies and clothing, (406) 646-9644.

# SECTION 6: WEST GATE, IDAHO

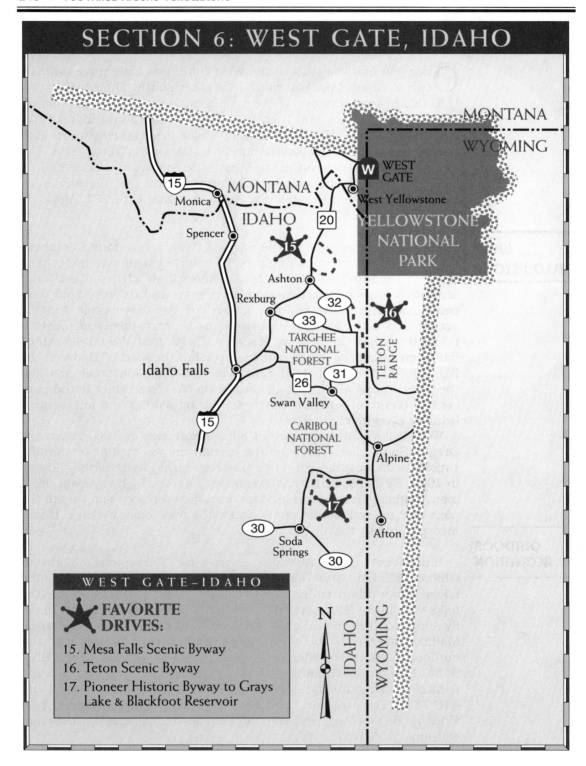

MONTANA

WYOMING

15
Monica

MONTANA

IDAHO

20

W WEST GATE
West Yellowstone

YELLOWSTONE
NATIONAL
PARK

Spencer

★ 15

Ashton

Rexburg

32

33

16 ★

TARGHEE
NATIONAL
FOREST

TETON RANGE

Idaho Falls

26    31

Swan Valley

CARIBOU
NATIONAL
FOREST

15

Alpine

17 ★

30
Soda
Springs

30

Afton

### WEST GATE–IDAHO

★ **FAVORITE DRIVES:**

15. Mesa Falls Scenic Byway
16. Teton Scenic Byway
17. Pioneer Historic Byway to Grays
    Lake & Blackfoot Reservoir

N

IDAHO    WYOMING

*Quake Lake, formed by an earthquake in 1959*

For a different scenic view, Yellowstone Aviation offers chartered flights over Yellowstone and Grand Teton National Parks. The lofty trip is an unforgettable experience, but not for white-knuckle flyers. For more information, write PO Box 178, Yellowstone Airport, West Yellowstone, MT 59758, or call (406) 646-7359.

Biking has become the new summertime pastime. The many trails and paved roads in West Yellowstone country provide scenic beauty and enjoyment of this relatively new sport. It's a lot easier to hang a mountain bike instead of a 4-wheel drive on the back of an RV. However, there are several rental shops in West Yellowstone if your bike was left behind. Freeheel & Wheel at 40 Yellowstone Avenue, (406) 646-7744; Yellowstone Activities in the Holiday Inn, 1-800-646-7365; and Yellowstone Bicycles (seasonal) at 132 Madison Avenue, (406) 646-7815, can help with rentals and information.

The wintertime recreation is snowmobiling, and it's big-time here. There are over 1,000 miles of groomed trails in the area surrounding West Yellowstone. The snowmobile season in Yellowstone National Park runs from mid-December to March. Outside the park in the National Forests, the season is longer, and trails are both groomed and ungroomed. Instruction and guides are available; ask the chamber for details.

Several companies specialize in snowmobile rentals; check out the following companies. Alpine West Snowmobiles, 1-800-858-9224. Big Western Pine, 1-800-646-7622. Rendezvous Snowmobile Rentals, Inc., 1-800-426-7669. Sawtelle Sales Service & Rentals, 1-800-273-1950. Travelers Snowmobile Rentals, 1-800-831-5741. Valley Motor Supply (Polaris), (406) 646-9567. Yellowstone Adventures, 1-800-231-5991. Yellowstone Arctic/Yamaha, 1-800-646-7365.

Another popular snow sport in West Yellowstone is cross-country skiing. The backcountry and telemark skiing is considered tops in the nation. The U.S. Nordic and Biathlon teams train in the area.

Wintertime visitors can enjoy the sights in Yellowstone National Park via a snowcoach tour. Guided tours from a ten-passenger heated snow vehicle journey to Old Faithful and the Grand Canyon of the Yellowstone. The sights, dressed in blazing winter white and brilliant blue colors, are spectacular. Information is available from Snocoach Tours, 555 Yellowstone Ave., West Yellowstone, MT 59758; (406) 646-9591.

The most original and unique tour is offered by Klondike Dreams Sled Dog Tours. "Mush" through the snow-covered land behind a team of dogs as the early mountain men once did. Contact Klondike Dreams at PO Box 999, 214 Faithful, West Yellowstone, MT 59758; or call (406) 646-4004.

**ATTRACTIONS**

Grizzly Discovery Center, a bear and wolf preserve, is located in the recently constructed Grizzly Park at the west entrance to Yellowstone. The center is an educational facility that affords the visitor a unique opportunity to view the grizzly bear and gray timber wolf as they interact in their separate, natural habitats. There are also many hands-on displays, videos and presentations, all of which are geared to enhance appreciation of the two threatened species. Preservation of the grizzly bear and wolf is the primary purpose of the facility. The center is open year-round, from 8:30 A.M. to 8:30 P.M. May through September, and 8:30 A.M. until dusk during October through April. A fee is charged. For information, call (406) 646-7001; 1-800-257-2570; or visit the website: http://www.avicom.net/grizzly

The Yellowstone IMAX Theatre is also at Grizzly Park. The excellent Academy Award-caliber presentation of "Yellowstone" tells the whole story behind America's first national park. Learn the history, and preview the wildlife, geothermal activity and scenic grandeur awaiting you on your visit, or find out what you missed. The 70mm movie filmed in IMAX format is shown on a six-story-high screen with stereo surround-sound. A food court and coffee bar service the area. The theatre is open year-round. Admission prices are adults, $6.50, juniors, $4.50. Call for hours and showtimes, (406) 646-4100.

Well worth a stop for inquisitive minds is the Museum of the Yellowstone. The museum is housed in the historic Union Pacific Depot, the perfect place to reveal the contribution of railroads to the development of Yellowstone National Park. Excellent exhibits on the U.S. Cavalry, trappers, cowboys and Native Americans, tell the history and the glory. Displays and videos about the region's largest earthquake in 1959 and the devastating 1988 fires tell the darker story. The museum, 124 Yellowstone Ave., West Yellowstone, MT 59758, is open Memorial Day to Labor Day; 1-800-500-6923; (406) 646-7814.

The 1903 Executive Railroad Car Museum is inside the West Yellowstone Conference Hotel at 315 Yellowstone Avenue. The free exhibit is the namesake of the Oregon Short Line Restaurant. For more information, 1-800-646-7365; (406) 646-7365.

West Yellowstone caters to visitors. Shopping for folks back home is a breeze with lots to choose from amid the town's dozens of gift shops, galleries and specialty stores.

Spend an enjoyable evening at the Playmill Theatre. The comedies, melodramas and musicals will entertain the whole family. The theatre, at 29 Madison in West Yellowstone, is open Monday through Saturday, May through September; call (406) 646-7757 for reservations (strongly recommended).

The World Snowmobile Expo is a snowmobiler's delight. The late-March event includes exhibits by equipment vendors, power pulls and drag racing. For more information, contact the West Yellowstone Chamber of Commerce.

## OVERNIGHTING

## CAMPGROUNDS & RV PARKS

▲ *Best Shot for a Camp Spot*
Brandin' Iron Motel & RV Park, at 201 Canyon, U.S. 191/20. 16 RV sites (pull-throughs), hook-ups, no dump station; hot showers and laundry; open May through October; busiest June 15 through September 15; (406) 646-9411; 1-800-217-4613; fax: 646-9436.

▲ *Best Shot for a Camp Spot*
Campfire Lodge & Resort, 8 miles north of West Yellowstone on U.S. 191, then 14 miles west on U.S. 287. 17 RV sites (1 pull-through), hook-ups, no dump station; hot showers and laundry; open May 30 through September 5; (406) 646-7258.

▲ *Best Shot for a Camp Spot*
Hideaway RV Campground, at the corner of Gibbon and Electric Streets. 14 RV sites (6 pull-throughs), hook-ups, no dump station; hot showers, cable TV; open May 1 through October 31; (406) 646-9049.

▲ *Best Shot for a Camp Spot*
Lionshead RV Resort, 7.5 miles west on U.S. 20. 166 RV sites (140 pull-throughs), hook-ups, no dump station; hot showers, laundry, restaurant, game room and playground; open May 1 through October 15; (406) 646-7662.

Madison Arm Resort & Marina, 3 miles north of West Yellowstone on U.S. 191, then 5 miles west on Forest Road 291. 52 RV sites (2 pull-throughs), hook-ups, dump station, hot showers, laundry, marina, lake swimming, fishing and boating on Hebgen Lake; open May 15 through October 1; (406) 646-9328.

▲ *Best Shot for a Camp Spot*

Rustic Wagon RV Campground & Cabins, on the west end of West Yellowstone. 42 RV sites (15 large pull-throughs), full hook-ups, hot showers, laundry, cable TV and playground; open April 1 through November 30, and open in winter for snowmobilers; (406) 646-7387; winter, (520) 680-7332.

Wagon Wheel Campground & Cabins, 1 block north of U.S. 20 at 408 Gibbon, West Yellowstone. 40 RV sites (7 pull-throughs), full hook-ups, hot showers, laundry, cable TV and game-recreation room; 10 separate tent sites; open May 31 through September 15; (406) 646-7872; winter, (520) 680-7332.

Yellowstone Cabins & RV Park, in West Yellowstone at 504 U.S. 20. 9 RV sites, hook-ups, no dump station; hot showers; open May 1 through September 30; (406) 646-9350.

Yellowstone Grizzly RV Park, in West Yellowstone at 210 S. Electric Street. 152 RV sites, hook-ups (electrical 20-30-50 amp each site), dump station, hot showers, laundry, store, recreation room and meeting room; open May 1 through October 31; (406) 646-4466; fax: (406) 646-4335.

*Campers enjoy the sunset near Yellowstone.*

Yellowstone Holiday Resort, 8 miles north on U.S. 191, then 5 miles west on U.S. 287. 35 RV sites, hook-ups, dump station, hot showers; 10 campsites, 6 modern cabins and 12 rustic cabins; 3 marinas, dock and boat rentals; open May 15 to October 15; (406) 646-4242.

Yellowstone Park KOA, 6 miles west on U.S. 20. 188 RV sites, hook-ups, dump station, hot showers, laundry, indoor swimming pool, hot tub, game room, rental bikes and mini-golf course; open May 15 through October 1; (406) 646-7606; 1-800-562-7591.

Baker's Hole—U.S. Forest Service Campground, 3 miles north of West Yellowstone on U.S. 191. RVs allowed (max. length 32 feet), no services; open May 27 through September 5; for reservations, call 1-800-280-CAMP.

Beaver Creek—U.S. Forest Service Campground, 8 miles north of West Yellowstone on U.S. 191, then 15 miles west on U.S. 287. RVs allowed (max. length 32 feet), no services; open May 2 through September 15; for reservations, call 1-800-280-CAMP.

Cabin Creek—U.S. Forest Service Campground, 8 miles north of West Yellowstone on U.S. 191, then 13 miles west on U.S. 287. RVs allowed (max. length 32 feet), no services; open May 22 through September 15; for reservations, call 1-800-280-CAMP.

Lonesomehurst—U.S. Forest Service Campground, 8 miles west of West Yellowstone on U.S. 20, 4 miles north of Hebgen Lake Road. RVs allowed (max. length 32 feet), no services; boat launch ramp for 2-wheel drive with trailer; open May 22 through September 15; for reservations, call 1-800-280-CAMP.

Rainbow Point—U.S. Forest Service Campground, 5 miles north of West Yellowstone on U.S. 191, then 3 miles west on Forest Service Road 610, 2 miles north on Forest Service Road 6954. RVs allowed (max. length 32 feet), no services; boat launch ramp for 2-wheel drive with trailer; open May 22 through September 15; for reservations, call 1-800-280-CAMP.

Wade Lake—U.S. Forest Service Campground, 8 miles north of West Yellowstone on U.S. 191, then 27 miles west on U.S. 287, 6 miles southwest on Forest Service Road 5721. 30 sites, RVs allowed (max. length 24 feet), no services except drinking water; boat launch ramp for 2-wheel drive; open June 1 through September 30.

Hilltop—U.S. Forest Service Campground, 8 miles north of West Yellowstone on U.S. 191, then 27 miles west on U.S. 287, 6 miles southwest on Forest Service Road 5721. 20 sites, RVs allowed (max. length 22 feet), no services except drinking water; open June 1 through September 30.

Cliff Point—U.S. Forest Service Campground, 8 miles north of West Yellowstone on U.S. 191, then 27 miles west on U.S. 287, 6 miles southwest on Forest Service Road 5721. 6 sites, RVs allowed (max. length 16 feet), no services except drinking water; boat launch ramp for 2-wheel drive; open June 1 through September 15.

## BED & BREAKFAST ESTABLISHMENTS

Osprey Shadows Inn, lodging with private entrance, hot tub and deck. The inn is located 5 minutes from town and has been operating since 1994. Open May through September, and January through March for snowmobiling; no credit cards accepted; pets allowed. Contact Susan and Simon Bowland, Box 751, 40 Central Ave., West Yellowstone, MT 59758; (406) 646-7786; fax: 646-7786.

Rainbow Point Inn, located on the shore of Hebgen Lake, Box 977, Rainbow Point Rd. #6954, West Yellowstone, MT 59758; (406) 646-7848; fax: (406) 646-7848.

Sportsman's High Bed & Breakfast is styled in antique country decor. The location is 8 miles from Yellowstone National Park off U.S. 20. The establishment has been operating since 1987. Open year-round; busiest summer and winter, slowest spring and fall; credit cards accepted; no pets allowed; children ages 12 up. Contact Gary and Diana Baxter, 750 Deer St., West Yellowstone, MT 59758; (406) 646-7865; fax: 646-9288.

## GUEST RANCHES

Bar N Ranch, on Targhee Pass Hwy., 5 miles from Yellowstone National Park. This 640-acre guest ranch has been operating since 1908. Features include trout fishing, Jacuzzi and artist's workshops. Open year-round; busiest summer and winter, slowest spring and fall; credit cards accepted; dogs allowed in cabins only, no cats allowed. Call (406) 646-7229; 1-800-BIG SKYS; fax: (406) 646-7229.

Firehole Ranch is located on Hebgen Lake Road, 15 miles from Yellowstone National Park. Features include fishing trips, horseback riding, hiking, boating and mountain biking. Contact Firehole Ranch, 11500 Hebgen Lake Rd., West Yellowstone, MT 59758; (406) 646-7294.

Parade Rest Guest Ranch, 10 miles from the West Gate to Yellowstone National Park. This recreation lodge has been in operation since 1978. Features include whirlpool tub, fly fishing, horseback riding, cookouts and outdoor games. Open May 30 through September, busiest July through August; credit cards accepted; no pets allowed. Contact Clyde Seely and Bill Howell, 7979 Grayling Creek Rd., West Yellowstone, MT 59758; (406) 646-7217; 1-800-753-5934.

West Yellowstone Hostel at the Madison Hotel, a historical hotel built in 1912. Free tours of the hotel and youth hostel rooms area available. Open May 30 through October 10; busiest July through August; credit cards accepted; no pets allowed. Contact Jim and Linda Christensen, 139 West Yellowstone Ave., West Yellowstone, MT 59758; (406) 646-7745; 1-800-838-7745; fax: (406) 646-9766; e-mail: jhc@sisna.com

**SUGGESTED DINING**

Three Bear, 205 Yellowstone Ave., West Yellowstone, MT; (406) 646-4132.

Coachman, 209 Madison Ave., West Yellowstone, MT; (406) 646-7381.

Trapper Inn, 315 Madison Ave., West Yellowstone, MT; (406) 646-9375.

Oregon Short Line, 315 Yellowstone Ave., West Yellowstone, MT; (406) 646-7365.

Silver Station, 105 S. Canyon St., West Yellowstone, MT; (406) 646-4241.

Rustler's Roost, 234 Firehole Ave., West Yellowstone, MT; (406) 646-7622, 1-800-646-7622.

**VISITOR INFORMATION & SERVICES**

West Yellowstone Chamber of Commerce and West Yellowstone Visitor Information Center are located just outside the west entrance to Yellowstone National Park on Canyon Street and Yellowstone Avenue. The mailing address and telephone are PO Box 458, West Yellowstone, MT 59758; (406) 646-7701; fax: 646-9691. While you're visiting the town's sights, you may park your RV at Grizzly Park.

Gallatin National Forest-Hebgen Lake Ranger District is on U.S. 191 North, or contact the office at PO Box 250, West Yellowstone, MT 59758; (406) 646-7369.

**MEDICAL SERVICES**

The Clinic at West Yellowstone, 236 Yellowstone Ave., West Yellowstone, MT 59758; (406) 646-7668, or after hours emergencies, call 911.

Yellowstone Apothecary, at Madison Crossing, 121 Madison Ave., West Yellowstone, MT 59758; (406) 646-7621.

**REPAIR & TOWING**

Repairs by O'B offers your-location or on-site service and repair; ASE certified and RVIA factory-trained; operates in West Yellowstone from June 1 to September 30. Call 1-888-646-9084.

Randy's Auto Repair, ASE Master Mechanics, Good Sam and ERS towing approval; 429 Yellowstone Ave., West Yellowstone, MT 59758; (406) 646-9353.

**VETERINARY SERVICES**

White and White Veterinary Hospital & Supply, on Gibbon Avenue, behind Blue Ribbon Flies, West Yellowstone, MT; open Monday and Wednesday, 8:30 A.M. to NOON, or call (406) 682-7151. The main office is at 5098 U.S. Highway 287, Ennis, MT 59729; (406) 682-7151.

# WEST YELLOWSTONE, BIG SKY, BOZEMAN: U.S. 287

The highway runs through forests of lodgepole pine, fir and spruce, eventually crossing back into Yellowstone National Park (no gate, no fee required) and then back out, following the Gallatin River most of the way north toward Bozeman. Initially the highway is in a narrow valley, with the Madison Range, including the Spanish Peaks, on the west, and the impressive Gallatin Range on the east.

**GALLATIN RIVER CANYON**

In 1805, the Gallatin River was named by Lewis and Clark in honor of Albert Gallatin, Secretary of the Treasury. Then in 1865, Gallatin County became one of Montana's original counties created by the First Territorial Legislature of 1865. The original boundaries have been altered with land absorbed into Yellowstone National Park, but the county still retains the contour of the Gallatin River. The world's largest forest of fossilized trees is located along the divide between the Gallatin and Yellowstone Rivers. Rockhounds search out valuable specimens of petrified and opalized wood, agates, jasper and various crystals. A permit from the Gallatin National Forest Ranger Station in Bozeman is required.

**BIG SKY**

Big Sky began as the development dream of NBC newscaster Chet Huntley in 1973. Initially known for winter skiing, Big Sky has much more, offering year-round sports and attractions. It is Montana's largest destination resort. It may remind you of Jackson, Wyoming; the lifestyle is much the same. To get there, go 9 miles west from U.S. 191 at the Big Sky turnoff; the road is paved, of course.

The Big Sky Ski and Summer Resort area is divided into Mountain Village and Meadow Village. Each is an adult playground. There are regular shuttles between the villages and the ski area and daily shuttles to Yellowstone National Park.

**OUTDOOR RECREATION**

Summer or winter, ride the Lone Peak Tram at Big Sky Resort; summer operation is June 1 through September 30. The incredible view at the summit of Lone Mountain, 11,150 feet, is truly inspiring. The ride up to the highest vertical ski drop in the United States is worth the fee of $20.

Summertime activities include golfing, swimming, horseback riding and white-water rafting. Call 1-800-548-4486 for a brochure and details.

The Big Sky Golf Course was designed by Arnold Palmer. The 18-hole public course at Meadow Village is 2 miles west of U.S. 191 in Big Sky. Call the Pro Shop, (406) 995-4706, for tee times.

Big Sky Resort Ski Area has 3,500 skiable acres with a vertical rise of 4,180 feet. It is one of the top ten largest ski resorts in the nation. The tram, quads, gondolas, chairlifts and surface tows take skiers where they need to be, faster. The average annual snowfall is an astounding 400 inches. Plus, there are more than 45 miles of groomed ski trails. Its excellent reputation is well deserved.

Snowmobilers will thrill at the 120-mile Big Sky Trail between Bozeman and West Yellowstone. Maps and information are available at the Bozeman Ranger District Gallatin National Forest; see page 258.

Cross-country skiing is touted as the "Best in the West." See Lone Mountain Ranch below.

**OVERNIGHTING**

### GUEST RANCHES

Big Sky Ski & Summer Resort, 44 miles from West Yellowstone, off U.S. 191 and then 9 miles on paved mountain road. This is Montana's largest destination resort, operating since 1972. See more on page 256. Credit cards accepted; no pets allowed; open May 15 through September 30, winter November 26 through April 15; for information, contact Big Sky Resort, Box 160001, 1 Lone Mountain Trail, Big Sky, MT  59716; (406) 995-5000; 1-800-548-4486; fax: (406) 995-5001.

Lone Mountain Ranch, 55 miles from West Yellowstone on Big Sky Road. Lone Mountain has operated since 1967. Features include vacation packages with naturalist-guided tours and hikes, horseback riding, kids' activities, Orvis-endorsed fly-fishing trips, 65 km cross-country ski trails, sleigh ride dinner, Yellowstone ski tours and more. Credit cards accepted; no pets allowed. Contact Lone Mountain Ranch, Box 160069, Big Sky, MT  59716; (406) 995-4644; 1-800-514-4644; fax: (406) 995-4670.
Website: http://www.lonemountainranch.com

Rainbow Ranch Lodge, 11 miles from Yellowstone National Park on the banks of Gallatin River. The lodge has been operating since 1994. Features include cross-country and downhill skiing, fly fishing and horseback riding. Credit cards accepted; no pets or smoking allowed; open year-round; busiest Christmas and summer, slowest in April. Contact Rainbow Ranch, Box 160336, Big Sky, MT 59716; (406) 995-4132; 1-800-937-4132; fax: (406) 995-2861.

## SUGGESTED DINING

Buck's T-4 Restaurant, U.S. 191, Big Sky, MT; (406) 995-4111.

Lone Mountain Ranch Lodge, a half mile off Big Sky Road, Big Sky, MT; (406) 995-2782.

Rainbow Ranch Lodge, 5 miles south of Big Sky, Big Sky, MT; (406) 995-4132.

## VISITOR INFORMATION & SERVICES

Big Sky Chamber of Commerce, Box 160100, Big Sky, MT 59716; (406) 995-3000; 1-800-943-4111; fax: (406) 995-2307.

Big Sky Ski and Summer Resort, PO Box 160001, 1 Lone Mountain Trail, Big Sky, MT 59716; (406) 995-5000; 1-800-548-4486; fax: (406) 995-5001; website: http://www.bigskyresort.com

## MEDICAL SERVICES

For medical services, see Bozeman Services, page 271.

Lone Mountain Pharmacy, in the Blue Mall, West Fork Meadows, Big Sky, MT; open Monday through Saturday, 10 A.M. to 5 P.M.; (406) 995-3149.

## REPAIR & TOWING

Big Sky Wrecker Service (AAA-rated), Big Sky, MT; 24-hour service; (406) 995-4711.

## VETERINARY SERVICES

See Bozeman Services (page 271).

*Fireweed is a common plant in the Yellowstone area.*

## GALLATIN GATEWAY AND VICINITY

Gallatin Gateway is 12 miles southwest of Bozeman. In the 1860s the settlement was named Salesville after the two Sales brothers. Alan was the storekeeper, and Zach ran the sawmill. Logging waned, and the settlement developed with the tourist trade. A post office was established in 1927. The community was named Gallatin for the river that flows the length of the county, and "Gateway" because it lies just outside the mouth of the canyon.

The Chicago Milwaukee Railroad's spur line stopped here. Passengers bound for Yellowstone National Park, visited the Gallatin Gateway Inn. The elegant, Spanish-style hotel looks as if it was built yesterday, not in 1927. The restorations have been carefully authentic. It's worth a stop to take a glimpse into the past and see how the eastern traveler "roughed it" out west. There is also exquisite dining at the restaurant.

## OVERNIGHTING

### CAMPGROUNDS & RV PARKS

Castle Rock Inn, 25 miles south of Bozeman on U.S. 191. 10 RV sites, hook-ups, hot showers, laundry, river frontage; open year-round, busiest summer, slowest winter; (406) 763-4243.

### BED & BREAKFAST ESTABLISHMENTS

Aspen Grove Bed & Breakfast, operating since 1993; open year-round; busiest summer, slowest spring; no credit cards accepted; no pets allowed. Contact Lloyd Milke and Alice Jones, 9 Rabel Lane, a quarter-mile east on U.S. 191 (gravel road), Box 98, Gallatin Gateway, MT 59730; (406) 763-5044.

Wild Rose Bed & Breakfast, in a peaceful country setting, operating since 1995; open year-round; busiest summer, slowest winter; credit cards accepted; pets conditional; horses boarded. Contact Dennis Bauer, 1285 Upper Tom Burke Rd., Gallatin Gateway, MT 59730; (406) 763-4692.

### GUEST RANCHES

320 Guest Ranch, within minutes of Big Sky and Yellowstone National Park. The ranch has log cabin accommodations. Features include trail rides, fly fishing, hay rides and sleigh rides, hiking and cross-country and downhill skiing. Credit cards accepted; pets are an additional fee. Contact Pat Sage, manager, 205 Buffalo Horn Creek, Gallatin Gateway, MT 59730; (406) 995-4283; 1-800-243-0320; fax: (406) 995-4694.

Cinnamon Lodge, 36 miles west of Yellowstone National Park, and 10 miles south of Big Sky. This lodge has been operating since 1992. Activities include snowmobiling, cross-country skiing, horseback riding, hunting, fishing and hiking. 6 RV hook-ups available; open year-round; busiest summer and winter, slowest in April; credit cards accepted; pets allowed. Contact Jim and Jo Snyder, 37090 Gallatin Rd., Gallatin Gateway, MT 59730; (406) 995-4253.

Covered Wagon Ranch, on U.S. 191. This log cabin ranch has been accepting guests since 1925. Features include horseback riding, fishing, hiking, pack trips and cookouts. Open year-round; busiest July through September, slowest November through December; no credit cards accepted; pets allowed. Contact Will King, 34035 Gallatin Rd., Gallatin Gateway, MT 59730; (406) 995-4237.

Nine Quarter Circle Ranch, family ranch in operation for 52 years. Features include horseback riding, fishing, hiking, swimming and pack trips. Open June 15 through December 15; no credit cards accepted; no pets allowed. Contact Kim and Kelly Kelsey; 5000 Taylor Fork Rd., Gallatin Gateway, MT 59730; (406) 995-4276.

**SUGGESTED DINING**

Gallatin Gateway Inn, U.S. 191, Gallatin Gateway, MT; (406) 763-4672.

**VISITOR INFORMATION & SERVICES**

See Bozeman Services (page 270).

**VETERINARY SERVICES**

All West Veterinary Hospital, Dr. Brian Peck, 81770 Gallatin Rd., (4 Corners), Bozeman, MT; 24 hours; (406) 586-4919.

# BOZEMAN AND VICINITY: MONTANA 84

As you head north on U.S. 191, Bozeman Hot Springs is the next major point on the map, about 5 miles from Gallatin Gateway. If you need to relax, the hot pools do the trick. Next comes your first awakening back to civilization, the four-corners traffic light. You have a choice to make at the junction of Highways U.S. 191 and Montana 84.

# FAVORITE DRIVE:
# HYALITE RESERVOIR

The Hyalite Canyon is reached by taking South 19th Avenue 7 miles to Hyalite Canyon Road. Hyalite Reservoir is 10.5 miles up the canyon. It was constructed in the 1940s and enlarged in 1993. There are three public campgrounds. One is on Hyalite Creek and the other two are on the shores of the reservoir.

Known predominantly for the extensive system of hiking trails, Hyalite Reservoir is one of the locals' best-kept fishing secrets. The beautiful forested peaks of the Gallatin Range surround the reservoir. It's not far from Bozeman, but the heavy timber and narrow, winding canyon easily eliminate the city hubbub. What's the reason so many local fishermen pick Hyalite? The deep, clear waters are not subject to the roaring, chocolate-milk syndrome that afflicts most Rocky Mountain streams during the spring runoff or raging summer thunderstorms. Weekdays are the best time to arrive, while those locals are slaving away 9 to 5. The reservoir is stocked with cutthroat trout, and fish range from 8 inches to an astounding 25 inches. Arctic grayling and brook trout are also there. The brookies are small, and the grayling are normally about 10 to 14 inches. Though the reservoir isn't well known by outsiders, Bozeman folks know it all too well. It's a good place to avoid on weekends and around holidays.

Rumor has it that the best place to fish is where the East Fork and Hyalite Creeks flow into the lake. Anything goes—fly fishing, lures and bait. Boats are allowed, and a "no wake" restriction is enforced. If you're using a float tube or wading, be sure to have good neoprene waders or other form of insulation. The water is extremely cold. Boaters should also be careful. A final warning: Watch for summer thunderstorms that can quickly blow over a sunny day. Be sure to check fishing regulations and seasonal closures of specific creeks. A Montana fishing license is required.

Hiking in Hyalite Canyon is renowned. The many signed trails are well maintained, and several are accessible to individuals with physical challenges. The Hyalite Challenge was a program sponsored by the Gallatin National Forest and the Gallatin Empire Lions Club in the 1980s. The successful project opened up outdoor opportunities for many people by providing special facilities. The difficulty of each of these trails is indicated on signs, and ranges from easiest to most difficult. The three trails listed here are all designated as wheelchair accessible. Palisades Falls is a 1- mile paved trail to a stunning falls on Palisade Mountain. West Shore Trail is a 1-mile trail that leads to a point overlooking the reservoir (hikers can continue about 3 miles around the west shore). Grotto Falls Trail is a 1.25-mile graveled trail beginning at Chisholm Campground that leads to Grotto Falls. More information on Hyalite Reservoir and hiking trails is available at the Gallatin National Forest office in Bozeman.

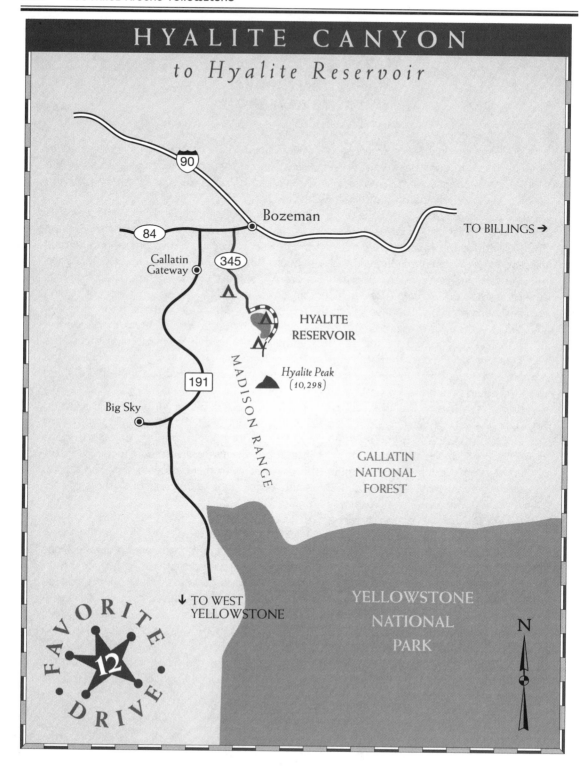

# HYALITE CANYON
## to Hyalite Reservoir

90

Bozeman

TO BILLINGS →

84

Gallatin
Gateway

345

HYALITE
RESERVOIR

Hyalite Peak
(10,298)

MADISON RANGE

191

Big Sky

GALLATIN
NATIONAL
FOREST

↓ TO WEST
YELLOWSTONE

YELLOWSTONE
NATIONAL
PARK

N

FAVORITE · DRIVE ·
12

## CAMPGROUNDS & RV PARKS

Langhor—U.S. Forest Service Campground, 11 miles south of Bozeman on South 19th Avenue and Hyalite Canyon Road (Forest Service Road 62), on Hyalite Creek. 12 camping sites, RVs allowed (max. length 32 feet), no services except drinking water; accessible trail fishing; open May 25 through September 15.

Hood Creek—U.S. Forest Service Campground, 17 miles south of Bozeman on South 19th Avenue and Hyalite Canyon Road (Forest Service Road 62), on Hyalite Reservoir. 18 camping sites, RVs allowed (max. length 16 feet), no services except drinking water; boating and fishing access; open May 25 through September 15.

Chisholm—U.S. Forest Service Campground, 18 miles south of Bozeman on South 19th Avenue and Hyalite Canyon Road (Forest Service Road 62), on Hyalite Reservoir. 9 camping sites, RVs allowed (max. length 55 feet), no services except drinking water; boating and fishing access; open May 25 through September 15.

*Hyalite Reservoir, south of Bozeman, Montana*
DONNIE SEXTON/COURTESY TRAVEL MONTANA

**BOZEMAN**

For several hundred years, the ancestors of the Shoshone, Nez Perce, Blackfeet, Flathead and Sioux thrived in this area. The rich hunting grounds, rivers and plants attracted the tribes. Similarly, French trappers are thought to have appeared in the 1700s. The Lewis and Clark Expedition crossed through the valley in 1805 and again on their return trip in 1806.

By far, the greatest movement of population through the area was attracted by gold, and later, silver. Bozeman, a fortune seeker himself, founded the Bozeman Trail to create a shorter route for prospectors to travel. Many prospectors turned into settlers when the booms went bust, and returned to form businesses or to farm. The town was founded in 1864. The city's Main Street (between Wilson and Rouse Avenues) was built on the actual Bozeman Trail.

In the early years, the town served as a regional supply and trade center. The Northern Pacific Railroad completed its line through Bozeman in 1883. The first classes were held at Montana Agricultural College in 1893. In the 1900s, the railroads began promoting Yellowstone National Park as a destination, and the town's tourism trade came of age. In later years, Bozeman established itself as the focus of economic activity in the Gallatin Valley.

Bozeman is the home of Montana State University, situated on a 1,170-acre campus. The 11,000 students influence the town, keeping it progressive and more liberal than other portions of the state. As in the past, Bozeman's 28,000 residents are the fortunate recipients of a more cultural setting, including a symphony, opera and the visual arts. The thriving city has a diversified economy based on agriculture, government, the university and tourism.

**OUTDOOR RECREATION**

Hiking, biking and cross-country trails are close to town at Lindley Park. The 15.9-acre park is at East Main and Cypress Streets. The picnic facilities, playground and trails provide a great opportunity to stretch your legs or to relax in the sun. The pavilion can be reserved for groups; contact the City of Bozeman Division of Parks, City Hall, 411 E. Main St., Bozeman, MT 59771; (406) 582-3200.

In town, the Sourdough Trail or Gallagator Linear Trail offer more hiking and biking challenges. Trails in the surrounding area include Hyalite, Bear and Sourdough Canyons, Stone Creek, Jackson Creek and Fairy Lake. Local bike rental shops have more details, or check with the Bozeman Recreation Department, (406) 587-4724.

The East Gallatin State Recreation Area, in the northeast corner of Bozeman, has summertime swimming and cross-country ski trails in winter. However, there's no overnight camping or open fires. Glen Lake has trout, perch and sunfish, and is enjoyable for all ages, especially youngsters. The Recreation Area is north of Griffin Drive on Manley Road.

Golfing is popular in Bozeman. There are two, 18-hole public courses: Cottonwood Hills Golf Course on River Road, (406) 587-1118, and Bridger Creek Golf Course at 2710 McIlhattan Road (just five minutes north of downtown), (406) 586-2333. Bridger Creek was selected by *Golf Digest* as one of the ten best public courses in Montana. The Riverside Country Club is a private course; the location is 2500 Springhill Road; call the Golf Shop at (406) 586-2251 for tee information and PGA member's reciprocity. Another private course, the Valley View Golf Course at 203 Kagy Blvd., can be reached at (406) 586-2145.

River rafting and kayaking on the Yellowstone, Gallatin and Madison Rivers are popular. In the spring, white-water enthusiasts meet their match as rivers rage with heavy runoff. There are many outfitters offering guided trips and instruction. Montana River Expeditions, 1-800-500-4538, and Montana Whitewater, 1-800-799-4465, are two experienced companies. Inquire at the Chamber of Commerce or Visitor Information Center for more outfits.

## ATTRACTIONS

A great reason to attend Montana State University, at least for a day, is to visit the Museum of the Rockies. At the museum, you can take a memorable journey through 4 billion years of time. The collection of exhibits illustrates the theme "One Place Through All of Time."

The displays are presented in the new Geology Hall, the Berger Dinosaur Hall and the Paugh History Hall. There are also special exhibits that showcase such fearsome creatures as the Tyrannosaurus Rex and Allosaurus, some of the fiercest carnivores to walk the earth. The dinosaur displays and fossil collections are particularly impressive. Maiasaura peeblesorum, Montana's state fossil, and her babies delight all ages. The newest exhibit, "T. Rex on Trial" is a wonderfully creative approach to uncovering the mysterious truth about these ancient beasts. Were they predators or scavengers? See for yourself.

The museum is on the campus at 600 West Kagy Blvd., Bozeman, MT 59717. From I-90 take the 19th Avenue Exit, travel through town to Kagy Boulevard, turn left and follow the street signs to the museum. Open year-round; from Memorial Day through Labor Day, the hours are 8 A.M. to 8 P.M. daily. The hours during the remainder of the year are 9 A.M. to 5 P.M. Monday through Saturday, and 12:30 P.M. to 5 P.M. on Sunday. The admission fee is $6 for adults, $4 for kids ages 5 to 18 (valid for two consecutive days). Call (406) 994-DINO or (406) 994-2251, to obtain information on current displays and traveling exhibits.

*Museum of the Rockies, near Bozeman*
DONNIE SEXTON/
COURTESY TRAVEL MONTANA

While you're on the MSU campus, visit the Taylor Planetarium. It offers an interesting show, using computer simulations that generate 3-D effects and flight through space. Feature presentations are changed quarterly, and every Friday night there are tours of the night sky. During winter, special laser shows are given. Planetarium hours are weekday afternoons and Friday and Saturday nights. Admission is the same as the Museum of the Rockies.

The American Computer Museum has won awards for turning normal citizens into cyberland techies. There are 6,000 square feet of outstanding quality exhibits, including thousands of artifacts and many hands-on attractions. The full gamut of humankind's technological development is covered, providing a better understanding of where it began and where it's headed. From sand-and-pebble calculators to NASA's first IBM electronic calculator weighing more than a ton, it's all here. Whether you feel trapped by the microprocessor phenomenon or thrilled by it, this is the place for you. Find yourself at home amid the wondrous collection of old-time typewriters and office equipment, the precursors to word processors. The museum is downtown, at 234 E. Babcock St., Bozeman, MT 59715. On Babcock Street, the museum's yellow building is one block off Main Street between Bozeman and Rouse Avenues. It is open all year except some holidays. Daily summertime hours are 10 A.M. to 4 P.M. From September to May, the facility is open Tuesday, Wednesday, Friday and Saturday from 12 noon to 4 P.M. The adult admission fee is $3, kids $2. There's room to park RVs on-site, or at the free public lot across the street on Rouse Avenue. Call for further details, (406) 587-7545; fax: 587-9620.

The north side of Historic Downtown Bozeman, on Main Street between Wilson and Rouse Avenues, has buildings dating back to the 1870s. Enjoy the quaint atmosphere and interesting architecture as you browse through the Rising Sun Leather and Shoes Company, Montana Gift Corral and the Great Rocky Mountain Toy Company.

While you're downtown, stop in the Emerson Cultural Center at 111 S. Grand. There is a parking lot that will accommodate RVs in the back. Situated in a refurbished elementary schoolhouse, the building houses both visual and performing arts. It is complete with studios for artists at work, as well as many fine galleries and shops.

Every Wednesday throughout the summer, the Lunch on the Lawn summer concert series takes place from 11:30 A.M. to 1:30 P.M. The free concerts are enjoyable for all ages. Pack a lunch, or try the delicacies from one of the food booths, and enjoy meeting the local talents. It's a fun way to top off the tour of downtown Bozeman. Call for a current schedule of Emerson events, (406) 587-9797.

*These Montana "badlands" seem barren and treeless but hold plenty of wildlife and plants.*

The downtown area provides an interesting combination of history lesson and shopping. For information about Bozeman's historic districts, contact the Chamber of Commerce or Visitor Information Center. Convenient shopping is available at the Main Mall, which has 60 stores; 2825 W. Main, on Hwy. 191 toward West Yellowstone.

The old county jail, built in 1911, is put to kinder purposes these days; the Gallatin Pioneer Museum offers an authentic look into yesteryear. The hanging of convicted murderer Seth Danner took place inside these walls, and many outlaws pined away their days in the cold cells. The story of John Bozeman, Native American artifacts and a fully furnished 1870s log cabin are among the displays. The resource library is available for those seeking their own family history. The former jail's location is 317 W. Main St. in downtown Bozeman. Free admission. Open daily, the summer hours are Monday through Friday, 10 A.M. to 4:30 P.M., Saturday, 1 P.M. to 4 P.M. For winter hours, call (406) 522-8122.

Built to protect settlers from raids, Fort Ellis was 3 miles east of Bozeman. The only existing model can be seen at the Gallatin Pioneer Museum, 317 W. Main St., Bozeman, MT; (406) 522-8122.

The Bozeman Fish Technology Center is more than a fish pond. A tour provides a look at the in-depth research and development efforts in fish culture techniques, fish diseases, diet testing and fishery management. Anglers will appreciate the programs from which they benefit most. There are many varieties of fish to observe, as well as a Native American program, National Historic Site on premises and picnic area. The center is at 4050 Bridger Canyon Rd., Bozeman, MT 59715; (406) 587-9265.

Savor the wares of Bozeman's restaurants at the Taste of Bozeman—Main Street is lined with food booths, creating a walk-around picnic. The street feast heads up the arts festival. The Sweet Pea Festival of the Arts fills the town during the first weekend of August. Art, crafts, music, parades and plenty of fun can be found citywide from downtown streets to Lindley Park. If you're around in late July to early August, this festival should be on your list. Information is available from the Chamber of Commerce, 1-800-228-4224.

Bozeman Hot Springs is a great place to relax. The pools are 8 miles west of Bozeman on U.S. 191, and are open year-round. For more information, write to 81123 Gallatin Rd., U.S. 191, Bozeman, MT 59715; (406) 586-6492.

## CAMPGROUNDS & RV PARKS

Bear Canyon Campground, 3 miles east of Bozeman, use I-90 Exit 313. 100 RV sites (pull-throughs), hook-ups, dump station, hot showers, laundry and heated pool; open May 1 through October 15; (406) 587-1575; 1-800-438-1575.

▲ *Best Shot for a Camp Spot*
Bozeman KOA, 8 miles west on U.S. 191, 8 miles south of Belgrade on Montana 85, at 81123 Gallatin Rd. (U.S. 191), Bozeman, MT 59715. 100 RV sites, hook-ups, dump station, hot showers, laundry and natural hot springs pools; open year-round; (406) 587-3030; 1-800-562-3036.

Sunrise Campground, off I-90 Exit 309, at 31842 Frontage Rd., Bozeman, MT 59715. 50 RV sites, hook-ups, dump station, hot showers and laundry; open April 1 through October 31; (406) 587-4797.

▲ *Best Shot for a Camp Spot*
Battle Ridge—U.S. Forest Service Campground, 22 miles northeast of Bozeman on Montana 86. RVs allowed (max. length 16 feet), no services; open June 10 through September 30.

Greek Creek—U.S. Forest Service Campground, 31 miles south of Bozeman on U.S. 191. RVs allowed (max. length 16 feet), no services; open June 15 through September 15.

Greycliff—Montana Department of Fish, Wildlife and Parks Campground, 23 miles west of Bozeman on Montana 84, then 6 miles north on Madison River Road. RVs allowed; no services; open year-round.

Moose Flat—U.S. Forest Service Campground, 32 miles south of Bozeman on U.S. 191. RVs allowed (max. length 16 feet), no services; open June 1 through September 15.

Red Cliff—U.S. Forest Service Campground, 48 miles south of Bozeman on U.S. 191. RVs allowed (max. length 40 feet), no services; open June 1 through September 15.

Spire Rock—U.S. Forest Service Campground, 26 miles south of Bozeman on U.S. 191, then 2 miles east on Forest Road 1321. RVs allowed (max. length 16 feet), no services; open June 15 through September 15.

Swan Creek—U.S. Forest Service Campground, 32 miles south of Bozeman on U.S. 191, then 1 mile east on Forest Service Road 481. RVs allowed (max. length 16 feet), no services; open June 15 through September 15.

## BED & BREAKFAST ESTABLISHMENTS

Bergfeld Bed and Breakfast Home, 10 minutes from town at mountain's edge, quarter-mile on gravel road. Operating since 1993; open year-round; busiest June through August, slowest October through November; credit cards accepted; pets allowed. Contact Dave and Faye Walters, 8515 Sypes Canyon Rd., Bozeman, MT 59715; (406) 586-7778; fax: (406) 582-8229.

Cottonwood Inn, open year-round; busiest July through October, slowest in May; credit cards accepted; no pets or smoking allowed. Contact Joe and Debby Velli, 13515 Cottonwood Canyon Dr., Bozeman, MT 59715; (406) 763-5452; 1-888-TRY-INNS.

Fox Hollow Bed & Breakfast, noted for panoramic views; operating since 1994. Open year-round; busiest July through August, slowest November and April; credit cards accepted; no pets allowed. Contact Michael and Nancy Dawson, 545 Mary Rd., Bozeman, MT 59715; (406) 582-8440; 1-800-431-5010.

Howlers Inn Bed & Breakfast, a wolf sanctuary with mountain views. The inn has been operating since 1994. Open year-round; busiest winter and summer, slowest spring and fall; credit cards accepted; no pets allowed. Contact Dan Astrom, 3185 Jackson Creek Rd., Bozeman, MT 59715; (406) 586-0304; 1-888-HOWLERS.

Kirk Hill Bed & Breakfast, in a ranch setting 6 miles south of Bozeman (sheep, llamas, goats). Open year-round; busiest May through September, slowest rest of year; credit cards accepted; no pets allowed. Contact Charles and Patricia Kirk, 7960 S. 19th Rd., Bozeman, MT 59715; (406) 586-0317; 1-800-240-3929. Website: http://www.avicom.net/kirkhill

Lindley House Bed & Breakfast, Victorian manor house in historic downtown area. Operating since 1994; open year-round; busiest in summer, slowest November through December; credit cards accepted; no pets allowed. Contact Stephanie Volz, 202 Lindley Place, Bozeman, MT 59715; (406) 587-8403; 1-800-787-8404.

Millers of Montana Bed & Breakfast; specialties are quilting, yoga and international cooking retreats. The lodge has been operating since 1991. Open year-round; busiest in summer, slowest October through February; no credit cards accepted; pets conditional. Contact Doug and Joyce Miller, 1002 Zachariah Lane, 1 mile off U.S. 191, Bozeman, MT 59715; (406) 763-4102; e-mail: millersinn@theglobalnet

Silver Forest Inn, 1930s lodge with mountain views and hot tub. The lodge has been operating since 1987. Open year-round; busiest winter and summer, slowest fall and spring; credit cards accepted; pets need pre-approval. Contact Silver Forest Inn, 15325 Bridger Canyon Rd., Bozeman, MT 59715; (406) 586-1882; fax: (406) 582-0492.

Voss Inn, 114-year-old inn. Open year-round; busiest in summer; credit cards accepted; no pets allowed. Contact Bruce and Frankie Muller; 319 S. Wilson, Bozeman, MT 59715; (406) 587-0982; (406) 585-2964.

### GUEST RANCHES

Bozeman Backpackers Hostel, bunk-style accommodations and private rooms. The hostel has been operating since 1989. Open year-round; busiest in summer, slowest in winter; no credit cards accepted; no pets allowed. Contact Bozeman Backpackers, 405 W. Olive St., Bozeman, MT 59715; (406) 586-4659.

**SUGGESTED DINING**

O'Brian's Restaurant, 312 E. Main, Bozeman, MT; (406) 587-3973.

John Bozeman's Bistro, 242 E. Main, Bozeman, MT; (406) 587-4100.

Spanish Peaks Brewery and Italian Cafe, 120 N. 19th, Bozeman, MT; (406) 585-2296.

**VISITOR INFORMATION & SERVICES**

Bozeman Chamber of Commerce, 1205 E. Main, PO Box B, Bozeman, MT 59771; (406) 586-5421; 1-800-228-4224; fax: (406) 586-8286.

Bozeman Visitor Information Center, 1001 N. 7th Ave., Bozeman, MT 59771; open Memorial to Labor Day; direct telephone calls to the Chamber of Commerce.

While you're visiting the sights, you may park on the north side of Main Street, or fairly easily in the many large parking lots around town.

Gallatin National Forest Headquarters, Bozeman Ranger District Office, 3710 Fallon St., Bozeman, MT 59715; open Monday through Friday, 8 A.M. to 5 P.M.; (406) 587-6920; 24-hour recording for the latest update on trail conditions, (406) 587-9784.

Montana Department of Fish, Wildlife and Parks, Region 3 Office, 1400 S. 19th Ave., Bozeman, MT; (406) 994-4042.

Montana State University, Information Office and Student Services, (406) 994-2452.

**MEDICAL SERVICES**

Bozeman Urgent Care Center, 1006 W. Main St., Bozeman, MT; (406) 585-8711.

Bozeman Deaconess Hospital, 915 Highland Blvd., Bozeman, MT; (406) 585-5000.

Albertson's Food & Drug, 200 S. 23 Ave., Bozeman, MT; (406) 587-8800.

Highland Park Pharmacy, adjacent to Bozeman Deaconess Hospital at 925 Highland Blvd., Bozeman, MT; open Monday through Friday, 8 A.M. to 6 P.M., and Saturday, 8 A.M. to 1 P.M.; (406) 585-1030.

**REPAIR & TOWING**

M & M Repair & Towing, 24-hour service, 1010 N. Rouse, Bozeman, MT; 1-800-447-8022.

C and T Trailer Supply and Service, Inc., 2000 N. 7th, Bozeman, MT; (406) 587-5000.

**VETERINARY SERVICES**

Creekside Vet Hospital, Dr. Connie Van Luchene, 8840 Chapman Rd., Bozeman, MT; (406) 586-8974.

# BELGRADE AND MANHATTAN: I-90

Follow the interstate west from Bozeman to Belgrade, and continue on to Manhattan. This is mostly ranching country, although much of it is being developed and sold to outside interests.

**BELGRADE**

The settlement began in 1883 as a grain trading stop along the rail line. Thomas Quaw founded the town with the aid of a group of Serbian financial backers. The name Belgrade was chosen by the Serbs for their native capital. The town has full services and visitor center, but its main feature is the airport, Gallatin Field, that serves Bozeman and the surrounding area. Air service is provided by Delta, Northwest and Horizon Air.

# John M. Bozeman: Pioneer and Pathfinder

John Bozeman came to Bannack, Montana, from Colorado in the gold rush of 1862. Bozeman formed a plan with John M. Jacobs to find a shorter route from Fort Laramie to Bannack.

In May 1863, the two men set out in search of their road, taking with them Jacobs's eight-year-old daughter. Together they suffered many hardships. They were captured by Natives and stripped of most of their possessions. The marauders were persuaded to take their horses, food supply and most of their clothing, leaving only small ponies behind. Eventually, the three arrived at Fort Laramie, Wyoming, in a near-starved condition.

The gold discovery on Grasshopper Creek, near Bannack, renewed their energy. Bozeman and Jacobs organized a wagon train of prospectors to lead back to Bannack via their new route, a shortcut that left the Oregon Trail. They claimed the cutoff saved 300 to 500 miles, had good water, rich grasslands and an abundant supply of wild game. The only drawback—hostile Natives.

In July 1863, Bozeman and Jacobs set out with a train of 46 wagons, 89 men and a French guide, Richards. The route began up the eastern side of the Bighorn Mountains. The party encountered Cheyenne and Sioux within two weeks' travel. A parley was held. The Natives promised not to attack if the wagon train retreated, but if it continued, all would be killed. A white man's road would not cross through the Native Americans' country. After a succession of small retreats and a denied request for a military escort, the prospectors yielded. At the end of July, the wagons headed back to the Oregon Trail.

The wagons went on, but John Bozeman and a group of nine men continued on the shorter route toward Bannack. They skirted the hostile tribes by crossing to the western side of Wyoming's Bighorn Range. The trip was a difficult one; the arid Bighorn Basin of the western side offered little aid. Eventually the group reached the Shoshone River and continued on without mishap. Bozeman Pass, a low route between the Yellowstone and Gallatin River Valleys, was discovered and named in his honor. (The pass is south of Livingston on Hwy. 89.)

The Bozeman Trail became a favorite, but dangerous, route to Montana for three years, and was often referred to as the Bloody Bozeman. In 1864 Bozeman and Jim Bridger were commissioned to guide expeditions to the Yellowstone River Valley and Virginia City. Bozeman, who had witnessed a terrible bread famine on a wagon train, conceived the idea to start a colony of farmers to till the fertile soil of the upper Gallatin Valley. His plan succeeded. Settlers were attracted to the valley, and a town site was established. At a meeting of the settlers in 1864, the town was named in honor of Bozeman.

In 1865, Bozeman was appointed probate judge of the newly created Gallatin County. Finally settled, he no longer led the wagons across the plains. Bozeman was his home, until he was murdered in 1867; the mystery of his death was never solved.

Prospectors and pioneers continued their pressure westward. In 1865, the U.S. Government sought to establish the Bozeman Road along the original route. Fort Phil Kearny and Fort C. F. Smith were built to fortify the trail, and other forts were intended. A shortage of manpower and the continuous siege of Sioux attacks under Chief Red Cloud prohibited use of the original Bozeman Trail. In 1868, the government abandoned the Bozeman Road under the Treaty of Fort Bridger.

## MANHATTAN

The current site of Manhattan was chosen by the railroad to serve as a station. As you might have guessed, it was named by a group of New York investors who purchased land in the area. Their primary business, the Manhattan Malting Company, ended during Prohibition.

## ATTRACTIONS

Our favorite gallery pick is the Big Sky Carvers Gallery, 324 E. Railroad Ave., South Manhattan, MT. The superior-quality products and images are created by master designers, artists and craftsmen—the nearly 150 members of the Big Sky Carvers workshop. The gallery offers a splendid collection of works, including wildlife woodcarvings, classic duck decoys, miniatures, trophy fish, the famous Big Sky Bears and much more. Regular hours are Monday through Friday, 8 A.M. to 5 P.M. For more information or a catalog, call (406) 284-3193.

**RV CAUTION:** Your Montana map shows a road from Manhattan to Maudlow via County Road 346, and then to Ringling. *Avoid this at all costs, whether the road is wet or dry.* This route winds through private ranchland, and though it's beautiful country, the road is badly rutted and potholed. When wet, it is treacherous.

## OVERNIGHTING

### CAMPGROUNDS & RV PARKS

▲ *Best Shot for a Camp Spot*
Lexley Acres, one-half mile south of I-90, exit at Belgrade. 23 RV sites (6 pull-throughs), hook-ups, dump station, hot showers; open year-round; busiest June 15 through August 15, slow rest of year; call (406) 388-6095.

### BED & BREAKFAST ESTABLISHMENTS

Heart Mountain Bed & Breakfast, on a gravel road. The establishment has been operating since 1992. Open year-round; busiest May through October, slowest November through April; no credit cards accepted; no pets allowed. Contact Julie Wagner, 10920 Corbly Gulch Rd., Belgrade, MT  59714; (406) 587-2004.

## SUGGESTED DINING

Sir Scott's Oasis, 204 W. Railroad Ave., South Manhattan, MT; (406) 284-6929.

The Mint Bar & Grill, 27 E. Main, Belgrade, MT; (406) 388-1100.

Country Kitchen, Belgrade, MT; (406) 388-0808.

Blair's Restaurant on Jackrabbit Lane, Belgrade, MT; (406) 388-4665.

| | |
|---|---|
| **VISITOR INFORMATION & SERVICES** | Belgrade Chamber of Commerce, PO Box 1126, 10 E. Main, Belgrade, MT 59714; (406) 388-1616; fax: 388-1616.<br><br>Manhattan Chamber of Commerce, PO Box 606, Manhattan, MT 59741. |
| **MEDICAL SERVICES** | For medical services, see Bozeman Services (page 271).<br><br>Price Right Drug Center, Main and Weaver, Belgrade, MT; open Monday through Friday, 9 A.M. to 9 P.M., Saturday, 9 A.M. to 6 P.M., and Sunday, 10 A.M. to 4 P.M.; (406) 388-4111. |
| **REPAIR & TOWING** | Cero Brothers Towing & Repair, 24-hour service, 150 Thunder Rd., Belgrade, MT; 1-800-377-4741. |
| **VETERINARY SERVICES** | Hardaway and Catlin Veterinary Hospital, 5650 Jackrabbit Lane, Belgrade, MT; (406) 388-8387. |

# BRIDGER BOWL: MONTANA 86

Head north from Bozeman on Montana 86 to explore the Bridger Range of the Gallatin National Forest.

Bridger Bowl is a nonprofit ski area, situated in the Bridger Mountains 16 miles northeast of Bozeman on Hwy. 86. The area was incorporated 40 years ago; if ever sold, all proceeds are pledged to Montana State University.

There are 1,200 skiable acres, 2,000 feet of vertical drop, and six chairlifts. The facilities include a base lodge, cafeteria and bar, mid-mountain chalet, ski school and rental shops. The longest run is 2.5 miles. Average annual snowfall is 350 inches. The season is from early December to early April. Call year-round: 1-800-223-9609; (406) 586-1518; website: http://www.bridgerbowl.com

Wildlife viewing of a unique nature is possible at Bridger Bowl. The Bridger Range is a significant flyway for 17 species of migrating raptors in the fall. The largest concentration of golden eagles in the lower 48 states can be viewed from two observation sites. However, there's a big hitch. Watching eagles classifies as more of a vigorous sport than eyes-only activity. The observation areas demand steep hiking. The more accessible post is reached by hiking up the

Bridger Lift area (2,100 feet) at the Bridger Bowl Ski Area. Best viewing is from 10 A.M. to 2 P.M. during the first two weeks of October. The Forest Service maintains a raptor monitoring station and personnel are available to answer questions. The experience is unforgettable. For raptor migration information and news on workshops, contact the Gallatin National Forest, (406) 587-6752.

# WEST YELLOWSTONE TO ENNIS: U.S. 287

This route heads due north out of West Yellowstone, and then forks, the north fork being U.S. 191 to Bozeman, and the west fork being U.S. 287. When you travel on the westerly fork, you'll see Hebgen Lake on your left, and soon you'll spot Quake Lake. As you continue, the road veers north, with the Gravelly Range on the left and the Lee Metcalf Wilderness Area on the right, within which are 11,286-foot Koch Peak and 10,860-foot Sphinx Peak. The Madison River parallels this highway on the west side to Ennis, where it then flows under the highway and courses along on the east side where it leaves Ennis Lake and the Beartrap Canyon. Note our "Favorite Drive" below that requires a short detour to Wade and Cliff Lakes.

Hebgen Lake offers great power or sail boating, fishing and wind surfing. The lake was created in 1915 by Hebgen Dam across the Madison River. The recreational area covers 12,000 acres and has all conveniences: boat rentals, marinas, camping and food service. There is plenty of access to fishing. See the list of campgrounds on page 278.

Madison River Canyon Earthquake Area is the site where a massive earthquake struck in 1959. Half the mountain slid into the canyon, killing 28 people. The slide area stretches over 37,800 acres; 80 million tons of rock came crashing down. Quake Lake was formed by the slide when huge slabs of rock crashed down and blocked the river. The earthquake caused a tidal wave that ripped across Hebgen Lake 6 miles away and poured over the dam. Luckily the dam held. The quake, the biggest in this region of the Rocky Mountains, measured 7.5 on the Richter scale. The quake area has a visitor center; open Memorial Day through Labor Day, (406) 646-7369. Maps for a self-guided tour show the route to Refuge Point, Cabin Creek Scarp area, the lake's east end "ghost village," and point out the turnouts where interpretive signs tell the whole story.

## FAVORITE DRIVE:
## WADE AND CLIFF LAKES

There's a loop road (Forest Service Road 8381) to Wade and Cliff Lakes off of Montana 87 from the south or accessed just north of the junction with U.S. 287. The 6-mile gravel road is in good condition and can be traveled by anything from RV to mountain bike. Fish for trout, hike some of the many ski trails or camp by the beautiful tree-lined lakes. There are private resorts or Forest Service campgrounds; see the Overnighting section for West Yellowstone (page 257). Fishing is outstanding in these deep, narrow lakes. Cliff Lake is about 4 miles long and a half-mile wide, while Wade Lake is only a mile and a half long and a quarter-mile wide. You can fish from shore or a boat. Many serious anglers use float tubes.

**CAMERON**

Settled by a pioneer family named Cameron in the year 1886, the community was originally known as Bear Creek. In 1919, the Camerons' store was bought out, and the building moved 6 miles down the road to the site of modern-day Cameron. The new owner sought the higher traffic passing along the route between Ennis and Yellowstone, a good plan then, and a good plan now.

The rock cliffs seen to the east collar around Sphinx Mountain, which rises to an elevation of 10,860 feet. On the lower slopes of this grand mountain are the pastures and hayfields of the valley ranchers. Although geologists gave the mountain a lofty foreign name, the locals called it simply "Old Red," because the rock cliffs glowed red in the sunset, a beautiful sight appreciated by all.

**ENNIS**

An Irishman by birth, William Ennis trekked across the Montana mountains from Bannack in the late 1870s. In 1879, he built a store on the Madison River and established the Ennis Post Office in 1881. For the next 86 years, the post office was managed by his family. Winifred (Ennis) Chowning Jeffers was the last of his line to hold the office of postmaster in 1967.

Ennis began as a supply stop for the gold miners at Virginia and Nevada Cities. When the gold panned out, the rich lands of the valley were put to use by ranchers. Eventually, ranching became the economic base of the community.

Today the junction site of U.S. 287 and Montana 287 is a rapidly growing commerce area. Gift and antique shops and real estate firms shoulder up to the old cafe and bars. Tourism, especially summer fishing, is very lucrative. The notoriety of Ted Turner's nearby buffalo ranch is bringing new faces and many changes to the Madison River Valley. Ennis's population of 775 faces the challenge of merging ways of the old and new days.

# WADE & CLIFF LAKES

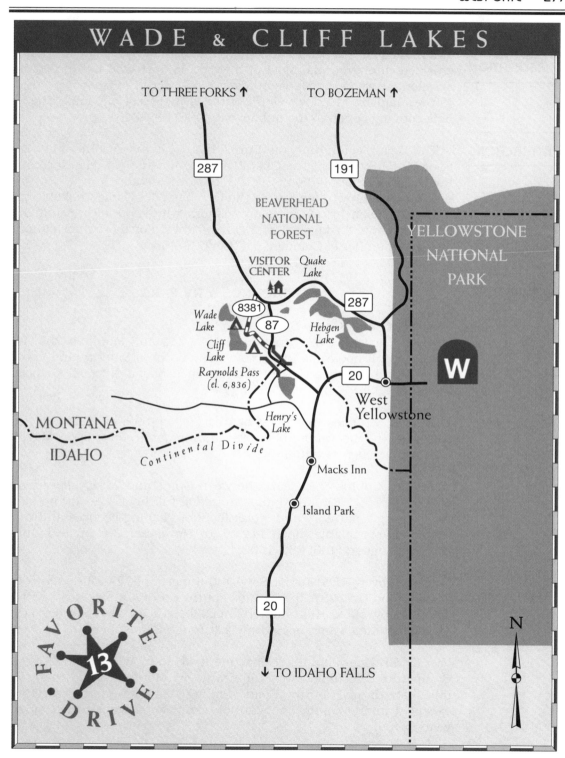

TO THREE FORKS ↑

TO BOZEMAN ↑

287

191

BEAVERHEAD
NATIONAL
FOREST

VISITOR
CENTER

*Quake
Lake*

8381

287

*Wade
Lake*

87

*Hebgen
Lake*

*Cliff
Lake*

*Raynolds Pass
(el. 6,836)*

20

YELLOWSTONE
NATIONAL
PARK

W

West
Yellowstone

MONTANA

IDAHO

*Henry's
Lake*

*Continental Divide*

Macks Inn

Island Park

20

FAVORITE 13 DRIVE

N

↓ TO IDAHO FALLS

## OUTDOOR RECREATION

Fishing along the Madison River is very popular. There are several fishing access points, but the popularity of the area can lead to crowded campgrounds. Most of the area is open and flat, providing excellent views of the Madison River.

The Madison Meadows Golf Course is just west of Ennis. The 9-hole course is open to the public; call (406) 682-7468.

## ATTRACTIONS

The small community of Ennis has a giant celebration at its Fourth of July Rodeo. The Chamber of Commerce, and the Northern Rodeo Association, (406) 252-1122, have the details.

Ennis has grown famous for the October Wild Game Cookoff. Fall hunting season brings in many visitors who serve as the judging panel and vote for favorite wild game dishes. For more information, call the Chamber of Commerce, (406) 682-4388.

## OVERNIGHTING

## CAMPGROUNDS & RV PARKS

▲ *Best Shot for a Camp Spot*
Camper Corner, at the junction of U.S. 287 and Montana 287. 20 RV sites, full hook-ups, dump station, showers, laundry and cable TV; walking distance to Main Street; open May 1 through October 31; (406) 682-4514; 1-800-755-3474.

Slide Inn, 30 miles northwest of West Yellowstone on U.S. 287. 23 RV sites, full hook-ups, showers, laundry and store; open May 1 through October 31; (406) 682-4804.

West Fork Cabins & RV Park, between Ennis and West Yellowstone on U.S. 287. 24 RV sites (pull-throughs), full hook-ups, dump station, showers, laundry and store; fly shop, fishing licenses and raft rentals are available; open May 1 to November 30; busiest July through August; (406) 682-4802.

Madison River—U.S. Forest Service Campground, 24 miles south of Cameron on U.S. 287, then 1 mile southwest on County Road 8381. 10 camping sites, RVs allowed (max. length 22 feet), no services except drinking water; open June 1 through September 30.

Varney Bridge—Montana Department of Fish, Wildlife and Parks Campground, 2 miles west of Ennis on Montana 287, then 10 miles south on County Road. Small RVs allowed, no services except drinking water; boat-launch ramp for 2-wheel drive; open year-round.

Ennis—Montana Department of Fish, Wildlife and Parks Campground, east of Ennis on U.S. 287, Milepost 48. Small RVs allowed, 25 sites, no services except drinking water; boat-launch ramp for 2-wheel drive; open April 1 through November 30.

Valley Garden—Montana Department of Fish, Wildlife and Parks Campground, quarter-mile south of Ennis on U.S. 287 at Milepost 48, then 2 miles north on County Road. Small RVs allowed, no services except drinking water; boat-launch ramp for 2-wheel drive; open April 1 through November 30.

West Madison—U.S. Bureau of Land Management Campground, 18 miles south of Ennis on U.S. 287, then 3 miles south on County Road. 22 sites, RVs allowed (max. length 35 feet), no services except drinking water; open year-round.

South Madison—U.S. Bureau of Land Management Campground, 26 miles south of Ennis on U.S. 287, then 1 mile west. 11 sites, RVs allowed (max. length 35 feet), no services except drinking water; boat launch ramp for 2-wheel drive; open year-round.

## BED & BREAKFAST ESTABLISHMENTS

9 T 9 Ranch, four minutes from the Madison River, licensed guide service available. Operating since 1990; open year-round; busiest June through September, slowest, November through May; has one RV hook-up; pets conditional. Contact 9 T 9 Ranch, 99 Gravelly Range Rd., Ennis, MT 59729; (406) 682-7659; fax: 682-7654; e-mail: jherrick@threerivers.net
Website: http://www.moscow.com.business/9t9

*Three Forks, Montana, where the Jefferson, Gallatin and Madison rivers form the Missouri River*
DONNIE SEXTON/COURTESY TRAVEL MONTANA

Rachie's Crow Nest, 100 U.S. 287, Ennis, MT 59729. The inn is located 1 mile south of Ennis and features a swimming pool and hot tub; (406) 682-7371.

Riverview, on the Madison River, has rooms with river view. Operating since 1997; open year-round; busiest July through September; no credit cards accepted; no pets allowed. Contact Harriet Pearson, PO Box 969, 321 Riverview, Ennis, MT 59729; (406) 682-4145; fax: 682-7402.

## GUEST RANCHES

Cliff Lake Resort, 4 miles off Montana 87, next to Cliff Lake. This resort has been operating since 1992. Features include 10 RV hook-ups; fishing, boating, canoeing, hiking, horseback riding, hunting and snowmobiling. Equipment rentals are available. Open May 30 through Labor Day; credit cards accepted; prefer no pets. Contact Cliff Lake Resort, PO Box 267, Cameron, MT 59720; (406) 682-4982.

Wade Lake Resort, 6 miles off U.S. 287 near Madison River on Wade Lake. The resort offers wildlife watching, fishing (both river and lake), hiking, boating and cross-country skiing. Open year-round; busiest in summer, slowest spring and fall; no credit cards accepted; no pets allowed. Contact Dave and Laurie Schmidt, PO Box 107, 963 Hwy. 287 North #1, Cameron, MT 59720; (406) 682-7560.

CB Cattle and Guest Ranch, in the Madison River Valley. The family-owned ranch is a working cattle ranch that features fishing and horseback riding. Contact CB Cattle and Guest Ranch, PO Box 604, Cameron, MT 59720; (406) 682-4954.

Lost Fork Ranch, guest ranch with new accommodations, 11-12 Hwy. 287 North, Cameron, MT 59720; (406) 682-7690.

Old Kirby Place, at West Fork Bridge. The riverside location is ideal for fly fishermen. Open in summer. Contact Old Kirby Place, PO Box 107, 963 Hwy. 287 North #1, Cameron, MT 59720; (406) 682-7560.

Centennial Guest Ranch, 10 miles east of Ennis. The ranch offers trail rides and pack trips and is an Orvis-endorsed expedition outfitter. Contact Centennial Guest Ranch, PO Box 360, Ennis, MT 59729; (406) 682-7292.

Diamond J Ranch, 12 miles east of Ennis. This family-owned ranch has been operating since 1959. Featured are private fishing; guided trips; horseback riding; tennis; heated pool; skeet, trap, and clay shooting; and seasonal bird hunting. Open June through September; busiest July and August; credit cards accepted; no pets allowed. Contact Pete and Jinny Combs, PO Box 577, Ennis, MT 59729; (406) 682-4867; fax: 682-4106.

T Lazy B Ranch, 10 miles east of Ennis. This ranch has been operating since 1978 and caters to those interested in fly fishing and upland bird hunting. The ranch also offers float trips on the Madison River. Open May 15 through October 15; no credit cards accepted; pets allowed. Contact Bob and Theo Walker, 532 Jack Creek Rd., Ennis, MT 59729; (406) 682-7288.

## SUGGESTED DINING

Continental Divide, Ennis, MT; (406) 682-7600.

Scottie's Supper Club at the Longbranch Saloon, Ennis, MT; (406)-682-5300.

## VISITOR INFORMATION & SERVICES

Ennis Chamber of Commerce, PO Box 291, Ennis, MT 59729; (406) 682-4388.

The Beaverhead National Forest, Ranger Station, 5 Forest Service Road, Ennis, MT 59729; (406) 682-4388.

## MEDICAL SERVICES

Madison Valley Hospital, 24-hour emergency room, Ennis, MT; (406) 682-4274.

Ennis Pharmacy, 124 Main, Ennis, MT; open Monday through Saturday from 6 A.M. to 6 P.M., (406) 682-4246.

## REPAIR & TOWING

M & B Auto & Towing (AAA-rated), Ennis, MT; (406) 682-7212; 1-800-823-7325.

## VETERINARY SERVICES

White & White, 5098 Hwy. 287, Ennis, MT; (406) 682-7151.

Dr. James Bond, Ennis, MT; (406) 682-4007.

# NORRIS, THREE FORKS AND TOWNSEND: U.S. 287

From Ennis, take U.S. 287 north to Norris. From there the road divides, and you can either take Montana 84 east to Bozeman, or head north on 287, where the highway splits again just north of Harrison. At that junction, you can take Route 359 northwest to Whitehall, or continue north on U.S. 287 to Montana 2 that takes you to Three Forks and I-15 to the east, or Cardwell to the west. U.S. 287 continues north out of Three Forks, running 30 miles to Townsend. From there you can stay on 287, passing Canyon Ferry Lake on the way to Helena, or instead, travel east out of Townsend on U.S. 12 to U.S. 89, which connects White Sulphur Springs to I-15.

## NORRIS

Norris, named for Alexander Norris, a local rancher, was a mining town that sat in the heart of cattle country. The post office opened in 1891. Cattle were driven here from the summer pastures to be shipped to market, and Norris was also the end of the line for the railroad.

## PONY

Ten times as many people lived in Pony back in the 1870s; today there are about 150 residents. The old metropolis of 1,000 was a mining town, and quartz discoveries in 1875 brought droves of prospectors. Tecumseh "Pony" Smith was the town's namesake; he was a rugged miner of relatively small physical build. He built his cabin on Pony Creek in 1869.

## OVERNIGHTING

### CAMPGROUNDS & RV PARKS

*Best Shot for a Camp Spot*

▲ Norris Hot Springs, quarter-mile east of Norris on Montana 84. Large natural hot springs pool; 15 RV sites (pull-throughs), full hook-ups and store; open year-round; (406) 685-3303.

Red Mountain—U.S. Bureau of Land Management Campground, 9 miles north of Norris on U.S. 289. RVs allowed (max. length 35 feet), no services except drinking water; hand-launch boat ramp; open year-round.

Harrison Lake—Montana Department of Fish, Wildlife and Parks Campground, 5 miles east of Harrison on County Road. 25 sites, RVs allowed, no services; boat-launch ramp for 4-wheel drive only; open year-round.

Potosi—U.S. Forest Service Campground, 3 miles southeast of Pony on County Road 1601, then 5 miles southwest on Forest Service Road 1501. 15 sites, RVs allowed (max. length 32 feet), no services except drinking water and toilets; open June 1 through September 30.

# NORRIS TO THREE FORKS: U.S. 287

The Three Forks area is unique in that it has three state parks in the vicinity. They are Lewis and Clark Caverns State Park, Headwaters of the Missouri State Park and Madison Buffalo Jump State Park.

## LEWIS AND CLARK CAVERNS STATE PARK

Despite its name, this park is one of the few places in the area that was not discovered by the exploring duo and their party. The caverns are 19 miles west of Three Forks on Montana 2.

Hidden along the Jefferson River, credit for the initial discovery is still undetermined. The Native Americans told stories about the caverns and surely knew of their existence. Local ranchers may have come upon the caves in the 1840s. There's a tale that a couple of hunters, Thomas Williams and Bert Pannell, found the caves in 1892, but D. A. Morrison put forth the first real effort and developed the site in the early 1900s. A prospector by trade, Morrison discovered the caverns by chance. He filed claims on the land and later charged the public for tours.

The caverns are distinguished as Montana's first and best-known state park. President Teddy Roosevelt declared the site a national monument in 1908, but little beyond the name was done. The state received control in 1935 and eventually committed financial resources. The park was finally developed and renamed Lewis and Clark Caverns State Park in 1946.

The park now includes a Visitor Center, interpretive displays, guided tours, group facilities, showers, dump station, shady picnic spots, cafe and gift shop. The 45-site campground is on an open grassy flat above the river. There are pull-through sites for large RVs but no hook-up services. Informative campfire talks are presented on Saturday nights in the amphitheater by park staffers.

*Lewis and Clark Caverns, near Three Forks, Montana*
CRAIG & LIZ LARCOM/COURTESY TRAVEL MONTANA

Cavern tours depart daily from May 1 through September 30. Tickets must be purchased at the Visitor Center. The guided tours take two hours and the charge per adult is $7, children $3. Even on the hottest summer day, the temperature inside the caverns remains a constant 48 degrees Fahrenheit. Take a light jacket along. The interior is wet and damp; hiking boots or rubber-soled shoes are best. The stalactites, stalagmites, columns and helictites are eerily fascinating and worth the price. With the aid of electric lights, the splendor of the cave's interior becomes visible and the tour much safer.

**RV CAUTION:** The paved road to the Visitor Center winds up a steep 3-mile switchback. Once you reach the top, be sure to park large RVs in the Visitor Center's first lower parking lot! The upper lot is small and could present problems. Reservations or additional information is available from the Park Headquarters, (406) 287-3541.

## HEADWATERS OF THE MISSOURI STATE PARK

This state park is one of the most inspiring landscapes in Montana. The union of three mighty rivers has the power of nature that makes one feel very small. The 560-acre state park is very RV-friendly. Go 3 miles east of Three Forks on I-90, then east on Highway 205, then 3 miles north on Highway 286. The day-use fee for out-of-state vehicles is $3, or use the Montana State Parks Passport, $15 per year.

As you might expect, fishing is a popular sport here; the boat launch is very convenient. Wildlife viewing and hiking along the trails are also enjoyable activities. The interpretive displays along the trails enhance the easy walk by providing an interesting narrative and descriptions of the vistas. The habitat is ideal for birds and fish. Have some mosquito repellent on hand; it can make the difference and ensure a pleasant stay.

Lewis and Clark arrived at the confluence of the three rivers in July 1805. Judging the three forks to be roughly equivalent in flow, Lewis and Clark determined this to be the headwaters of the Missouri. They named the southwest fork Jefferson's River in honor of President Thomas Jefferson. The middle fork was called Madison's River for Secretary of State James Madison and the southeast fork was dubbed Gallatin's River after Albert Gallatin, Secretary of the Treasury. The geographical hub was significant as a crossroads to Native Americans, mountain men and early pioneers.

*Headwaters of the Missouri River, at Three Forks, Montana*

*Missouri River headwaters, near Three Forks, Montana*
DONNIE SEXTON/
COURTESY TRAVEL MONTANA

Even during the peak of the summer season, the state campground is a reliable spot to camp. Although RVs must remain self-contained, the site is beautiful and convenient for visiting the surrounding area. (See Overnighting, page 287.) Be sure to explore the area. The park land lies on both sides of Highway 286, running along the east shore of the Madison and Missouri Rivers. There are several designated vista areas and many trails. The only drawbacks to returning home with wondrous pictures are the annoying power lines that seem impossible to keep out of the picture. Mankind encroaches where it has never gone before.

**MADISON BUFFALO JUMP STATE PARK**

It takes imagination to appreciate the cliffs at Madison Buffalo Jump State Park. However, the scenic view of the Madison River Valley and peaks of the Tobacco Root Mountains require only a clear day. Archaeological digs have revealed that several Native American tribes used the cliffs for a buffalo jump. The Blackfeet, Nez Perce, Northern Shoshone and Crow were among the tribes who gathered their meat and other necessities in this manner. The jump is called a *pishkun*. The interpretive displays fittingly explain the "jump" process, its necessity and historical importance.

A visit to the site enhances understanding of the land and Native peoples but requires some stoic endurance.

**RV CAUTION:** The washboard gravel road is pretty rough. It's better to break away in a towed car, if one is available. If you're traveling during peak season, it's better to park at the lower turn-around area, and walk up to the overlook. Maneuvering an RV to turn around at the top is difficult when the small lot is filled with vehicles. To visit the primitive park, get off I-90 at the Logan Exit (283), then go 7 miles south on Buffalo Jump Road. (406) 994-4042.

## THREE FORKS

The annals of the Three Forks area are filled with the most colorful and famous characters in American history. The tribes of Sacajawea were accosted by outsiders here. Lewis and Clark came upon the river junction in 1805. Five years later, John Colter guided the French fur traders to establish the first trading post in the territory. Although these famous people passed through here, the building of a permanent community was a slow process.

The area was rich in wildlife, especially the fur-bearing type. The natural crossroads led to fierce battles when the Blackfeet, Gros Ventre, Flathead, Crow or other tribes met. The Blackfeet especially were no kinder to the white intruders.

Lewis and Clark left their legacy by naming the three rivers that join to form the Missouri: the Madison, Gallatin and Jefferson. John Colter, along with Andrew and Pierre Menard built the first trading post, but it was abandoned after three years. The men at Fort Three Forks were so continuously harassed by the Blackfeet that trapping and trading became impossible. In 1811, the discouraged mountain men abandoned the post.

The area remained a crossroads, losing out to rapidly growing commerce in nearby towns like Bozeman. Slowly, Three Forks claimed its own, and a post office was established in 1882. Today, the wholesome community of 1,800 retains the true character of Montana. The current major employers are the Luzenac Talc Mine and Plant (150), Holnam Cement Plant (100), School District (50) and Wheat Montana Farms (40). Visit Three Forks by leaving I-90 at Exit 278.

## OUTDOOR RECREATION

This area has unsurpassed access to fishing hundreds of miles of blue-ribbon trout streams. The Madison, Gallatin, Jefferson and Missouri Rivers have become world famous. See more fishing details on page 288.

Headwaters Public Golf Course has 9 holes, lots of water, a putting green and driving range. Play in view of the Tobacco Root Mountains. Call the full-service golf shop, (406) 285-3700, for tee times, or just stop in. The course is at 225 7th Ave. E., Three Forks, MT.

Eight miles west of Three Forks is the Parker Homestead. The authentic sod-roofed cabin was typical of frontier homes built on the prairie. The day-use-only site is included in the state park system. For more information, call (406) 994-4042.

## ATTRACTIONS

Headwaters Heritage Museum is a quaint museum that covers local history and nostalgia. Constructed in 1910, the building was one of the town's first banks. The unusual assortment of exhibits include a display of the 701 different types of barbed wire and the largest fish ever caught in the state. The whopper was a $29\frac{1}{2}$-pound brown trout caught by a Three Forks resident. There's a picnic area in back next to the 1860s log cabin from Gallatin City. The address is 202 S. Main, Three Forks, MT 59752; (406) 285-4778. Take either of the Three Forks Exits off I-90; the museum is at the corner of Main and Cedar Streets. It's easier to park down on Cedar Street. The free museum is open May to September, Monday through Saturday, 9 A.M. to noon, 1 P.M. to 5 P.M. and Sunday, 1 P.M. to 5 P.M.

Stop in Headwaters Floral and Gifts for that special gift or to remember someone back home. The shop, at 20 Main St. (406) 285-4177, also has a wire service. Be sure to tell Ralph and Jeri that the Zumbos say hello!

The Wheat Montana Farms are listed in the Guinness Book of World Records for the amazing feat of taking wheat in the field to bread on the table in 8 minutes, 13 seconds. However, on a normal basis, it takes somewhat longer. If you're hungry, stop in at the bakery and deli, 10778 U.S. 287, Three Forks, MT; (406) 285-3614. They have over 80 varieties of the freshest bread, and the sandwiches are great. There's plenty of RV parking too.

The third weekend in July marks the time of the Three Forks Rodeo Weekend. The special event is held at the Rodeo-Fair Grounds. The town's summer celebration includes the rodeo, a parade and flea market.

If you're traveling through in August, the Antique Air Show flies the skies during the first full weekend (Thursday through Sunday). Stop in at the Visitor Center for details.

Visit the three wonderful state parks near Three Forks: Headwaters of the Missouri State Park, Lewis and Clark Caverns State Park and Madison Buffalo Jump State Park; see pages 283-285.

The Sacajawea Inn at 5 N. Main in Three Forks is a beautiful historical inn built in 1910. The inn has been completely restored to its original elegance and is listed on the National Register of Historic Places. Although the facility is closed as this book is being published, we hope it will reopen soon. When the Sacajawea Inn resumes operations it will feature lodging, a gift shop and an excellent restaurant.

## OVERNIGHTING                    CAMPGROUNDS & RV PARKS

▲ *Best Shot for a Camp Spot*
Three Forks KOA, 15 KOA Rd., Three Forks, MT 59752, off I-90, Exit 274, then 1 mile south on U.S. 287. 50 RV sites (pull-throughs), hook-ups, dump station, hot showers, laundry, swimming pool and sauna; open May to October; busiest June 15 through August 15; (406) 285-3611; 1-800-562-9752.

▲ *Best Shot for a Camp Spot*
Missouri Headwaters—Montana Department of Fish, Wildlife and Parks Campground, 3 miles east of Three Forks on Route 205 (Logan Exit from I-90), then 3 miles north on Montana 286. 21 campsites, RVs allowed, no hook-ups; dump station, interpretive signs and hiking trails, boat launch and fishing access; open year-round.

▲ *Best Shot for a Camp Spot*
Lewis and Clark Caverns—Montana Department of Fish, Wildlife and Parks Campground, 19 miles west of Three Forks on Montana 2, Milepost 271. 50 campsites, RVs allowed, no services except drinking water; open year-round.

Fort Three Forks, off I-90 at the Helena Exit (274), then north on U.S. 287. The new resort is named for Three Forks, one of the first trading posts built in the region. The RV park has full hook-ups, meeting facilities, laundry and ample truck parking; credit cards accepted; small pets welcome; (406) 285-3233.

Fairweather—Montana Department of Fish, Wildlife and Parks Campground, 1 mile west of Logan on Route 205, then 3 miles north on Logan-Trident Road, 7 miles northeast on Clarkston Road. RVs allowed; no services; open year-round.

### GUEST RANCHES

Bud Lilly's Angler's Retreat, fishing inn catering to anglers. The original "hotel" was built in 1910, and the Lilly family has operated the business since 1914. Bud Lilly also owns an internationally known fly shop in West Yellowstone. Services include fishing itinerary for the numerous rivers, lakes and creeks nearby; tips on fishing methods and flies; and guide services. Credit cards accepted; no pets allowed; open year-round; busiest spring to late fall. Contact Bud Lilly, PO Box 983, 16 W. Birch, Three Forks, MT 59752; or call (406) 285-6690; Bud Lilly (406) 586-5140; Dave Miller (406) 285-3412.

**SUGGESTED DINING**

Wheat Montana Farms, Bakery & Deli, 10778 U.S. 287, Three Forks, MT; (406) 285-3614.

Custer's Last Rootbeer Stand, 23 W. Date, Three Forks, MT; (406) 285-6713.

Longhorn Café, Hwy. 10, Three Forks, MT; (406) 285-4106.

Stageline Pizza, 198 Main, Three Forks, MT; (406) 285-3614.

**VISITOR INFORMATION & SERVICES**

Three Forks Chamber of Commerce, PO Box 1103, Three Forks, MT 59752; (406) 285-4556; fax: (406) 285-4724.

In the summer, stop at the Three Forks Visitor Information Center. Look for the Orange Caboose.

**MEDICAL SERVICES**

Three Rivers Clinic, 223 1st Ave. E., Three Forks, MT; open Monday through Thursday, 8 A.M. to 5 P.M., Friday until noon; walk in or call for appointment; (406) 285-3251.

Three Forks Pharmacy, 207 Main Street between Date and Cedar Streets, Three Forks, MT; (406) 285-6575.

**REPAIR & TOWING**

Ron's Diesel Repair, 10769 Hwy. 287, Three Forks, MT; (406) 285-6913.

**VETERINARY SERVICES**

Headwaters Veterinary Clinic, Dr. Slyngstad, 11370 Montana 287, Three Forks, MT; day or night, (406) 285-6672.

# THREE FORKS TO TOWNSEND AND CANYON FERRY: U.S. 287

**TOWNSEND**

Townsend is another town with roots tied to the railroad. Developed for the coming railroads, the first passenger train stopped at the station in September 1883. Officials had named the town in honor of the company president's wife; Townsend was the maiden name of Charles Wright's wife.

Farmers and ranchers settled the area and have maintained a western grace within the town. It is the seat for Broadwater County, established in 1897. Still a ranching community, the 1,600 residents also cater to tourism and recreation activities on nearby Canyon Ferry Lake.

*Canyon Ferry Reservoir*
DONNIE SEXTON/COURTESY TRAVEL MONTANA

**OUTDOOR RECREATION AND ATTRACTIONS**

The Old Baldy Golf Course with 9 holes is on Delger Lane, 1.5 miles north of Townsend.

Canyon Ferry Wildlife Management Area is a 5,000-acre wetlands on the southeast end of Canyon Ferry Lake. The watchable wildlife includes ospreys, loons and migrating waterfowl, beavers and whitetail deer. The location of the area is east of Townsend on Highway 12 to Harrison Road, then north 1 mile.

Canyon Ferry Lake has over 80 miles of shoreline. The dam, built in 1950 by the U.S. Bureau of Reclamation, backs up 25 miles of the grand Missouri River. Townsend sits on the south end of the lake, which is stocked with rainbow trout. Although the majority of tourism development is on the north end of the lake, there are facilities on the southern end.

*Canyon Ferry Reservoir*
DONNIE SEXTON/
COURTESY TRAVEL MONTANA

**OVERNIGHTING**

## CAMPGROUNDS & RV PARKS

▲ *Best Shot for a Camp Spot*
Goose Bay Marina, on the east shore of Canyon Ferry Lake on Montana 284. 68 RV sites, water and electric hook-ups, dump station, showers, store, docks, gas and propane; open April 1 through November 1; (406) 266-3645.

Road Runner RV Park, on U.S. 287 on the north side of Townsend. 20 RV sites, full hook-ups, dump station, showers and laundry; open year-round; (406) 266-3278; (406) 266-9900.

Silos RV Park & Store, 8 miles north of Townsend on U.S. 287. 32 RV sites, full hook-ups, dump station, showers, laundry and store; open year-round; (406) 266-3100.

Canyon Ferry RV Park & Storage, on the northeast edge of Canyon Ferry Lake. 7 RV sites, full hook-ups, showers and laundry; open May 1 through October; (406) 475-3811.

Kim's Marina & RV Resort, 20 miles east of Helena on Canyon Ferry Road. 60 RV sites, full hook-ups, dump station, showers, laundry, store, boat rentals, tennis and volleyball; open April 1 through October 1; (406) 475-3723.

Indian Road—U.S. Bureau of Reclamation Campground, 1 mile north of Townsend on U.S. 287, Milepost 75. 25 sites, RVs allowed, no services except drinking water; boat-launch ramp for 2-wheel drive; open year-round.

Skidway—U.S. Forest Service Campground, 23 miles east of Townsend on U.S. 12, then 2 miles south on Forest Service Road 4042. 11 sites, RVs allowed; no services except drinking water; open June 1 through October 1.

Toston Dam—U.S. Bureau of Land Management Campground, 13 miles south of Townsend on U.S. 287, then east to Toston Dam. 10 sites, RVs allowed (max. length 24 feet), no services; boat-launch ramp for 2-wheel drive; open year-round.

*The following Canyon Ferry Reservoir Campgrounds are maintained by the U.S. Bureau of Reclamation/U.S. Bureau of Land Management (USBR/USBLM).*

Chinaman's Gulch—USBR/USBLM, 9 miles east of Helena on U.S. 287, then 10 miles northeast on Montana 284. 40 sites, RVs allowed, no services except drinking water; boat-launch ramp for 2-wheel drive; open year-round.

Court Sheriff —USBR/USBLM, 9 miles east of Helena on U.S 287, then 9 miles northeast on Montana 284. 25 sites, RVs allowed, no services except drinking water; boat-launch ramp for 4-wheel drive; open year-round.

Hellgate—USBR/USBLM, 9 miles east of Helena on U.S. 287, then 18 miles northeast on Montana 284. 130 sites, RVs allowed, no services except drinking water; boat-launch ramp for 2-wheel drive; open year-round.

Jo Bonner—USBR/USBLM, 9 miles east of Helena on U.S. 287, then 12 miles northeast on Montana 284. RVs allowed, no services except drinking water; boat-launch ramp for 4-wheel drive; open year-round.

Ponderosa—USBR/USBLM, 9 miles east of Helena on U.S. 287, then 9 miles northeast on Montana 284. 40 sites, RVs allowed, no services except drinking water; open year-round.

Riverside—USBR/USBLM, 9 miles east of Helena on U.S. 287, then 9 miles northeast on Montana 284, 1 mile northwest on Forest Service Road 224 toward power plant. RVs allowed, no services except drinking water; boat-launch ramp for 2-wheel drive; open year-round.

Silos—USBR/USBLM, 7 miles north of Townsend on U.S. 287, Milepost 70, then 1 mile east on County Road. 80 sites, RVs allowed, no services except drinking water; boat-launch ramp for 2-wheel drive; open year-round.

White Earth—USBR/USBLM, 13 miles north of Townsend on U.S. 287 to Winston, then 5 miles east on County Road. 40 sites, RVs allowed, no services except drinking water; boat-launch ramp for 2-wheel drive; open year-round.

*Camping near Canyon Ferry*
DONNIE SEXTON/COURTESY TRAVEL MONTANA

## BED & BREAKFAST ESTABLISHMENTS

The Bedford Inn, operating since 1997. Open year-round; busiest in summer; no credit cards accepted; pets allowed. Contact Richard and Renee Majszak, Box 772, 7408 Hwy. 287, Townsend, MT 59644; (406) 266-3629.

Lambs Rest Guest House, private guest house on a working sheep and cattle ranch. The guest house has been operating since 1996. Open year-round; busiest summer and fall, slowest November through May; no credit cards accepted; no pets or smoking allowed. Contact Gary and Judy Olsen, 16 Carson Lane, Townsend, MT 59644; (406) 266-3862; 1-888-526-2778.

Litening Land Bed & Breakfast, cabins, fishing, horseback riding and western hospitality. Contact Litening Land B & B, 290 Litening Barn Rd., Townsend, MT 59644; (406) 266-3741; 1-800-654-2845; fax: (406) 266-3741.

## GUEST RANCHES

Battle Creek Ranch is a working cattle ranch. Featured are horseback riding, cattle working, fishing, spring varmint hunting and side tours. The ranch has been operating since 1988. Open May through September; pets conditional; no credit cards accepted. Contact Lary and Shelly Richtmyer; 199 South Fork Ray Creek, Townsend, MT 59644; (406) 266-4426; fax: 266-3787; website: http://www.binet.net/~bcranch/index.html

Hidden Hollow Hideaway Ranch, working cattle ranch on 12,000 acres located 17 miles northeast of Townsend. The ranch offers participation on cattle drives, horseback riding, gold panning, tours, hunting and fishing. Contact Hidden Hollow Hideaway Ranch, PO Box 233, 211 Flynn Lane, Townsend, MT 59644; (406) 266-3322; (406) 266-3580.

## VISITOR INFORMATION & SERVICES

Chamber of Commerce (in the City Office), 129 S. Spruce, Townsend, MT 59644, (406) 266-3911; fax: (406) 266-4042.

## MEDICAL SERVICES

Broadway Health Center, 24-hour emergency room, 110 N. Oak, Townsend, MT; (406) 266-3187.

Francisco Pharmacy, 223 Broadway, Townsend, MT; open Monday

through Saturday, 9 A.M. to 5:30 P.M.; (406) 266-3325.

**REPAIR &
TOWING**

Four Seasons Towing (AAA), 320 Broadway, Townsend, MT; (406) 266-4747.

Sparky RV Repair, 302 N. Front, Townsend, MT; (406) 266-3142.

Valley Sales & Service, on U.S. 287, Townsend, MT; (406) 266-5207.

**VETERINARY
SERVICES**

Elkhorn Veterinary Services, Dr. Sorensen, 7687 U.S. 287, Townsend, MT; (406) 266-5794.

# ENNIS TO VIRGINIA CITY AND NEVADA CITY: MONTANA 287

As you leave Ennis on Montana 287 and take the winding road up, stop at the overlook on the pass and look down on the sprawling Madison River Valley. Be sure to have your camera. On the steep drive down to Virginia City and Nevada City, note the dry and barren-looking landscape. It's hard to imagine that this region once bustled with tens of thousands of people during the peak of the gold rush.

**VIRGINIA CITY
AND
NEVADA CITY**

Virginia City is an unusual town where the western boardwalks meander between vacant ghost buildings and thriving businesses. The old building fronts all look alike, but some are cleared of cobwebs and waiting for guests. The setting is the same in Nevada City, 1 mile down the road. If you've ever had a hankering to live in the past, this is the place for you.

Charles and Sue Bovey began the project of preserving and restoring the old mining towns shortly after their first visit in 1944. The authentic restorations have created a setting rich in history, capturing the tale of the 1863 Alder Gulch Gold Rush.

Gold ore was discovered by six prospectors on the lam with the Crow in pursuit. Worn out and hungry, the men stopped to share an antelope shot by one of the prospectors, Bill Fairweather. Panning at the spot revealed the lucky color. The men staked claims, swore secrecy and headed to Bannack for provisions. But, no matter when or where, gold finds were impossible to keep secret. On the return trip, most of the miners in Bannack followed. Within one year, the towns grew to 10,000, and they reached a massive population of 30,000 by the end of the second year.

Montana's first incorporated town was Virginia City. In 1865, the Second Territorial Congress met at the town, which was the state's largest population base. Virginia City remained the capital until 1875. Gold mining continued under advanced mining technology for 65 years until 1928.

Most of the buildings preserved by the Bovey Restoration have stood for 150 years. The impressive restoration site has served as the filming location for movies such as *Missouri Breaks*, *Little Big Man* and *Return to Lonesome Dove*. The Gilbert Brewery, Bale of Hay Saloon, Fairweather Inn and Montana Post are some of the interesting sights. The Virginia City Players give enjoyable vaudeville performances weeknights at 8 P.M. and Saturdays at 6 P.M. and 9 P.M. Some of the world's unique mechanical musical instruments, such as the calliope, can be heard at Nevada City Music Hall. A ride on the Alder Gulch Railroad, a narrow-gauge line between the two cities, is fun. You can pan for gold at the Alder Gulch River of Gold Mining Museum. There's several great places to dine: try the Copper Palace, Wells Fargo and Pioneer Cafe. For reservations or to obtain more information, contact the Bovey Restoration, PO Box 338, Virginia City, MT 59755; 1-800-648-7588; (406) 843-5377.

## OVERNIGHTING

### CAMPGROUNDS & RV PARKS

Alder-Virginia City KOA, 9 miles west of Virginia City on Montana 287. 39 RV sites, 9 full hook-ups, 11 water and electric sites, dump station, showers, laundry and store; open year-round; busiest May through September; (406) 842-5677.

Virginia City Campground, at the east end of town (toward Ennis). 19 RV sites, 10 pull-through sites, 10 full hook-up sites, dump station, showers, mini-golf and horseshoes; open April 15 through October 1; (406) 843-5493.

### BED & BREAKFAST ESTABLISHMENTS

Stonehouse Inn, Victorian charm, antiques and brass beds. Contact John and Linda Hamilton, PO Box 202, 306 E. Idaho, Virginia City, MT 59755; (406) 843-5504.

Virginia City Country Inn, 1879 Queen Anne-style home furnished with Victorian antiques. Current management has been operating since 1992. Open year-round; busiest June through September, slowest in winter; credit cards accepted; no pets or smoking allowed. Contact Max and Donna Quigley, PO Box 61, 115 E. Idaho,

Virginia City, MT 59755; (406) 843-5515; 1-888-843-5515.

Just An Experience B & B, guest rooms furnished with antiques and fully furnished cabins. Families welcome. Operating since 1990; open year-round; busiest in summer, slowest October through April; credit cards accepted; no pets allowed inside. Contact John and Carma Sinerius, PO Box 98, U.S. 287 West, Nevada City, MT 59755; (406) 843-5402.

### GUEST RANCHES

Broken Arrow Lodge, off the beaten path 25 miles south of Alder on the Upper Ruby River. This ranch has been operating since 1994. Features include family accommodations in a homey atmosphere; guided or unguided wade fishing, float trips, horseback riding, tours and hiking. Open year-round; busiest June through December; credit cards accepted; pets allowed. Contact Erwin and Sherry Clark, PO Box 177, 2200 Upper Ruby Rd., Alder, MT 59710; (406) 842-5437; 1-800 775-2928; fax: (406) 842-5437;
e-mail: brokenal@threerivers.net
Website: http://www.recworld.com/broken-arrow/

Tate's Upper Canyon Ranch, in the Beaverhead National Forest. Featured are horseback trips, fly fishing, hunting, hiking and swimming. The ranch is accessible for the disabled. Contact Mr. McDonald, PO Box 109, Alder, MT 59710; (406) 442-8410; 1-800-735-3973.

**VISITOR INFORMATION & SERVICES**

Bovey Restoration, PO Box 338, Virginia City, MT 59755; 1-800-648-7588; (406) 843-5377.

For other services, see Ennis Services (page 281).

## ALDER, SHERIDAN AND TWIN BRIDGES: MONTANA 287

This route parallels the Ruby River that joins with the Beaverhead River just south of Twin Bridges.

**ALDER**

Alder was once the end of the line for the Northern Pacific spur that shipped ore and livestock out of the Ruby Valley. Beginning in 1901, extensive dredging projects produced tons of gold ore and were the key reason for the railroad branch. Today, tons of talc ore, seen as heaps of white material piled near the railroad lines, are shipped worldwide on Burlington Northern trains.

**SHERIDAN**

The Alder Gulch mining activity attracted Civil War veterans to the gold works. Sheridan was established in 1866 and named for Union Cavalry leader General Phillip H. Sheridan. Rozelle Bateman, one of the first settlers, picked the name. In 1868, Rozelle obtained the official job as postmaster, and he was given rights to move the cigar box that contained all the postal supplies to the Bateman cabin.

**TWIN BRIDGES**

The quiet community of Twin Bridges sits at the intersection of Highways 41 and 287. You'll find full services, a grocery store, laundromat, pharmacy and cafe here.

Times were livelier back in the mid-1800s. Twin Bridges was at the crossroads of transportation from Whitehall in the north, Dillon to the southwest and the boom town of Virginia City. Three stagecoaches passed through on a daily basis. The Lott brothers, who also established Sheridan, built two bridges and charged a toll. They improved the Native trails and turned them to roads. The Lotts donated land to build the area's first normal school in 1889. Eventually the college was moved to Dillon, and the Twin Bridges building became the state orphanage. Before it closed in 1975, the building was home to some 5,000 children.

**OUTDOOR RECREATION**

Ruby Reservoir lies just a few miles south of Alder on Route 357. The surrounding country is lush agricultural land. Fishing and boating on the lake is good as long as the water level is not drawn too low for local irrigation use.

**RV CAUTION:** The road continues south of Ruby Reservoir and becomes Forest Service Road 100. The gravel road winds along the Ruby River, crossing the Gravelly Range and eventually comes out at Red Rock Lakes National Wildlife Refuge. The road is a fair-weather road, and the complete trip across is not recommended for RV travel.

A great time can be had in Twin Bridges on the third weekend in July. The Twin Bridges Floating Flotillas and Fish Fantasies festival has something for all ages. There are fly casting and fishing contests, theatre, games and lots of entertainment. The wader races are hilarious. Not the most artful race—it's more like watching a herd of hippos rather than graceful gazelles. The big event is the floating parade on the Beaverhead River. For more details, contact the Chamber of Commerce, (406) 684-5259, or (406) 684-5701.

*Nevada City* DONNIE SEXTON/COURTESY TRAVEL MONTANA

Sacajawea's people named the huge landmark Beaverhead Rock, but it takes imagination to see the beaver's head. The Beaverhead Rock State Park day-use area is a cultural stop along Montana's portion of the Lewis and Clark Trail. Sacajawea pointed out the rock formation while traveling with the expedition in 1805. She recognized the landmark, and knew her people, the Lemhi Shoshone, were in the area. Lewis and Clark welcomed the news. The expedition was in dire need of horses and knew Sacajawea's people would supply the animals. The park's location is 14 miles south of Twin Bridges on Hwy. 41. For more information, call (406) 834-3413.

## OVERNIGHTING

### CAMPGROUNDS & RV PARKS

Branham Lakes—U.S. Forest Service Campground, 6 miles east of Sheridan on County Road 1111, then 5 miles east on Forest Service Road 1112, 3 miles north on Forest Service Road 1110. 6 sites, RVs allowed (max. length 22 feet), no services; boat-launch for 2-wheel drive; open July 1 to September 15.

Mill Creek—U.S. Forest Service Campground, 7 miles east of Sheridan on Mill Creek Road. 13 sites; RVs allowed (max. length 22 feet), no services except water; open June 1 to October 31.

Stardust Country Inn & RV Park, on Montana 41 North, 409 N. Main St., Twin Bridges, MT. 9 RV sites, water, full hook-ups, dump station and showers; open year-round; (406) 684-5648.

Ruby Reservoir—U.S. Bureau of Land Management Campground, south of Twin Bridges on Montana 287 to Alder, then south to east shore of Ruby River Reservoir. 10 sites; RVs allowed (max. length 35 feet), no services except drinking water; boat launch for 2-wheel drive; open year-round.

### BED & BREAKFAST ESTABLISHMENTS

The Old Hotel, on Main and Fifth Streets, built in 1870; operated under current management since 1995; geared to anglers; credit cards accepted; pets conditional. Contact Jane Waldie, 101 E. 5th, Twin Bridges, MT; (406) 684-5959.

### GUEST RANCHES

Country Roads, Inc., features access to nearby fishing lakes and rivers; PO Box 710, Sheridan, MT 59749; (406) 842-7101; fax: 842-7104.

Tobacco Root Land Livestock Company, features access to nearby fishing; PO Box 497, 374 Mill Creek Rd., Sheridan, MT 59749; (406) 842-5566.

Zak Inn Guest Ranch, 4 miles south of Sheridan in the Ruby Valley. Featured are fishing, hunting, snowmobiling and fishing on Ruby River within the ranch. The ranch has a 3,800-foot grass airstrip. Contact Zak Inn Guest Ranch, 2905 Hwy. 287, Sheridan, MT 59749; (406) 842-5540.

## SUGGESTED DINING

The Old Hotel, on Main St., Twin Bridges, MT; (406) 684-5959.

Blue Anchor Bar & Grill, on Main St., Twin Bridges, MT; (406) 684-5655.

## VISITOR INFORMATION & SERVICES

Twin Bridges Chamber of Commerce, PO Box 134, Twin Bridges, MT 59754; (406) 684-5259 or 5701; fax: (406) 684-5687.

Tourist information is available at the City Library on Main St., Twin Bridges, MT; open weekdays, 2 P.M. to 7:30 P.M.

## MEDICAL SERVICES

Ruby Valley Hospital, 24-hour emergency room, 220 E. Crowfoot, Sheridan, MT; (406) 842-5454.

Twin Bridges Clinic, 104 S. Madison, Twin Bridges, MT; open weekdays except Wednesday, 1 P.M. to 5 P.M.; (406) 684-5642.

McAlear Pharmacy & Grocery, on Main St., Twin Bridges, MT; open Monday through Saturday, 8 A.M. to 7 P.M., and Sunday, 11 A.M. to 4 P.M.; (406) 684-5671; 1-800-378-5671.

## REPAIR & TOWING

Twin Tire & Towing, on Main St., Twin Bridges, MT; (406) 684-5631.

## VETERINARY SERVICES

Lott Veterinary Hospital, Dr. Robert Lott, on Main St., Twin Bridges, MT; (406) 684-5513.

Mountain View Veterinary Services, Dr. Wayne Carlson, S. Montana 287, Twin Bridges, MT; (406) 684-5513.

# TWIN BRIDGES TO SILVER STAR AND WHITEHALL: MONTANA 41

At the junction of Montana 287 and 41 in Twin Bridges, you can take 41 south to Dillon and I-15, or you can drive north on Montana 41 and Montana 55 to Whitehall, following the Jefferson River. Or, 4 miles past Silver Star, you can stay on Montana 41, which will take you to Montana 2.

**SILVER STAR**

One of the oldest towns in the state, Silver Star was a mining camp. A branch line of the Northern Pacific brought supplies, and Silver Star distributed them to miners from Virginia City to Helena. The post office was established here in 1869.

**WHITEHALL**

The settlement of Whitehall began as a stage stop for the run between Helena and Virginia City. E. G. Brooke built a big white ranch house and named his stop "Old Whitehall." The Union Pacific brought a branch line through in 1889, and the community began to grow. Today, the town has roughly 1,200 residents.

**ATTRACTIONS**

A tour of the Golden Sunlight Mine provides an interesting picture of the miners' life. The mine is located off I-90 at the Whitehall Exit, then east 4.3 miles on Highway 2 to Mine Road, then 2 miles to the Golden Sunlight Mine. The free tours are available weekdays, 8 A.M. to 4:30 P.M. from June through September. Reservations made at least 24 hours in advance are recommended, (406) 287-2026.

**OVERNIGHTING**

### CAMPGROUNDS & RV PARKS

Jefferson River Camp is located 1 mile south of Silver Star on Highway 41, on the Jefferson River. There are 14 RV sites, full hook-ups, shower facilities and fishing access. Open April 1 to December 1; (406) 684-5577.

Pipestone Campground, 6 miles west on I-90 at Pipestone Exit 241. 55 RV sites, full hook-ups (30- and 50-amp electric), dump station, showers, laundry and store; playground, pool, spa and game room; open April 1 to October 5; (406) 287-5224.

Toll Mountain—U.S. Forest Service Campground, 15 miles west of Whitehall on Montana 2, then 3 miles north on Forest Service Road 240. RVs allowed (max. length 22 feet), primitive, no services or drinking water; open May 25 to September 15.

## Homestake Pass

The Northern Pacific had a station on the Continental Divide near Butte. The station was named after an old mining camp that had been there—Homestake. Prospectors were fond of the word **stake**. The act of marking a claim site was known as "staking out a claim." When a prospector got a loan to buy food while prospecting, it was called a "grub stake." Most important, when the prospector struck it rich and found enough gold to return home, wherever that might be, the gold find was dubbed a "homestake."

Homestake Pass is just outside Butte on I-90. Unlike its glory-hole namesake, the slow climb to the pass summit at 6,375 feet has posed a problem for many an RVer as well as other motorists. In the winter, the pass can be treacherous with windblown white-outs and iced-over pavement.

**RV CAUTION:** There is another Forest Service Campground 5 miles south on Forest Service Road 668, and it is not recommended for RVs.

## BUTTE

The heritage of Butte will always hover before it. Unlike other towns that have hidden the scars of their birth, Butte must bear hers openly. At the base of the hill for which Butte was named ran the chaste, clear waters of a creek shaped like a bow. The ripples glistened in the sunlight, like silver, and the creek was known as Silver Bow.

Native Americans and mountain men fur traders were the first explorers in the area. Only a few of these pioneers settled permanently. Precious metals made the change. Gold, silver and copper brought the masses to Montana; silver and copper kept them in Butte.

The early placer gold rush days lured prospectors to Butte in the 1860s, but, overall, the arid lands were not conducive to placer mining. Prospectors didn't have enough water to pan the gravel beds in their customary manner. Their water ditches were costly and insufficient. By 1870 placer mining dwindled; gold prospectors and their followers moved onward.

Silver and copper had been discovered as early as 1874. The claims had been abandoned because the metals were buried within quartz ore. Smelters and new technology were needed to recover these riches. A whole new game was afoot, one to be played by shrewd investors, industrial development, labor unions and state and federal politics.

*Butte, Montana, was one of the largest mining towns in the West.*
BILL RAUTIO/ COURTESY BUTTE SILVER BOW CHAMBER OF COMMERCE

*Mine frames near Butte, a common site in the old mining days*
BILL RAUTIO/ COURTESY BUTTE SILVER BOW CHAMBER OF COMMERCE

William Andrews Clark and Andrew Jackson Davis brought the investment capital to develop Butte's mines. Davis became Montana's first millionaire, and Clark soon followed. Clark continued his interests, buying out many other mine claims. By 1876, the meager settlement grew to 1,000 and attracted attention from Utah. Marcus Daly came, representing the Walker brothers from Salt Lake City. These entrepreneurs purchased the Alice Mine and the town of Walkerville, on top of Butte Hill, was born.

Daly eventually sold his interests with the Walkers and bought the first of several properties, the Anaconda Mine. This time his backers were from the Hearst family of San Francisco. Clark too built up his empire and found investors in Denver and the east. It wasn't long before capitalists in New York, Boston and nationwide all had a piece of Butte. The Union Pacific Railroad, known as the Utah Northern and Northern Pacific back then, provided the final key element in 1881: transportation and shipping. Heavy machinery at a reasonable cost and shipping to smelters were needed to claim the riches of the mountain. Butte was called the "richest hill on earth" and, in the next decade, became the largest producer of copper in the world.

Clark and Daly became the leaders of the silver and copper mining industry. The rivalry of the two remarkable men became a bitter feud turned spectacle. Clark was sophisticated, educated, traveled abroad and had great political ambitions. It's said he was jealous of Daly's successes and tried every trick to stop him. Daly, an Irish-born, hard-working, simple man, whose associates became his friends, and whose workers were treated justly, had an unquenchable temper when it came to Clark. Daly, a dedicated Democrat, even renounced his party rather than support Clark in his race for

Congress. The antagonism continued throughout their lives. Daly died in 1900, Clark in 1925. A third copper king, Augustus Heinze, showed up as the peak of Butte's glory days started to recede. In 1900 he bought judges and craftily manipulated laws to claim for himself properties legally owned by Daly. The covert action worked, and Heinze became wealthy, but it wised up Daly's company to its weaknesses, prompting them to modernize the huge corporation.

*Anselmo Mine Yard in Butte*
DONNIE SEXTON/COURTESY TRAVEL MONTANA

A tremendous labor force was needed for the deep hardrock mining. Immigrants from Ireland, Italy and Asia came seeking jobs. During World War I, the steady employment drew Serbians, Poles, French Canadians, Finns, Germans, Mexicans and others. The city spread rapidly, reaching a male population of 41,611 in 1920. This was nearly double the next largest city, Great Falls. (Estimates put the total area population, including women and children, at 100,000. Modern-day Billings, the largest city in Montana, has about the same area population today.)

It was a wild time. The people of many different cultures grappled on the slopes and in the dark tunnels, grabbing hard to claim a life in the New World. The raucous and boisterous town was the largest ethnic convergence west of Chicago. As the immigrants poured in, the sulfurous smoke poured thickly out of the smelters. The sky turned ominously dark with the toxic fumes.

The next phase of Butte's history was suffering through the trials of economic exploitation and union misrepresentation. In 1899, one year before Daly's death, Anaconda Mine merged with Rockefeller's Standard Oil and Amalgamated Copper Mining Company was born. By 1910, the giant company consolidated more individual interests and gained control of the town. The name was changed to the Anaconda Copper Mining Company. The huge national trust controlled Butte interests from the east. Known simply as "the Company," it would dominate Butte for the next 70 years. In the early 1900s, Anaconda controlled politics statewide. Nearly every daily newspaper, except the *Great Falls Tribune*, was owned by Anaconda.

The labor movement came about in response to the working conditions underground and the lack of response by the faceless Anaconda. Butte's miners formed the Western Federation of Miners (WFM). Between 1893 and 1906, the WFM leaned more and more toward socialism and radical action. When the union sent a delegation to the Chicago convention in 1906, the leaders joined with the Industrial Workers of the World (IWW). The socialist organization came to be called the "Wobblies," and actively spoke out against capitalism.

Meanwhile, Anaconda had gained complete control of Butte's mines and smelters. The company had also surreptitiously worked its way into the union and controlled the leaders. Management began a system of "rustling cards." Each miner had to have a card

*The Berkeley Pit near Butte, once the site of one of the busiest mines in the United States*
BILL RAUTIO/COURTESY BUTTE SILVER BOW CHAMBER OF COMMERCE

indicating advance company approval in order to work in the mines. The cards could be pulled at any time by the company or a foreman, thus ruining a man's chance to make a living. The miners hated this system and wanted to strike. The management-controlled union leaders refused, and violence erupted. In 1914, Miners Union Hall was dynamited. The riots and internal fighting killed the union. The National Guard kept Butte quiet. Anaconda stepped up and gained total control.

In 1917, another union formed. The Wobblies (IWW) were in the news agitating against World War I, denouncing it as a capitalist's fight. Then the Wobblies tried to take advantage of the June 8, 1917, mining tragedy. The world's worst hardrock-mining disaster, a deep fire in the Speculator Mine, left 168 miners dead. In part, poor safety conditions were to blame. The angry miners wanted to strike. The IWW sent an aggressive organizer, Frank Little, to bolster membership strength. He raged against the company, the capitalists and the war. But his seditious talk turned the miners against him. Frank Little was lynched.

Montana's Governor Samuel Stewart called a special legislative session. Federal troops were sent in to keep peace. The U.S. Government, at the outset of war, needed copper. The strikers were admonished. The Montana Sedition Law made it a crime to speak against the government, and civil rights were curtailed until after the end of the war. The company prevailed and grew.

Anaconda expanded operations outside of Butte. In 1923, it bought one of the world's largest copper mines in Chile. During the Great Depression years, copper prices plummeted. Anaconda began to

*A pair of old businesses in historic Butte, Montana*
BILL RAUTIO/COURTESY BUTTE SILVER BOW CHAMBER OF COMMERCE

alter its focus in Butte. By 1955, mining operations changed from underground works to the open-pit method. The truck-operated excavation was a more cost-effective extraction method. The pit swallowed up entire communities like Meaderville, McQueen and Columbia Gardens. An astounding $1\frac{1}{2}$ billion tons of material were taken to form the Berkeley Pit. Of that, 290 million tons were copper ore.

Anaconda merged with Atlantic Richfield (ARCO) six years before the Berkeley Pit was closed in 1983. In 1985, ARCO's holdings were bought by millionaire Dennis Washington, who has developed new methods for extracting profits from the ore. The Berkeley Pit remains a tremendous challenge for Butte. ARCO, past mine owners, the Environmental Protection Agency and state wildlife and other agencies are working for a solution.

Butte was the center of Montana's primary development in terms of industry, population growth and political progress. The city honors its mining heritage and its pride is obvious, seen through the mining-related attractions, museums and points of interest. The 33,000 residents are now building a diversified economy based on medicine, tourism and waste-treatment technology.

## OUTDOOR RECREATION

Golf the Butte Country Club, which has an 18-hole course. Guests are welcome; phone (406) 494-3383 or 494-2394 for fees, directions and reservations. West of Butte, another 18-hole course is at the Fairmont Hot Springs Resort; call (406) 782-2349 for more information. The Highland View Golf Course, at Stodden Park in Butte, has a 9-hole course; call (406) 494-7900 for tee times.

Tennis courts, walking trails and picnic grounds are convenient at the city parks. Stodden and Father Sheehan are the two largest. Stodden Park is down Harrison Avenue to Dewey Street, then west just over a half-mile to Utah Street. Father Sheehan Park is on the north side of I-90 at Exit 127, off Harrison Avenue. The Butte Visitor Center is just completing a new paved walking trail that runs along Black Tail Creek. It's a great place to exercise and stretch out.

Serious and novice rock climbers will find a place to climb in the Butte area. Spire Rock and Humbug Spires are two famous spots, and there are many other climbing routes in the mountain ranges nearby. Butte offers a challenge for subscribers of the upcoming new sport of rock climbing. Several shops have gear and information on climbs. One such shop is Pipestone Mountaineering at 829 S. Montana St. in Butte, (406) 782-1994.

**RV CAUTION:** The roads to the climbing areas are not all RV-friendly. Be sure to check with the pros before making the drive.

The Humbug Spires Primitive Area is south of Butte off I-15. Hiking around the unusual limestone formations provides a milder means of appreciating the landscape. The nine white granite steeple-like spires rise up to heights of 600 feet, a spectacular sight. To get there head south on I-15 for 25 miles to Moose Creek or Selway Springs Road, then go east to reach the primitive area.

**RV CAUTION:** Road conditions are much better suited to regular vehicles, are fair weather only and not recommended for large RVs.

Fishing access to streams, rivers or lakes surrounds the Butte area. Many of the prime rivers are in the direction of Yellowstone National Park. Fran Johnson's Sport Shop at 1957 Harrison Ave. in Butte, (406) 782-3322, has guide services, equipment and up-to-date fishing information.

An easily accessible wildlife watching site is 14 miles north of Butte on I-15. The Sheepshead Mountain Recreation Area has trails, fishing and campgrounds; all are accessible to persons with disabilities. The area is open from late May through September. Elk and moose can often be seen in the fall. Migrating waterfowl, mountain bluebirds, nuthatches and birds of prey are commonly seen.

Winter sports include ice fishing, downhill skiing, snowmobiling and cross-country skiing. The sport shops in Butte will tell you where and provide the gear.

The U.S. High Altitude Sports Center is in Butte, (406) 723-2234. This workout center, an acclaimed speed-skating facility, is open all year. The public is welcome when training sessions and competitions are not scheduled.

Every weekend during February and March, Butte hosts a competitive sports festival. The festival celebrates the different winter activities by hosting competitions for participants of all ages and skill levels. The Winternational X Sports Festival featured 17 events and nearly 3,500 participants. Events are open to the public. For information on eligibility, fees, and the essentials, contact Winternational Sports Festival, 1000 George St., Butte, MT 59701; (406) 723-3177.

*Ice skating is one of many activities around Butte.*
ANTHONY DI FRONZO/
COURTESY BUTTE SILVER BOW CHAMBER
OF COMMERCE

**ATTRACTIONS**

Everyone, not just rockhounds, can appreciate the Mineral Museum. It's at the Montana College of Mineral Science and Technology. The impressive displays show about 1,300 of the collection's 15,000 worldwide mineral specimens. The Highland Centennial Gold Nugget, found during placer mining, is on display. The gold nugget weighs a hefty 27.475 troy ounces and was found in the Highland Mountains south of Butte. Another interesting display shows fluorescent minerals in illuminated cases with both long- and short-wave ultraviolet light. The Mineral Museum is open daily, 8 A.M. to 5 P.M., June through Labor Day, and weekdays and Sunday afternoons the rest of the year. Contact the college, (406) 496-4414, for more information. The college is located on Park Street near the World Museum of Mining. RV parking at the college is possible but limited.

Step back in time to 1899 and Butte's peak mining days at the World Museum of Mining and Hell Roarin' Gulch. The site of the 12-acre outdoor and indoor mining camp is an inactive silver and zinc mine named Orphan Girl. The camp is an historically accurate replica dedicated to the city's mining roots. The Orphan Girl Mine headframe is the centerpiece of the outdoor museum. Hell Roarin' Gulch, a life-size camp rendition, has over 24 old-time offices, stores, saloon, Chinese laundry and even a funeral parlor. A real tribute to the past, the museum is open from 9 A.M. to 9 P.M., April 1 through Labor Day, and 10 A.M. to 5 P.M. (closed Monday) the rest of the year. Admission is $3 per person; children under 12 are free. The location of the historic site is at the end of West Park and Granite Streets. There's plenty of room to park an RV. Depart I-90 at Montana Street, Exit 126, go north to West Park Street and head west all the way to the museum. For complete brochures, write to the World Museum of Mining, PO Box 3333, Butte, MT 59701; (406) 723-7211.

There are more mining sites and interesting exhibits of Butte's history. The Anselmo Mine Yard and Headframe are in the Historic District at Excelsior and Caledonia Streets. The mine headframe, like the skeleton of a giant elevator, is the remnant of the surface support for the underground tunnels. View the Belmont Mine diorama in the Butte Courthouse at 155 W. Granite Street. Visit the Granite

*The World Museum of Mining, near Butte*
DONNIE SEXTON/COURTESY TRAVEL MONTANA

Mountain Memorial, a site dedicated to the 168 men killed in the worst disaster suffered in hardrock mining. The direct road up to the memorial, at over 6,000 feet, is quite long and steep; ask the staff at the Visitor Center for alternative route directions. Visiting hours and information are available from the Butte Visitor Center (406) 494-5595; 1-800-735-6814; fax: (406) 494-5188.

The Butte Silver Bow Chamber of Commerce has put together a walking tour of the uptown historic district. It takes about two hours to follow the selected route, covering 40 buildings listed on the National Register of Historic Places. The tour map is available in the "Visitor's Guide" from the Butte Silver Bow Visitor Center. RV parking in the uptown district can be a challenge, but sights like the Belmont Mine diorama, Arts Chateau and Copper King Mansion make it worth the effort.

The Arts Chateau was originally the home of Charles Clark, the son of one of Butte's copper kings. The 1898 mansion is recorded on the National Register of Historic Places. The once-great home is now a community arts center (first floor galleries) and museum. The Chateau is in the historic uptown Butte section at the corner of Washington and Broadway. The facility is open June through August, Tuesday through Saturday, from 10 A.M. to 5 P.M., and Sunday from noon to 5 P.M. During winter (September through May), the hours are Sunday through Saturday, 11 A.M. to 4 P.M., open Sunday from noon until 5 P.M., and closed Monday. For the current exhibit schedule, contact the Chateau at 321 W. Broadway, Butte, MT 59701; (406) 723-7600.

The Copper King Mansion was the first home in Montana registered as a historic site. There's no doubt the Victorian mansion deserves a place in the annals of history. It was claimed as "A Place Fit for a King" in a 1976 *National Geographic* magazine article. The lavish structure was constructed in 1884–88 for millionaire copper baron William A. Clark. French beveled glass, Tiffany-style stained-glass windows, parquet floors, hand-painted fresco ceilings, nine fireplaces, and bronze, silver and copper walls are just some of the embellishments. If you're feeling cramped in the RV, stroll through this pioneer's palace. The location at 219 W. Granite St. is in the

*Copper King Mansion, in Butte*
COURTESY BUTTE SILVER BOW
CHAMBER OF COMMERCE

*Inside the Copper King Mansion*
LEFT: DONNIE SEXTON/ COURTESY TRAVEL MONTANA
RIGHT: COURTESY BUTTE SILVER BOW CHAMBER OF COMMERCE

upper historic district. Guided tours are given from 9 A.M. to 4 P.M., 7 days a week from May 1 through September 30; fee charged. From October through April, the mansion is open by appointment. For information, call (406) 782-7580.

The Dumas Brothel, or "parlor house" as it was termed in certain circles, is quite a place to visit. Built in 1890, the house was operational until 1982. The red lights burned long in this neighborhood. The location of the infamous property is 45 E. Mercury St. in Butte. RV parking is not a problem here on the side streets. Admission is free; guided tours are $2. The parlor is not open at night these days; hours are 9:30 A.M. to 5 P.M., 7 days a week.

Another way to get around and see Butte is via the Old No. 1 Trolley Tours. The 90-minute ride with narrative is interesting in itself,

plus it provides a great preview of places to investigate more fully. The tours depart from 1000 George Street, by the Butte Silver Bow Chamber of Commerce. Tours run June through September, daily at 10:30 A.M., 1:30 P.M., 3:30 P.M., and 7:00 P.M. Fees are adults, $4, and children ages 4 to 12, $2.50. For information and reservations, call (406) 723-3177; 1-800-735-6814.

*Old #1 streetcar, in Butte*
DONNIE SEXTON/COURTESY TRAVEL MONTANA

*Our Lady of the Rockies
statue overlooks Butte.*
ANTHONY DI FRONZO/
COURTESY BUTTE SILVER BOW
CHAMBER OF COMMERCE

A touching sight high above Butte is the white statue of Our Lady of the Rockies. Visible at night, the lighted statue casts a serene glow above the city. The 90-foot non-denominational statue is the likeness of Mary, Mother of Jesus. The six-year project was built in honor of women everywhere, especially mothers. Daily tours to the statue on top of the mountain are made during the summer season. Access is not allowed by private vehicles. Memorials continue to be the primary source of support. The Lady of the Rockies Center, at 434 N. Main, Butte, MT 59703, 1-800-800-LADY, 1-800-800-5239, (406) 782-1221, has all information on tours and memorials.

Butte owes its past growth to mining, and mining companies owe a lot more than that to Butte, and all of Montana. The Berkeley Pit is 7,000 feet long, 5,600 feet wide and 1,600 feet deep. From 1955 to 1982, the Anaconda Company conducted truck-operated, open-pit copper mining operations. During the latter years, Anaconda was bought out by Atlantic Richfield Company (ARCO). More than 290 million tons of copper ore were removed from the enormous pit. When underground mining operations were stopped, the pumping system was abandoned. Groundwater began rising through the thousands of miles of tunnels honeycombed throughout Butte Hill. The pit filled with toxic, acidic water. Today, cleanup efforts are being made among the Environmental Protection Agency, state agencies, ARCO and other past mine owners. There is no charge to view the awesome pit from an observation stand at 200 Shields St. in Butte. The Visitor Center is open from late spring to early fall, dawn to dusk. There's also plenty of room to park. Call for information, 1-800-735-6814; (406) 723-3177.

*(Left):
This Butte church once bustled with activity during the mining era.*
BILL RAUTIO/COURTESY BUTTE
SILVER BOW CHAMBER OF COMMERCE

*(Right):
This statue of copper king Marcus Daly is one of the many reminders of Butte's mining past.*
TONY DI FRONZO/
COURTESY BUTTE SILVER BOW
CHAMBER OF COMMERCE

## CAMPGROUNDS & RV PARKS

▲ *Best Shot for a Camp Spot*
Butte KOA, off I-90 at Exit 126, one block north, then one block east on Kaw Ave., Bozeman, MT. 100 RV sites, full hook-ups, dump station, showers, laundry, store, playground, fishing and swimming; open April 15 to October 31; (406) 782-0663.

LaRue Mountain View RV Park, 2.1 miles south on Montana 2, then on Harrison. 10 RV sites, full-hook-ups and dump station; adult entertainment room with cable TV; open year-round; (406) 494-3211.

Pipestone Campground, 6 miles west on I-90 at Pipestone Exit 241. 55 RV sites, full hook-ups (30- and 50-amp electric), dump station, showers, laundry, store, playground, pool, spa and game room; open April 1 to October 15; (406) 287-5224.

Lowland—U.S. Forest Service Campground, 8 miles northeast of Butte on I-15, then 8 miles west on Forest Service Road 442, 2 miles south on Forest Service Road 9485. 11 sites; RVs allowed (max. length 22 feet), no services except drinking water; open May 25 to September 15.

Beaver Dam—U.S. Forest Service Campground, 5 miles west of Butte on I-90, then 12 miles south on I-15, 6 miles west on Forest Service Road 96. 15 camping sites; accommodates large RVs (max. length 50 feet), no services except drinking water; open May 25 to September 15.

## BED & BREAKFAST ESTABLISHMENTS

Copper King Mansion, National Historic Site, built in 1884, with Victorian charm. Operating as a bed & breakfast since 1953. Open year-round; busiest in summer, slowest in winter; credit cards accepted; no pets allowed. Contact John Thompson and Erin Sigl, 219 W. Granite, Butte, MT 59701; (406) 782-7580.

Scott Bed & Breakfast, extraordinary view and beautiful rooms. Located at 15 W. Copper, Butte, MT 59701; (406) 723-7030; 1-800-844-2952.

Victoria Joy's Bed & Breakfast & Tea House, beautiful mountain view from the historical uptown area. Open May 1 through September 30. Located at 627 N. Main, Butte, MT 59701; (406) 723-6161; 1-800-484-2258, code 3996.

**SUGGESTED DINING**

Lydia's, Five Mile and Harrison Streets, Butte, MT; (406) 494-2000.

War Bonnett, 2100 Cornell, Butte, MT; (406) 494-6031.

Gold Rush Casino, 22 W. Galena, Butte, MT; (406) 782-5652.

**VISITOR INFORMATION & SERVICES**

The Butte Silver Bow Chamber of Commerce Visitor and Transportation Center is located off I-90 at Exit 126, at the corner of Montana and George Streets. The address is 1000 George, Butte, MT 59701; (406) 494-5595; 1-800-735-6814; fax: (406) 494-5188. The best thing about the Butte Visitor Center is that there's plenty of room to park an RV. If you're towing a pleasure car, the center is happy to have you park the RV while you visit the city. The staff will fill you in on the sights and provide good information on how to get around. The center is open May 30 through Labor Day, 7 days a week, from 8 A.M. to 8 P.M. During September, it's open 7 days a week from 8 A.M. to 5 P.M. The remainder of the year, the center is open Monday through Friday, 9 A.M. to 5 P.M.

The Beaverhead-Deerlodge National Forest offices are in Butte, (406) 494-2147.

The U.S. Bureau of Land Management, Butte District Office, may be reached at (406) 494-5059.

The Butte Area Resource Office has limited hours; call for times (406) 494-1953.

**MEDICAL SERVICES**

St. James Community Hospital has 24-hour emergency room, 400 S. Clark St., Butte, MT 59701; (406) 723-2500.

Osco Drug, 1275 Harrison Ave., Butte, MT 59701; open Monday through Saturday, 8 A.M. to 9 P.M., and Sunday, 10 A.M. to 6 P.M.; (406) 723-9408.

**REPAIR & TOWING**

Milo's Towing & Repair (capable of towing big RVs), 200 Centennial, Butte, MT 59701; (406) 723-4140.

AL's RV Center, full-service repair shop with mobile unit for on-site 24-hour repairs; 5041 Harrison Ave., Butte, MT; (406) 494-2902; 1-800-449-2902.

## VETERINARY SERVICES

The Animal Hospital, 2330 Amherst, Butte, MT 59701; (406) 494-4044.

Animal Medical Clinic, 3302 Monroe, Butte, MT 59701; (406) 494-3630.

Dr. Darrell Turley, 11 Dewey Blvd., Butte, MT 59701; (406) 494-2020.

# BUTTE TO HELENA: I-15

From Butte you can make a nice drive north on I-15 that will take you through Basin, Boulder and into Helena, Montana's state capital. You can also exit I-15 at Boulder and take Montana 69 back down to Whitehall on I-90.

## BASIN

Basin, a small community in the Boulder River Basin, was established by a couple of miners in the 1880s. The ore mined there was sent to Butte, allowing the community to prosper and a trading center to become established. There is very little active ore mining these days. Similar to Boulder, the mines have been tapped for radon gas (see page 314), and the town is known as a site for therapeutic treatments.

## OVERNIGHTING

### CAMPGROUNDS & RV PARKS

O'Neill Campground, in Basin, two blocks west on Basin Creek Rd.; 30 RV sites, full hook-ups and dump station; open April 1 to November 1; (406) 225-3220.

Mormon Gulch—U.S. Forest Service Campground, 4 miles west of Basin on I-15, 2 miles west on Forest Service Road 82. 16 sites; RVs allowed (max. length 16 feet), no services except drinking water; open May 25 to December 1.

Ladysmith—U.S. Forest Service Campground, 4 miles west of Basin on I-15, then 4 miles west on Forest Service Road 82. 6 sites; RVs allowed (max. length 16 feet), no services except drinking water; open May 25 to December 1.

Whitehouse—U.S. Forest Service Campground, 4 miles west of Basin on I-15, then 8 miles west on Forest Service Road 82. 5 sites, RVs allowed (max. length 22 feet), no services except drinking water; open May 25 to December 1.

Basin Canyon—U.S. Forest Service Campground, 5 miles northwest of Basin on Forest Service Road 172. 2 sites, RVs allowed (max. length 16 feet), no services; open May 25 to September 15.

## BOULDER

An 1860s stage station, Boulder's namesake lay strewn about the valley. The large stones were an obstacle course for the Native trails, trapper's mules, wagon roads and stages that coursed through the frontier. Originally called Boulder Valley, the town served both mining and agriculture in the surrounding area. The Great Northern Railway came through in 1888, adding new growth to the trade center. The name was changed to Boulder in 1897.

Boulder is the Jefferson County Seat. The courthouse, an 1889 structure, is listed in the National Historic Register and shows the local architect's German training. The impressive stone structure is complete with gargoyles that are reminiscent of the European Dark Ages.

## ATTRACTIONS

Boulder Hot Springs offers refreshing hot and cold soaking pools to visitors and overnight guests. Radon gas found in the pool area has a following among the health-conscious. It is believed to have beneficial qualities, particularly for the ailments of arthritis and emphysema. The practice of radon gas treatments began in 1952; it is widely popular with Europeans where similar practices are common. Certain soaking pools and lounge areas have been designed for this added dimension. One of the first resorts in the state, Boulder Hot Springs has been refurbished many times throughout the years. It also serves as a bed & breakfast.

The silver mining boom swept through the Elkhorn Mountain area in the 1880s. Now only a ghost town remains. Just two buildings from the frontier town still stand, a town that once held 2,500 people. Elkhorn State Park is a day-use only facility. From I-15 at the Boulder Exit, go 7 miles south on Highway 69, then 11 miles north on County Road. Check the weather and road conditions with local authorities before heading out to the site.

*A sheepherder's wagon on the prairie*

**CAMPGROUNDS & RV PARKS**

▲ *Best Shot for a Camp Spot*
Free Enterprise Health Mine and Campground, 2 miles west of
Boulder. 15 RV sites, water and electric hook-ups, dump station,
showers and laundry; open March 1 to October 31. Contact Free
Enterprise Health Mine and Campground, 149 Depot Hill Rd., Boul-
der, MT  59632; (406) 225-3383.

**BED & BREAKFAST ESTABLISHMENTS**

Boulder Hot Springs, 3 miles south of Boulder on Montana 69. This
newly restored century-old hotel has been operating since 1989.
Features include mineral water in indoor and outdoor pools and
steam rooms, hiking, fishing and cross-country skiing in nearby
Beaverhead-Deerlodge National Forest. Sunday buffets are offered.
Open year-round; alcohol-free; credit cards accepted; no pets
allowed. Contact Ann Wilson Schaef, president, Rt. 69, Box 930,
Boulder, MT  59632; (406) 225-4339; fax: (406) 225-4345.

**SUGGESTED DINING**

Mountain Good, 124 N. Main St., Boulder, MT; (406) 225-3382.

Legal Tender, #7 Legal Tender Lane, Clancy, MT; (406) 933-8449.

# BUTTE TO DILLON: I-15, MONTANA 43, COUNTY ROAD 278

Head south from Butte on I-15, then drive over Deer Lodge Pass,
which is 9 miles south of the I-90 junction. The summit is at
5,902 feet, and the pass itself normally is not a problem for an RV.
If you're in a hurry, stay on the interstate to Dillon and, ultimately,
the Idaho border. If you have the time—and you really should see
this—exit the interstate at Divide, turning west on Montana 43. At
Wise River, head south on the Pioneer Mountains Scenic Byway
through Polaris, and turn east on County Road 278, which you
must turn off for a few miles to see Bannack. From there, continue
to Dillon on County Road 278.

# BUTTE TO DIVIDE: I-15

The interstate crosses rolling country, hemmed in by the Deer-lodge National Forest and beautiful snow-capped peaks. Deer Lodge Pass is a fairly gradual ascent and descent.

## DIVIDE

The town began as a Union Pacific station. Established in 1873, the station was a central stock shipping point for the Big Hole Valley. Divide was named for the Continental Divide.

The Divide Ridge Recreation Area is just a few miles west of Divide. The area is popular with anglers, and there is easy fishing access to the Big Hole River as well as many camping sites.

## OVERNIGHTING

### CAMPGROUNDS & RV PARKS

Dickie Bridge—U.S. Bureau of Land Management Campground, 18 miles west of Divide on Montana 43. 8 sites, RVs allowed (max. length 24 feet), no services; open year-round.

Divide Bridge—U.S. Bureau of Land Management Campground, 2.5 miles west of Divide on Montana 43. 25 sites, RVs allowed (max. length 24 feet), no services; boat-launch ramp for 2-wheel drive; open year-round.

Humbug Spires—U.S. Bureau of Land Management Campground, on I-15 south of Divide, take Moose Creek Exit, then 3 miles northeast on Moose Creek Road. RVs allowed (max. length 24 feet), no services except drinking water; open year-round.

## FAVORITE DRIVE:
## THE PIONEER MOUNTAINS SCENIC BYWAY

The Pioneer Mountains Scenic Byway makes a good day side-tour. The 35-mile drive begins from Wise River and heads south through the Pioneer Mountains, connecting from Montana 43 to County Road 278. The paved or oiled gravel road is in good condition, with the last 12 to 15 miles scheduled for completion by the spring of 1998. (Dillon Visitor Center will have complete details; see Visitor Information, page 326, for the center's address and telephone number.) Not only is there good fishing along the Wise River, but the road passes through scenic country. Crystal Park, Elkhorn Hot Springs, Maverick Mountain Ski Area and the small town of Polaris are along the route. The Forest Service also has several campgrounds along the way. Begin by exiting I-15 at Divide and going west to Wise River.

# DIVIDE TO WISE RIVER: MONTANA 43

This route follows the Big Hole River, one of the most famous in the west. The highway winds about through a canyon for some time, with a steep cliff on the south and the river on the north. The canyon opens up and spreads out before the town of Wise River.

## WISE RIVER

The Wise River flows into the Big Hole River at the town of Wise River. Originally the Big Hole was named the Wisdom River, and some say the smaller river was named after that. The town followed suit when the post office was opened in 1913.

Fly fishing and big-game hunting are the big attractions throughout the Beaverhead National Forest area. Wise River is no exception, and there are several outfitters to guide visitors down the Big Hole River. The Dillon Visitor Information Center has extensive information on outfitters in the region, (406) 683-5511. The following list of Wise River outfitters contains but a few (all are in area code 406). The Complete Fly Fisher, 832-3175. Craig Fellin's Big Hole River Outfitters, 832-3252. The Fishhook, 832-3317. Troutfitters, 832-3212.

## WISE RIVER TO BANNACK

This road is called the Pioneer Mountains Scenic Byway. It runs south through lovely timbered country in the Beaverhead National Forest, paralleling the Wise River along much of its route. As the road approaches Bannack, the countryside becomes drier, typical of many gold towns.

Montana has more than just precious metals. Fortune seekers came for the gemstones hidden in the hills. Crystal Park offers the chance to hunt for gems such as garnets and amethysts. All it takes is a small shovel and piece of screen to sift the diggings. The Forest Service site also has picnic facilities and plenty of trails to hike. Depending on weather conditions, Crystal Park is open May 15 to September 30. The area, located 3 miles north of Polaris, is a great lunch stop while touring along the Pioneer Mountains Scenic Byway. The Forest Service has built a parking lot to accommodate RVs on the west side of the area near some of the designated digging sites.

**RV CAUTION:** Just before you reach Crystal Park, which is at the top of a pass, there's a gravel road turnoff to the ghost town of Coolidge. This one's not for RVs. The rough and rocky road is better suited to a mountain bike—wheels without the oil pan. The remains of the mine and mining camp settlement are about three-quarters of a mile from the main road.

The Elkhorn Hot Springs Resort provides a relaxing getaway for summer visitors as well as winter skiers. Hikers can soak their weary muscles in the outdoor mineral pools or use the sauna. For old-time fun, the resort features stagecoach rides where you can bounce along like the area's first tourists once did. For more information, call 1-800-722-8978, and see page 319. Forest Service campgrounds are nearby, or commercial RV parks are near Maverick Mountain. There are also several guest ranches in the area; see page 319.

## ATTRACTIONS

Maverick Mountain Ski Area is the popular destination for downhill skiers in the winter, and hikers in the summer. In winter, the day-use ski area is open Thursday through Sunday. There are 16 runs: 40 percent intermediate, 40 percent advanced, and 20 percent beginner class. The vertical drop is 2,120 feet from a top elevation of 8,620 feet to the base of 6,500 feet. The average snowfall is 180 inches at this ski resort in the Beaverhead National Forest.

## POLARIS

Nearly a ghost town now, the Polaris Mine was once a thriving silver mine. From the 1880s to the 1920s, various owners operated the mine. A fire destroyed the smelter in 1922, and it was downhill from there. The town's post office, opened in 1898, still operates and serves the current population of five.

## OVERNIGHTING

### CAMPGROUNDS & RV PARKS

**Wise River Area**
Wise River Club, in Wise River on Montana 43. 4 RV sites, full hook-ups, dump station, showers, laundry, bar and cafe; open May 1 to November 15; (406) 832-3258.

Boulder—U.S. Forest Service Campground, 12 miles southwest of Wise River on Pioneer Mountains Scenic Byway. 12 sites, RVs allowed (max. length 22 feet), no services; boat-launch ramp for 2-wheel drive; open June 15 to September 15.

Fourth of July—U.S. Forest Service Campground, 11 miles southwest of Wise River on Pioneer Mountains Scenic Byway. 5 sites, RVs allowed (max. length 24 feet), no services except drinking water; open June 15 to September 15.

Lodgepole—U.S. Forest Service Campground, 13 miles southwest of Wise River on Pioneer Mountains Scenic Byway. 11 sites, RVs allowed (max. length 16 feet), no services except drinking water; open May 25 to September 15.

Willow—U.S. Forest Service Campground, 14 miles southwest of Wise River on Pioneer Mountains Scenic Byway. 9 sites, RVs allowed (max. length 16 feet), no services except drinking water; open June 15 to September 30.

Little Joe—U.S. Forest Service Campground, 20 miles southwest of Wise River on Pioneer Mountains Scenic Byway (Forest Service Road 484). 4 sites, RVs allowed (max. length 16 feet), no services except drinking water; open May 25 to September 15.

Mono Creek—U.S. Forest Service Campground, 23 miles southwest of Wise River on Lower Elkhorn Road 2465. 5 sites, RVs allowed (max. length 16 feet), no services except drinking water; open June 15 to September 30.

### Polaris Area
Maverick Mountain RV Park, 11 miles north on Pioneer Mountain Scenic Byway from Montana 278. 15 RV sites, full hook-ups, dump station and showers; credit cards accepted; open year-round; (406) 834-3452.

## GUEST RANCHES

### Wise River Area
Sundance Lodge, near the Anaconda-Pintler Wilderness. Featured are fishing, hiking, hunting, cross-country skiing, trail rides and hot tub. Open year-round. Contact Sundance Lodge, 4000 LaMarche Creek Rd., Wise River, MT 59762; (406) 689-3612.

Toussaint Ranch, 500-acre homestead ranch that was established in 1906. Features include hiking, mountain biking, nature photography, fishing, ghost town exploring, crystal digging and horseback riding. Contact Toussaint Ranch, PO Box 39, Wise River, MT 59762; (406) 832-3154.

### Polaris Area
Elkhorn Hot Springs and Trail Creek Lodge, west of Dillon in the Pioneer Mountains. Features include two hot mineral pools, sauna, restaurant, hiking, snowmobiling and cross-country skiing. Primitive cabins; open year-round. Contact Elkhorn Hot Springs, PO Box 514, Polaris, MT 59746; (406) 834-3434; 1-800-722-8978; or (517) 684-0592; 1-800-275-3017 outside Montana.

Grasshopper Inn features fishing, horseback riding, hunting, skiing, snowmobiling and cross-country skiing. Restaurant, lounge and game room are on-site. Open year-round. Contact Grasshopper Inn, Box 460511, Polaris, MT 59746; (406) 834-3456.

ZW Ranch, 34 miles west of Dillon, 4 miles off Montana 278. The working cattle ranch features fishing, hunting and excellent riding. Open March through September; busiest June through August; credit cards accepted; pets conditional. Contact Calvin and Laurie Zimdars, 4300 Polaris Rd., Polaris, MT 59746; (406) 834-3487.

## BANNACK

The Pioneer Mountains Scenic Byway finishes out at Montana 278. Head east and turn on the County Road for the easiest route to Montana's first capital and biggest ghost town, Bannack.

## BANNACK STATE PARK

A visit to Bannack State Park is undoubtedly one of the most fascinating side trips to take. Steeped in villainous history, the ghost town once held the true spirit of the Wild West. The tale of those who ventured west seeking fortune first, then settling for the land's more permanent riches was made here.

*Gold.* The word was whispered, but still couldn't be contained. Prospectors came by the hundreds after hearing news of Montana's first big gold strike on Grasshopper Creek. It was July 1862. The rush was on, and one of the wildest, Wild West towns was born. The population of Bannack rapidly grew to over 3,000. A crooked sheriff, Henry Plummer, ran a gang of outlaws (his Road Agents) that killed over 100 men. Vigilantes formed to rectify the wrongs. The result of all the ensuing bloodshed and lawlessness was the formation of stronger government. As control was sorely needed, the U.S. Government granted the petition for territorial status in 1864. Bannack became the first capital of the new Territory of Montana.

*Bannack Days attracts many superb musicians.*
DONNIE SEXTON/
COURTESY TRAVEL MONTANA

*A woman demonstrates her spinning wheel during Bannack Days.*
DONNIE SEXTON / COURTESY TRAVEL MONTANA

The Bannack rush was short-lived. Miners began drifting on to richer claims in Virginia City, and the town residents soon followed. By 1900, the wind whistled through many empty buildings, as in the ghost town you see today. Visitors are free to roam through the 60 well-preserved buildings. It's better than any Hollywood ghost story you can dream up. Or if you prefer a little company, the annual celebration, Bannack Days, is great fun. Held the third weekend in July, the event includes shootouts, lynchings, melodramas and skits, wagon and stagecoach rides, gold panning, dancing, mountain men and old-time music.

Bannack State Park is a National Historical Landmark. The park is open year-round in good weather, daylight to dark. Fees are $3 per vehicle, or 50 cents per person. The Visitor Center, open seasonally through October 31, has informative self-guided tour maps. It takes just under an hour to get there from Dillon. The best way is to take I-15 south to Exit 59, go northwest on Highway 278 for 21 miles, then 4 miles south on County Road (gravel). RV camping is available at the Bannack Campground. Call the Bannack State Park Visitor Center, (406) 834-3413, for more information.

## OVERNIGHTING

### CAMPGROUNDS & RV PARKS

Bannack—Montana Department of Fish, Wildlife and Parks Campground, 5 miles south of Dillon on I-15, then 21 miles west on Montana 278, 4 miles south on County Road. 30 camping sites, RVs allowed, no services except drinking water; open year-round.

# DIVIDE TO DILLON: I-15

If you're in a hurry and don't have time for the Pioneer Mountains Scenic Byway described above, stay on the interstate and continue south to Dillon. You'll note more and more sagebrush along the highway, and you should be able to spot some antelope.

**MELROSE**  The small community is located about halfway between Butte and Dillon. Trout fishing on the Big Hole River is its claim to fame. Exit I-15 at Melrose, and turn onto the County Road at Milepost 93 to access the Maidenrock Campground and fishing on the Big Hole River.

**OVERNIGHTING**

### CAMPGROUNDS & RV PARKS

Sportsman Motel & RV Park, off I-15, Melrose Exit, between Butte and Dillon, on the Big Hole River. 10 RV sites, full hook-ups, showers and laundry; open April 1 to December 1; (406) 835-2141.

Maidenrock—Montana Department of Fish, Wildlife and Parks Campground, off I-15 at Melrose, Milepost 93, then 6 miles west and north on County Road. 30 sites; RVs allowed; no services except drinking water; boat-launch ramp for 4-wheel drive; open year-round.

### GUEST RANCHES

Canyon Creek Ranch, 18 miles from Montana 43. Featured are trout fishing, river floating and alpine lake fishing, pack trips, trail rides and hunting. Contact Dave Duncan, Outfitter, PO Box 126, Melrose, MT 59743; (406) 496-9155; 1-800-291-8458.

**DILLON**  Dillon is a traditional western town in that ranching and farming are the mainstays. The area is Montana's largest producer of cattle and ranks fourth in the industry nationwide. Dillon is also first, statewide, in production of hay. In past years, Dillon was the largest wool shipping point in the state, and it still ranks second largest in sheep ranching. Mining is also represented. Barrett Minerals, a talc mine, is one of the area's largest employers. The high-quality talc is used in medicines, cosmetics and other materials. Education has always had its role here, too. Montana's Normal College was moved from Twin Bridges in 1893. Since then, the quality teacher's school was renamed Western Montana College. In recent years, the school has affiliated with the University of Montana in Missoula.

Beaverhead County is the largest county in Montana, and one of the top ten largest in the nation. That's in terms of land mass, of course. The county covers 5,551 square miles; that's approximately the size of Connecticut and Rhode Island combined. Dillon, and its 4,300 residents, has the honor of being the Beaverhead County Seat. This diversified town calls itself the "Entrance to Montana," and welcomes visitors to its varied styles.

Lewis and Clark spent the greatest amount of time in any one location here in the Beaverhead River Valley. The expedition found it extremely difficult tracking upstream, hauling boats and supplies. It was a tremendous relief when Sacajawea's people, who could supply horses, were found.

Early prospectors and settlers came to this part of Montana in the 1860s. The first gold rush booms in Bannack and Virginia City spurred growth in the area. By 1880, the transportation needed for continued prosperity, the Utah and Northern Railroad, was close at hand. However, construction of the railroad came to a halt when a rancher refused to allow the rails to cross his land. Some resourceful men formed a partnership and overcame the problem by buying out the rancher. The partners then gave permission for the railroad to come ahead to their new town, Terminus. One year later, the name was changed to Dillon for Sidney Dillon, then president of the Union Pacific Railroad. Dillon is distinguished as the "Cradle of Montana" because so much of the state's history began here.

## OUTDOOR RECREATION

The Beaverhead Golf Course, a public course with 9 holes and 18 tees, is on the north edge of Dillon on Montana 41. For tee times, call (406) 683-9933.

Fishing the rivers and lakes around Dillon is rapidly gaining national attention, with plenty of outstanding fishing in the area. Areas include the Big Hole with its main tributary, the Wise River; Blacktail Deer Creek in the south; Clark Canyon Reservoir; Ruby Reservoir; and the Beaverhead and Ruby Rivers that join the mighty Jefferson. Try your hand or get some local know-how, and a float trip too. A full list of guides and outfitters is at the Dillon Visitor Center, (406) 683-5511.

In the Dillon area, Maverick Mountain is the place for downhill skiing. The area is only 45 minutes from Dillon. For more information, call (406) 834-3454.

The Clark Canyon Recreation Area, about 20 miles south, is a favorite fishing and camping spot in this area. There are lots of outdoor activities; see page 327.

The Beaverhead County Museum focuses on local and southwestern Montana history. The outdoor interpretive exhibit includes an 1885 pioneer cabin depicting the early settlement days. The indoor displays include artifacts, photographs and taxidermy. For those seeking a bit of exercise, there's a walking tour through the town's historic buildings. The museum is at 15 S. Montana, Dillon, MT, (406) 683-5027. During the summer months, the museum is open daily, and weekdays only during the remainder of the year. RVs can park behind the buildings; there's plenty of room.

Clark's Lookout is an undeveloped day-use cultural park in the Montana State Park system. The site has a rocky outcrop above the Beaverhead River where members of the Lewis and Clark Expedition were able to look ahead and see their route. The location makes a pleasant, stretch-your-legs stop. Locals call it Lover's Leap, and the county road is named Lover's Leap Road. In Dillon, exit I-90 at Highway 41, go a half-mile east, then a half-mile north on the county road.

Beaverhead Rock State Park is a day-use area. The familiar landmark was named by Sacajawea's people, and visited by Lewis and Clark in 1805. To visit the site, head north of Dillon on Montana 41, about 14 miles.

A diorama of the Lewis and Clark Expedition at the Beaverhead is displayed at the Dillon Visitor Center in the old train depot. The diorama scene depicts the expedition at Beaverhead Rock. Originally built for the Historic Society in Helena in 1953, the wax figurines were created by artist Rudy Audio. The complete scene was restored and brought to its current site.

Western Montana College features the Seidenssticker Wildlife Collection, which has North American, Asian and African taxidermy mounts and an art gallery. The college is at 710 S. Atlantic in Dillon. The free museum is open Monday through Thursday from 10 A.M. to 3 P.M., Tuesday and Thursday evenings from 7 P.M. to 9 P.M. For information, call (406) 683-7126.

The Rancher Roundup Days is a different kind of rodeo. The festival began as a way for locals to have some fun, and blossomed into a grand Memorial Day weekend event. Unusual contests, such as the Rope-n-Stroke (a mixture of golf and team roping) and wild cow milking, are held along with traditional saddle bronc riding. This is the most fun-filled rodeo around. For details, ask the Dillion Visitor Center, (406) 683-5511.

Labor Day weekend brings about one of Montana's biggest celebrations, the Beaverhead County Fair. The Dillon Jaycee Rodeo is held at the same time, and there's fun for all ages. The rodeo, a parade, barbecue and top-name entertainment at the rodeo are featured. Contact the Dillon Visitor Information Center, (406) 683-5511, for details. The fair runs Tuesday through Saturday; the rodeo is on the weekend.

## CAMPGROUNDS & RV PARKS

▲ *Best Shot for a Camp Spot*
Armstead Campground, 20 miles south of Dillon on I-15; take Clark Canyon Exit 44. 50 RV sites (pull-throughs), 18 full hook-ups, dump station, showers and laundry facility; lake activities and access to Beaverhead River are a plus; open April 1 through November 30; busiest in May; (406) 683-4199.

▲ *Best Shot for a Camp Spot*
SkyLine RV Park, 2.5 miles north of Dillon on Montana 41 North. 38 RV sites (pull-throughs), full hook-ups, dump station, showers and laundry; open year-round; busiest June through October, slowest January through February; (406) 683-4692.

Dillon KOA, off I-15 in Dillon; take Exit 63 to Montana Street, right on Reeder to Park Street. 68 RV sites, full hook-ups, dump station, showers, laundry, store, pool, fishing and playground; open year-round; (406) 683-2749.

Dinner Station—U.S. Forest Service Campground, 12 miles north of Dillon on I-15, then 12 miles northwest on Birch Creek Road. 7 sites, RVs allowed (max. length 16 feet), no services except drinking water; open May 15 to September 15.

Grasshopper—U.S. Forest Service Campground, 4 miles south of Dillon on I-15, then 27 miles west on Montana 278, 11.5 miles north on Pioneer Mountains Scenic Byway. 24 sites, RVs allowed (max. length 16 feet), no services except drinking water; open June 15 to September 15.

*A fisherman tries his luck on Canyon Ferry Reservoir near Helena.*

## BED & BREAKFAST ESTABLISHMENTS

The Centennial Inn, 122 S. Washington, Dillon, MT  59725; (406) 683-4454.

Rivers Edge Lodge Bed & Breakfast; contact Rod and Jennifer, 765 Henneberry, Dillon, MT 59725; (406) 683-2649; fax: 683-4467.

## GUEST RANCHES

Hildreth Livestock Ranch, on the Medicine Lodge/Big Sheep Creek. This working cattle ranch has been operating since 1984. Featured are hunting, fishing and rock hunting. Open year-round; busiest October through November, slowest in winter; no credit cards accepted; no pets allowed. Contact Hildreth Company, Box 149, Dillon, MT 59725; (406) 681-3111.

Horse Prairie Ranch, on Bachelor Mountain Road. One of southwest Montana's oldest working cattle ranches, it has been operating as a guest ranch since 1995. Open year-round; busiest June through September, slowest in winter. Contact Kenneth and Marie Duncan, 3300 Bachelor Mountain Rd., Dillon, MT 59725; (406) 681-3155, 681-3160; 1-888-RANCHLIFE; fax: (406) 681-3222. Website: http://www.netvoyage.com/hpr

## SUGGESTED DINING

Buffalo Lodge, 19975 Hwy. 91 South, Dillon, MT; (406) 683-5535.

Paradise Inn, 660 N. Montana, Dillon, MT; (406) 683-4966.

Lions Den, 725 N. Montana, Dillon, MT; (406) 683-2051.

Crosswinds, 1004 S. Atlantic, Dillon, MT; (406) 683-6370.

## VISITOR INFORMATION & SERVICES

Dillon Visitor Information Center (at the Old Railroad Depot), 125 S. Montana, Dillon, MT; (406) 683-5511.

The Visitor Information Center is also a state travel center and has complete tourism information for the entire state. Small RVs can park in front of the building, and large RVs will find plenty of room behind the facility. The center is open year-round: June through August, 8 A.M. to 8 P.M., 7 days a week; May and September, 8 A.M. to 5 P.M., 7 days a week; October through April, Monday through Friday, 8 A.M. to 5 P.M.

Beaverhead-Deerlodge National Forest, Dillon Ranger Station, Dillon, MT; (406) 683-3900.

U.S. Bureau of Land Management, Dillon Resource Area, Dillon, MT; (406) 683-2337.

Bannack State Park Visitors Center, (406) 834-3413.

**MEDICAL SERVICES**

Barrett Memorial Hospital, 1260 S. Atlantic, Dillon, MT; (406) 683-2323.

Area is served by 911.

**REPAIR & TOWING**

Big Bear Road Service & Repair, full-service, 24-hour towing; cellular phone: (406) 660-1133.

Paul's Motor Company, 675 N. Montana, Dillon, MT 59725; (406) 683-2371.

Big Sky Motors, 790 N. Montana, Dillon, MT; (406) 683-2347.

**VETERINARY SERVICES**

Veterinary Hospital, Inc., 935 S. Atlantic, Dillon, MT 59725; (406) 683-2385.

# DILLON TO MONIDA (IDAHO BORDER): I-15

Just 4 miles south of Dillon is Montana 278, the back road to Bannack State Park, that will take you on to Wisdom and the Big Hole Battlefield. If you didn't visit Bannack before, be sure to go. The County Road from Montana 278 is the shortest route to Bannack State Park. As you continue down I-15, Clark Canyon Dam should be your next stop.

**CLARK CANYON RECREATION AREA**

The Clark Canyon Recreation Area has lots of outdoor activities. The lake has rainbow trout, brown trout and ling. Fishing in the lake is reputedly excellent. Also, try fishing the blue-ribbon Beaverhead River below Barretts Dam (12 miles north), which is popular with streamside anglers. A marina on-site is convenient for boaters. There is a fee to use the facilities. Several public campgrounds make it easy to spend awhile and enjoy hiking around the area.

The Cattail Marsh Nature Trail, at the north edge of the recreation area, is a favorite area for birding. Look for waterfowl, the colorful yellow-headed and redwing black birds and snipes. Below the dam there is a wheelchair-accessible trail. As always, marsh areas tend to be buggy; remember the insect repellent.

**RV CAUTION:** As you explore around the recreation area on the paved road, there are back roads leading over Lemhi Pass and south into the Tendoy Mountains. Although the Lemhi Pass road starts out mildly, the last few miles get rugged. The pass is not recommended for large RVs or trailers. It's best to hike the last mile. Temporary parking at the small, non-RV campground, Sacajawea Memorial Camp, is available just below the pass.

The southern backcountry route between the Bitterroot and Tendoy Mountains is also a potentially hazardous drive. Forest Service Road 302 is known as Big Sheep Creek Road. The U.S. Bureau of Land Management has declared that the route can only be taken by large RVs in perfect, dry weather. If a storm comes up, do not try to continue driving. Have a supply of food and water and wait until the storm passes. When the road dries, it's safe to continue.

The Clark Canyon Recreation Area, (406) 683-6472, is south of Dillon; take Exit 44 off I-15 and follow the signs.

## OVERNIGHTING

## CAMPGROUNDS & RV PARKS

▲ *Best Shot for a Camp Spot*
Armstead Campground, 20 miles south of Dillon on I-15; take Clark Canyon Exit 44. 50 RV sites (pull-throughs), 18 full hook-ups, dump station, showers and laundry facility; lake activities and access to Beaverhead River are a plus; open April 1 through November 30; busiest in May; (406) 683-4199.

*The following Clark Canyon Reservoir Campgrounds are maintained by the U.S. Bureau of Reclamation (USBR).*

Barrets Park—USBR Campground, 5 miles south on I-15. RVs allowed, no services except drinking water; boat-launch ramp for 4-wheel drive; open year-round.

Beaverhead—USBR Campground, at Clark Canyon Reservoir. RVs allowed, no services except drinking water; boat-launch ramp for 2-wheel drive; open year-round.

Cameahwait—USBR Campground, at Clark Canyon Reservoir. RVs allowed, no services except drinking water; open year-round.

Fishing Access—USBR Campground, at Clark Canyon Reservoir. RVs allowed, no services except drinking water; boat-launch ramp for 2-wheel drive; open year-round.

Hap Hawkins—USBR Campground, at Clark Canyon Reservoir. RVs allowed, no services except drinking water; open year-round.

Horse Prairie—USBR Campground, at Clark Canyon Reservoir. RVs allowed, no services except drinking water; boat-launch ramp for 2-wheel drive; open year-round.

Lewis and Clark—USBR Campground, at Clark Canyon Reservoir. RVs allowed, no services except drinking water; open year-round.

Lonetree—USBR Campground, at Clark Canyon Reservoir. RVs allowed, no services except drinking water; boat-launch ramp for 4-wheel drive; open year-round.

West Cameahwait—USBR Campground, at Clark Canyon Reservoir. RVs allowed, no services except drinking water; open year-round.

**DELL**   This remnant of a town, lying just off I-15, has one of our all-time favorite eating spots. Called the Calf-A, (406) 276-3380, the building was an old schoolhouse. The interior hasn't been changed much; there are still blackboards and all the appointments you'd find in a pioneer school. While enjoying this look at the past, you'll enjoy the food and the prices, too. Count on homemade chow, and then take a walk outside and look at the zillions of pieces of antique farm equipment and other items lying around in barns and on the ground.

# MONIDA TO RED ROCK LAKES NATIONAL WILDLIFE REFUGE: I-15, MONTANA 509

As you continue south on I-15, you reach Monida, which lies close to the border between Montana and Idaho. The name was created from the first three letters of each state. At Monida, state route Montana 509 heads east to Red Rock Lakes National Wildlife Refuge, one of our favorite drives. Another option is to continue south on I-15 and head over the summit of Monida Pass, which crosses the Continental Divide at 6,870 feet. Although troublesome in winter, this is a relatively gentle pass that was the primary access for settlers and miners moving up into Montana's gold country. The first town in Idaho is Spencer, and from there you may return to the Island Park/West Yellowstone area via Idaho A-2 east out of Spencer (see page 365). Another option is to proceed south along I-15, where you'll descend into a broad valley that extends to Idaho Falls. For the story on Idaho, see page 333.

# FAVORITE DRIVE:
# HENRY'S LAKE TO RED ROCK LAKES
# NATIONAL WILDLIFE REFUGE

July and August are the most congested months in Yellowstone National Park, but you don't always have a choice on when to take your vacation. Red Rock Lakes National Wildlife Refuge is the place to go for a day's drive or a week's serenity; a calm within the storm of continuous traffic. The 51-mile drive winds from Henry's Lake up to 6,000 feet at the refuge. Gas up at Mack's Inn on U.S. 20, and head out for a pleasant adventure beneath the Continental Divide. From Mack's Inn, head north, then turn west on Red Rock Road (Forest Service Road 053), or go north and then northwest on Montana 87 and turn west again onto Henry's Lake Road (Forest Service Road 055). The two roads merge at the northwest corner of Henry's Lake and become Red Rock Road (Forest Service Road 053). If you're coming from West Yellowstone on U.S. 20, gas up there and again turn northwest on Montana 87, and west onto Henry's Lake Road. The trip over Red Rock Pass (elevation 7,120) and on to the refuge is a moderate drive; the improved gravel road is in good condition. The drive from Henry's Lake to Monida on I-15 can be made in about three hours, which gives you plenty of time to enjoy the scenery and wildlife.

Red Rock Lakes National Wildlife Refuge was established in 1935 to protect the rare and majestic trumpeter swan. At that time only 69 swans existed in the Greater Yellowstone Ecosystem. The success of the 40,300-acre refuge and preservation program can be measured by the current year-round population of about 600 swans. The winter population increases to 2,000, when more swans arrive on their annual migration from Canada. The refuge offers outstanding wildlife observation opportunities, and the remote location allows a tranquil intimacy not found inside Yellowstone.

The Upper Lake Campground, nestled in a stand of aspens, is an excellent place to camp if your RV is under 24 feet. You can look across the lake for trumpeter swans, or you can see moose often swimming about or feeding along the willows and marsh areas. Oddly enough, moose are avid swimmers and can outmaneuver a two-man canoe quite handily. Canoeing, kayaking or travel via other non-mechanized vessels is an exciting way to view the wildlife. Be sure to check up on boating rules and access restrictions established by the U.S. Fish and Wildlife Service.

Travel on Red Rock Pass Road to Rush's Lakeview Guest Ranch. Stop in and say hello to Keith and Leah Rush. Their ranch offers a variety of activities, including horseback riding, fishing, a guide school and outfitted hunts (see page 331).

The River Marsh Campground, at Lower Red Rock Lake, is 2.5 miles down a fair-weather, dirt-gravel road. There is no drinking water available at this area. There are many side roads to explore, such as Elk Lake Road, that are good, and others that are only good on a clear day (a muddy quagmire if it's wet). The Refuge Headquarters in Lakeview has refuge maps and information on weather and recent wildlife sightings.

# HENRY'S LAKE TO RED ROCK LAKES NATIONAL WILDLIFE REFUGE
## (CONTINUED)

There are a wide variety of birds, over 250 species. Bird species include shorebirds such as willets, avocets, long-billed curlews, terns and gulls; fishers such as great blue herons and white pelicans; others such as sandhill cranes and the intensely colored mountain bluebirds. Raptors such as ferruginous hawks, red-tailed hawks and peregrine falcons are fascinating to watch while they fly and hunt their prey. Sandhill cranes can be seen feeding in the open grassy areas, and bluebirds commonly sit on the fenceposts watching for insects to devour. There's a vast amount of insects, especially mosquitoes. If there weren't any insects, there wouldn't be any birds to watch. So, be prepared. Bring along repellent, use it according to manufacturer's directions and really enjoy your stay.

There are also plenty of elk, mule deer and whitetail deer in the Centennial Valley, and farther east in the sagebrush prairie, you'll find pronghorn antelope. The elk can usually be heard bugling about mid-September through early October. Year-round, look for whitetails along the lake and mule deer in the sagebrush areas on the upper side of the road opposite the lake.

The drive from Lakeview ends up at Monida, Montana, and from there you can proceed up I-15 to Dillon, or turn south into Idaho. Once in Idaho, you can keep traveling south to Idaho Falls and the city life, or make a loop back to the Henry's Lake area via Spencer to Idaho A-2 (a good-condition gravel road) to Mack's Inn on U.S. 20.

## OVERNIGHTING

### CAMPGROUNDS & RV PARKS

▲ *Best Shot for a Camp Spot*
Red Rock Lakes NWR, Upper Campground—U.S. Fish and Wildlife Service. camp sites, RVs allowed (max. length 24 feet), no services; open July 15 to September 30.

### GUEST RANCHES

Rush's Lakeview Guest Ranch is a great place to stay while visiting Red Rock Lakes Wildlife Refuge. Keith and Leah Rush own and operate the ranch. Activities include pack trips, photography workshops, fishing, hunting, swimming, canoeing, hiking, horseback riding, sauna, cross-country skiing, snowmobiling and just about anything outdoors that you want to do. A professional outfitter and guide school, horsemanship school and bird-watching on the refuge are also offered. For more information, contact Keith and Leah Rush, Monida Star Route, Lima, MT 59739; (406) 276-3300; 1-888-624-3300; or, winter, 2905 Harrison, Butte, MT 59701; (406) 494-2585.

# HENRY'S LAKE

## to Red Rock Lakes National Wildlife Refuge

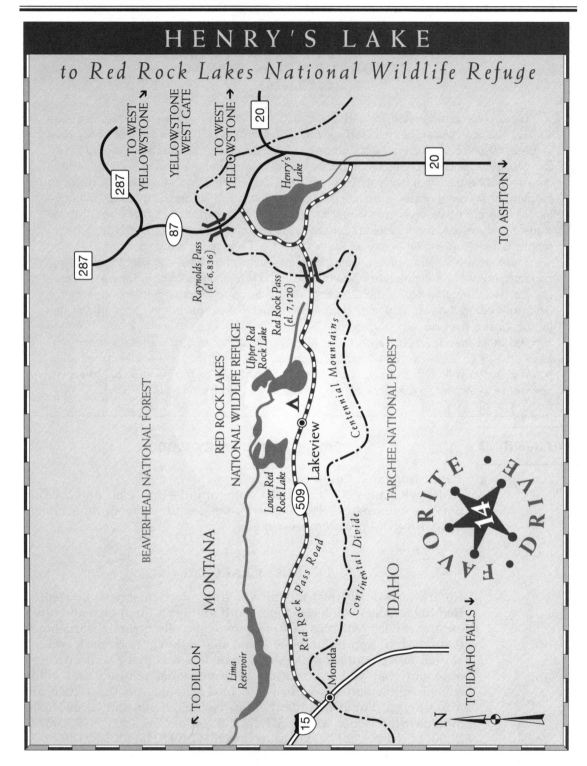

*Lakeview Guest Ranch, near Red Rock Lakes*

Elk Lake Resort, 40 miles west of West Yellowstone on northeast edge of Red Rock Lakes National Wildlife Refuge. This resort has been in operation since the 1930s. Featured are fishing, hiking, bird-watching, snowmobiling, cross-country skiing and ice fishing in winter. Open year-round; busiest winter and summer; credit cards accepted; pets allowed. Contact Elk Lake Resort, PO Box 1662, West Yellowstone, MT 59758; (406) 276-3282.

**VISITOR INFORMATION & SERVICES**

Red Rock Lakes National Wildlife Refuge, U.S. Department of the Interior, Fish and Wildlife Service, is responsible for the area. Camping is allowed at the Upper Lake and River Marsh campgrounds only. Outside established areas, camping is not permitted. The refuge address is Monida Star Route, Box 15, Lima, MT 59739; (406) 276-3536.

# WEST YELLOWSTONE, GREATER ISLAND PARK AREA, ASHTON, REXBURG AND IDAHO FALLS: U.S. 20

Once you exit West Yellowstone, via U.S. 20, you drive only 10 miles through Montana and then into Idaho. Actually, in less than 20 miles, you drive three states, a fact that few people realize. Wyoming ends just a few miles from West Yellowstone, you have the short distance through Montana, and then you're in Idaho. This is a beautifully paved road meant for year-round use, and it's well maintained in the winter. You'll see "moose crossing" signs along this highway. These aren't meant to be humorous but are deadly serious. Be on the lookout for these animals, especially early in the morning and late in the afternoon when they're most active and moving around.

Just a few miles into Idaho, you can turn north on Montana 87 and drive over Targhee and Raynolds Passes, and then to Ennis. Don't let the term "pass" intimidate you; these passes are not RV hindrances. If you continue down U.S. 20 into Idaho, you'll drive through Island Park, which contains a couple of fishing holes known as the "Mother of All Trout Waters" to trout anglers around the country. Henry's Lake, which is just off the highway, has enormous trout and is easily fished via boat, float tube or from shore. Henry's Lake State Park exists essentially for fishing access. The lake was named after Major Andrew Henry, who traveled and explored the area in 1910. Realizing the rigors of winter, Henry established a winter post in St. Anthony where the valley climate was a bit more hospitable. There's a campground at Henry's Lake that offers good access to the water. For one of our favorite drives through the Henry's Lake area to Red Rock Lakes National Wildlife Refuge, see page 330.

**MACK'S INN AND ISLAND PARK AREA**

Island Park Reservoir has exceptional fishing, but it's overshadowed by Henry's fly-fishing notoriety. From Mack's Inn to Island Park, you'll see lots of fishing shops along the highway and plenty of traffic. The two towns form a 30-mile stretch of highway loaded with resorts, restaurants and RV parks and services. This is a popular place not only for Idahoans, but also for plenty of Salt Lake City area residents and tourists from distant places. You'll note several signs along the highway indicating forest plantations, the years the trees were planted, and interpretive signs that describe old fires or logging practices. Be aware that campgrounds in the entire area are extremely busy and almost always full. Best bet is to get back away from the highway, but be aware that some of the more remote campgrounds have RV size restrictions and may have no hook-ups.

Island Park is actually a geological feature—a 20-mile-wide volcanic basin called a *caldera*. The caldera was formed from the collapse of a volcano that erupted for thousands of years. It is, in fact, the world's largest caldera.

**OUTDOOR RECREATION AND ATTRACTIONS**

Even though Island Park is best known as a fisherman's paradise, golfers also can enjoy the scenery while playing a round. For details, call the Island Park Village Club House, Island Park, ID; (208) 558-7550.

You'll want to check out Big Springs, just a short drive east of Mack's Inn. It's an amazing spot where water gushes from the ground at the rate of almost 100,000 gallons per minute. The springs are a major source of the Henry's Fork River. At that spot you can see huge rainbow trout cruising about and gleefully accepting food from strangers, but don't put a hook in that food. Fishing is a no-no here, but you can watch all you want. For a relaxing float trip with plenty of opportunities to view wildlife, take the Big Springs National Water Trail—a four-hour trip. There's also a lovely campground here as well as the Big Spring Water Trail, which is a water trail that is open from May through the end of September.

You can also visit the Johnny Sack cabin near Big Springs, which was built in 1939 by a German immigrant. It features lovely hand-carved furniture and unique flooring. It's open only in July and August.

Jewelry lovers and rockhounds will enjoy hunting opals at the Spencer Opal Mines. Take a drive across the basin on Idaho County Route A-2, which starts halfway between Mack's Inn and Island Park. The well-maintained gravel road takes you to Kilgore, and then south to Spencer, where it connects into I-15. Lots of locals use this road as a good shortcut over to the interstate, but if you're traveling very early or late in the season, be sure to ask authorities the condition of the road. For more information on the gemstones, see page 365.

Harriman State Park is worth a stop if you're interested in seeing wildlife, horseback riding and fishing in legendary waters. Historians tell us that the area was bought in 1902 by the Oregon Short-line Railroad, a branch of the Union Pacific, to transport tourists to West Yellowstone. It was later purchased by several wealthy individuals, including Edward H. Harriman. Unfortunately, Edward died before he ever saw the property, but his wife and three children moved to the ranch in 1911. Plenty of cowboys and cows made this an authentic cattle operation, but this was a harsh land with enormous amounts of snow and extreme cold. Cattle were moved back and forth from summer pastures to wintering areas. In 1977, a deal was struck between the Harrimans and the Idaho Parks and Recreation Department. Ownership was given to the state, and the park was open to the public in 1982. Now known as the "Railroad Ranch," it offers peace and quiet to a region normally full of tourists in the summer and hundreds of snowmobilers in the winter. Avid trout anglers bow their heads in respect when they murmur the words "Railroad Ranch." If fishing isn't your thing but you like wild critters, you can spot plenty of creatures at the Harriman Wildlife Refuge. The sanctuary hosts bald eagles, endangered trumpeter swans, ospreys, sandhill cranes, and even elk and moose. There are horses available for riding here, and this spot gets our vote as one of the prettiest places in the region for horseback riding.

## OVERNIGHTING

### CAMPGROUNDS & RV PARKS

**Henry's Lake**

▲ *Best Shot for a Camp Spot*

Redrock RV & Camping Park, above the "Cliffs" on Henry's Lake, from U.S. 20 turn west on Red Rock Pass Road, Milepost 398, then 5 miles. 44 RV sites (24 pull-throughs), hook-ups, dump station, showers, accessible to the disabled, and mini-mart; pets allowed; open May 15 through September 30; 1-800-473-3762; (208) 558-7442.

## FAVORITE DRIVE: MESA FALLS SCENIC BYWAY

Take a detour off U.S. 20 and turn onto Idaho 47. You'll get away from the frenetic pace of the highway and travel down a peaceful gravel road that runs through the mountains for 26 miles, and parallels the main highway and the Henry's Fork of the Snake River. This was the primary route to the west entrance of Yellowstone in the 1950s, before U.S. 20 was built. There are four campgrounds (see the Overnighting section, page 339) along Idaho 47 with a possible 103 RV sites—a good bet to find a campsite. The bulk of traffic is generally carried along U.S. 20 at the major RV centers throughout Island Park, Mack's Inn and Henry's Lake.

Along Idaho 47, you'll want to visit two gorgeous waterfalls: Upper and Lower Mesa Falls. You can drive to observation points, and at the upper falls, you can walk an extensive well-made boardwalk that allows you to see and photograph the falls from different angles. The upper falls cascades 114 feet, while the lower drops some 65 feet. You can easily see the lower falls from a vantage point aptly named Grandview, which allows RV parking. As you leave the falls area, you'll pass beyond Three Rivers Canyon where Warm River and Robinson Creek flow into the Henry's Fork, then the highway descends into rolling farmland. The Tetons are visible in the distance to the east.

Staley Springs Lodge, on the northwest shore of Henry's Lake. 44 RV sites, hook-ups; dump station and showers, restaurant and mini-mart; lake- and riverfront access; pets allowed; (208) 558-7471.

▲ *Best Shot for a Camp Spot*
Valley View General Store & RV Park, on U.S. 20 at Henry's Lake. 53 RV sites (pull-throughs), hook-ups, laundry, showers, LP gas and mini-mart; credit cards accepted; pets allowed; open May 1 through November 30; (208) 558-7443.

Jared's Wild Rose Ranch, on the north shore of Henry's Lake on Montana 87 at 340 W. 7th South, Island Park. 45 RV sites (max. length 30 feet), full hook-ups, cable TV and restaurant; credit cards accepted; pets allowed; open May 23 through October 31; (208) 558-7201.

Henry's Lake State Park, 15 miles south of West Yellowstone on U.S. 20. 50 RV sites (max. length 40 feet), pull-throughs, hook-ups, dump station, showers, toilets and laundry; hiking, lake- and riverfront access, boating and fishing; open May 30 through September 30.

# MESA FALLS SCENIC BYWAY

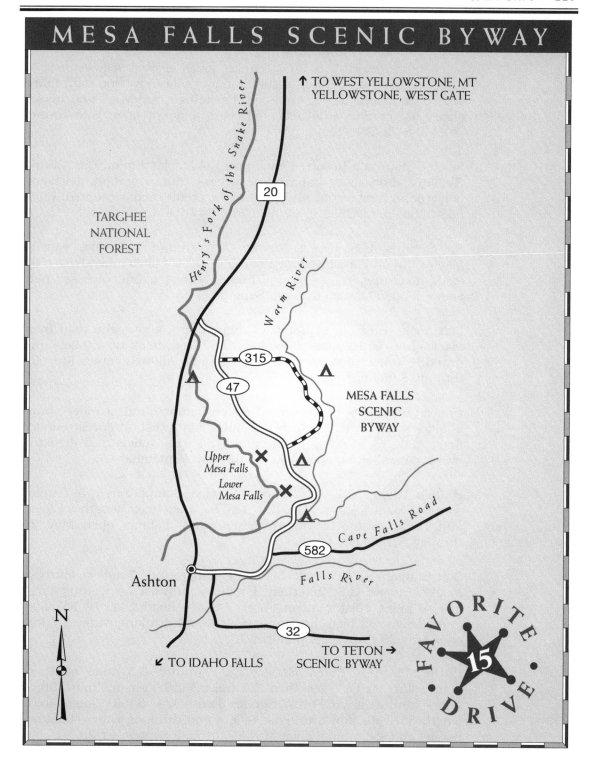

Henry's Fork of the Snake River

↑ TO WEST YELLOWSTONE, MT
YELLOWSTONE, WEST GATE

20

TARGHEE
NATIONAL
FOREST

Warm River

315

47

MESA FALLS
SCENIC
BYWAY

Upper
Mesa Falls

Lower
Mesa Falls

Cave Falls Road

582

Falls River

Ashton

N

32

↙ TO IDAHO FALLS

TO TETON →
SCENIC BYWAY

FAVORITE · DRIVE

15

**Mack's Inn**

▲ *Best Shot for a Camp Spot*

Mack's Inn Resort, U.S. 20, 20 miles south of West Yellowstone. 73 RV sites, hook-ups, dump station, showers, laundry and mini-mart; float trips, paddleboats, mini-golf, basketball, volleyball and horse-shoe pits; credit cards accepted; pets allowed; open year-round; (208) 558-7272.

Sawtell Mountain Resort, 1 mile north of Mack's Inn on U.S. 20. 60 RV sites, hook-ups, barrier-free access, dump station, showers, playground, restaurant and mini-mart; credit cards accepted; (208) 558-9366; fax: (208) 558-9235; 1-800-547-0404.

Big Springs—U.S. Forest Service Campground, 4.5 miles east of Mack's Inn on Forest Service Road 059. 19 RV sites (max. length 32 feet), hook-ups, toilets and drinking water; fishing access; pets allowed; open May 25 through September 15.

Flat Rock—U.S. Forest Service Campground, across the road from Mack's Inn. 40 RV sites (max. length 32 feet), hook-ups, toilets and drinking water; boating and fishing; pets allowed; open May 25 through September 15.

Upper Coffee Pot—U.S. Forest Service Campground, 2 miles south of Mack's Inn on U.S. 20, then 2 miles southwest on Forest Service Road 130. 15 RV sites (max. length 32 feet), toilets and drinking water; pets allowed; open May 25 through September 15.

Buffalo Loops A-G—U.S. Forest Service Campground, 5.5 miles south of Mack's Inn on U.S. 20. 127 RV sites (max. length 34 feet), pull-throughs, toilets and drinking water; fishing; open May 25 through September 15.

Box Canyon—U.S. Forest Service Campground, 7 miles south of Mack's Inn on U.S. 20, then 3 miles southwest on County Road 134, 9 miles northwest on Forest Service Road 284. 19 RV sites (max. length 32 feet), hook-ups, toilets and drinking water; hiking; open May 25 through September 15.

Buttermilk—U.S. Forest Service Campground, 3.5 miles south of Mack's Inn on U.S. 20, then 2.2 miles northwest on Idaho 30, 4 miles southwest on Forest Service Road 334. 54 RV sites (max. length 32 feet), pull-throughs, toilets and drinking water; boating, fishing and swimming; open May 25 through September 30.

McCrea Bridge—U.S. Forest Service Campground, 3.5 miles south of Mack's Inn on U.S. 20, then 2.2 miles northwest on County Road 30. 25 RV sites (max. length 32 feet), toilets and drinking water; boating and fishing; open May 25 through September 30.

### Island Park

Aspen Lodge, on U.S. 20 and U.S. 191, Milepost 397-1/2. 8 RV sites, hook-ups, dump station; restaurant and mini-mart; credit cards accepted; pets allowed; open year-round; (208) 558-7406.

Snowy River Campground, on U.S. 20. 50 RV sites, pull-throughs, hook-ups, dump station and showers; lake- and riverfront access; (208) 558-7112.

Ponds Lodge, 25 miles south of West Yellowstone on Buffalo River, three-quarters of a mile from Henry's Fork and Island Park Reservoir. 64 RV sites, full hook-ups; restaurant, lounge and grocery store; fishing in lakes and reservoir; open May through October; (208) 558-7221.

### Mesa Falls Area

Riverside—U.S. Forest Service Campground, 16.5 miles north of Ashton on U.S. 20, then 1 mile southeast on Forest Service Road 304. 57 RV sites (max. length 34 feet), pull-throughs, drinking water; fishing access; pets allowed; open June 1 through September 30.

Pole Bridge—U.S. Forest Service Campground, 12 miles northeast of Ashton on Idaho 47, then 5 miles north on Forest Service Road 294, 7 miles north on Forest Service Road 150. 10 RV sites (max. length 22 feet), drinking water; pets allowed; open June 1 through October 31.

Grand View—U.S. Forest Service Campground, 12 miles northeast of Ashton on Idaho 47, then 2 miles north on Forest Service Road 294 at Lower Mesa Falls. 20 RV sites (max. length 22 feet), drinking water; pets allowed; open June 30 through October 31.

Warm River—U.S. Forest Service Campground, 10 miles northeast of Ashton on Idaho 47. 17 RV sites (max. length 24 feet), hook-ups, barrier-free access and drinking water; fishing access and hiking; pets allowed; open June 1 through September 30.

## GUEST RANCHES

Elk Creek Ranch, 2 miles from Island Park on U.S. 20; open during fishing season; no credit cards accepted; pets allowed. Contact Elk Creek Ranch, Box 1, Island Park, ID 83249; (208) 558-7404.

Jacob's Island Park Ranch, on Shotgun Valley Road. This authentic working cattle spread has been operating since 1990. Features include horseback riding, pack trips, sleigh rides, cattle drives, boat rides, swimming, cross-country skiing and snowmobiling. Open year-round; busiest July through August, slowest October and May; credit cards accepted; no pets allowed. Contact Mitch Jacobs, owner, 2496 N. 2375 E., Hamer, ID 83433, or Brad Rhoads, manager, Shotgun Valley Rd., Island Park, ID 83249; (208) 662-5567.

**SUGGESTED DINING**

Henry's Fork Landing, U.S. 20, Mack's Inn, ID; (208) 558-7672.

Aspen Lodge, U.S. 20, Island Park, ID 83429; (208) 558-7407.

Pond's Lodge, U.S. 20, Island Park, ID 83429; (208) 558-7221.

Wild Rose, U.S. 87, Island Park, ID 83429; (208) 558-7201.

Staley Springs Lodge, northwest shore of Henry's Lake on Highway 87, Island Park, ID 83429; (208) 558-7471.

Henry's Fork Lodge, U.S. 20 at Mack's Inn Bridge, Island Park, ID 83429; (208) 558-7953.

Shotgun Store & Cafe, 5 miles west of U.S. 20 on Yale-Kilgore Road (Idaho A-2), Island Park, ID 83429; (208) 558-7090.

Cowbell Bar & Grill, 2 miles west of U.S. 20 on Yale-Kilgore Road (Idaho A-2), Island Park, ID 83429; (208) 558-9606.

**VISITOR INFORMATION & SERVICES**

Island Park Area Chamber of Commerce, PO Box 83, Island Park, ID 83429; (208) 558-7755.

Idaho Department of Parks and Recreation, Harriman and Henry's Lake State Parks, HC 66, Box 33, Island Park, ID 83429; (208) 558-7368.

Henry's Lake Fish Hatchery, on the southern shoreline of Henry's Lake; open to visitors by appointment; (208) 558-7202.

**MEDICAL SERVICES**  See West Yellowstone, Ashton or Rexburg Services (page 348).

**REPAIR & TOWING**  Tony's Wrecker, Island Park, ID; (208) 558-7755.

**VETERINARY SERVICES**  See West Yellowstone or Ashton Services (page 348).

# ASHTON, TETONIA, DRIGGS AND VICTOR: U.S. 20, IDAHO 32, IDAHO 33

As you continue driving south on U.S. 20, you'll arrive in Ashton where you can then continue to Idaho Falls and meet up with I-15. If you have time and want to take a nice side trip, turn your RV east at Ashton, and head over to the Tetonia, Driggs and Victor area on Idaho Highways 31, 32 and 33. If you continue south on Idaho 31, you'll come to U.S. 26, which will take you either west to Idaho Falls, or east through Swan Valley to Alpine; see page 344.

The Driggs and Tetonia area have absolutely gorgeous grainfields, most of them on rolling slopes mingled with strips of forests here and there. Try to see this country early in the morning or late in the afternoon, preferably when the light adds the special effect that photographers die for—the alpenglow.

This area was once known as Pierre's Hole by early trappers and mountain men who gathered there from 1819 to 1840. As you can imagine, this was the scene of some wild parties and fistfights as these tough characters bartered and traded their furs, and also had regular skirmishes with Native Americans. The valley was named for "Old Pierre" Tevanitagon, an Iroquois trapper who worked for the Hudson's Bay Company.

**OUTDOOR RECREATION AND ATTRACTIONS**  Just 28 miles east of Ashton is the Cave Falls and Bechler Meadows Area of Yellowstone National Park. The only way to reach this southwestern corner of Yellowstone is through Idaho. The beautiful drive along Idaho 47 passes through fields and mountain meadows on an improved gravel road. Although a little rough in spots, the road is accessible to RVs in that it is not exceedingly steep or winding. Cave Falls are on the Fall River, and there is a campground on the riverbank. Trailheads for nonmotorized access into Yellowstone are here. If you aren't into hiking, this is a beautiful drive nonetheless. Yellowstone National Park services, (307) 344-7381, will have additional trail information.

The Hess Heritage Museum is a complex of interesting structures, including a one-room log schoolhouse and a carriage house. The 1890s Heritage Home and Implement Barn is filled with historical implements, such as horse-drawn and mechanized farm equipment, sleighs, buggies and a vintage T-Model Ford, and it provides a complete view of pioneer life. The museum is 1 mile south of Ashton, one-quarter mile west of U.S. 20 on the Fish Hatchery Road. Open from April through October, there is an admission fee to enter the museum, and hours are by appointment every day except Sunday and Tuesday; (208) 356-5674, 652-7353.

The biggest annual celebrations in Driggs take place over the Fourth of July weekend during the Mountain Men Rendezvous Days and Hot Air Balloon Fest. The mountain men's festival reenacts the gatherings of fur traders and trappers of the 1820s. Main Street and the Driggs's City Park swing into action with the mountain art celebration, fine art exhibit, live music entertainment, chuckwagons and more. You can also watch the launches of the two-day Balloon Fest and enjoy a morning picnic.

For information on the history of Idaho's Teton area, pay a visit to the Teton County Historical Museum on Main Street in Driggs. The museum, which is behind the county courthouse, specializes in artifacts from early ranches. The Chamber of Commerce has current hours of operation.

Golfers have a choice. Aspen Acres Golf Course in Ashton on Northwest Squirrell, (208) 652-3524, or the Targhee Village Golf Course in Driggs. Targhee Village is a 9-hole community golf course open to the public. The season is April 20 to November 1. Call for tee times, during season (208) 354-2621, or 354-8577; or winter, (208) 356-5353. To get to the course, go east from Driggs on Ski Hill Road about 4 miles to Alta, turn onto Stateline Road and continue three-quarters of a mile to Golf Course Road.

Grand Targhee Ski and Resort Area is reached through Driggs. With 2,200 vertical feet and 626 runs on two mountains, this is a major ski destination. One mountain provides 3,000 acres of skiing, and the other is reserved exclusively for powder snowcat skiing. The annual snowfall is over 500 inches. Cross-country ski enthusiasts will enjoy the many groomed trails. Grand Targhee also offers summer recreation with a multitude of activities, including horseback riding, mountain biking, music festivals and more. Be sure to visit. Call 1-800-TARGHEE, 1-800-827-4433, for resort information.

Trout fishing the Teton River in the summer and running snowmobiles in the winter are the favorite outdoor activities. The Teton Valley Chamber of Commerce has information on fishing guides and snowmobile trails in Fremont County.

## FAVORITE DRIVE:
## TETON SCENIC BYWAY

The Teton Scenic Byway provides a different view of the Grand Teton Range, and one less apt to be viewed bumper-to-bumper behind another vehicle. This route, which begins from Ashton heading east on Idaho 32, eventually connects with Wyoming 22 out of Jackson Hole and will take you to that famous town via the lovely Teton Pass. The route offers great views of the back sides of the Teton Range.

**RV CAUTION:** Be aware that both sides of Teton Pass are very steep in spots, often having grades up to 10 percent. Be sure your RV is in top condition to tackle this road. You can avoid the pass and take a much longer route to Jackson by driving to Rigby and taking U.S. 26 southeast to Alpine, Wyoming, and north to Jackson.

## OVERNIGHTING

## CAMPGROUNDS & RV PARKS

### Ashton
Aspen Acres Golf Club & RV Park, 9 miles east/southeast of Ashton, 4179 E. 1999 North, Ashton, ID. 40 RV sites, hook-ups, dump station and showers; pets allowed; (208) 652-3524.

▲ *Best Shot for a Camp Spot*
Jessen's RV and Bed & Breakfast, on U.S. 20, 1.5 miles south of Ashton, 1146 N. 3400 East, Ashton, ID. 22 RV sites (pull-throughs), 14 full hook-ups, dump station, showers, LP gas and workout facilities; cottages and camping; pets allowed; (208) 652-3356.

Cave Falls—U.S. Forest Service Campground, 6 miles east of Ashton on Idaho 47, then 5.5 miles northeast on Cave Falls Road, 11 miles northeast on Forest Service Road 582. 16 RV sites (max. length 24 feet), pull-throughs, hook-ups and drinking water; fishing access, Wyoming license required; pets allowed; open June 1 through September 30.

West End—U.S. Forest Service Campground, 18 miles north of Ashton on U.S. 20, then 15 miles northwest on Forest Service Road 167. 19 RV sites (max. length 22 feet), boating, fishing and swimming; open June 1 through September 15.

# TETON SCENIC BYWAY

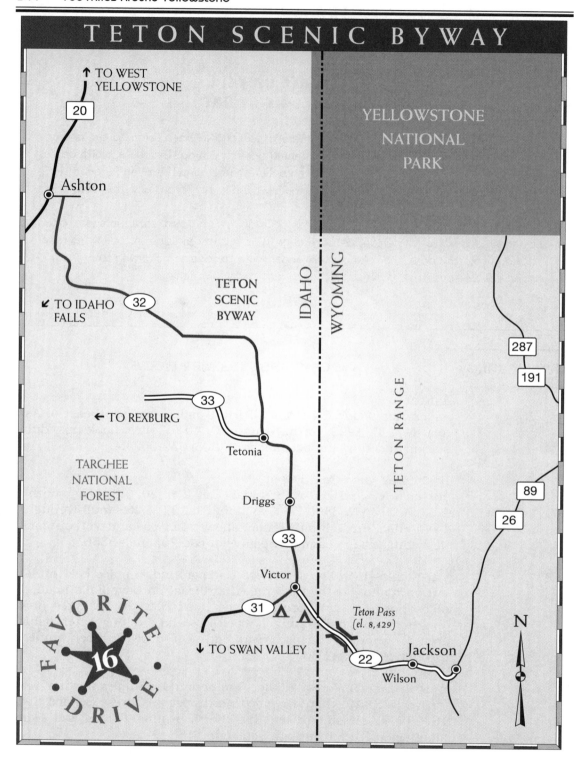

↑ TO WEST
YELLOWSTONE

20

YELLOWSTONE
NATIONAL
PARK

Ashton

↙ TO IDAHO
FALLS

32

TETON
SCENIC
BYWAY

IDAHO

WYOMING

287

191

33

← TO REXBURG

Tetonia

TARGHEE
NATIONAL
FOREST

TETON RANGE

89

26

Driggs

33

Victor

31

Teton Pass
(el. 8,429)

N

↓ TO SWAN VALLEY

22

Jackson

Wilson

FAVORITE • DRIVE

16

### Driggs

Teton Canyon—U.S. Forest Service Campground, 6 miles northeast of Driggs on County Road 009, then 4.5 miles east on Forest Service Road 009. 20 RV sites (max. length 24 feet), pull-throughs, hook-ups, toilets, dump station and drinking water; fishing and hiking; pets allowed; open June 15 through September 15.

Reunion Flat—U.S. Forest Service Campground, 10 miles east of Driggs in Teton Canyon. 2 RV sites (max. length 35 feet), pull-throughs, toilets, dump station and drinking water; boating, fishing and hiking; pets allowed; open June 15 through September 15.

### Victor

Teton Valley Campground, 1 mile southwest of Victor on Idaho 31, PO Box 49, Victor, ID 83455. 30 RV sites, hook-ups, dump station, showers and laundry; swimming pool and mini-mall; credit cards accepted; pets allowed; (208) 787-2647; fax: (208) 787-2647.

Mike Harris—U.S. Forest Service Campground, 4 miles southeast of Victor on Idaho 33, then one-half mile on Forest Service Road 239. 12 RV sites (max. length 20 feet), pull-throughs, dump station and toilets; hiking and fishing; pets allowed; open June 15 through September 15.

Pine Creek—U.S. Forest Service Campground, 6.5 miles west of Victor on Idaho 31. 9 RV sites (pull-throughs), hook-ups, drinking water and toilets; hiking and fishing; pets allowed; open June 15 through September 15.

Trail Creek—U.S. Forest Service Campground, 6 miles southeast of Victor on Idaho 33. 11 RV sites (max. length 20 feet), pull-throughs, dump station, drinking water and toilets; fishing and hiking; pets allowed; open year-round.

## BED & BREAKFAST ESTABLISHMENTS

### Ashton

Jessen's Bed & Breakfast, 1.5 miles north of Ashton along U.S. 20; open year-round; busiest June through August; no credit cards accepted; no pets allowed. Contact Jack and Nieca Jessen, 1146 N. 3400 East, Ashton, ID; (208) 652-3356.

Stegelmeier Farm House Inn, 10 miles east of Ashton; operating since 1997; open year-round; credit cards accepted; pets conditional. Contact manager, 1357 N. 4350 East, Ashton, ID 83420; (208) 652-3363.

### Driggs

Teton Creek, a large ranch house with grand room and outdoor hot tub. This small ranch is 40 miles from Jackson. Operating since 1990; open year-round; busiest June through September; credit cards accepted; no pets allowed. Contact Val and Naomi Christensen, Southeast Idaho 33, Driggs, ID 83422; (208) 354-2584.

Willowpine Bed & Breakfast and Guest House, private sundecks, secluded patios, and accessible to the disabled; operating since 1988; open year-round; busiest in summer, slowest late fall and early spring; no credit cards accepted; no pets allowed. Contact Darla Neely, 136 E. Little Ave., Box 105, Driggs, ID 83422; (208) 354-2735.

Alta Lodge Bed & Breakfast, a country home with hot tub; operating since 1994; open year-round; busiest in summer, slowest in November; credit cards accepted; no pets allowed. Contact Judy, Susie and Robert Blair, 590 Caghee Town Rd., Box 135, Alta, WY 83422; (307) 353-2582; fax: (307) 353-2582.

Wilson Creekside Inn, a historic country farmhouse with hot tub; operating since 1992; open year-round; busiest July through August and December through March, slowest March through June, and October through November; no credit cards accepted; no pets allowed. Contact Janice Wilson, Ski Hill Rd., Alta Rt., Box 3620, Alta, WY 83422.

## GUEST RANCHES

### Tetonia

Beard Mountain Ranch, in Moran, 1 mile from U.S. 287 on the west slope of the Tetons. This small ranch has been operating since 1967. Featured are trail rides, overnight pack trips, fishing and big-game hunting. Open year-round; busiest June through August, slowest October through December; pets allowed; no credit cards accepted. Contact Lyle Beard, Box 84, Tetonia, ID 83452; (307) 576-2694.

### Driggs

Teton Teepee Lodge, near Grand Targhee Ski Area; family lodge with rustic charm; operating since 1973. Features include winter ski packages and summer mountain bike tours, fishing, hiking and white-water rafting. Open year-round; slowest in November and April; credit cards accepted; no pets allowed. Contact Mark Melehes and Brent Palmer, Rt. 1, Box 3475, Alta, WY  83422; (307) 353-8176; 1-800-353-8176; fax: (307) 353-8176.

Teton Ridge Ranch, on Dry Ridge Road, 10 miles north of Driggs; small guest ranch operating since 1985. Features include horseback riding, hiking and fishing. Open May 15 through October, and December 15 through March, closed November through December 15 and April; no credit cards accepted; well-behaved pets only. Contact Albert and Chris Tilt, managers, 2000 Valley View Rd., Tetonia, ID  83452; (208) 456-2650.

Moose Creek Ranch Bed & Breakfast, 18 miles west of the Tetons on Idaho 33; hot tub in winter, heated pool in summer; dude ranch open June through September; bed & breakfast open year-round; credit cards accepted; no pets allowed. Contact Kelly and Roxanne Van Orden, Box 350, Victor, ID  83455; (208) 787-2784; 1-800-676-0075.

**SUGGESTED DINING**

Trails Inn, 213 Main, Ashton, ID; (208) 652-9918.

Fall River Café, Idaho 33, Ashton, ID; (208) 652-7871.

Glades, 1370 U.S. 20 North, Ashton, ID; (208) 652-7869.

Joe's Place, 10 N. Main, Driggs, ID; (208) 354-2293.

O'Rourke's, Little Road to Grand Targhee, Driggs, ID; (208) 354-8115.

Toni's Pizza & Pasta, Main St., Driggs, ID; (208) 354-8829.

Trail's End, Main St., Tetonia, ID; (208) 652-9918.

Knotty Pine Bar & Restaurant, 58 S. Main, Victor, ID; (208) 787-2866.

Timberline Bar & Café, 14 W. Center, Victor, ID; (208) 787-2639.

Victor Steak Bank, 13 S. Main, Victor, ID; (208) 787-2277.

Old Dewey House, Victor, ID; (208) 787-2092.

**VISITOR INFORMATION & SERVICES**

Ashton Chamber of Commerce, PO Box 151, 604 Main St., Ashton, ID 83420; (208) 652-3987. You may park your RV at the Chamber of Commerce while viewing the town's sights or fairly easily around town.

Teton Valley Chamber of Commerce, Second Floor, Outfitters Building on Main and Ashley Streets, PO Box 92, Driggs, ID 83422; (208) 354-2292.

Teton Information Center, staffed by volunteers, irregular hours; (208) 354-2500.

**MEDICAL SERVICES**

Ashton Family Clinic, 235 8th St., Ashton, ID 83420; open Monday through Friday, 9 A.M. to 5 P.M.; (208) 652 7471.

City Drug, 235 8th St., Ashton, ID 83420; open Monday through Saturday, 9 A.M. to 6 P.M.; (208) 652-3932, after hours (208) 652-7985.

Teton Valley Hospital, 24-hour emergency room, 238 N. 1st E., Driggs, ID 83422; (208) 354-2334.

Corner Drug, 10 S. Main, Driggs, ID; open Monday through Saturday, 9 A.M. to 6 P.M.; (208) 354-2334.

**REPAIR & TOWING**

Amen Wrecker, Ashton, ID; (208) 652-7242.

**VETERINARY SERVICES**

Fremont Veterinary Clinic, Dr. John Sharps and Dr. Bert Elsworth, 3349 U.S. 20, Ashton, ID; (208) 652-7218, after hours, (208) 652-7903.

## ST. ANTHONY AND REXBURG: U.S. 20

As you continue on U.S. 20 out of Ashton, plan to spend time viewing sights along the highway. They're worth it. If you see huge fields of crops that look unfamiliar to you, they might very well be potatoes. This is the eastern edge of Idaho's legendary potato country, which extends across the southern part of the state. The air and soil temperature are perfect for potatoes, as is the well-drained and light-textured soil. You'll also begin noticing long, low-slung buildings on farms. These are potato barns that store the

*Fields of potatoes in Idaho, near Rexburg*

crop in darkness to prevent the formation of green chlorophyll in the skin. Optimum temperatures keep the potatoes from sprouting, and optimum humidity keeps them moist, preventing them from drying.

St. Anthony is next on the route after Ashton and lies close to unique sand dunes. These are real dunes, constantly shifting and blowing with the winds. The dunes, which consist of clear white quartz sand, extend over 11,000 acres.

About 13 miles farther is Rexburg, the largest town in the valley. Rexburg is best known for Rick's College, which was established in 1888 by the Mormons. Initially the school was intended to provide a safe refuge for young Mormons who were being persecuted for their beliefs. Rick's is now one of the biggest private two-year colleges in the country and has almost 7,000 students.

## OUTDOOR RECREATION

St. Anthony Sand Dunes covers an area 35 miles long and 5 miles wide. The blowing sand provides a fun recreation area for dune buggy riders. Park your RV and try walking in these dunes, but be prepared for some strenuous work. Even worse, try hiking uphill, but only if you're in decent physical condition. Do you recall how difficult it is to walk a beach with deep sand? That's nothing compared to doing it up a steep hill; some of these hills ascend to 400 feet or more. These dunes are among the highest in the United States. For information about the dunes area, call (208) 523-1012, or the U.S. Bureau of Land Management, (208) 524-7500.

The Fremont County Golf Course, 674 Golf Course Rd., St. Anthony, is a public course 5 miles north of town; (208) 624-7074. Golfers can also enjoy the public course at Teton Lakes Golf Course, N. Hibbard Hwy., Rexburg; (208) 359-3036.

Wintertime visitors love snowmobiling in the Targhee National Forest. There are 1,400 miles of groomed trails that lead from Rexburg to Island Park and on through West Yellowstone. Check with the Eastern Idaho Visitor Information Center, 1-800-634-3246, for details.

## ATTRACTIONS

The Idaho International Folk Dance Festival begins the last weekend in July and continues through the first weekend in August in Rexburg. Beautiful indoor night performances are contrasted by fun-filled street dances and parades in the daytime. The festival is nationally recognized for bringing together cultures from around the world. Call (208) 356-5700 for dates on this wonderful annual event.

While in Rexburg, don't miss the Teton Flood Museum located in the old tabernacle building. You'll see artifacts as well as a dramatic real-life video of the disastrous flood that occurred when nearby Teton Dam collapsed in 1976. About 80 billion gallons of water rushed downstream in just a few hours, and killed anywhere from 6 to 14 people (depending on which source you believe). That loss of life was miraculously low when you consider the incredible surge of water that engulfed several small towns with very little warning. The video at the museum shows the whole thing and will bring goose bumps. This is a bit like the popular movie *Hard Rain*, but it differs in that this was no staged event but reality.

The Teton flood movie is shown in a basement room that feels like a concrete bunker. As you sit in the darkness, allow yourself to forget the calendar. Step into the past and relive the catastrophe of the dam breaking, hear the frantic voice of the newscaster warning people to run, just run; the unbelievable has happened. Disastrous events happen and affect people generations after most evidence disappears. This movie provides an insight into the people of the area from Rexburg to Rigby. The residents' strength of spirit resembles that of their forefathers. You can drive out to the Teton Dam site 25 miles east of Rexburg on Idaho 33, where all that remains is the conical-shaped center section. Before you go, watch the video and you'll have a better appreciation of this incredible disaster.

The flood museum also has a nifty collection of artifacts, including a unique assortment of some 350 salt-and-pepper shakers. The Teton Flood Museum is in the basement of the Rexburg Tabernacle, 51 North Center, Rexburg, ID 83440; (208) 356-9101.

Also in Rexburg, check out the Idaho Centennial Carousel in Porter Park. This New York-built merry-go-round was received in 1952; unfortunately, it was a victim of the Teton Dam flood and also vandalism. It has since been restored. Broken legs and horse's tails were replaced by carver Sherrill Anderson, who did a beautiful job. The fully operational carousel is well decorated with Idaho logos and memorabilia. If you're traveling with your kids or grandkids and they're feeling a little cooped up in the RV, let them ride the carousel. It's open in the summer Monday through Saturday, weather permitting.

A site that remains largely undiscovered and worth a look is the Menan Butte area southwest of Rexburg. Two buttes rising 500 and 800 feet out of craters a half-mile wide and 300 feet deep offer hiking on good trails as well as unique sightseeing. Reach them by taking Idaho 33 west of Rexburg.

## OVERNIGHTING

### CAMPGROUNDS & RV PARKS

### St. Anthony
Eagin Lakes—U.S. Bureau of Land Management Campground, St. Anthony Sand Dunes Main Entrance. 30 RV sites, no hook-ups, no services, vault toilets; open except during winter.

Sand Hills Resort, 865 Redroad, St. Anthony, ID 83445. RV sites, hook-ups, hot showers and laundromat; (208) 624-4127; winter, (801) 393-2246.

### Rexburg
▲ *Best Shot for a Camp Spot*
Sheffield House RV Park, on U.S. 191, 5362 S. U.S. 20, Rexburg, ID 83440. 18 RV sites, 15 pull-throughs, showers; putting green, beach volleyball and horseshoes; credit cards accepted; pets allowed; open year-round; (208) 356-4182.

▲ *Best Shot for a Camp Spot*
Thompson RV Park, 4 miles south of Rexburg on U.S. 20, Rexburg, ID 83440. 12 RV sites (pull-throughs), laundry; open in summer; (208) 356-6210.

Rainbow Lake & Campground, .25 mile west and 1.25 miles south of Rexburg on Idaho 41, 2245 S. 2000 W., Rexburg, ID 83440. 60 RV sites, hook-ups, dump station, laundry and showers; lake fishing and paddle boats; pets allowed; open April 15 through October 10; (208) 356-3681.

### BED & BREAKFAST ESTABLISHMENTS

### Rexburg
Sheffield House & RV Park; hot tub; operating since 1996; open year-round; credit cards accepted; pets allowed. Contact Val Moss, 5362 S. U.S. 20, Rexburg, ID 83440; (208) 356-4182.

**SUGGESTED DINING**

Relay Station, 593 N. 2600 E., Rexburg, ID; (208) 624-4640.

Craigo's Pizza, 121 W. 4th S., Rexburg, ID; (208) 359-1123.

Silver Horse Bar & Grill, 22 N. Bridge St., St. Anthony, ID; (208) 624-2850.

**VISITOR INFORMATION & SERVICES**

South Fremont Chamber of Commerce, 110 W. Main, Ste. A, St. Anthony, ID 83445; (208) 624-3411.

Targhee National Forest: Campgrounds, Trails and Visitor Information, PO Box 208, St. Anthony, ID 83445; (208) 624-3151.

Rexburg Chamber of Commerce and Cottontree Conference and Tourist Information Center, 420 W. 4th S., Rexburg, ID 83440; (208) 356-5700.

**MEDICAL SERVICES**

Madison Memorial Hospital, 24-hour emergency room, 450 E. Main, Rexburg, ID 83440; (208) 356-3691.

Boyles Pharmacy, Broulim Mall, Main St., Rexburg, ID; open Monday through Friday, 9 A.M. to 7 P.M., and Saturday, 9 A.M. to 5 P.M.; (208) 356-5416.

**REPAIR & TOWING**

Taylor Chevrolet, Towing & Repair, 871 S. U.S. 191, Rexburg, ID; (208) 356-6600.

**VETERINARY SERVICES**

Upper Valley Veterinary Clinic, Dr. Neil Call, 12226 N. Salem, Rexburg, ID; open Monday through Friday 8 A.M. to 5 P.M.; (208) 356-4848.

# RIGBY, SWAN VALLEY AND VICINITY: U.S. 20, U.S. 26

As you near Rigby, you'll see billboards proclaiming it to be the birthplace of television. Your first reaction, like ours, might be that someone is putting you on. But it's true. Rigby is the home of Philo T. Farnsworth, an amazing guy who invented the cathode ray tube. Rigby is worth a stop to investigate the story.

From Rigby the most traveled route is on U.S. 20 to Idaho Falls. The more scenic path through the countryside heads east on U.S. 26 to Swan Valley, following along the Snake River to Palisades Reservoir. The reservoir is shared by Idaho and Wyoming, with the bulk of it in Idaho.

## OUTDOOR RECREATION AND ATTRACTIONS

The Jefferson County TV and Pioneer Museum has the whole story on Philo T. Farnsworth—the father of television. The nicely done museum displays his ideas and works that led to the invention of the cathode ray tube. When he was 21, the Utah-born Farnsworth proved his bizarre notion that he could transmit a single horizontal line from a camera in one room to a screen in another room. As the story plays out, it seems that RCA offered Farnsworth $200,000 for his invention, but he turned it down. Then, as the allegation continues, an RCA employee by the name of Vladimir Zworykin visited Farnsworth's lab and was later credited with being TV's inventor. Farnsworth's camp maintains that Zworykin stole Farnsworth's ideas, but that will always remain arguable. Before Farnsworth's death in 1971, he had 300 patents, one of them for a baby incubator. The only drawback is that the museum has very short hours, 1:00 P.M. to 5:00 P.M., and is closed Sunday and Monday. Look for the tall tower at the museum on 118 W. 1st S., Rigby, ID; (208) 745-8423.

The Heise Hot Springs are east of Ririe and just 3 miles north of U.S. 26 on Heise Road. The hot springs were once used by Native Americans. In 1896 a German immigrant, Richard Heise, decided to homestead in the area near the therapeutic waters. After World War II, the property was sold to the Quinn family, who have managed it ever since. The scenic 40-acre resort is a beautiful spot, with a 9-hole golf course, huge swimming pool with water slides and excellent fishing on the Snake River. Licensed guides are on the premises. There is also an RV campground. For information, contact Heise Hot Springs, 5116 E. Heise Rd., Ririe, ID 83443.

As you depart Rigby and head east along the South Fork of the Snake River on U.S. 26, you'll travel through lush cottonwood bottomlands. Be sure to watch for bald eagles and great blue herons in this area. Moving east, the river flows through a deep canyon, and the views are quite impressive. Fall Creek Falls, which can be seen from the Swan Valley Bridge, is a good place to stop, rest and take a picture. After you cross the bridge and continue upriver to the southeast, you come to Palisades Dam and a long 18-mile lake known as Palisades Reservoir. Fishing, hiking and just enjoying the scenery are great pastimes here. The native cutthroat trout fishery is rated as excellent. And, yes, this is a popular area, but a well-developed one. There are 9 campgrounds and 181 family units in the combined Palisades Reservoir and Alpine, Wyoming, areas. Almost always, you'll find a spot.

## CAMPGROUNDS & RV PARKS

### Ririe

▲ *Best Shot for a Camp Spot*
7 N Ranch RV Park, 21 miles from Idaho Falls on Idaho 26, 5156 E. Heise Rd., Ririe, ID 83443. 48 RV sites, 10 pull-throughs, full hook-ups, dump station and showers; open April 15 to October 15; (208) 538-5097.

Heise Hot Springs & RV Park, 3 miles northeast of Ririe on Idaho 26, 5116 Heise Rd. Ririe, ID 83443. 50 RV sites, laundry, showers, swimming pool, spa and hot tub and restaurant; lake- and riverfront access; (208) 539-7312.

Kelly's Island—U.S. Bureau of Land Management Campground, 2 miles east of Heise on access road, north side of river. 16 RV sites (max. length 40 feet), hook-ups, drinking water and toilets; boating; open May 1 through October 31.

Ririe Reservoir—U.S. Bureau of Reclamation Campground, 1 mile east of Ririe off Idaho 26, then south on County Road to Headquarters. 49 RV sites (max. length 35 feet), pull-throughs, barrier-free access, drinking water, dump station and showers; hiking, boating, fishing and swimming; pets allowed; open May 15 through October 15.

Table Rock—U.S. Forest Service Campground, 12 miles southeast of Ririe on U.S. 26, then 1.5 miles southeast on Forest Service Road 218, 1.3 miles southeast on Forest Service Road 217. 9 RV sites (max. length 22 feet), drinking water and vault toilets; hiking; open May 21 through September 7.

### Swan Valley

*Best Shot for a Camp Spot*
▲ Timberwolf Resort on U.S. 26, 3781 Swan Valley Rd., Swan Valley, ID 83449. 30 RV sites (12 full hook-ups), gas station, cafe, cabins, boat and RV storage; open spring thaw to freeze; (208) 483-3581.

South Fork Lodge, 4 miles west of Swan Valley on U.S. 26, Box 22, Swan Valley, ID  83449. 48 RV sites, hook-ups, dump station, showers, mini-mart and restaurant on-site; lake- and riverfront access; credit cards accepted; pets allowed; (208) 483-2112; 1-800-483-2110.

Falls—U.S. Forest Service Campground, 4 miles west of Swan Valley on U.S. 26, 2.3 miles south on Forest Service Road 076. 23 RV sites (max. length 24 feet), drinking water and toilets; open May 21 through September 7.

Falls Group Area—U.S. Forest Service Campground, 4 miles west of Swan Valley on U.S. 26 then 2.6 miles south on Forest Service Road

076. 1 RV site (max. length 22 feet), drinking water and toilets; open May 21 through September 7.

## Palisades Reservoir Area to Alpine

Big Elk Creek—U.S. Forest Service Campground, 5.4 miles southeast of Palisades on U.S. 26, then 1.4 miles northeast on Forest Service Road 262. 21 RV sites (max. length 22 feet), no services; drinking water, vault toilets and restaurant; swimming, hiking, boating and fishing; open May 21 to September 7; reservations accepted, call 1-800-280-CAMP.

Blowout—U.S. Forest Service Campground, 9 miles southeast of Palisades on U.S. 26. 19 RV sites (max. length 32 feet), no services; drinking water and vault toilets; swimming and boating; open May 21 to September 7.

Calamity—U.S. Forest Service Campground, 2.6 miles south of Palisades on U.S. 26, then 1.1 miles southwest on Forest Service Road 058. 41 RV sites (max. length 32 feet), no services; drinking water and vault toilet; swimming, boating and fishing; open May 21 to September 15; reservations accepted, call 1-800-280-CAMP.

Palisades—U.S. Forest Service Campground, 2 miles northeast of Palisades on Forest Service Road 255. 8 RV sites (max. length 22 feet), no services; drinking water and vault toilets; hiking and fishing; open May 21 to September 15.

Elbow—U.S. Forest Service Campground, 14 miles east of Alpine on U.S. 89. RV sites, no pull-throughs, no services; open June 10 to September 10.

Station Creek—U.S. Forest Service Campground, 11 miles east of Alpine on U.S. 89. 15 RV sites, no pull-throughs, no services; open June 10 to September 10.

## GUEST RANCHES

Granite Creek Guest Ranch, operating since 1991; open June through August; no credit cards accepted; pets conditional. Contact Carl and Nessie Zitlau, PO Box 340, Ririe, ID 83443; (208) 538-7140.

Hanen-Silver Guest Ranch, 957 Rainey Creek Rd. This ranch has been operating since 1989. Features include hot tub, horseback riding and guided fishing trips. Open year-round; busiest June through October; credit cards accepted; no pets allowed. Contact Que Hansen, Box 112, Swan Valley, ID 83449; (208) 483-2305.

SUGGESTED
DINING

Mountain River Ranch, 18 miles northeast of Idaho Falls on road to Heise, 98 N. 5050 E., Ririe, ID; (208) 537-7337.

Heise Hot Springs Restaurant, 3 miles northeast of U.S. 26, 5116 Heise Rd., Ririe, ID; (208) 538-7312.

The Fox's Corner'd Inn and Saddlesore Saloon, 2998 Swan Valley Hwy., Swan Valley, ID; (208) 483-2510.

South Fork Lodge, Swan Valley, ID; (208) 483-2712.

The Sandy-Mite Cafe & Fly Shop, 3333 Swan Valley Hwy., Swan Valley, ID; (208) 483-2609.

**VISITOR INFORMATION & SERVICES**

Rigby Area Chamber of Commerce, PO Box 217, 120 E. Main St., Rigby, ID 83442; (208) 745-8701.

Swan Valley Chamber of Commerce, PO Box 19, Swan Valley, ID 83449; (208) 483-3972.

**MEDICAL, REPAIR & TOWING, VETERINARIAN**

For Medical, Repair & Towing and Veterinary Services, see Idaho Falls or Swan Valley Services (page 364).

# ALPINE, WYOMING, TO SODA SPRINGS, IDAHO: U.S. 89, IDAHO 34

The border town of Alpine presents a choice between alternate routes. U.S. 26/89 heads east back to the Jackson Hole area, or U.S. 89 takes you south to Freedom, Wyoming, where you'll need to pick one of two possible beautiful drives. For information about the drive through Wyoming's Star Valley, see page 203. The other beautiful drive is the 57-mile Pioneer Historic Byway that goes from the Wyoming border along Idaho 34 east to Soda Springs. This is a two-lane paved road; however, there is a moderately steep grade from the Wyoming border to Wayan. In the winter, this section is often blanketed with heavy snow and will occasionally be closed; otherwise, the route is open year-round. At Soda Springs you can continue the Pioneer Historic Byway on Idaho 34 to Franklin, or go west along the Bear Lake-Caribou Scenic Byway on U.S. 30, or head east on Idaho 30 to I-15, and eventually to Pocatello and Idaho Falls.

## FAVORITE DRIVE:
## PIONEER HISTORIC BYWAY

Cruising along Idaho 34, there's scenery we never tire of seeing as the road winds through ranches, farms and lovely aspen forests. Officially called the Pioneer Historic Byway, the paved road passes by Grays Lake and Blackfoot Reservoir. The 127-mile byway continues past Soda Springs to Franklin and then the Utah border.

## SODA SPRINGS AND VICINITY

This community was a site on the Oregon Trail, making it one of Idaho's earliest towns, dating back to 1863. Nothing much happened here until Brigham Young, the leader of the LDS church, built a cabin in 1870. Soda Springs was named for several nearby geothermal springs that had carbonated water. The city park preserves one of them named Hooper Springs, whose effervescent waters were sold commercially for a century.

Today the town's economy is based on the phosphate industry. The Monsanto Company, which opened in 1953, produces phosphorus that is used in detergents, fertilizers and water-treatment agents. Monsanto also produces an undesirable byproduct: huge mounds of slag that you'll see on the north side of town.

## OUTDOOR RECREATION AND ATTRACTIONS

The Grays Lake National Wildlife Refuge is a federal refuge and important breeding area for sandhill cranes. A fascinating wildlife story surrounds the refuge. In an attempt to increase the population of the endangered whooping crane, biologists concocted a scheme to place whooping crane eggs in sandhill crane nests. They hoped that the baby birds would imprint with the adopted parents and fly off with them during migration time. The object of this plan was to create an entirely new flock and a new migration route. The project initially worked as young whoopers grew and flew off with their sandhill parents, but the story has no happy ending. Several successive droughts hampered efforts, and the adult whoopers never joined together to mate. The project was scrapped in 1991, but plenty of sandhills are still very much evident as you make this drive. For information about the refuge, contact Refuge Manager, Grays Lake National Wildlife Refuge, 74 Grays Lake Rd., Wayan, ID 83285; (208) 574-2755.

Blackfoot Reservoir is a favorite angling spot. Rainbow trout and big cutthroat trout are the catch. The reservoir is 20 miles north of Soda Springs on Idaho 34.

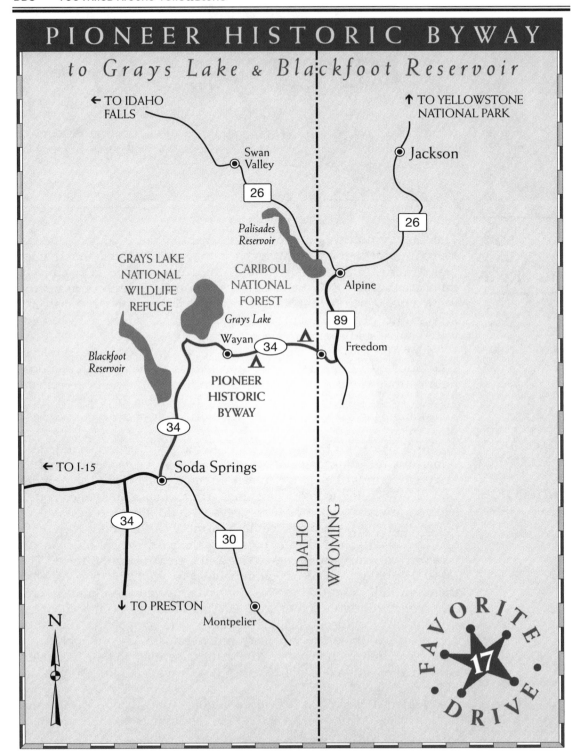

# PIONEER HISTORIC BYWAY

### to Grays Lake & Blackfoot Reservoir

← TO IDAHO FALLS

↑ TO YELLOWSTONE NATIONAL PARK

Swan Valley

Jackson

26

*Palisades Reservoir*

26

GRAYS LAKE NATIONAL WILDLIFE REFUGE

CARIBOU NATIONAL FOREST

*Grays Lake*

Alpine

89

Wayan    34

Freedom

*Blackfoot Reservoir*

PIONEER HISTORIC BYWAY

34

← TO I-15

Soda Springs

IDAHO

WYOMING

34

30

↓ TO PRESTON

Montpelier

N

FAVORITE · DRIVE ·

17

At the Oregon Trail Country Club, you have a choice of three public courses, the 18-hole course or one of two 9-hole courses. The country club is west of Soda Springs on U.S. 30; (208) 547-2204.

The biggest attraction in Soda Springs is an inadvertent man-made geyser. In 1937, a drilling crew that was looking for water to supply the town hit a pocket of carbon dioxide some 300 feet down, and water shot over 100 feet into the sky. The town has since capped this geyser, which is controlled by a timed valve to erupt on a regular schedule.

## OVERNIGHTING

### CAMPGROUNDS & RV PARKS

Trail Motel and Restaurant, 213 E. 200 W., Soda Springs, ID 83230. 17 RV sites, hook-ups, barrier-free access and restaurant; credit cards accepted; (208) 547-3909.

White Locks Marina and RV Park, on Idaho 34, 18 miles north of Soda Springs, 3429 Hwy. 34, Soda Springs, ID 83230. 50 RV sites, pull-throughs, full hook-ups, dump station, showers, laundry facilities, LP gas and restaurant; lake- and riverfront access; pets allowed; (208) 574-2208.

Tin Cup—U.S. Forest Service Campground, on Idaho 34 about 16 miles east of Wayan. 5 camping sites, RVs allowed, no services; timbered setting; fishing on Tincup Creek; open June 1 to September 30.

Pine Bar—U.S. Forest Service Campground, on Idaho 34 about 6 miles east of Wayan. 5 camping sites, RVs allowed, no services; timbered setting; fishing on Tincup Creek; open June 1 to September 30.

Gravel Creek—U.S. Forest Service Campground, about 8 miles south of Grays Lake Wildlife Refuge Headquarters, take Idaho 34 to Forest Service Road 191. 9 camping sites, RVs allowed, no services; timbered setting; fishing on Gravel Creek; open June 1 to September 30.

Mill Canyon—U.S. Forest Service Campground, 10.1 miles north of Soda Springs on Idaho 34, then 11.4 miles east on County Road 30C, 1.9 miles east on Forest Service Road 095, 6 miles west on Forest Service Road 099. 10 RV sites (max. length 32. feet), pull-throughs; open June 1 through September 30.

Diamond Creek—U.S. Forest Service Campground, 10.1 miles north of Soda Springs on Idaho 34, then 11.4 miles east on County Road 30C, 4.9 miles northeast on Forest Service Road 095, 12.5 miles southeast on Forest Service Road 102. 20 RV sites; hiking and fishing; open June 1 through September 30.

Dike Lake—U.S. Bureau of Land Management Campground, 11 miles north of Soda Springs on Idaho 34 at southeast end of Blackfoot Reservoir. 35 RV sites (max. length 25 feet), drinking water and toilets; lake- and riverfront access, boating and fishing; open May 15 through October 31.

Eight Mile—U.S. Forest Service Campground, 9.2 miles south of Soda Springs on County Road 30C, 4 miles south on Forest Service Road 425. 11 campsites, RVs allowed (max. length 16 feet), drinking water and toilets; fishing and hiking; open May 31 through October 30.

**SUGGESTED DINING**

Trails, 213 E. 200 W., Soda Springs, ID; (208) 547-3909.

White Locks, 3429 Idaho 34, Soda Springs, ID; (208) 547-3909.

**VISITOR INFORMATION & SERVICES**

Soda Springs Chamber of Commerce, PO Box 697, Soda Springs, ID 83726; (208) 547-4964.

Soda Springs Ranger District, 421 W. 2nd S., Soda Springs, ID 83726; (208) 547-4356.

**MEDICAL SERVICES**

Caribou Memorial Hospital, 24-hour emergency room, 300 S. 3rd W., Soda Springs, ID; (208) 547-3341.

Eastman Drug, 116 S. Main St., Soda Springs, ID; open Monday through Friday, 9 A.M. to 6 P.M., and Saturday, 9 A.M. to 3 P.M.; (208) 547-3585.

**REPAIR & TOWING**

R & R Transport, west of Soda Springs on Idaho 30; (208) 547-4616.

Rocky Mountain RV Repair, 590 E. 2nd S., Soda Springs, ID; (208) 547-4698.

**VETERINARY SERVICES**

Soda Springs Pet Care, Dr. Lisa Vanpelt, 1950 Oregon Rd., Soda Springs, ID; (208) 425-3269.

Soda Springs Animal Clinic, 2607 Idaho 30, Soda Springs ID; (208) 547-5981.

# IDAHO FALLS AND VICINITY: JUNCTION OF U.S. 20 AND I-15

At Idaho Falls you can take a more southerly roundabout route to Jackson and avoid the steep Teton Pass. U.S. 26 takes you to Swan Valley, where it parallels the Snake River upstream to Palisades Reservoir. This is a pretty drive on an excellent road; see page 352. Also, from Idaho Falls you can continue south on I-15 to Pocatello and connect into I-86.

**IDAHO FALLS**

Idaho Falls has an interesting history because the falls were built to fit the name rather than the reverse. Originally, the city was named Taylor's Bridge after J. M. Taylor, who built a toll bridge across the Snake River in 1865. Then the community was named Eagle Rock after the bald eagles that fished the nearby Snake River. But in 1911, clever entrepreneurs took advantage of a 20-foot-high weir that created an artificial falls, thus changing the name. This is the third-largest city in Idaho, coming in behind Boise and Pocatello, which lies about 50 miles to the south.

Idaho Falls is the county seat and largest city in Bonneville County. Although agriculture is the state's number-one industry, agribusiness accounts for 41 percent of the county's employment. Nuclear research, engineering, education, and tourism and recreation provide a diversified economy.

If you continue 30 miles south of Idaho Falls on I-15, you'll come to Blackfoot, named for the Blackfeet tribe. Historians say the Natives were given this name because they habitually walked in ashes after fires had burned the land. Today, modern Blackfooters claim their town to be the Potato Capital of the World.

You'll invariably spot a sign along the interstate near Blackfoot that says, "Free Taters for Out of Staters." If you follow the directions, you'll end up at a railroad depot built in 1913, which has now been converted into Idaho's World Potato Exposition. This is perhaps the only museum in the country dedicated to the potato, complete with all sorts of things that you've always wanted to know but were afraid to ask about potatoes. You can also view the world's largest potato chip and buy potato ice cream. A small donation as you enter is suggested.

**OUTDOOR RECREATION AND ATTRACTIONS**

A golfer's haven, Idaho Falls has four courses nearby. The Sandcreek Golf Course is an 18-hole course maintained by the city at 5230 Hackman Rd., (208) 529-1115. The other two city courses are also 18 holes: the Pinecrest Golf Course at 701 Elva, (208) 529-1485; and the new Sage Lakes Golf Course, 100 E. 65 N., (208) 528-5535. The fourth is a private course south of the city, the Idaho Falls Country Club, (208) 523-5757.

An attractive strip of lawn, flowers and trees runs about a mile along the downtown portion of the Snake River. Aptly named the Idaho Falls Greenbelt, this is a comfy spot for businessfolks to relax and eat lunch in the cool recesses of the strip. Travelers commonly park nearby as well. They enjoy the vegetation as well as the hundreds of ducks and geese that are always willing to beg food. It's also one of the preferred spots to view the Fourth of July Fireworks. If you're in town on the big weekend, get there early for a good view of the display over the water.

The Bonneville Museum has some interesting exhibits, depicting the area's early history and its explorers. You can stroll through an early-day replication of Eagle Rock, and see artifacts on early pioneer lifestyles. The museum at 200 North Eastern Ave. is in the Andrew Carnegie Library Building, which was added to the National Register of Historic Places. The hours are 10 A.M. to 5 P.M. weekdays, and 1 P.M. to 5 P.M. on Saturdays; (208) 522-1400.

Idaho Falls has one of the Mormon temples that exist in select cities around the world. A visitor's center is open daily from 9 A.M. to 9 P.M., featuring various attractions of Mormon history.

The Idaho Falls Zoo is located in Tautphaus Park and has numerous large cats, as well as many other animals and exotic birds—over 250 species in all. The zoo is open daily, May 1 through October 1, and weekends during October, November and April. For more information, call (208) 529-1470.

If you want to stretch a bit, you might try walking or biking at Freeman, Eastbank and Westbank parks that are located along Science Center Drive. For picnicking, try Lincoln Park, which is along Lincoln Road. It also has tennis courts, a playground and baseball diamonds.

A big chunk of Idaho Falls's residents work at the Idaho National Engineering Laboratories, which is about 45 miles west toward Arco along U.S. 20. The visitor center there features all sorts of nuclear displays, including a control room, reactors, remote handling tools and Geiger counters. You can also take a guided tour. The center is open from 8 A.M. to 4 P.M. from Memorial Day to Labor Day. For more information, call (208) 526-0111.

The area stretching north of Idaho Falls on I-15 through Roberts and Hamer has several wildlife management areas that are wonderful for birding and wildlife watching. Information on the best times to visit Market Lake and Mud Lake Wildlife Management Areas can be obtained from (208) 522-7783. For the Camas National Wildlife Refuge, call (208) 662-5423. Of course, as with all backcountry roads, check the weather and road conditions before venturing to these wild areas.

## CAMPGROUNDS & RV PARKS

### Idaho Falls

▲ ***Best Spot for a Camp Spot***
Shady Rest Campground, 2200 N. Yellowstone, Idaho Falls, ID. 30 RV sites, 6 pull-throughs, full hook-ups and laundry; open year-round; busiest June through September; (208) 524-0010.

Idaho Falls KOA, I-15 Exit 119E, then one-eighth mile to Lindsay, 1440 Lindsay Blvd., Idaho Falls, ID 83402. 180 RV sites, full hook-ups, LP gas, heated pool, hot tub and mini-golf; (208) 523-3362.

Sunnyside Acres Park, 905 W. Sunnyside Rd., Idaho Falls, ID. 25 RV sites (pull-throughs), hook-ups, dump station and showers; (208) 523-8403.

### Mud Lake

Haven Motel and Trailer Park, 1079 E. 1500 N., Mud Lake, ID. 13 RV sites; (208) 663-4821.

Birch Creek—U.S. Bureau of Land Management Campground, 25 miles northwest of Mud Lake on Idaho 28. 16 RV sites (max. length 25 feet), no services except toilets.

Summit Creek—U.S. Bureau of Land Management Campground, from Howe, then 40 miles northwest on County Road 22. 12 RV sites (max. length 30 feet), fishing and hiking; open May 1 through October 31.

### Blackfoot

Cutthroat Trout—U.S. Bureau of Land Management Campground, 7 miles north of Blackfoot on U.S. 91, then 10 miles east on Wolverine Road, right on Cedar Creek Road for 13 miles, right on Trail Creek Bridge Road for 6 miles, road turns into Lincoln Creek Road, then 3 miles to access to campground. 5 RV sites (max. length 15 feet), no services except toilets; lake- and riverfront access and fishing; open May 1 through October 31.

Graves Creek—U.S. Bureau of Land Management Campground, 7 miles north of Blackfoot on U.S. 91, then 10 miles east on Wolverine Road, right on Cedar Creek Road for 13 miles, right on Trail Creek Bridge Road for 6 miles, road turns into Lincoln Creek Road, then 1 mile to access to campground. 5 RV sites (max. length 15 feet), no services except toilets; lake- and riverfront access and fishing; open May 1 through October 1.

Sage Hen Flats—U.S. Bureau of Land Management Campground, 7 miles north of Blackfoot on U.S. 91, then 10 miles east on Wolverine Road, right on Cedar Creek Road for 13 miles, right on Trail Creek Bridge Road for 6 miles, road turns into Lincoln Creek Road, then 6 miles to access to campground. 5 RV sites (max. length 15 feet), hook-ups and toilets; lake- and riverfront access and fishing; open May 1 through October 31.

## BED & BREAKFAST ESTABLISHMENTS

Little Bush Inn, five minutes from downtown; open year-round; busiest summer through fall, slowest late winter; no credit cards accepted; no pets allowed. Contact Terry Bousquet, 498 Maple St., Idaho Falls, ID  83403; (208) 529-0567.

**SUGGESTED DINING**

Rondezvous, 325 River Parkway, Idaho Falls, ID; (208) 528-5458.

Garcia's Mexican, 2180 E. 17th, Idaho Falls, ID; (208) 522-2000.

Smitty's Pancake & Steak House, 645 W. Broadway, Idaho Falls, ID; (208) 529-5542.

Jakers Steak, Rib & Fish House, 851 Lindsay Falls, Idaho Falls, ID; (208) 524-5240.

**VISITOR INFORMATION & SERVICES**

Eastern Idaho/Yellowstone and Teton Visitor and Convention Bureau, 505 Lindsay Blvd., Idaho Falls, ID 83405; 1-800-634-3246; (208) 523-1010. The visitor center is a joint cooperative effort between the U.S. Forest Service, U.S. Bureau of Land Management and Idaho Falls Chamber of Commerce—a one-stop shop! While you're visiting the sights, you can park your RV at the Visitor Center, or along the river on Memorial Drive, one block away.

Targhee National Forest: Campgrounds, Trails and Visitor Information, PO Box 208, St. Anthony, ID 83445; (208) 624-3151.

Idaho Department of Fish and Game, 1515 Lincoln Rd., Idaho Falls, ID; (208) 522-7783.

Idaho Guide and Outfitters Board, Boise, ID; 1-800-847-4843.

**MEDICAL SERVICES**

Columbia Eastern Regional Medical Center, 24-hour emergency room, 3100 Channing Way, Idaho Falls, ID 83403; (208) 529-6210, 529-6111.

Family Emergency Center—East, 1995 E. 17th, Idaho Falls, ID; open Monday through Saturday, 9 A.M. to 9 P.M.; (208) 529-5252.

Family Emergency Center—West, 250 S. Skyline Dr., Idaho Falls, ID; open Monday through Saturday, 9 A.M. to 9 P.M.; (208) 525-2600.

Prescription Center, Inc., 25 N. Placer, Idaho Falls, ID; open Monday through Friday, 8 A.M. to 6:30 P.M., and Saturday, 8 A.M. to 1 P.M.; (208) 523-3360, 3361.

**REPAIR & TOWING**

H & H Diesel, 24-hour towing, 3409 N. 15th E., Idaho Falls, ID; (208) 529-3746.

Lindsey Truck & Towing/Repair, 6754 Overland Dr., Idaho Falls, ID; (208) 523-6618.

**VETERINARY SERVICES**

Sunnyside Veterinary Clinic, 629 W. Sunnyside Rd., Idaho Falls, ID; (208) 523-2513.

Skyline Animal Clinic, 1378 S. Grizzly, Idaho Falls, ID; (208) 529-3244.

## Spencer Opal Mines

The opal deposits were discovered by two hunters in 1948, and the Stetler family purchased the open-pit mine in 1964. Today, the Stetler family, under Claudia Stetler Couture, still owns and operates the mine, which covers about eight acres. Rockhounds and jewelers will appreciate this site. The high-quality opal is considered in the precious stone category.

The headquarters of the Spencer Opal Mines are in Spencer, 65 miles north of Idaho Falls on I-15. You can also reach the town from the Island Park area on Idaho County Route A-2, which is halfway between Mack's Inn and Island Park. The well-maintained gravel road runs through the valley to Kilgore and connects into I-15 at Spencer. As with any backcountry gravel road, if you're traveling very early or late in the season, be sure to ask locals the condition of the road.

The Stetlers offer a "mini-mine" at their shop and sell rough-cut stone, or you can sign up for the prescheduled group digs at the mine site. These folks are serious about their business but are loads of fun to be around and familiar with RVers. There is a convenient 18-site RV park, with full hook-ups at the shop located at the north end of Main Street in Spencer. Main Street runs to a dead-end at the Spencer Opal Mine Shop, so you can't miss it. To sign up for a group dig ($25 per day per 5 pounds), or for more information, contact Claudia Stetler Couture, Spencer Opal Mines, HCR 62, Box 2060, Dubois, ID 83423; (208) 374-5476, May through September; or PO Box 521, Salome, AZ 85348; (520) 859-3752, October through April.

## OVERNIGHTING

## CAMPGROUNDS & RV PARKS

Spencer Opal Mine Shop, north end of Main Street in Spencer. 18 RV sites, full hook-ups; open May through September, (208) 374-5476; off-season, call (520) 859-3752.

Steel Creek Group Area—U.S. Forest Service Campground, 3.5 miles north of Spencer on I-15, then 17 miles southeast on Forest Service Road 006, 1.2 miles west on Forest Service Road 478. 1 RV site, hook-up, barrier-free access, drinking water and toilets; fishing and hiking; open May 25 through October 15.

Stoddard Creek—U.S. Forest Service Campground, 3.5 miles north of Spencer on I-15, then 1 mile northwest on Forest Service Road 003. 24 RV sites (pull-throughs), hook-ups, drinking water and toilets; fishing; open May 15 through October 15.

# APPENDIX:
# INFORMATION AND
# ROADSIDE ASSISTANCE NUMBERS

### State Road Reports

| | |
|---|---|
| Wyoming: Cody area | (307) 587-9966 |
| Wyoming: Worland area | (307) 347-9966 |
| Wyoming: Jackson Hole area | (307) 733-9966 |
| Montana | 1-800-332-6171 |
| Idaho | (208) 336-6600 |

### Weather Reports

| | |
|---|---|
| Wyoming: Cody area | (307) 587 9966 |
| Wyoming: Worland area | (307) 347-9966 |
| Wyoming: Jackson Hole area | (307) 733-9966 |
| Montana | (406) 444-6339 |
| Idaho | (208) 336-6600 |

### Lost or Stolen Credit Cards

| | |
|---|---|
| American Express | 1-800-528-4800 |
| Citicorp Diner Club | 1-800-234-6377 |
| Discover Card | 1-800-347-2683 |
| Ford Citibank | 1-800-950-5114 |
| GM Credit Card | 1-800-947-1000 |
| Mastercard | 1-800-826-2181 |
| VISA | 1-800-336-8472 |
| Bank of America | 1-800-219-9147 |
| Traveler's Checks, American Express | 1-800-221-7282 |
| Thomas Cook Mastercard | 1-800-223-7373 |
| Mastercard International | 1-800-223-9920 |
| American Express International | 1-800-492-8596 |
| Western Union | 1-800-325-6000 |
| Money Gram, wiring | 1-800-926-9400 |
| Money Order | 1-800-999-9600 |
| General number, lost card information | 1-800-221-7282 |

## Tourism Departments

Wyoming Division of Tourism, 1-25 at College Drive, Cheyenne, WY 82002; (307) 777-7777.

Travel Montana, 1424 9th Ave., Box 200533, Helena, MT 59620-0533; (406) 444-2654; 1-800-847-4868; website: http://travel.mt.gov/

Idaho Travel Council, Division of Tourism Development, Idaho Department of Commerce, 700 W. State St., PO Box 83720, Boise, ID 83720; 1-800-635-7820; travel information: (208) 334-2470.

# ABOUT THE AUTHORS

Jim and Madonna Zumbo live in the mountains just 30 miles from Yellowstone National Park with their two labradors, Shike and Rosey. The Zumbos maintain a publishing business from their home and, in their free time, explore the vast region surrounding Yellowstone.

Jim has written 17 books and is also a staff editor with *Outdoor Life* magazine—a position he has held for 20 years. This is Madonna's second book. She was formerly Vice President and General Manager of International Sportsmen's Expositions, a West Coast company that produces boat, travel and sportsmen's shows.

*AUTHOR PHOTO (BACK COVER) BY JUDGE AND MARIANNE GAMBILL*

# INDEX